CITIZEN-IN-CHIEF

ALSO BY LEONARD BENARDO AND JENNIFER WEISS

*Brooklyn by Name: How the Neighborhoods, Streets,
Parks, Bridges and More Got Their Names*

CITIZEN-IN-CHIEF

The Second Lives of the American Presidents

—⁓—

**LEONARD BENARDO
AND
JENNIFER WEISS**

𝓌𝓂
WILLIAM MORROW
An Imprint of HarperCollins*Publishers*

HarperCollins books may be purchased for educational, business, or sales promotional use. For information please write: Special Markets Department, HarperCollins Publishers, 10 East 53rd Street, New York, NY 10022.

FIRST EDITION

Designed by Lisa Stokes

Library of Congress Cataloging-in-Publication Data

Benardo, Leonard.
   Citizen-in-chief : the second lives of the American presidents / Leonard Benardo and Jennifer Weis. — 1st ed.
      p. cm.
   Includes bibliographical references and index.
   ISBN 978-0-06-124496-4
1. Ex-presidents—United States—History.
2. Ex-presidents—United States—Biography. 3. Retirees—United States—Biography.
4. Presidents—Retirement—United States—History. 5. Presidents—United States—
History. 6. Presidents—United States—Biography. I. Weiss, Jennifer. II. Title.
   E176.1.B444   2009
   973.09'9—dc22   2008036145

---

09   10   11   12   13   WBC/RRD   10   9   8   7   6   5   4   3   2   1

FOR FELIX AND ANYA—

whose warmth and decency is our
greatest legacy

In free governments the rulers are the servants and the people their superiors and sovereigns. For the former therefore to return among the latter is not to degrade them but to promote them.

BENJAMIN FRANKLIN

CONTENTS

CITIZEN-IN-CHIEF

INTRODUCTION

~

An Exploration of the Ex-Presidency

The American Presidency . . . is merely a way station en route to the blessed condition of being an ex-President. In office, Herbert Hoover made the nation feel drastically insecure; out of office, he has radiated for thirty years a positively archangelic calm. While Harry Truman was residing in the White House, he gave the impression of being an unnerved riverboat gambler improvising his way through the biggest crap game in Western history; back home in Independence, he gets wiser every year, until in retrospect it seems that we had a combination of von Clausewitz, Macaulay, and Ty Cobb supervising our destinies in that harried era.

John Updike

Whatever vestiges of power went with the retiring President—the grant of $375,000, the office space, the mailing frank, the military helicopter, the Secret Service—the real power was gone.
Doris Kearns, *Lyndon Johnson and the American Dream*

There are things I can do as a private citizen, in an unofficial capacity, that the President of the United States cannot do.
Jimmy Carter

. . . . . .

SPEAKING IN CHICAGO ON THE ONE HUNDRED AND SEVENTY-FIFTH anniversary of George Washington's birth, former president Grover Cleveland, a decade out of office and a year shy of death, wryly summed up his conception of the ex-presidency. "What shall be done with our ex-presidents? It has been suggested that they be taken out in a five-acre lot and shot. It seems to me, however, that an ex-president has already suffered."

Cleveland's mordant observation points to what was until recently a perennial concern in American history: What's to become of our former presidents? These sometimes revered, sometimes notorious, but always famous figures once stood at the pinnacle of American political power; yet the futures they plunged into after leaving office have often been uncertain, and this fact alone has frequently left Americans uneasy. Absent any formal position for ex-presidents—any "president emeritus" chair giving them a defined role in public life— would the nation have any way of benefiting from their experience? On the other hand, was it even appropriate for ex-presidents to continue to influence American policy after their terms had expired? And, on a more personal level, what would become of the men themselves— these descendants of our Founding Fathers? Should a respectful public arrange to provide for them, or should their lives be left simply to chance?

The question of what should become of former presidents has long provoked impassioned debate. In his classic 1888 study *The American Commonwealth*, the British jurist Lord Bryce advocated emulating Roman practice and inviting ex-presidents to join the Senate. "They managed things better at Rome," Bryce argued, "gathering into their Senate all the fame and experience, all the wisdom and skill of those who had ruled and fought as consuls and praetors at home and abroad." With their reservoir of leadership experience, he argued, former presidents could prove a boon to Congress's upper house. Others disparaged such ideas. Rutherford B. Hayes argued that the

Senate was already turning into a "rich man's place" and that including ex-presidents would run roughshod over "the principle of popular government."

Years later, populist leader William Jennings Bryan became the first major American political figure to propose that former presidents become ex-officio members of the Senate. (A three-time presidential nominee, Bryan was probably envisioning such a position for his own future.) Yet critics were swift to dismiss Bryan's suggestion. William Howard Taft, late of the presidency himself, snickered, "If I must go and disappear into oblivion, I prefer to go by the chloroform or lotus method. It's pleasanter and less drawn out." There was enough chatter in the Senate as it was, he added; it needn't be augmented by "the lucubrations of ex-Presidents."

Despite such protests from former presidents, over the years there were numerous legislative efforts to make them permanent "representatives at large," nonvoting salaried members of Congress. Before the Twenty-second Amendment established presidential term limits in 1951, offering former presidents a lifetime congressional perch seemed like a clever way to preclude second-term presidents from launching third-term runs. Still, the legislation went nowhere. When asked about the prospect, Herbert Hoover threw cold water on it: "Twenty years ago, I would have been enthusiastic," he said. "But at my time of life, I don't look on the prospect of sitting on a hard cushion for several hours a day and listening to speeches as being attractive." During the Cold War, there was one final variation on the theme, a proposal to make all former presidents members of the National Security Council. When that failed, the long-standing quest to harness the wisdom and experience of ex-presidents had met its end.

By the late twentieth century, this durable public yearning to find a meaningful official role for former chief executives had been answered by the efforts of the past presidents themselves. Many people may have concluded that the examples of public engagement presented by Jimmy Carter and Bill Clinton in our time are anomalous.

If anything, though, the opposite is true: most American presidents have found ways to occupy themselves in the public sphere after leaving office—whether politically, philanthropically, remuneratively, or redemptively. The image of the former leader retiring to a bucolic life was always a half-truth, with only a minority yielding to the blandishments of a tranquil existence. In fact, their lives have been far richer and varied than is customarily assumed.

Few, if any, of our former presidents would have required a ceremonial post to continue their influence on American life. Some postpresidential undertakings are a familiar part of American history, among them Thomas Jefferson's founding of his great Virginia university, John Quincy Adams's astonishing sequel as an antislavery congressman, Ulysses S. Grant's heartrending last days racing the clock to finish his memoir, and Teddy Roosevelt's flamboyant return to political life—not to mention the wholesale reimagining of the ex-presidency launched by Carter and Clinton. Less celebrated, but equally compelling, are the considerable postpresidential activities of others: Andrew Jackson's studied manipulation of electoral politics, Rutherford B. Hayes's varied progressive reforms on behalf of African Americans, William Howard Taft's inspired peace-building efforts, Herbert Hoover's heroic overseas relief work, and Dwight Eisenhower's strategic advice on Cold War policy among them.

The reality is that just a handful of former presidents have withdrawn into anonymity. Some presidents returned to the political arena as elected officials, one even signing on to the Confederacy. Others sought to regain presidential power via third parties of varying ideological stripes. Several adopted the mantle of éminence grise and offered their successors wisdom and counsel; more than a few found their métier in public service both at home and abroad; and many campaigned actively on behalf of potential successors.

Recent years have seen a sea change in what journalist James Fallows calls "the structure, expectations, and opportunities that come with being an ex-President." The examples of Carter and Clinton have led us to embrace the image of an engagé ex-president who places primacy on the global commonweal. Whether through securing support for natural disaster victims, speaking out against genocide, or identifying funding for public health crises, high-profile public service is now seen as the natural fulfillment of a former president's responsibility to the world. No longer do we worry what will be done with former presidents; instead, we wonder what they might do for humankind.

It should be noted that Carter and Clinton didn't invent this playbook. Herbert Hoover's international food relief efforts spoke to the same lofty aspirations. But the recent ex-presidents have amassed such large portfolios of diplomatic and humanitarian activities that they stand in a class by themselves. The information revolution has obviously contributed to their fame, helping these former presidents become "celebrity statesmen," permanent features of the current-affairs landscape. "Whether we like it or not, they're guests in our home, 24/7," says historian Richard Norton Smith. In the digital age, the concept of a former head of state slinking quietly into the post-presidential night is drifting into obsolescence.

THE POWER AND INFLUENCE OF AN EX-PRESIDENT

The conventional wisdom says that Jimmy Carter's presidency, in retrospect, was merely a stepping-stone for greater things. Political commentators never tire of referring to Carter's post–White House period as his "second term," and many have dubbed him "our greatest ex-president." As Carter himself noted, "Every President has had a different attitude toward the post-presidential years." But he signaled his own approach by declaring that he wasn't interested in "going into the corporate world or on the permanent lecture tour"; instead, he compiled a résumé of triumphs that many Americans found significantly more presidential than his single term as commander-in-chief.

Kris Kristofferson's rueful observation that "freedom's just another word for nothing left to lose" could easily apply to Carter's post-presidential convictions. "I have infinitely more freedom to speak now than when I was president," Carter has admitted. "An ambassador speaks for the State Department and the White House; constraints that are very severe. I don't have to speak for my country." Whether mediating conflicts or fighting epidemics, Carter has been widely applauded for his globe-trotting efforts; and in 2002 he became the first former president to win the Nobel Peace Prize. (Teddy Roosevelt and Woodrow Wilson won theirs during their presidency.)

The outspoken Carter doesn't lack for critics. By inserting himself, particularly on the diplomatic side, into contested and politicized waters, Carter has invited unsparing attacks, with opponents savaging everything from his soft-pedaling of despots such as Slobodan Milosevic or Kim Il-Sung to his alleged anti-Zionism. One conservative detractor, Joshua Muravchik, has dubbed Carter "Our Worst Ex-President." Journalist Robert Kaplan has dismissed Carter's self-styled diplomacy as a series of "high profile stunts" and critiqued his extensive writing for its "diminishing returns." Carter's 2006 book, *Palestine: Peace Not Apartheid*, fanned the flames of anti-Carter invective, leading to the resignation of fourteen members from the Carter Center's Board of Councilors and igniting thunderous condemnation from some precincts of America's Jewish community.

Although few could have foreseen the success of Carter's charitable undertakings after his anguished defeat by Ronald Reagan in 1980, the issues animating his single term in office offered a clue. Carter committed his administration to advance and enforce human rights norms as a tool of foreign policy and to strengthen the legitimacy of human rights institutions worldwide. And his Herculean negotiations at Camp David to broker a deal between Egypt and Israel—not to mention his evangelical background—always reflected an ardor for the holy land. Nevertheless, Carter's extraordinary service these last decades was hardly imaginable when he left the White House.

Similarly unexpected have been the accomplishments of Bill Clinton. The youngest former president since Teddy Roosevelt, the man from Hope had everyone wondering what he might do for an encore: University president? Talk-show host? World Bank president? Secretary General of the United Nations?

"When you leave the presidency," Clinton said, "you lose your power but not your influence." Nevertheless, that influence "must be concentrated in a few areas." Clinton recognized that "Jimmy Carter had made a real difference in his post-presidential years, and I thought I could too." The forty-second president has divided his philanthropic endeavors into several discrete categories, from combating high drug prices as a key factor in overcoming public health calamities like HIV/AIDS to shining a light on children's nutrition. Seeking to address his administration's blind spots, Clinton's foundation maintains a clarity of vision and seriousness of purpose.

Fortunately for Clinton—one former president who savors the limelight—a commitment to social change need not come at the cost of diminished public attention. The Clinton Global Initiative is an example of such a high-profile enterprise: a mass annual convocation where world leaders, major capitalists, and international celebrities meet at the same time as the UN General Assembly to make substantial financial pledges toward helping to solve the earth's problems. Clinton's multifaceted role as impresario, spin doctor, auctioneer, and salesman is the necessary glue that makes the initiative a success.

Until the 2008 presidential election, Clinton's demeanor during his postpresidency bore a striking resemblance to Hillary Clinton's deportment in the U.S. Senate: little rancor, an absence of hostility, and bipartisanship being its principal features ("Like me, she believes in working with Republicans," Clinton once pointed out). After suffering the slings and arrows of the GOP's demagogic wing—especially

1994's incoming "Contract with America" class—and the dubious attempt to impeach him in 1997, the former president might have been expected to strike out to clear his name. Instead, Clinton took the high road and kept focused on delivering good deeds and preferring charitable acts to ad hominem attacks. Yet Hillary Clinton's bruising 2008 nomination fight against Barack Obama showed another side of the former president. Returning full-on to the rough-and-tumble world of electoral politics, the consummate politician riddled his stump speeches with divisive and uncompromising language—only to become a liability to his wife, who was forced to rein him in. It was a considerable stain on Clinton's postpresidential halo.

The Road to Financial Stability

Bill Clinton's influence has been striking in another realm, too: making money. Though he didn't set the standard, Clinton's success as rainmaker for himself and others has raised the bar significantly. Often charging hundreds of thousands of dollars for a single speech and accumulating north of $100 million since leaving office, he is now a man of profound wealth. Clinton also employs his postpresidential influence to raise funds innovatively—as when he invited the Rolling Stones to play at his birthday party and used the event to solicit contributions for the William J. Clinton Foundation. Motivational speeches at corporate gatherings now seem quaint by contrast.

As Clinton has demonstrated, former presidents are uniquely positioned to exploit their status for beneficent purposes. Yet, in recent decades, ex-presidents have also proved increasingly adept at raising funds for their own benefit, a practice long deemed out of step with the virtuous traditions of the Founding Fathers.

The modern-day practice of using one's postpresidential years for excessive personal enrichment was inaugurated by Gerald Ford.

Thrilled at the opportunity to accumulate capital after years of a modest middle-class lifestyle, Ford rapidly joined an array of corporate boards, marketing his name to the highest bidder. Never a flashy man during his years in public office, as a former president Ford relished the accoutrements of high living, purchasing homes in Palm Springs, Vail, and Rancho Mirage. Although his acquisitive behavior attracted criticism for retailing "the prestige of the presidency," Ford's revenue-generation machine plowed forward unabated.

In the late 1980s, however, Ronald Reagan—once Ford's great rival—redefined postpresidential cupidity. In Reagan's all-too-brief compos mentis life after the White House, one striking number stands out: the $2 million he earned for a handful of speaking engagements in Japan in 1989. A junket in extremis that made Ford's avarice look respectable by comparison, Reagan's Japanese adventure stands lamentably as a defining moment of his ex-presidency. Reagan's successor, George H. W. Bush, a former director of the Central Intelligence Agency, took an understandably more circumspect path to financial reward: the private equity concern for which he consulted for five and a half years, the once predominantly military- and aerospace-invested Carlyle Group, is not at liberty to divulge the level of Bush's compensation.

Faced with the examples of Ford and Reagan, Bush and Clinton, it's easy to forget that U.S. presidents didn't always have such an easy time of things after leaving office. Virginians such as Thomas Jefferson, James Madison, and James Monroe lived at best in declining economic circumstances and often in relative poverty. Monroe, in fact, spent his postpresidential half decade fighting tooth and nail to get congressional reimbursement for his work as minister to France. Though he was eventually paid back, he died in New York City, where he had relocated, empty-handed and destitute. That these towering figures, the drafters of the Declaration of Independence and the Constitution among them, could fall into such exiguous circumstances confounds the modern sensibility. Yet the early presidents reentered private life at a time when their young nation was undergoing challenges to its plantation-based agricultural economy, and their livelihood suffered as a direct result.

There were cultural transformations as well. Whatever their financial hardships, the early southern presidents all remained wedded to the institution of slavery, regardless of its human or economic costs. Only George Washington put forward a plan to manumit all his slaves (at his wife Martha's death). Six other southerners—Jefferson, Madison, Monroe, Jackson, Tyler, and Polk—had postpresidencies that were burdened by the peculiar institution. In an effort to resolve the nation's conflict between the Scylla of states' rights and the Charybdis of federal rule, James Madison in retirement tried unsuccessfully to fashion some form of legal remedy. Emphasizing the fragility of the union and determined to explain that slavery wasn't a political imposition but a way of life, Madison sought other ways to address "the dreadful calamity which has so long afflicted our country and filled so many with despair." Madison saw colonization to Africa as a means to that end; Monroe agreed, and vociferously enough that during his presidency the capital of the new state of Liberia was named Monrovia in his honor. Nevertheless, slavery remained a drag on the already deteriorating plantation life of our former presidents.

Until the end of the Civil War, it was considered improper to deploy one's presidential résumé in the pursuit of private profit. In line with the tenets of early republicanism, a former president was expected to shield himself from commercial opportunities. After the war, as competitive capitalism took root within American society, these expectations changed. Serving on corporate boards, writing for popular publications, and, of course, speechifying soon became routine. Though the prospect of today's earning potential was still years away, the opportunities for an ex-president to use his symbolic power for surplus income burgeoned during the Gilded Age.

Not everyone was pleased with this development. In the first half of the twentieth century, concerned members of Congress periodically introduced legislation to secure a guaranteed pension for former presidents, to help offset the temptation to exploit their fame commercially. Yet such overtures were met with resistance. To many legislators, a pension was tantamount to royal privilege.

By the mid-1950s, the pendulum had swung back toward offering some kind of financial security to former presidents. The journalist Richard Rovere wrote of the need to repair "one of the great deficiencies in our political system: the failure to provide either a living or a dignified function for those who have served as President. Most retired politicians get pensions; many superannuated generals get automobiles, valets and a good many lifetime perquisites. But we cut off our Chief Magistrates and Commanders-in-Chief without a thin dime and, what is in some ways worse, with the terrible knowledge that they will demean the high office they have held if they scratch for a living as most mortals do."

The principal cause for Rovere's concern was Harry Truman, who arrived home to Independence, Missouri, in straitened circumstances. As Truman told House Speaker Sam Rayburn, "I'm so poor, I don't have a pot to piss in, or a window to throw it out of." The news that the former haberdasher-turned-president was unable to pay even the postage on his voluminous mail finally forced the hand of Congress, and in 1958 it passed the Former Presidents Act, mandating a guaranteed salary and a number of perks: a small staff, travel funds, and a furnished office. Later measures would ensure Secret Service protection and a transition budget to help former presidents make the adjustment back to private life. With this range of lifetime supports in place, the informal office of the ex-presidency was born.

Trotsky famously said that every revolution has its Thermidor—the moment when the revolutionary spirit gives way to counterrevolutionary forces. By the 1980s, the steadily increasing privileges in the economic livelihood of our former presidents began to generate significant resistance. There were charges that taxpayer-supported perquisites afforded to former presidents (and their spouses) had spiraled out of control and must be sheared. Each new administration seemed to present some new disgrace: Richard Nixon received two hundred thousand dollars in transition expenses despite resigning the office; Jimmy Carter purchased a twelve-thousand-dollar Oriental rug; Jerry Ford got his car washed—all on the taxpayer's nickel. In an age when ex-presidents can earn millions, guaranteeing them a salary and benefits equal to those of a cabinet secretary ran counter to logic.

PRESERVING THE LEGACY

Just a few years before the Former Presidents Act was passed, Congress established a private-public partnership for building and maintaining presidential libraries. The enduring challenge of how presidents should be preserved both financially and in terms of their legacy thus found two answers in rapid succession. Not surprisingly, the presidential library, once a humble venue for housing a chief executive's materials, has become a form of big business.

The swelling of the presidential library system has been a boon to former Oval Office residents eager to manage the narrative of their presidency. Before the Presidential Libraries Act of 1955, the catch-as-catch-can quality of material preservation was a recipe for disaster. Untold numbers of documents from at least a few dozen presidents were lost forever due to the absence of a formalized archival process. Today, all presidential records belong to the people, and the National Archives and Records Administration is the government's caretaker, overseeing the twelve existing libraries from coast to coast, from Franklin Roosevelt's in Hyde Park, New York, to Ronald Reagan's in Simi Valley, California.

Since the early, unpretentious repositories for presidential materials, library complexes have galloped ahead in size and monumentality. Lyndon Johnson's papers are enshrined in a windowless monolith at the University of Texas; Ronald Reagan's in a ninety-thousand-square-foot hangarlike pavilion housing Air Force One; and Bill Clinton's in his elaborate "bridge to the twenty-first century" showpiece in Little Rock, Arkansas. The funds to build these increasingly outsized structures come from the private sector, in which transparency requirements are largely nonexistent. Foreign corporations and sovereign governments can pay what they wish, even before a president's term in office is over—raising problematic questions of conflict of interest. There have long been calls for legislation to make such donor funds public, but to date Congress has made only meager advances in that direction.

The George W. Bush Presidential Library, reportedly budgeted at $500 million, will become the thirteenth library in the system when completed at Southern Methodist University (SMU) in Dallas. Most contentiously, it will have a public affairs body, provisionally called the Freedom Institute, which will operate largely outside the jurisdiction of SMU's general administration. Similar to the 1980s conflicts over Ronald Reagan's proposed library and think tank at Stanford University and Richard Nixon's planned museum and archives at Duke University, George W. Bush's complex has provoked heated protest and debate. Eventually, Reagan and Nixon were forced to turn elsewhere and set up shop in Southern California; George W. Bush, however, has prevailed, winning the day in Dallas. Despite faculty anger that a campus-based think tank would serve to burnish an unpopular president and misguided war, the prize of the Bush library and its associated institute proved too big a draw for SMU to reconsider.

The proposed cost of the Bush library raises the obvious question of how to identify adequate funds for such a venture. Bush's low approval ratings and a series of GOP scandals put a damper on the effort during Bush's time in office. Yet at least one former presidential library fund-raiser felt that Bush's fund-raising assignment "won't be that difficult," suggesting that "the least the corporations that [benefited from] Bush's war could do for him is to put up a few million dollars."

Despite the downturn in the fortunes of neoconservatism, political analyst Rhodes Cook believes that the "power of being proven right" will still influence the Right to give generously: "A lot of conservatives continue to respect Bush and will work hand in glove to fund his ex-presidency to prove their rectitude."

STUMPING FOR THE PARTY

Whereas George W. Bush's projected think tank will be a repository for Republican ideas, at some point Bush will also be asked to campaign on behalf of the Republican Party. Presidents with low approval ratings—think of Richard Nixon and Jimmy Carter—are often shunned once they leave office. Eventually, though, the Republican National Committee and individual candidates will solicit the former president's backing when running for election, and Bush will return to the political stage in earnest. For conservative districts in beet red states, there may not even be a time delay.

Stumping for political candidates became a formal pursuit for former presidents toward the end of the nineteenth century. In early America, the very notion of parties and partisanship was perceived as unrepublican, a departure from virtuous behavior. But behind the scenes, George Washington himself, who explicitly professed an antipathy to factionalism, was unable to resist backing favorite horses like Patrick Henry. He wasn't alone. Other out-of-office Founding Fathers voiced their concerns about parties and elections through letters and other channels.

From his plantation perch in Nashville, Tennessee, Andrew Jackson helped secure the Democratic nomination and eventually the presidency for his fellow Tennessean slaveholder and Texas annexationist James Polk—over another of his former protégés, Martin Van Buren. During the Civil War period, all five living ex-presidents voted in lockstep against Lincoln. Reconstruction Era and Gilded Age ex-presidents offered their services, making public addresses on behalf of their parties; in one memorable case, exiting Democratic stalwart Grover Cleveland even bolted the party at the nomination of progressive reformer William Jennings Bryan. And Teddy Roosevelt's thunderous return to the political scene following his well-publicized African trip in 1910 began a tradition of ex-presidents stumping loudly for favorite candidates.

Since Teddy Roosevelt, few former president have failed to campaign for fellow partisans. Sometimes former leaders have tried to reanimate interest in their own positions. Herbert Hoover, for example, recovered from the abyss of the Great Depression and his accompanying loss to Franklin Roosevelt to spend three decades pressing candidates to conform to his flavor of conservatism. From convention stump speech to radio address to campaign stop, Hoover worked tirelessly to raise the fortunes of his Grand Old Party. His confidence that he alone possessed the keys to Republican salvation left little room for robust debate. Nonetheless, his contrarian voice was a constant feature of America's political firmament until well after World War II.

While Hoover felt little compunction about airing his views, regardless of who was listening, Harry Truman had a harder time adjusting to the realities of political life after the presidency. Lending his political support to dark-horse candidates in 1956 and 1960—instead of the Democratic Party's prophets of change, Adlai Stevenson and John Kennedy—Truman held out hope for a replay of an earlier era while seeking affirmation of his continued relevance.

A select few former presidents have actually had the chance to campaign for immediate family members. A late octogenarian when his son triumphed over Andrew Jackson in the notorious election of 1824, John Adams was able to offer little more than moral support. His fellow New England Brahmin George H. W. Bush also kept an arm's-length relationship and played only a modest role on the campaign trail, but was thrilled to have his friend and former secretary of state

James Baker help his son triumph in another notorious election at the dawn of the twenty-first century.

Bill Clinton took another tack entirely. After leaving office, Clinton said, "I made up my mind that I would not be someone who spent the rest of his life wishing I were still president. That seemed to be a stupid way to waste a day and also an arrogant thing." Instead, he spent at least some of his time wishing that someone else would become president—his wife. Toward the end of his second term, Clinton suggested that the next twenty years would be his wife's time to lead. He played a front-and-center role during Hillary Clinton's campaigns for reelection to the Senate in 2006 and, as noted, the Democratic presidential nomination in 2008—and employed a small army of campaign workers whose job it was to vet any document that might have offered fodder to her enemies.

REINHABITING POLITICAL OFFICE

As the Clintons left the White House, one persistent rumor was that the former president might consider running for mayor of New York. Though the idea of one of the world's greatest politicians tackling the "second hardest job in America" was intriguing, in contemporary America it was also farfetched. In the postwar period, only Gerald Ford had seriously entertained seeking political office once again, coming startlingly close to forging a deal to become Ronald Reagan's running mate in 1980.

Returning to electoral politics was not always an aberration. There are four cases of presidents who have won political office after the White House: John Quincy Adams's radical turn to the House of Representatives in 1831; John Tyler's ignominious election to the Confederate Congress sixteen years after leaving power; Andrew Johnson's securing of a Senate seat in 1875 following his impeachment-plagued completion of

Lincoln's presidency; and Grover Cleveland's nonconsecutive second term, which rendered him the only president to achieve two postpresidencies. (After his loss in 1888, Cleveland's wife, twenty-seven years his junior, presciently told a White House servant, "I want you to take good care of all the furniture and ornaments in the house, for I want to find everything just as it is now when we come back again.")

A number of former presidents have also made significant efforts to reclaim the presidential mantle. Martin Van Buren ran for the office under the Free Soil Party's banner in 1848; Millard Fillmore campaigned under the nativist American Party (also known as the Know-Nothings) in 1856; U. S. Grant fell short in his bid for a third term at the 1880 Republican convention (though he was leading after thirty-five ballots); and Teddy Roosevelt made his fantastic insider/outsider run on the Bull Moose ticket in 1912's "election of the century."

On occasion, such aspirations have been marked by delusions of reelectability on the part of politicians who might have known better. In 1923, ten months before his death, a battered Woodrow Wilson still fantasized that a third term was in reach. Teddy Roosevelt quietly expected to launch another comeback in 1920, a prospect complicated by his untimely death in 1919. Most shocking of all was Herbert Hoover's illusory hope of a rematch against FDR: as the Republican Party met in Philadelphia's steamy Convention Hall in July 1940, Hoover sat in the stands, calmly indulging a romantic fantasy that he would be anointed as that year's GOP dark horse.

A Commitment to Public Service

Even without returning to elected office, many former presidents have found ways to impart their knowledge and experience both at the behest of sitting presidents and in their own right as private citizens. Thomas Jefferson's late work of genius, the University of Virginia, is an example of the latter. Bothered by the religious concentration of his alma mater, William and Mary, Jefferson set out to establish an institution that would not be undergirded by religious precepts. Chartered by the Commonwealth and publicly funded, the university gathered its first class in 1825, a year before Jefferson's death. Sadly, the former president—who had hoped to find his new institution populated by civic-minded Jeffersons in miniature—was confronted instead with drunken blowhards whom he was forced to reproach. Despite the cold shower, Jefferson's accomplishment in Charlottesville is nothing short of astonishing, and the university he founded stands as an eloquent final testament to his ideals.

More than half a century later, Rutherford B. Hayes picked up Jefferson's pedagogical mantle—this time promoting education not for the sons of the elite, but for the offspring of the enslaved. After his single term in office, Hayes oversaw a foundation that advanced the vocational and general learning of African Americans. Paternalistic in tone, the fund nonetheless ensured that many Negro colleges were kept afloat, and no less a figure than W. E. B. DuBois extolled the former president for his "tireless energy and single-heartedness for the interests of my Race." Despite Hayes's noble efforts, he could never escape the stigma of the infamous 1876 election that ended Reconstruction and gave him the presidency.

Herbert Hoover also knew from stigma. Over his long postpresidential life, Hoover never lived down his ineffectual performance during the worst economic crisis of the twentieth century. As a result, Hoover's staggering humanitarian relief work both before and after his catastrophic term in office has often been overlooked. In three months alone in 1946, he and his pro bono staff logged fifty thousand miles in trying to tackle Europe's perilous food shortages and help stabilize its famine emergency. The following year, Hoover devised a school meals program in America that eventually served forty thousand tons of food and 3.5 million meals to children. No matter the success of the "Hoover-meals," it was the Depression era's notorious "Hoovervilles" that entered the lexicon instead, the former president's laudable relief efforts largely ignored by posterity.

Rehabilitation and Vindication

Historian Joan Hoff has observed that one constant in the story of the American postpresidency is the urge of middling or failed presidents to transcend their legacy. As Carter and Clinton have demonstrated, humanitarianism is an obvious way to turn the page. But other presidents have tried other means—the locus classicus among them being Richard Nixon, who dispensed with humanitarian gestures and spent his remaining years in a long and concerted campaign to refurbish his tarnished reputation.

Resurrection was the central leitmotif of Nixon's ex-presidency. Once called "the political figure who has been revived more times than *Oklahoma!*," Nixon managed a partial, but substantial, metamorphosis from the disgraced progenitor of Watergate to the Sage of Saddle River, a fount of realpolitik sought out by presidents from Reagan to Clinton. (Small wonder his presidential library used to screen the film *Never Give Up.*) By publishing a string of instruction manuals on foreign affairs, seizing opportune moments for op-ed contributions, and making high-profile visits to China, Russia, and elsewhere, Nixon bought back respectability with strategic segments of the *bien-pensant*. Bill Clinton, who profited from Nixon's advice on Russia during the first year of his presidency, provided the capstone by proffering an overly indulgent eulogy at Nixon's funeral: "May the day of judging President Nixon on anything less than his entire life and career come to a close," Clinton pronounced. In death, Nixon's final comeback was complete.

The postpresidency of Nixon's liberator, Gerald Ford, demonstrates a more indirect route to upgrading one's legacy. Though Ford's life after the Oval Office certainly involved its notable share of moneymaking ventures and golf tournaments, it also confirmed his long-standing tendency to back political positions that were out of step with the Republican Party establishment. Ford favored affirmative action, supported the Equal Rights Amendment, questioned the GOP's rigid pro-life stance, addressed (with Carter) the subjectivity of the Palestinian people, and even tried—unsuccessfully—to broker a deal to end the attempted impeachment of Bill Clinton. In today's polarized ideological climate, Ford can be justly hailed as a sane voice of the moderate middle.

The memoir is one more potential tool for any president bent on burnishing his legacy. The genre has seen few unqualified successes: U. S. Grant's stirring literary recollections of his life before the presidency are usually acknowledged to have set the standard for the field, but many others—including Herbert Hoover's impenetrable four volumes—are read only by the most fanatical aficionados. What should have been a master class in the machinations of power politics, Lyndon Johnson's memoir, *The Vantage Point*, is instead an anodyne, lightweight account of little general interest. Yet now and then a variation on the theme has emerged that has an impact on public consciousness: Merle Miller's bestselling oral biography of Harry Truman, *Plain Speaking*, stirred a longing for the "truth-telling" of Truman's time during the Watergate era of distrust and cynicism. Despite later challenges to the veracity of Truman's remarks, the book had long made its mark on the general population.

GEORGE W. BUSH'S FUTURE?

It is an open question how the forty-third commander-in-chief will shape his own postpresidency—whether he will conform to the modern model, in which charitable activities and the pursuit of money take pride of place, or whether he will chart some new course. To what extent will George W. Bush's presidency, racked as it has been by global indignation, undermine his potential for humanitarian engagement? What means exist to rehabilitate a legacy scarred by an unpopular war? Will lucrative consultancies and speeches offer the tempting path of least resistance?

Only sixty-two when leaving office in 2009, Bush confronts a wide open, and thus uncertain, future. He has said little about his aspirations, aside from expressing a general interest in his presidential complex and a desire to make money—"replenishing the ol' coffers," as he told one journalist. Seasoned observers of the Texas scene, like political journalists Louis Dubose and Robert Bryce, are at a loss to predict his next move. "What strikes me about Bush is his lack of a character arc," Dubose explains. "He's the same guy who was governor here, who was then the same guy with whom I occasionally played basketball at the downtown Y in Houston in the 70s. . . . Bush is a character in stasis, which makes gaming his next move so challenging." Bush's personality and temperament while in the White House seem to mirror these sentiments. He was a man outwardly untroubled by the usual stresses and anxieties of executive power. Sustaining a rigorous certitude that history will prove him right, and unfazed by the Sturm und Drang of even a wartime presidency—a psychological strain that demoralized LBJ and tormented Nixon—Bush has always evinced a righteousness untouched by ambivalence.

Bush will probably take time before settling on his future. He plans to live near his Dallas presidential library, but will likely spend considerable time at his Crawford ranch. "I can just envision getting in the car, getting bored, going down to the ranch," he says. Returning to the ranch probably won't be as sharp a departure for Bush as it was for Lyndon Johnson in 1969. ("He's become a goddamn farmer," one Johnson friend complained at the time. "I want to talk Democratic politics, he only talks hog prices.") Bush has spent more time at home during his tenure in office than any other modern president.

It seems doubtful that George W. Bush will follow the path of Richard Nixon, who wrote a series of policy books in a concerted effort to vindicate the catastrophe of Watergate. There is also strikingly little in Bush's background to suggest that international humanitarian work, à la Carter and Clinton, could become a passion. And in contrast with Eisenhower and even his own father, Bush's foreign affairs record is unlikely to lead to invitations to consult on geostrategic policy in the near term.

Among postwar heads of state, the closest model for Bush could be Gerald Ford, whose predilection for the good life he may yet prove to share. As noted, however, Ford remained a political moderate—a kind of maverick bipartisan—until his death. Bush may be more likely to continue his calls for democracy promotion American-style, reviving his presidency's "freedom on the march" homilies for a hard-core conservative audience. Ultimately, the nearest point of comparison for Bush may be James Buchanan, the copperhead president from Pennsylvania, who spent his post–White House years unapologetically fighting for exculpation of his Civil War sins.

Should the next legislature seek to investigate claims that his administration engaged in abuses of power, George W. Bush may repeat a common refrain of his presidency: the invocation of executive privilege. Harry Truman was the first former president to invoke executive privilege after the White House. During the McCarthy period, Truman rebuffed a subpoena to testify about his appointment of Treasury Department official Harry Dexter White—then suspected of spying for the Soviets—on the grounds of executive privilege. In the late 1970s, Nixon did the same over Vietnam. Bush may yet face similar challenges as he struggles to fend off congressional investigations into the conduct of the war on terrorism.

Speculation about Bush's future does suggest one tantalizing wild-card prospect, a job Bush coveted long before the onset of his political career: commissioner of Major League Baseball. A managing general partner of the Texas Rangers from 1989 to 1994, Bush has long been entranced by the sport. "I never dreamed about being president," he says. "When I was growing up, I wanted to be Willie Mays."

After Bush family friend Fay Vincent was ejected as commissioner in September 1992, Vincent recalls Bush asking him, "Fay, what do you think about me becoming commissioner? Do you think I'd make a good commissioner?" Bush added that Bud Selig, then acting commissioner and head of Major League Baseball's Executive Council, "would love to have me be commissioner and he tells me that he can deliver it." Vincent tried to set the wheels in motion, but he soon gathered that Selig was being disingenuous—that in fact he wanted the job for himself. "I'm afraid Selig is bullshitting you," he was finally forced to tell Bush.

If Bush had been offered the commissioner's slot, he might have forgone his gubernatorial run against Ann Richards in 1994. (One wonders how different the world would look today had Bush gotten the job.) But he may still get his opportunity: as chance would have it, Bud Selig plans to step down for good in 2012 at the age of seventy-eight. After enduring a thousand days out of office, Bush could be primed to go after the position he has wanted for years. The pay, at least, would be hard to beat: in 2006 Selig pulled down $15 million. That kind of salary might relieve Bush of the obligation to keynote rubber-chicken dinners for Bechtel and Halliburton.

From leader of the free world to commissioner of baseball? It's a thought-provoking notion—and yet probably a long shot. It's unlikely that Major League Baseball, hugely profitable in the recent past, would run the risk of what would surely be a politically divisive choice. Moreover, a former president could never attend a game without an enormous security envelope. Former Reagan and Bush senior aide Marlin Fitzwater is hard-pressed to imagine Bush committing to such an all-encompassing role. "He will have so many choices and options," Fitzwater says. "I don't think any former president would want to tie himself down with a full-time job."

Ultimately, of course, we can only watch and wait. For the familiar caveat applies as surely to former presidents as it does to financial funds: past performance is no guarantee of future results.

GETTING SOLVENT

~

The Financial Journey of Past Presidents

It is a national disgrace that our Presidents . . . should be cast adrift, and perhaps be compelled to keep a corner grocery for subsistence. . . . We elect a man to the Presidency, expect him to be honest, to give up a lucrative profession, perhaps, and after we [are] done with him we let him go into seclusion and perhaps poverty.

Millard Fillmore

I never had a nickel to my name until I got out of the White House, and now I'm a millionaire, the most favored person for the Washington Republicans. I get a tax cut every year, no matter what our needs are.

Bill Clinton

[Gerald Ford] has become the presidential equivalent of Joe Louis, who ended his days as a greeter for a Las Vegas hotel.

Richard Cohen, *The Washington Post*

· · · · · ·

RETURNING BY TRAIN ON HIS OWN DIME AND MOVING INTO HIS mother-in-law's house, Harry Truman found his January 1953 exit from the White House a sobering experience. With no Air Force

One to guarantee a soft landing, no million-dollar transition fund to help him segue into private life, no plush office awaiting administrative staff, the former president confronted a subdued and humbling homecoming.

Nearly half a century later, Bill Clinton's departure could not have been more different. Forsaking Little Rock and removing to New York, Clinton left office blessed with a rich array of perks and a wide-open opportunity to capitalize on his fame. Waiting in the wings were a host of record-setting book deals for him and his wife, unprecedented speaking fees (over $9 million his first year alone), and an eight-thousand-square-foot office space in Harlem that would become headquarters for his worldwide fund-raising operations. The ex-presidency, once a burden to bear, now had the marks of la dolce vita.

Compensation for presidents and ex-presidents alike has long been a contested question. The opening salvo in the debate occurred during the Constitutional Convention of 1787, when Benjamin Franklin proposed that a president receive no recompense whatsoever. Franklin wanted to diminish what he believed was human nature's overriding passion: avarice. Two stays in England before the Revolution convinced him that corruption was inherent to English political life, and helped seed his "Utopian Idea" of a nonsalaried chief magistrate in America. "That we can never find men to serve us in the Executive department, without paying them well for their services," he declared, was a false premise and one that risked creating institutional birth defects.

Franklin's advice went unheeded. The convention decided to grant the commander-in-chief a twenty-five-thousand-dollar salary and a rent-free mansion. Yet what appeared to be a generous offer was not generous enough. Although Congress occasionally allocated separate funds, presidents were generally expected to use their personal income to finance the standard accoutrements of White House life—public receptions, banquets, furnishings, and staff. Many ended up saving nothing during their tenure, and most left the office deep in debt. Thomas Jefferson found himself eight thousand dollars in the hole simply from the invoices accrued during his final year in power.

Compounding the pain of debt, once out of power most presidents were loath to engage in the kinds of commercial pursuits that might have restored them financially. Republican ideas of virtue, nurtured and fostered by the Founding Fathers, held that commerce was a stain on the reputation of the presidency and something to be shunned. For decades, most departing presidents felt compelled to uphold an informal obligation to refrain from exploiting the symbolic power of their former position.

Not until after the Civil War were the financial restraints on former presidents finally adjusted. The new capitalist ethic altered the playing field: generating income from commercial transactions was no longer perceived as antithetical to the country's value system. The ruthless accessories of capitalism's forward march—graft, acquisitiveness, and inequality—benefited the ex-presidential class. According to historian Henry Graff, "Puritan America was trying to find moral justification for the relatively easier accumulation of money," and singled out robber barons, corrupt bosses, and rapacious industrialists as villainous exceptions to the rule. For the rest of America, there was no shame in turning a legitimate business profit—and former presidents were hardly blamed for pursuing a decent living after leaving office, whether in law, business, writing, or speaking for pay.

SURPLUSES AND DEFICITS OF THE VIRGINIA FOUNDERS

In the beginning, George Washington acknowledged his kismet. The only one of the early Virginia presidents not to be enveloped by the tyranny of arrears, Washington wrote in 1799 that "Were it not for occasional supplies of money in payment for lands sold within the last four or five years to the amount of upwards of $50,000," he too would have been mired "in debt and difficulties."

Washington's good fortune was a product of diligence and foresight. Having acquired his first piece of land in western Virginia's Shenandoah Valley before turning twenty, and educated himself on Pennsylvania investments during the French and Indian War, Washington was seasoned in the burgeoning business of land speculation. (He also bore witness to the regrettable circumstances of others who gambled poorly and landed in debtors' prison—friends like Henry Lee and Robert Morris, the latter who, before meeting such a fate, had been celebrated as the "Financier of the Revolution.")

Out of office, Washington ventured conservatively and forswore borrowing on assets purchased with loans, pledging "never [to] undertake anything without perceiving a door to the accomplishment in a reasonable amount of time with my own resources." His prudence paid off. Moreover, Washington was rarely beset by the challenge of managing distant lands; there was never a shortage of people eager to assist the retired general-president in administering his real estate. Reluctant to use his position for financial gain when in power, once out of office he became "shameless, asking government officials and private individuals to assess the value of tracts, see to surveying and improvements, advise him as to the reliability of respective buyers, [and] collect sums due to him."

Despite his acumen and land-holding successes, especially compared with his Virginia successors, Washington was nevertheless cash poor; he often resorted to selling property to make money, but frequently failed to receive full payment. The refurbishing of Mount Vernon, and the mouths he had to feed there, only aggravated his burden. Washington left half his slaves in Philadelphia when he returned home in 1797, planning to rent out parts of his plantation to freedmen. But the scheme was unsuccessful: by 1798 Washington was forced to secure a bank loan, his lack of ready cash forcing him into what he considered "a ruinous mode of obtaining money."

Despite its rundown state when Washington left Philadelphia, Mount Vernon did provide the former president with an income. In his first year out of office, Washington established a 2,250-square-foot distillery that produced twelve thousand gallons of corn and rye whiskey and fruit brandy, and became one of the new republic's largest whiskey distillers. (Early Americans were mighty imbibers, consuming three times as much alcohol as their counterparts today.)

At his death, Washington's estate was valued at more than half a million dollars, predominantly in land and stock, making him one of the wealthiest persons in the country. His twenty-seven-page will, written on watermarked paper in the summer of 1799, liberated his slaves, with additional provisions for the elderly and young, upon his wife's passing. As the foremost historian of Washington's finances concluded: "His greatness, in the last analysis, rests upon the fact that he was by nature and by thorough training the greatest businessman of his time."

The same could not be said, alas, for Washington's successors. Thomas Jefferson, James Madison, James Monroe, and Andrew Jackson were besieged by debt for almost their entire postpresidential life. Confronted by the prospect of relative poverty, they borrowed money, sold off land, and marketed their personal collections. As relatively large slaveholders, the early presidents were also held back by the intensifying contradictions and economic inviolability of plantation life. The vast landholdings and slave workforce of the plantation model required a level of oversight and investment causing many to become "prisoners of their own plantations." In this era before agricultural innovation had made more efficient plowing and harvesting possible, gentlemen farmers like James Madison soon concluded that slavery and farming were incompatible. Yet these slaveholding ex-presidents rarely divested themselves of their human property.

Virginia underwent profound economic changes in the period after Washington's death. In the first quarter of the nineteenth century, the profitable Virginia lifestyle, driven for two centuries by slaveholding and major cash crops like tobacco, was nearing obsolescence. The emergence of a world economy, the rise of the Kentucky region as a source of competition, and the advent of cotton as a marketable commodity all contributed to the attenuation of the Virginia way of life. The Old Dominion dropped from first to fifth among the states in population, had almost no resident growth (while the country exploded), and developed only the meagerest of industry. With the peculiar institution exacerbating its decay, Virginia was a state in radical decline—and the early Virginia presidents were caught in the transition.

Suspicious of the commercial and market forces that were overturning his agricultural conventions, Thomas Jefferson clung to his belief in the ideal of the yeoman farmer; the rash of competitive commerce streaking through the North left him cold. While he grudgingly accepted new forms of exchange, such as the sale of cash crops abroad, Jefferson viewed the new institutions of capitalism—banks and stock markets—as inherently foreign and dangerous.

Although they accelerated the deterioration of his condition, the changes in Virginia's economic profile were hardly Jefferson's only problem. Far more immediate and significant were the debts he had accumulated—from outstanding liabilities on his father-in-law's estate and pre–Revolutionary War loans from British firms, to his unsustainable affinity for the good life. Though he owned two hundred slaves and more than ten thousand acres of land, Jefferson's life out of office was economically unforgiving.

Jefferson felt the oppression keenly. "Instead of the unalloyed happiness of retiring unembarrassed and independent, to the enjoyment of my estate," he said regretfully upon his retirement, "I have to pass such a length of time in a thraldom of mind never before known to me." Yet he did little to address the problem. Jefferson was constitutionally incapable of curbing his spending, his polymathic interests motivating purchases far and wide. His personal debt was ironic, given his political conviction that any form of governmental debt was an injustice to be avoided at all cost. "I place economy among the first and most important virtues," he wrote, "and public debt as the greatest of dangers to be feared." Still, his righteous disdain for public debt never figured into his private habits.

The constant flow of visitors to Monticello—he sometimes hosted more than a hundred at a time—presented a further burden. And there were more permanent guests: Jefferson's only surviving child from his marriage to Martha Skelton, Martha (Patsy) Randolph, lived there with her underemployed husband (whose debt exceeded even Jefferson's) and children. Selling land was Jefferson's only practical source of income and sole means to pay off his debts—especially since he refused any form of paid labor.

Jefferson was also faced with crippling litigation in his later years. Landholder Edward Livingston filed suit against him in Richmond, Virginia, in the circuit court of Jefferson's foe and second cousin, John Marshall. The issue concerned a Livingston-owned New Orleans river property that Jefferson had ordered federal marshals to seize during his presidency, arguing that it obstructed access to the Mississippi River. Livingston sued for one hundred thousand dollars, but he really just wanted his land back. While the suit was thrown out, the case was costly to Jefferson in time and resources alike.

By 1814, Jefferson's economic situation had become so parlous that he was forced to sell to Congress his treasured personal library of over six thousand volumes. The timing was right: the British had torched the Library of Congress not long before, and Congress's need for books dovetailed with Jefferson's need for cash. The final price Jefferson received, just under twenty-four thousand dollars, was half its market value. The bulk of the funds went to repay Jefferson's creditors, including Polish Revolutionary War general Tadeusz Kosciuszko and former private secretary William Short. Though Jefferson took no credit for the Library's rebirth, "the institution that emerged from the ashes after the war" was essentially his creation, as biographer Dumas Malone noted.

Yet Jefferson's solvency was eventually overcome by his acquisitiveness. Tormented by the loss of his collection—"I cannot live without books," he wrote—he soon began building another library, though the costs would surely diminish the remaining proceeds from his sale to Congress. Whatever his financial circumstances, Jefferson retained an abiding faith that all things must pass. "Somehow or other these things find their way out as they come in and so I suppose they will now." Jefferson saw his economic problems as "an approaching wave in a storm," but remained determined to "live as long, eat as much, and drink as much, as if the wave had already glided under the ship."

But even Jefferson could only cling to such optimism for so long. When the young nation entered its first financial crisis, the panic of 1819, Jefferson's longtime escape hatch—his ability to generate income by selling land—was finally closed off. His status in Virginia allowed him to run up bills that he never paid, but that was small consolation. Although he was bailed out by friends, Jefferson's situation continued its descent—especially after he invested in a local flour mill that would generate virtually no net value. Worse, he was forced to pay compound interest on an ill-advised loan to his grandson's father-in-law. Even his monumental labors to establish the University of Virginia were financed with borrowed funds.

The last months of Jefferson's life may have been his most emotionally taxing. Faced with a hovering debt of a hundred thousand dollars, he was forced to appeal to the Virginia General Assembly for the legal right to sell off Monticello itself (though not the slaves who lived there). A letter to a friend, sitting Virginia legislator Joseph Cabell, presents the evidence in painful detail: "My application to the legislature is for permission to dispose of property . . . in a way which, bringing a fair price for it, may pay my debts, and leave a living for myself in my old age, and leave something for my family. . . . To me it is almost a question of life and death." A public lottery was planned to support the third president, but Jefferson was reluctant to accept the proceeds. Though his friends finally raised enough money to save Jefferson from the humiliation of selling his estate, he nevertheless ended his life bankrupt and debt-ridden.

Till the end, Jefferson clung to the belief that "the earth belongs to the living," and that every generation must start afresh—with new laws, constitutions, and, yes, a financial slate cleared of all debt. His own debts were not settled until 1831, five years after his death, when Monticello and its slaves were sold to James Turner Barclay for seven thousand dollars after Jefferson's daughter could not pay her creditors. It was one of history's astringent ironies: the "apostle of liberty," as Dumas Malone called him, had his posthumous arrears wiped out by the sale of human life.

After he left office in 1817, James Madison visited frequently with Jefferson at Monticello (just thirty miles away from his own home, Montpelier). The two men endured similarly harsh circumstances in their postpresidential years. Beset by the general hard times in Virginia, Madison was also overwhelmed by the panic of 1819, with its string of foreclosures and bank failures. The years that followed brought further anguish. Though Madison took a forward-looking interest in the science of farming, a combination of lackluster markets, an uncooperative Mother Nature, and a dramatic downturn in agricultural fortunes cast doom on his economic well-being. In ten years, Madison experienced nine crop failures. After a streak of bad luck, including insects, early frost, and torrential rains, in 1825 he was forced to make supplications to Nicholas Biddle and the Bank of the United States for a six-thousand-dollar loan to tide him over—a loan that was never even granted.

By the late 1820s, Madison had disposed of enough land and assets to reclaim, barely, his former lifestyle. Maintaining his hope that slavery would be eliminated by gradual means, he held off selling any slaves until 1834, two years before his death—and came to regret the transaction. Convinced that the races were irreconcilable, Madison helped to found the American Colonization Society, which advocated the deportation of liberated slaves to West Africa. A rigid constitutionalist, he always held that slaves were legal property and that slaveholders should be guaranteed adequate compensation upon their sale.

Madison's economic condition was weighed down by an additional drain: the painful liability of his wife Dolley's wastrel son from her previous marriage. Saddled with gambling debts and other trappings of a spendthrift existence, Payne Todd made several visits to debtors' prison and left his stepfather with forty thousand dollars in unpaid bills. Madison even began to contemplate the loss of his Washington home. "He still talks of the last resort, 'the house in Washington,'" Dolley bemoaned. Madison did retain one increasingly valuable set of documents: his private notes on the 1787 constitutional debates, which he pledged not to publish while any Founders were still alive. Despite his straitened circumstances, he stuck to the promise, and the notes went unpublished until his death.

Things were hardly better for James Monroe. The last of the original Virginians, Monroe left office seventy-five thousand dollars in the hole. According to one account, he "tottered from the White House . . . wrinkled, bent, old, and poverty-stricken," an ignoble end to the life of the fifth president. And unlike Jefferson and Madison—who managed, with great struggle, to hold on to some of their property—Monroe was forced to dispose of his.

Jefferson may have spent his retirement years chasing away creditors, but he remained committed to earthly pleasures, imbibing the wines (a "necessary of life") and food ("we seldom repent of having eaten too little") that deepened his economic plight. By contrast, Monroe's half decade after the presidency was dominated by his pursuit of what he felt was just compensation for the diplomatic missions he had conducted on behalf of the government. Where Jefferson soothed his despair with the pleasures of the sweet life, Monroe was gripped by a single idée fixe: getting repaid.

Monroe had known easier times, especially during his postings to France in 1794–96 and 1803–7. In those days he was considered extravagant in his habits, living abroad "infected by a spirit of emulous ostentation." Monroe laid out substantial funds to the government on these trips, fully expecting to be paid back. In general, however, American ministers abroad were treated shabbily when it came to financial provision. Though the cost of a European posting was outlandish, the most Monroe could expect in return was nine thousand dollars per year. By the time he left the presidency, with his land largely sold off, he was in dire need of that long-postponed reimbursement—his only real prospect of new income. When his initial requests went unheeded, he became convinced that he was being swindled—and getting paid back became a matter of honor as well as survival.

Monroe's duress played out in Congress in the mid-1820s, and members squared off for and against him, largely along party lines. Sensing that the political tides were turning toward Andrew Jackson—and that associating himself with President John Quincy Adams and his 1824 "stolen" election would torpedo congressional support for his repayment—Monroe rejected Adams's offer to participate in the 1826 Panama Congress, and categorically refused to serve as Adams's vice president in 1828. Monroe had lost interest in politics; he wanted only what he felt he was owed.

To pay his debts, in 1826 Monroe sold his primary residence, Highland, in Albermarle County, and moved to Oak Hill, Virginia. Fortunately, that same year Congress finally endorsed half of his overall claim, nearly thirty thousand dollars. Four years later, after his wife's death and without any funds remaining, Monroe left for New York City to move in with his daughter and son-in-law. While there he received another thirty thousand, actually exceeding his original request. The funds helped Monroe square his debts, but even this windfall was insufficient to rescue his standard of living: he was now a destitute man. Upon his death, his family lacked even the funds to ship his body home to Virginia from New York. Twenty-seven years would pass before Monroe would be reburied on his native soil.

After winning election to the House of Representatives in November 1830, John Quincy Adams—who had served as Monroe's secretary of state—stopped to visit the ailing Monroe in New York while traveling from Massachusetts to Washington, D.C. "Mr. Monroe is a very remarkable instance of a man whose life . . . has received more pecuniary reward from the public than any other man since the existence of the nation, and is now dying, at the age of seventy-two, in wretchedness and beggary."

THE ADAMS FAMILY FINANCES

Not all early presidents hailed from Virginia. The two President Adamses were America's first northern presidents, and their financial fortunes would differ from those of their Virginia colleagues in important ways. John Adams and his son John Quincy Adams were raised in Massachusetts against a Puritan landscape of sobriety and moderation, not the unsustainable economic model of colonial slavery—a key difference that made things generally easier for the Adamses once they left office.

John Adams was careful with his finances—so much so that, unlike other early presidents, he was actually eleven thousand dollars in the black when he left the presidency in 1801. He returned to a home he had purchased in 1787, known variously as the Mansion, Peacefield, or simply the Big House, a reasonably sized estate on seventy-five acres that sometimes roomed more than twenty persons.

Adams sometimes fantasized about the wealth he might have earned as a lawyer if he hadn't gone into political life. The attorney who took over his practice, Adams mused, had "made a fortune of two or three hundred thousand dollars" from the business he had founded. Attending board meetings of the American Academy of Arts and Sciences, Adams seethed with envy at those around him, who by his account were "all but me very rich," with "their city palaces and country seats, their fine gardens, and greenhouses and hot houses."

Though Adams lived a quarter century after his presidency, his single financial crisis happened in 1803, two years into his retirement.

In that year John and Abigail Adams lost most of the thirteen thousand dollars they had cautiously invested in a banking house at the recommendation of their son John Quincy. The firm, Bird, Savage & Bird, was based in London, but since it traded in U.S. Treasury funds they thought it a safe bet. John Quincy's guilt at the firm's foreclosure was so intense that he ended up selling his own Boston home and making up the difference on his parents' losses. "The error of judgment was mine," he wrote, "and therefore I shall not refuse to share in the suffering." Despite being "penny poor," the Adamses stayed afloat with the income from the farms they tended in Quincy and the securities Abigail wisely purchased over the years.

The Bird, Savage & Bird fiasco foreshadowed John Quincy's own postpresidential setbacks. Although the sixth president was without an institutional income for only two and a half years between leaving the White House in 1829 and moving to the House of Representatives at the end of 1831, congressmen at that time were paid on a per diem basis, earning nothing when Congress was not in session. Though his father had left him the family mansion, Adams still had to sell land around Boston to make ends meet. Only when his son Charles Frances Adams took over the family's portfolio, overseeing everything from rents to investments, did John Quincy's situation stabilize. Through the end of his long life he would remain on relatively sure footing.

Staring Down Poverty Again

Andrew Jackson, who took office in 1829, was America's first outsider president—the first who was neither a Virginia Founder nor an Adams from Massachusetts. But he shared the experience of several of his forerunners in one crucial respect. Haunted by financial problems, he spent his ex-presidency at his Hermitage plantation outside Nashville, Tennessee, trying to shore up his fortunes. "I carried five thousand dollars when I went to Washington," Jackson wrote. "I returned with barely ninety dollars in [my] pockets."

As with the other early presidents, Jackson had been forced to lay out most of his presidential salary to cover the upkeep of the White House. And like Madison, who left office only to be greeted by the economic hurricane of the 1819 panic, Jackson was plunged headlong into the depression of 1837 upon leaving office that year. Also like Madison, who bailed out his reckless stepson time and again, Jackson repeatedly extricated his adopted son, Andrew Jackson Jr., from financial disaster. (Madison, at least, recognized the waywardness of his wife's offspring; Jackson refused to accept his son's failings, convinced that his namesake was being swindled by malevolent associates.)

Similar to his Virginia predecessors, Jackson suffered primarily from cash-flow poverty. He retained scores of slaves and multiple property holdings that he could have sold to ensure his family's livelihood, but his reluctance to sell off the slaves—and a series of unsatisfying harvests—kept his finances unstable. Only after a number of bad cotton crops did the former president contemplate what he called his "great sacrafice" [sic]: selling any of his "one hundred and fifty odd negroes, old and young large and small." Yet it never came to that: Jackson went to any length to preserve his slave workforce. He even went so far as to borrow a thousand dollars to defend his slaves when four of them were called up on murder charges.

Jackson's money woes caused him endless distress. Planning a January 1840 trip to Louisiana to celebrate the silver anniversary of his victory in the Battle of New Orleans, Jackson appealed to a friend: "I am out of funds . . . and I cannot bear to borrow or travel as a pauper." (Eventually he managed to cobble together the resources for the trip without resorting to loans.) The Whig Party gleefully exploited Jackson's financial predicament, scolding him publicly for one particularly large debt even though Jackson swore that nothing would stop him from repaying it—including "all the calamities that may befall a nation, or individuals, except earthquakes."

Such financial challenges followed Andrew Jackson to the final months of his life. To his newly elected protégé, James K. Polk, Jackson confessed his situation: "Poverty stares us in the face," he told him. After Jackson's death, his son's troubles forced the sale of the former president's beloved Hermitage—an apt coda to a life of unease.

RETIRING IN (RELATIVE) COMFORT

The ex-presidencies of Martin Van Buren and John Tyler offer a departure from the unforgiving circumstances of most of their precursors. Van Buren arrived in Washington with a comfortable reserve of two hundred thousand dollars and led a relatively well-heeled life after leaving the White House. Indeed, his situation was so fortunate that he actually opted to take his four years' worth of presidential salary in a lump sum upon leaving office. Virginia slave owner John Tyler, who took office after the eye-blink presidency of William Henry Harrison, retired to his twelve-hundred-acre Tidewater plantation, Sherwood Forest, owning anywhere from sixty to ninety slaves. Like Van Buren, Tyler was in favorable financial health for most of the years he spent out of office and faced little of the damaging economic circumstances of the earlier Virginia presidents. After the death of his first wife, Letitia, in 1842, Tyler remarried well: his new wife, Julia Gardiner, came from a wealthy New York family and protected him during his cash-poor stretches. Unlike the Virginia Founders, Tyler never had to contemplate selling his plantation. Deeply involved in the management of his farm and constantly seeking new methods to improve the soil, Tyler actually accumulated both an additional four hundred acres of land and an increased number of slaves after leaving office.

During Tyler's retirement, gold rush mania gripped the country. His wife's relatives excitedly lit out for the West to pursue new fortunes. Tyler himself could not be bothered. "The President" was underwhelmed by the "California fever," Julia wrote her mother. "He thinks a good farm on James River with plenty of slaves is gold mine enough." It is hardly a shock, then, that Tyler called for none of his slaves to be released upon his death. On the contrary, he made clear in his will that "my wife will upon each of our children (the boys) attaining the age of twenty-one years, select for each a Negro boy as his own separate property."

Like Tyler, Millard Fillmore came to power on the death of a Whig president (in Fillmore's case, Zachary Taylor). Also like Tyler, he helpfully married a wealthy widow after the death of his first wife. Born into abject poverty, Fillmore had entered a thriving law practice in western New York before assuming a life in politics. After a two-and-a-half-year presidency, he opted not to return to the law, instead traveling, participating in civic activities in his native Buffalo, New York, and running again for the White House in a third-party bid. One of the earliest proponents of a presidential pension, Fillmore was badly scarred by the Panic of 1857, which wrecked the portfolio of railroad securities in which he had invested much of his savings. His second wife, Caroline Carmichael McIntosh, helped bail him out. After signing a prenuptial agreement that paid Fillmore ten thousand dollars a year to manage his new wife's finances, the former president spent his remaining years in fine fiscal health, ultimately leaving an estate in excess of two hundred thousand dollars.

The postpresidency of Fillmore's successor, Franklin Pierce, may be captured best by one clarifying personal admission: "After the White House," he asked, "what is there to do but drink?" In time, alcohol so deeply corroded Pierce's vital organs that he died of cirrhosis of the liver in 1869, twelve years after stepping down from office. Pierce had wisely stashed away around half of his presidential salary, which together with some shrewd investments provided him with a reasonably comfortable retirement, the ability to travel abroad freely, and the resources to tend to his ailing wife. He had lost two sons early on, and lost his thirteen-year-old in a freak railway accident two months before his inauguration—events that doubtless spurred his deepening alcoholism.

Abraham Lincoln's predecessor, James Buchanan, shared with Pierce a despondency upon leaving office—though in Buchanan's case the reasons were political, not personal. The only unmarried president, Buchanan was in a comfortable economic situation from the end of his term in office until his death in 1868, and passed most of that time trying to rehabilitate his political reputation. Shortly before he died he calculated carefully the value of his Wheatland estate: "Making all reasonable deductions," he wrote, "I am worth about $250,000." His fastidiousness on pecuniary matters bordered on the obsessive: after a land sale that brought him fifteen thousand dollars, Buchanan groused to the buyer, "You have made a mistake. Your check is ten cents too little."

Cautious and deliberate in financial matters, Buchanan managed the affairs of several relatives, and was generous to associates in need. Upon learning that Robert Tyler, the son of the former president and once a Democratic Party leader from Buchanan's state of Pennsylvania, had landed in difficult straits, he swiftly dispatched him a thousand-dollar check. Their different ideologies gave him no pause: "Though I could not approve your course in favor of the secessionists," Buchanan wrote Tyler, "I have never doubted the sincerity of your belief and the purity of your motives." This turned out to be an act of courage on Buchanan's part: a defender of the slaveocracy, Robert Tyler was a despised man in the North, threatened with lynching and hanged in effigy. He fled back to his native Virginia to save his life.

The first president to leave office after the Civil War, Andrew Johnson had a largely favorable financial profile despite the Panic of 1873. Though initially devastated by a large investment in a failed bank, he later recouped most of his losses. Buoyed by a portfolio of state bonds and real estate holdings, Johnson finished his days in reasonable security.

Johnson's fate, however, stands in stark contrast to that of his rival, Ulysses S. Grant. In fact, no postpresidential life matches in intensity the parabolic narrative of the dazzling Civil War general and controversial two-term president. The story's familiarity is testament to its disastrous denouement—and the lucrative phoenix that saved Grant's family following his painful death. At once tragic and transformative, the saga of U. S. Grant stands as one of the great stories of the American ex-presidency.

PRECARIOUS ENDINGS

Ulysses S. Grant had entered the White House in 1869 a war hero, one of the great men of his age. Yet a scant eight years later he finished his second term enveloped by scandal, his administration having succumbed to the temptations of graft, that scourge of Gilded Age politics. It was a mighty fall. His second term saw a series of debilitating setbacks: the Credit Mobilier affair, the Indian Trading scandal, the Sanborn incident, and the Whiskey Ring. Though he was never personally implicated, Grant was condemned for tolerating widespread corruption within his administration, and his reputation was forever tarnished.

Ten weeks after leaving office, Grant and his wife, the former Julia Dent, embarked on a worldwide tour to leave such indignities behind. At the beginning of Grant's second term, Congress had doubled the presidential salary to fifty thousand dollars, and the Grants had saved enough to finance much of their twenty-eight-month trip.

Upon their return, however, the Grants found themselves unexpectedly compromised. Though hardly impoverished—minor investments brought in around six thousand dollars a year—Grant felt compelled to turn to the corporate world to improve his finances. By now, former presidents were no longer expected to rely on favorable investments and generous friends: the era of competitive capitalism was in full bloom, and Grant looked forward to profiting from the nation's expanding markets.

Ferdinand Ward was a Wall Street guru-cum-fraudster who established corporate relations in a brokerage house with Grant's financially successful son, Ulysses Jr. (known as Buck). Persuaded by Buck, the former president signed on as a silent partner with the house—and soon invested the bulk of his savings there, in an all-or-nothing gamble that proved disastrous. Though initial returns appeared rewarding—with promised gains sometimes approaching 40 percent—it was a shell game. "Ward was kiting the firm's assets, pledging the same securities as collateral against multiple loans," biographer Jean Edward Smith explains. Ward's firm was keeping two sets of books; the firm's valuation was entirely fabricated, and in 1884 it collapsed.

Convicted of larceny, Ward was sentenced to ten years at Sing Sing. The extraordinary fleecing left Grant one hundred thousand dollars in debt. (Adding insult to his already injured pocketbook, Grant's final major investment, Wabash Railroad bonds, vanished when the company went bankrupt.) Having forfeited his military pension when he chose to resign his commission rather than retire, the Union Army hero was now reduced to accepting handouts from former colleagues and friends. William H. Vanderbilt offered to underwrite Grant's losses without asking for repayment; a disconsolate Grant reluctantly agreed, but insisted on paying Vanderbilt back (which he eventually did, at least in part, by selling his property and offering Vanderbilt such treasures as elephant tusks from the king of Siam and a congressional gold medal). The year before his death, Grant accepted a number of writing gigs with *Century Magazine* to stay above water. Generating five hundred dollars an article for a series of Civil War essays, Grant unknowingly started down his path to financial salvation.

Enter Mark Twain. With encouragement and publishing support from the esteemed author and friend, Grant accepted an assignment he had ducked for years: writing his memoirs. With his family's livelihood now at issue, Grant set down to work—but during the course of his writing the general learned that he had developed cancer, which had begun in his tongue and then swept through his mouth and throat. (At his peak, Grant smoked twenty cigars a day.) His pain grew so relentless that his doctor was forced to spray a cocaine solution on his tumor just to allow him to swallow. Grant was in a race against time.

The federal government took pity on the former president. Just minutes before leaving office, President Chester Arthur reinstated the dying Grant as a general, thus affording him the financial safety net of a military pension. Members of Congress stood to applaud the bill's passing.

Ulysses S. Grant died on July 23, 1885, just days after his war chronicle's second and final volume was sent to the printers. Twain marketed Grant's *Personal Memoirs* by subscription, and within months a staggering quarter million copies had been sold. Julia Dent Grant and her family received around four hundred and fifty thousand dollars in royalties; their first check was for two hundred thousand, supposedly the largest royalty check ever paid out to that point. By the end of the nineteenth century, Grant's best-selling memoirs had outsold another enduring classic of American literature—Twain's own *Adventures of Huckleberry Finn*.

Though nowhere near as dramatic, Rutherford B. Hayes's postpresidency had its own precarious moments. Hayes was already knee-deep in debt upon beginning his single term in office—a situation exacerbated by the high-end entertaining he and his wife did at the White House. However, Hayes was sanguine about his fortunes by the end of his term: "I shall leave here in debt from twenty thousand to twenty-five thousand dollars," he considered, "but with a good credit, plenty of property, and in no sense needing pecuniary aid or sympathy." Hayes failed to predict that one of his major investments—the Fremont Harvesting Company—would go bust in 1885, or that his local bank, where he kept much of his cash, would soon be in danger of foreclosure. The former president's financial woes would even prevent him from attending the February 1885 dedication of the Washington Memorial—a project he had championed personally.

TRADING ON ONE'S NAME

After Hayes's departure in 1881, it would be many decades until an ex-president again encountered privation in his personal life. With the institutionalization of benefits still decades off, former presidents now availed themselves of opportunities that once were socially verboten. One case in point is Grover Cleveland, who escaped financial trouble after leaving office for the second time. Having sold his home outside Washington, D.C., for a large profit, he purchased a comfortable house in Princeton, New Jersey, and a summer residence in Cape Cod. Cleveland's net worth was estimated to be north of three hundred thousand dollars, savings one biographer considered a "moderate fortune" and another called "not rich, but well-to-do." With most of his funds tied up in equity, Cleveland agreed to write about his presidency for magazines and other publications to generate income. Journals as wide-ranging as the *Century,* the *Atlantic,* and *Ladies' Home Journal* paid handsomely for his efforts.

The late nineteenth century was an era of commercial expansion, and Cleveland embraced economic opportunities that came his way. Recognizing the growth in America's insurance industry, he joined the board of the Equitable Life Assurance Corporation and chaired the Association of Life Insurance Presidents. The insurance industry was overrun by fraud and graft, under constant pressure to reform from voices like future Supreme Court Chief Justice Charles Evans Hughes, and Cleveland set about to restore confidence in the sector. The insurance bosses remunerated him accordingly: Equitable paid him twelve thousand dollars annually for his trustee duties (making him their only compensated board member) and another twelve-thousand-dollar annual fee to help adjudicate company disputes. The Association of Life Insurance Presidents sweetened Cleveland's bankbook with a twenty-five-thousand-dollar annual paycheck. Though he was criticized for taking such handouts, Cleveland died leaving his family well provided for—and was rewarded for his troubles by having his visage appear on the thousand-dollar bill from 1928 to 1946.

Cleveland's successor (and predecessor), Benjamin Harrison, was equally ready to trade on his name. As he relaunched his law practice, he resolved to consider only cases worth at least five thousand dollars. From the Indianapolis Street Railway, Harrison earned a sizable twenty-five-thousand-dollar fee for his services, roughly doubling his net worth. Even more rewarding were requests from sovereign governments: Venezuela hired the former president to represent its interests against Great Britain in a boundary dispute with the British colony of Guiana. Though he lost the case, he earned eighty thousand dollars for his spirited defense, offering a closing argument that lasted five days and twenty-five total hours. While a breed apart from Grover Cleveland's insurance-greased sinecure, Harrison's presidential résumé served him well out of power. By the time of his death, his estate had ballooned to four hundred thousand dollars.

At the dawn of the twentieth century, public speaking and writing for publication had become, like law and business, legitimate financial prospects for former presidents. Theodore Roosevelt was uniquely positioned to take full advantage of these opportunities. A skillful writer, Roosevelt had penned everything from social criticism to the four-volume adventure series *The Winning of the West*. Before long, writing would become his bread and butter.

Popular perception to the contrary, Roosevelt was not a man of means; though his small paternal inheritance kept him afloat, he was obliged to pursue independent sources of income. Soon after leaving the White House, TR contracted with the magazine *Outlook* to be a contributing editor for twelve thousand dollars a year. Offering signed editorials on politics, economics, and society, he submitted around a dozen pieces annually, which secured a reasonable safety net for his family. Writing with historical acumen and literary skill, Roosevelt garnered substantial sums for his commentary on events of the day.

Expanding on an already outsized reputation as tribune of the people and man of adventure, Roosevelt was flooded with offers when word spread of his planned trip to Africa. For fifty thousand dollars, *Scribner's Magazine* won the rights to publish the former president's reports on his African sojourn. (*Collier's* had offered twice as much, but TR chose *Scribner's* for its prestige.) During his yearlong safari tour of 1909–10, Roosevelt penned fourteen pieces, from five to fifteen thousand words each, reliving his East African escapades in minute detail. In one six-week stretch he poured out a logorrheic forty-five thousand words. The American public ate it up, devouring his depictions of lion hunting and his close-up encounters with rhinos, hippos, hyenas, and giraffes—not to mention his killing of more than five hundred animals. Roosevelt's good friend Senator Henry Cabot Lodge reported that "the people follow the account of your African wanderings as if [you] were a new Robinson Crusoe."

TR's writings sold sensationally. His *African Game Trails: An Account of the African Wanderings of an American Hunter-Naturalist*, a compilation of the *Scribner's* pieces published in 1910, produced royalties of forty thousand dollars in a single year. Upon hearing of Roosevelt's windfall, England's Edward VII scorned such profits as unbecoming for a former president, but Roosevelt wasn't troubled by the appearance of indecency. With sales topping two hundred thousand dollars, an all-time high for the firm, neither was *Scribner's*. Roosevelt's magazine writing also provided him with a platform to rail against the alleged iniquities of his once protégé, now rival, William Howard Taft. Until his death in 1919, and despite a headlong return to electoral politics, Roosevelt continued to write, agreeing to syndicate his fortnightly ruminations to the *Kansas City Star* in the last year of his life.

After the astonishing 1912 election, in which Woodrow Wilson prevailed over Roosevelt and William Howard Taft, the latter left office with a hefty three-hundred-and-forty-pound frame—and an equally robust one hundred thousand dollars in his bank account. Taft's wife, Nellie, managed their expenses effectively during his term in office, carefully setting aside monies from Taft's seventy-five-thousand-dollar paycheck (the presidential salary had been bumped up again the year Taft assumed office). Within a year after leaving the White House, Taft had shed seventy pounds, bringing him to a fitter two hundred and seventy. His salary dropped the same amount, falling to five thousand dollars when he joined the Yale Law School.

Taft supplemented his modest income by a now commonplace feature of the ex-presidential repertoire: the lecture circuit. The former president trekked the country with a stock set of thirty talks on subjects ranging from contemporary issues ("The Initiative and Referendum") to boilerplate Americana ("Duties of Citizenship"). Taft received invitations from civic groups, soi-disant ladies' clubs, conventions, and Chautauqua agencies, most of them paying around four hundred dollars a pop. He also wrote for popular magazines like the *Saturday Evening Post*, earning a thousand dollars an article. His finances finally settled into a more straightforward pattern in 1921, when he began collecting a scheduled paycheck as chief justice of the United States Supreme Court.

Maintaining Integrity at a Cost

As he left the White House, Taft said to his successor, Woodrow Wilson, about the savings possibilities inherent to the presidency, "You will find that Congress is very generous with the President. You have all your transportation paid for and all servants in the White House except such valet and maid as you and Mrs. Wilson choose to employ. . . . [Even] your laundry is looked after in the White House."

After more than a century, Congress had finally begun picking up many of the operating costs of White House life.

Sadly, Wilson had little opportunity to enjoy any such savings. Felled by a stroke in the fall of 1919, he never physically returned to form and spent his thousand days after the Oval Office in fragile health. Nevertheless, as in his unceasing quest to rally support for the League of Nations, Wilson soldiered on, forming a law partnership with Bainbridge Colby, his final secretary of state.

Colby was eager to reap the financial rewards he expected to accrue from partnering with a former president. Wilson was more reluctant to exploit his position. Worried about appearances of impropriety, Wilson declined most of the lucrative offers that came to their F Street offices. In one example, the Ecuadorian government sought their services to secure a $12 million loan from the United States. While Colby considered the offer "a very fine piece of business," Wilson saw the invitation to help a foreign government procure U.S. monies as a clear conflict of interest. The same was true when the short-lived West Ukrainian Republic appealed to Wilson for help with recognition from the League of Nations. Neither the financial recompense nor Wilson's passion for the League were sufficient to overcome his scruples. "Day after day I sit in my office and see a procession walk through—thousands and thousands of dollars—and not one to put in our pockets," Colby complained to Edith Wilson. "It is a sublime position on the part of your husband."

Wilson's weakened health also forced him to reject financially rewarding writing projects—including an offer of a hundred and fifty thousand dollars to pen the history of World War I's Paris peace negotiations. He also declined an offer to write about Jesus Christ, and even writing his own autobiography proved too onerous: "There ain't going to be none," he told an interested publisher. Wilson ultimately managed to punch out only a single piece, a brief meditation inspired by the Bolshevik uprising, called "The Road Away from Revolution."

When Wilson grew short on capital, his friends stepped in to help finance his handsome Georgian brick S Street town house above

Washington's Dupont Circle. (Two years later many of them reconvened, this time joined by banker Bernard Baruch, to share the cost of a permanent ten-thousand-dollar annuity for the former president.) His wife, Edith, would live there for thirty-seven years after her husband's death, but Wilson himself had little time to enjoy the new home: he died in the District of Columbia in 1924, and remains the only president to be buried in the nation's capital.

Working the System

Less consumed than Wilson by the need to maintain the integrity of the ex-presidency, Calvin Coolidge didn't allow his New England–style prudence to interfere with his desire to make money. Just a day after leaving office, Coolidge revealed that he had inked several lucrative magazine contracts: fifteen-thousand-dollar articles for *Ladies' Home Journal* and *American* magazine, and a sweetheart deal from *Encyclopedia Americana* that offered him a dollar a word for anything he put on paper, on top of a twenty-five-thousand-dollar annual salary. Silent Cal also signed on to write his autobiography, for which he reportedly received a hefty sixty-five-thousand-dollar advance. (The book he turned in would conclude in 1924, omitting his entire elected term in office.) Coolidge pocketed one hundred and ten thousand dollars for his writing in his first postpresidential year alone. The next was even better: he agreed to bang out a column, "Calvin Coolidge Says," for nationwide syndication. Though panned by critics as an exercise in banality, the column paid more than two hundred thousand dollars during the early days of the Great Depression.

Coolidge found other ways to enrich his accounts after his time in office. He enjoyed special relations with leading bankers, which enabled him to benefit sizably from equity acquisitions. Acting on insider tips—such practices were not yet illegal—he purchased thousands of shares of J. P. Morgan stock below market value. Coolidge recognized that such special treatment was a direct result of his former office: "These people are trying to [curry favor not with] Calvin Coolidge, but a former President of the United States," he observed. (Harry Truman and Dwight Eisenhower would later echo the sentiment.)

Despite his privileged investments, however, the parsimonious Coolidge retired to a thirty-two-dollar-a-month flat in Northampton, Massachusetts. Only the constant exposure to prying journalists and sightseers forced him to dip into his four-hundred-thousand-dollar reserve and eventually purchase a secluded forty-thousand-dollar home above the Connecticut River.

It was Coolidge who famously proclaimed that "the business of America is business." His successor, Herbert Hoover, might not have signed on to that sentiment expressly, but he showed great acumen in profiting from America's business-friendly environment. By the age of forty, Hoover had amassed a net worth of $4 million in his extraordinarily successful career as a mining engineer. The wealthiest man to become president until that time, Hoover also became the richest ex-president. He had come a long way from the meager three-room cottage of his birth in West Branch, Iowa.

Preferring to lob bombs at the New Deal, Hoover wasn't as involved in the mining industry after his presidency. His interventions were largely confined to investments—whether in mines in the western United States or in Central American ore deposits—though he did retain a foothold in his former business. And like Cleveland, who forged relations with the world of insurance, Hoover joined the board of the New York Life Insurance Company—where, curiously, he was paired with Al Smith, the man he had defeated for president in 1928.

Hoover lived in comfort, whether at his house on S Street in Washington, D.C., or at his primary residence in Palo Alto, California. After Franklin Roosevelt's third consecutive win in 1940, Hoover and his wife sold their Washington home and moved permanently to Suite 31-A at the Waldorf-Astoria, Manhattan's high-end hotel. There the

Hoovers lived among celebrities including the Shah of Iran, Queen Juliana of the Netherlands, General Douglas MacArthur, and Cole Porter. Hoover even joined the Waldorf's board, which became a point of amusement for him: as a Quaker who had enforced Prohibition, he liked to joke that he would now be responsible for controlling "the biggest bar in the world."

PENSIONS AND THE MODERN EX-PRESIDENCY

After World War II, Herbert Hoover's status as a self-made millionaire, coupled with the expanded financial opportunities for ex-presidents, papered over the unresolved issue of pensioning our former heads of state. For years the wisdom of guaranteeing ex-presidents a lifetime income had been a subject of debate among the general public and members of Congress alike. How could the president of the United States leave office without even a minimal retirement income—particularly when such compensation was afforded to the legislative and judicial branches?

From the outset there were detractors. Early Americans considered it inappropriate for presidents who serve at the behest of the people to receive a lifetime income guarantee. The profound example of George Washington, who exited after his second term never to return, resonated powerfully with the American public. That one would leave office, yet continue to receive an income, seemed to contradict the bedrock principles Washington embodied.

To some, a postpresidential guarantee of income also smacked of royal privilege, the kind of thing many Americans felt they had rightly left behind with their European forebears. This abiding fear of regal signifiers, real or imagined, kept the pension issue from emerging during America's first century. Though there were sporadic mentions of retirement funds—Millard Fillmore, for example, had suggested a twelve-thousand-dollar annual pension—it took until the last quarter of the nineteenth century to jump-start the discussion.

The change in America's relations with England, along with the passage of time, helped strip away fears of falling back into monarchy. Revolutionary War holidays such as Evacuation Day, which commemorated Britain's removal from New York after the war, faded into obscurity. No longer apprehensive that former presidents were likely to retain any kind of royal power, Americans now realized that a pension would serve an important objective: preventing former presidents from turning to commercial quick fixes that could sully the reputation of the office.

The broad issue of pensions emerged as a political football during Grover Cleveland's presidency. Convinced that the Pensions Bureau, created under Lincoln for Civil War veterans, was turning into a Republican slush fund for unworthy applicants, Cleveland decided to review all the Bureau's proposals personally. His uncompromising stance on the matter was a factor in his loss to Benjamin Harrison in 1888.

Cleveland strongly supported granting financial security to former presidents, but his frustration with the military pension issue kept him from pushing it forward while in office. Out of power, Cleveland embraced the idea of a presidential pension, though he still resisted equating it with a military pension: giving a military-style pension to a president who hadn't served in the armed forces ran the risk of stigmatizing the benefit itself.

Cleveland tried to square the circle. While "I am not in need of aid from the public treasury," he said, "our people ought to make a definite and generous provision for all cases alike." Since former presidents were still obliged to uphold "a certain dignity" and could not easily follow the opportunism that the market allowed, Cleveland argued that "a reciprocal connection [exists] between the curtailment of opportunities on one side and a reasonable obligation of indemnification on the other." Using France as an example, he pointed out that its privileges helped ensure "a dignified and unperplexed future for its ex-president." Was there a way to grant a former president a salary, but ask him in return to refrain from all activities except those that contributed to the betterment of the country?

The matter fell to Congress to decide. Massachusetts Republican William Croad Lovering, one of the earliest members to raise the issue, introduced a bill in 1902 to provide former presidents with a salary of twenty-five-thousand dollars, but the legislation quickly died. A few years later another pension bill was introduced, but this one, too, was met with scorn: "Why shouldn't they earn their living as well as other folks?" one newspaper asked. "The reputation the Presidency gives them will secure twice as much for the articles they write as the articles are worth." Yet not everyone was so dismissive. As the *Boston Post* remarked, "When [a president] goes out of office he is not entirely free to choose his line of work among occupations which are most lucrative." That he might discredit himself and the institution of the presidency were he to accept what the market brought to bear was thus of continued concern.

Congressional discussion was revived in 1910 on the question of how to provide for the nation's former first ladies—but despite the plights of the widows Harrison and Cleveland, the proposed pension legislation didn't pass. As for former presidents, only Teddy Roosevelt was alive, and few thought the indomitable Rough Rider incapable of fending for himself. Roosevelt "would probably not consider it a compliment to be put on the retired list," the *Los Angeles Times* wrote, "and we feel sure that he would not consent to live as a pensioner upon the people of the United States." In this environment, there was little grist for the pension mill.

In the fall of 1912, however, steel magnate and philanthropist Andrew Carnegie tossed a grenade into the debate. Hoping to set a fire under Congress, which he considered derelict for not providing former presidents a proper pension, Carnegie personally offered to guarantee a twenty-five-thousand-dollar annual pension to any living former president and the same to their unmarried widows. Carnegie was said to have been appalled to learn that Grover Cleveland had taken his insurance jobs strictly for money, and shocked at how many former presidents had ended their lives in poverty; his offer was a daring attempt to shame Congress into action.

Shown up by the industrialist, a number of senators flew into a rage. The idea of a wealthy titan paying for presidential retirement funds didn't sit very well with many, including some who may have taken a certain nativist umbrage that the offer came from a born Scotsman. Georgia senator Hoke Smith bellowed that "it is a piece of impudence on [Carnegie's] part to suggest such a thing, and a reflection on the people that it should be considered." William E. Borah of Idaho added that "any man who would accept the Carnegie pension would prove conclusively by doing so that he was not fit to be President." And Senator Thomas Gore (Gore Vidal's maternal grandfather) concluded, "I do not think Mr. Carnegie's pension will reflect any credit on our ex-Presidents, and I am not sure that an ex-President who would accept such a pension would receive or be entitled to the continued respect of the people of the United States. The idea of giving a pension to the widows of ex-Presidents to secure to the country the benefit of their knowledge and experience in public affairs is possibly a joke, but not a very good one."

William Howard Taft, who would have been the first beneficiary of Carnegie's pension, tried to strike a middle ground. Speaking in New York, he put the onus on Congress to offer the former presidents a living wage. "Unless it is the policy of Congress to enable [the president] in his four years to save money enough to live in adequate dignity and comfort thereafter," Taft argued, "then the salary [of the president] is all that it ought to be." Taft, who was soon to leave office, had special reason for concern: having appointed most of the currently seated Supreme Court justices, he knew he would be effectively proscribed from appearing before them as an attorney.

Taft ultimately refused Carnegie's pension. But a decade later, after Carnegie's death, the Hearst newspapers announced that the former president had accepted an annuity of ten thousand dollars a year bequeathed by the industrialist. Though Taft tried to ascribe the decision to his wife—"Mrs. Taft wishes me to do it and she is an interested party"—the grant immediately raised ethical questions about Taft, who by then had become chief justice of the Supreme Court. Fearing damage to his beloved Court ("next to my wife and children . . . the nearest thing to my heart in life"), Taft redirected all financial support from Carnegie's bequest to Yale University.

At the time of the Carnegie proposal, a stroke of positive public relations fell into the hands of pension proponents. In a newly unearthed 1869 letter, it appeared that Abraham Lincoln's wife, Mary Todd Lincoln, had dispatched a poignant plea to Congress. Writing from Germany, where she had traveled for her health, she explained, "I am a widow of a President of the United States whose life was sacrificed in his country's service. . . . [It is my hope that] a yearly pension may be granted me, so that I may have less pecuniary care." A year after she had written the letter, Mrs. Lincoln's pension was granted: three thousand dollars per year until her death in 1882. It was a fortuitous find, but unsuccessful: less than a fortnight later, the Appropriations Committee blocked a bill that would have provided a pension of seventeen thousand five hundred dollars per year and a lifetime congressional seat to former presidents.

In the early 1920s, Senator William M. Calder of New York and Representative Leonidas C. Dyer of Missouri introduced new pension legislation, this time offering a more meager ten thousand dollars per year, and the *Chicago Daily Tribune* came out strongly for a "liberal pension for ex-presidents," but the bill still went nowhere. "It may be un-American to condemn our ex-Presidents to a life of slothful inactivity," another newspaper commented. Once again the pension issue was stalled.

Two decades passed before the next serious congressional push. In 1945 House Republican leader Joseph W. Martin Jr. of Massachusetts revisited the idea of a twenty-five-thousand-dollar annuity. The concept was later picked up by Ohio's Senator Robert Taft, who advocated substantial pensions and returned to Grover Cleveland's theme that former presidents should live in a dignified manner. After a protracted period of debate and deliberation, with multiple bills floating through Congress over more than a decade, it took Harry Truman's plight upon his homecoming to Independence, Missouri, to create the necessary momentum for the pension's ultimate passage.

With little money to his name—he lacked even the funds to hire a secretary to answer his abundant mail—Truman worried openly about his capacity to sustain a viable livelihood. Beleaguered by financial problems throughout his life, Truman had good reason to be nervous: he had invested poorly (in zinc mines) before World War I, failed as a haberdasher, and saved little during his years of public service. When he left Washington, D.C., for Missouri, he even paid for the ticket himself. (These days, Air Force One is dispatched to provide a more refined segue to civilian life.)

Despite their sympathy for Truman's predicament, the members of Congress did not decide to send the bill to President Eisenhower without first battling among themselves. Opponents of the legislation thought it tainted the Constitution to establish an informal office of the ex-president. House Republican August Johansen, who was instrumental in watering down some of the initial privileges, argued that the bill would mark "the beginning of the buildup of a bureaucracy around a nonexistent office," that "For the first time in American history it means that a non-office holding citizen is to have a . . . permanent entourage of federal personnel." It required the persistent importuning of House Speaker Sam Rayburn, House Minority Leader Joseph W. Martin Jr., and Senate Majority Leader Lyndon Johnson to push the legislation to passage.

It had taken 171 years since the nation's founding to arrive at a pension for former presidents. Signed by President Dwight D. Eisenhower on August 25, 1958, the Former Presidents Act was the first official measure providing ex-presidents with a lifetime salary, as well as compensation for staff, travel, phone bills, office space, and other amenities. Until this point the president had remained virtually the only federal government employee without a retirement package. Twenty-seven previous heads of state who left office had no guaranteed income whatsoever from their labors as commander-in-chief. Herbert Hoover, who accepted the pension only out of deference to Truman, applauded Ike for signing the legislation. "No man can make any substantial savings from being president," he noted, and with some self-importance added, "I have made it a practice to devote all personal compensation derived from our government to public service or charity."

With a pension and associated perquisites now mandated by law, the informal office of the ex-president was born. Within a few years, additional perks expanded the catalog of postpresidential benefits. In the early 1960s, Congress legislated for each outgoing president "transition expenses" in the Presidential Transition Act to cushion their landing to private life; shortly thereafter it introduced a lifetime Secret Service provision for ex-presidents and their spouses and widows. Where just a few years before, the former presidents had stood bereft, now they were lavished with rewards at last.

SCALING BACK

The years that followed, perhaps predictably, saw a rash of stories spotlighting the excesses the former presidents were enjoying at taxpayer expense. *U.S. News & World Report* made it a personal mission to expose the most egregious examples: a twelve-thousand-dollar Asian rug for Jimmy Carter's Atlanta office; a thirty-four-thousand-dollar phone bill for Jerry Ford; a five-hundred-dollar replacement key for Richard Nixon's filing cabinet (not to mention repairs to his electric golf cart). When Congress passed a $1 million supplemental appropriation to cover twelve agents' round-the clock shielding of Lady Bird Johnson and friends as they vacationed in the Greek Isles, it became clear that something had to be done.

In the early 1980s, Congress introduced a flurry of bills to reform the bloated ex-presidential office. Spearheading the challenge, Florida senator Lawton Chiles derided the new "era of the 'imperial' former presidency with [its] special staffs and benefits, around-the-clock Secret Service protection for life and other badges of privilege." By 1984, the costs of the ex-presidency had reached $27 million annually. "To take care of former presidents and their wives," Chiles complained, "we are paying more than we are paying for the office of the president itself." Chiles recommended allowing the government a percentage on presidential memoirs, limits on Secret Service protection, and stricter guidelines in the selection of office space.

The lower chamber handily approved legislation that curbed some of the central perks. Sponsoring the bill, Florida's Bill Nelson reasoned, "We need to send a clear message that our former presidents should not live royally at the taxpayers' expense." Under his plan, the pensions themselves would remain untouched (they were now pegged to the level of a cabinet secretary's salary), but the longer a president was out of office, the greater the reductions would be in his overall benefits.

Indiana representative Andrew Jacobs wanted to go further. He called for Congress to wipe the perquisite slate clean, suggesting that former presidents no longer needed special coddling. "These guys, with their . . . pensions alone," Jacobs said, "have greater personal income than about 97 percent of their fellow Americans who are paying the taxes to pay the pension." Jacobs introduced the whimsically named "Former Presidents Enough Is Enough and Taxpayers Relief Bill of 1983," which asked: "How many presidents can the American public afford at one time?" Not unlike the ice-cream impresarios Ben and Jerry, who had pledged not to make more than ten times the salary of their lowest-paid employee, Jacobs called for the "care and feeding" of ex-presidents not to exceed more than ten times the poverty level for a four-person family. "They're ornaments, curiosities, someone to have at your convention," Jacobs sneered.

No one expected Jacobs's bill to go anywhere, but Chiles's more serious proposals also failed to garner enough support. Though he was modestly successful in paring down the steroidlike growth of presidential libraries, Chiles had little effect on most other ex-presidential privileges. The airtight solidarity of the presidential class fiercely protected its self-interest. Using their combined muscle, former presidents Ford and Carter prodded Senate Majority Leader Howard Baker to weaken the resolve of lawmakers pushing the legislation. Then the Reagan administration stepped in to play the heavy, asking the Senate to remove the bill from its agenda altogether. Though the legislation swept through the Senate Governmental Affairs Committee, Reagan's back-door manipulation prevented it from going to the full Senate.

The debate reignited in the mid-1990s. This time the Former Presidents Act was successfully amended to guarantee ex-presidents office and staff costs for only five years. Just before the bill was about to take effect, however, Gerald Ford—anxious to retain his Rancho Mirage digs—stepped in once more to militate against the changes, and the amendments never saw the light of day. As a consolation prize for the reformers, Secret Service protection for presidents whose terms began after 1997 was reduced to ten years. (Andy Rooney later quipped, "If anyone hated a president enough to try to harm him, they'd get over it in ten years.") George W. Bush will be the first ex-president to be granted only a decade's worth of taxpayer-supported security detail.

THE TELEVISION AND PUBLISHING BOON

Harry Truman, whose financial condition provoked the formation of the ex-presidential office, ended up all right. In the same year that the

Former Presidents Act came into force, it was later revealed, he received a hefty fee for his appearance on Edward R. Murrow's television program *See It Now*, making him the first ex-president to cash in on this revolutionary new medium. Yet Truman retained a frugality that placed him at odds with most of his successors, accepting no posts on corporate boards, no commercial endorsements, and no consulting deals. "I could never lend myself to any transaction, however respectable, that would commercialize on the prestige and dignity of the office of the presidency," he declared. His successors felt otherwise.

Dwight Eisenhower wasted little time before accepting a large payment for television interviews on CBS with Walter Cronkite just months after stepping down in 1961; he did a second round in 1964. Ike had been financially comfortable before taking office, in large part due to income from his best-selling wartime memoir, published in 1948 (a tax-exempt income source, thanks to Harry Truman). After the White House, Eisenhower retired to a farm in Gettysburg, Pennsylvania, spinning out additional reminiscences of his presidential years that paid impressively and sold well. At his death in 1969, his estate was worth around a million dollars.

Like Herbert Hoover, the next president to survive the office, Lyndon Johnson, had come a long way from humble beginnings. "I know what poverty means to people," Johnson said, shortly after taking office. "I have been unemployed. . . . I have shined shoes as a boy. I have worked on a highway crew from daylight until dark for a dollar a day." Upon leaving the White House, however, Johnson retook control of a communications empire that included the Texas Broadcasting Company, and a ranch of fifteen thousand acres.

LBJ's accounts were augmented quickly after he left power. Days after Nixon's inauguration, he and Lady Bird signed on for book deals that brought them well over $1 million. And, like Ike, Johnson sat for interviews with Walter Cronkite, accepting three hundred thousand dollars to discuss seven predetermined topics. (Most of the fees were donated to his public affairs school at the University of Texas–Austin.)

In 1972, however, Johnson was forced to sell off his television station when an FCC ruling forbade one owner to control a cable company and a television station within a single market. He made $9 million from the sale. Leonard Marks, who represented the Johnsons' media interests, was blunt in his appraisal of the former president's financial wizardry: "God—if he hadn't been president, he would have been the biggest tycoon this world has ever seen." Despite Johnson's massive estate—he was worth in excess of $20 million, making him the most affluent former president since Hoover—Lady Bird elected to receive her pension until her death in 2007 (presidential widows can receive twenty thousand dollars annually if they give up all other pension opportunities).

Richard Nixon was not a man of exorbitant wealth when he left Washington, D.C., in disgrace in 1974, but neither was he strapped for cash. Moving to his western redoubt of San Clemente, California, Nixon was the fortunate beneficiary of approximately two hundred thousand dollars in transition expenses. (Nixon came by that provision only narrowly: such support is provided to all former presidents unless they are impeached and convicted. Nixon, who faced an impeachment vote before he resigned, surely had other considerations in mind when he decided to leave office, but his decision did preserve this welcome windfall.)

Not all members of Congress were happy with the arrangement. After Nixon's resignation, there were several unsuccessful efforts to prevent Nixon from receiving a pension and staff. Yet time heals most wounds, and by the summer of 1978 the Senate had decided to preserve Nixon's benefits package by a resounding vote of eighty-nine to two. Several years later, out of contrition or perhaps a heartfelt belief in small government, Nixon unilaterally ditched some of the benefits, including the costliest of the bunch: his $3 million annual Secret Service detail.

Nixon quickly learned that leaving office under a cloud didn't impair his earning potential. The first financially rewarding aspect of Nixon's postpresidency came in 1977, with the famous Nixon-Frost interviews. Marking Nixon's post-Watergate debut, the interviews netted him six hundred thousand dollars plus a percentage of the profits—not a bad take for four conversations. (He even won an Emmy for best spoken-word performance—a first for a president.) These funds were important because Nixon faced enormous litigation, with over sixty lawsuits filed against him in his first years out of power. He would eventually sign over all income from the Frost interviews to his lawyers and agent.

The $2.5 million advance Nixon secured for his memoirs, thanks to agent Swifty Lazar, placed Nixon in better standing. It was a smart bet for the publisher, too: the book became the best-selling presidential memoir ever, with three hundred and thirty thousand copies purchased in the first six months. Clocking in at nearly eleven hundred pages, the memoir meant a lot of heavy lifting for the staff working on the text, including former White House aide Diane Sawyer. Over the course of his postpresidency Nixon would publish another eight books, most of which were best sellers.

After initially moving to New York to be close to his daughters, Nixon soon crossed the Hudson to lead a quieter life in Saddle River, New Jersey, where he bought a fifteen-room, five-acre homestead for $1.2 million. To most people in this conservative leafy suburb, he was "the lonely figure with the flashlight, walking his dogs at night." In 1984 Nixon came close to purchasing a twelve-room co-op on Park Avenue and Seventy-second Street for $1.8 million; Pat Nixon had suffered a second stroke, and the Nixons thought life would be easier in an apartment. (Some cynics also jibed that the move was part of the former president's strategy to be closer to the action.) Ninety-three-year-old resident Jacob Kaplan, a building trustee and founder of the J. M. Kaplan Fund, procured a temporary restraining order to block the move, writing to his neighbors that there "are nutty people around . . . some who might want to do Nixon harm. Should we be exposed to these possible threats against our lives?" Kaplan also worried that "our only little elevator" would be dominated by the Secret

Service. Though their application was eventually approved by the board, the Nixons withdrew from consideration, citing the widespread publicity around the affair.

EXPLOITATION

While Richard Nixon was careful about capitalizing on his infamy, the man who stepped in to complete his term in office, Gerald Ford, was eager to cash in any way he could. In a span of weeks, Ford accepted a representation offer from the William Morris Agency; signed a million-dollar contract to appear on NBC television; and agreed to an additional million for his and his wife's memoirs. Even his former press secretary, Jerald terHorst, saw it as a stunning example of "the huckstering of an ex-president." Flabbergasted at Ford's shamelessness, terHorst came out with a savage piece in the *Washington Post* entitled "President Ford, Inc." Nearly broke when he moved into the White House, forced to borrow ten thousand dollars to stay afloat, Ford transformed "the former First Family into something of a conglomerate," terHorst declared. Many were appalled that the understated, middle-income public servant who had resided in a quiet home in the Virginia suburbs for more than a quarter century was now busily marketing his eight hundred and ninety-five days of occasional glory. Ford's "nice guy" image, terHorst said, was "getting harder and harder to see behind that pile of money on his Palm Springs doorstep."

Ford now had three homes: his primary residence and office on a golf course in Rancho Mirage, California; a ski chalet in Vail, Colorado; and a sizable apartment in Los Angeles. Between his time as president, his tenure in Congress, and his stint in the military, he also had three pensions that would eventually deliver him more than three hundred thousand dollars per year. And during the years when Ford gave frequent speeches, he required almost $4 million worth of annual

Secret Service protection. Instead of charging a fee for his speech, Lawton Chiles joked, it would be cheaper for the American taxpayer "to pay President Ford to stay home."

Ford's response to his critics was unequivocal: "I'm a private citizen now. It's nobody's business." Ford insisted that "this is what the free enterprise system is all about." For the major corporations whose boards he graced, of course, it was also about corporate prestige. Ford set a postpresidential record for holding the most seats on company boards, including the American Express Company, the Sante Fe International Corporation, the Texas Commerce Bank, Tiger International Inc., the Beneficial Corporation of New Jersey, and the 20th Century Fox Film Corporation (which paid him fifty thousand a year). By 1983, when the former president made a cameo appearance on the TV hit *Dynasty*—a program celebrating conspicuous consumption— Ford's climb into the ranks of the prosperous was complete.

Ford's conduct made the Former President Act's warnings about demeaning the office appear almost quaint. Richard Nixon often grumbled at the moneymaking proclivities of his once pardoner. "He's busy making speeches for big money, like the rest of them," Nixon said. "I have never taken a dime for a speech since 1952. Of course no one gives me credit for that. . . . I know it's tempting, but it's just not right."

STEERING CLEAR OF TEMPTATION

When it came to money, Ford could not have made a greater contrast with his peanut-farming Georgian successor. While Ford lent his name to a growing list of major corporations, Jimmy Carter turned his attention to the humanitarian sphere after leaving office, steering clear of all temptations to get bought off. Calling his friend a "pure Calvinist," Carter's UN ambassador, Andrew Young, lamented that Carter made him "feel guilty for serving on corporate boards because he's shunned all that." Carter was explicit about refusing to use his ex-presidency as a platform to grow rich—"a naïve and sincere commitment," he said, and one he's honored in the years that followed. At a reunion of many of his former administration officials, Carter's secretary of transportation, Neil Goldschmidt, saluted him: "You have carried the dignity and character of the American Presidency to high ground—on which is posted a sign: 'Not for sale.'"

It could not have been easy—especially not at the start of his retirement, when Carter found himself in thorny financial straits. Having long run a successful agricultural business, the Carters had placed their assets in a blind trust before heading to Washington. Beset by drought—and Carter's infamous brother Billy's mismanagement—the Carters' peanut operation imploded and they landed in a million dollars' worth of debt. They were forced to sell the business to free themselves from crushing interest payments. "Just as almost two decades of political life were about to end," Rosalynn Carter ruefully recounted, "we found that the results of the preceding twenty-three years of hard work, scrimping and saving, and plowing everything back into the business, were now also gone."

Selling the warehouse to Archer Daniels Midland for around six hundred thousand dollars protected Carter from having to give up the family farms (instead, they were leased out to others). To pay down his debts, Carter took the now-familiar route of procuring a book deal. Regardless of his unpopularity, publishing offers started appearing even before he left office, and by the summer of 1981, he and Rosalynn had signed his-and-hers book contracts. (Carter allegedly included a clause in his contract prohibiting the size of his advance from being revealed, but most put the figure somewhere between $1 million and $2 million.) Carter's William Morris agent had big ideas about lecture fees—"If he and Mrs. Carter appear as a double, they can probably get $25,000 a night," he surmised—but the former president just wanted to be solvent. "How much money I make in a year is really not important to me," he said. "I'm determined my life ahead will be just as meaningful to me and, I hope, to the public." After selling his business and getting his first advance, he could turn to those core issues that preoccupied his second act.

At the dawn of Carter's postpresidency, few would have predicted that publishing would become his largest income-generating source, but he would spin off more than twenty books, most of them best sellers, on a diverse array of subjects—works of fiction, poetry, and memoir, books on Middle East politics and aging. A man of substantial means, Carter continues to live in his relatively modest 1961 ranch house in Plains, Georgia. "I'm a farmer still," he says. "I get up at five o'clock. I will write until I get tired, until ten or eleven o'clock. Then I have a woodshop twenty feet away, and I go there and I build furniture, and I paint."

RAISING THE ANTE

Ronald Reagan, in his few active years after the White House, was more comfortable going back to the Jerry Ford model: ex-president as moneymaking machine. Nine months after stepping down, Reagan starred in one of the crowning examples of postpresidential excess. As the honored guest of the Fujisankei Communications Group, a media giant with rock-solid conservative credentials, Reagan received a $2 million fee for a couple of twenty-minute speeches and a handful of public appearances. Fujisankei also underwrote an additional $5 million for the twenty-person team that accompanied the former president, including Nancy Reagan and Julius the hairdresser. Startled at the outlay, Jimmy Carter quipped, "I've been telling the press that I never criticize another former president. But . . . if you hear of another deal like that, let me know. I believe idealism and practicality go together."

At least Reagan earned his keep. During a period when Japanese investment was inciting fierce protectionist backlash in America, Reagan sounded the trumpet for open borders. "If America looks like a good investment," he said, "why, we should be pleased and proud of it. Who are we to bellyache about somebody else wanting to [invest]?" Certainly Reagan's generous comments must have satisfied his hosts, who eagerly accepted the former president's support. On a Fujisankei-owned station, Reagan was asked about the headline of the day: Sony's takeover of Columbia Pictures. Showing no compunction about criticizing his former home turf, Reagan said, "I just have a feeling that maybe Hollywood needs some *outsiders* to bring back decency and good taste to some of the pictures that are being made." For a mere $2 million, the Japanese "outsiders" got their message driven home by a master.

Reagan's run for the money wasn't fueled by financial exigency. His prepresidential investments had paid off generously—from the almost $2 million sale of his home to 20th Century Fox (a house originally purchased for one-twentieth the cost) to his careful savings from his years as a B-movie actor (during the 1940s, he had pulled down a hundred fifty thousand dollars a year on average). With the negotiating help of George Scharffenberger, who oversaw his blind trust investments when president, Reagan secured a reported $5 million deal for his memoirs and a book of speeches. Nancy got another $2 million for hers. Reagan lived out his days in a seventy-two-hundred-square-foot home in Bel Air, California.

When it was reported that Reagan would earn millions for his writings, George H. W. Bush was asked if he thought his forerunner was "cashing in" on his time in office. "I don't know that I'd call it 'cashing in,'" Bush snapped. "I expect every President has written his memoirs and received money for it. . . . Grant got half a million bucks. That's when half a million really meant something." Of course, even in 1989 half a million dollars still "meant something" to most Americans—as it still does today—but Bush's history was altogether wrong. Grant was an anomaly, the only former president until Teddy Roosevelt to produce a memoir. And since he finished it only days before expiring, the considerable income the book earned went to his family, not Grant himself.

It's curious, then, that Bush is the only modern president to have forgone writing a memoir. Instead, Bush has concentrated on other means to profit from the symbolic power of the Oval Office. In his first years out of power, Bush leaped on the bandwagon of corporate opportunity. Often charging a hundred thousand dollars for an overseas speech, Bush worked to benefit dozens of companies, especially in Asia, traveling to China at least eight times in his initial years out of office. The first former commander-in-chief to have professional experience with the CIA and the oil sector, not to mention close personal relations with the Saudi royal family, Bush was ideally suited to play rainmaker. These relationships helped forge what Michael Lewis aptly dubs "access capitalism," or what William Power describes as "Beltway alchemy: turning global connections into gold."

One of the most convincing illustrations of access capitalism at work is found in the highly secretive and hugely successful private equity firm known as the Carlyle Group. Founded in 1987, Carlyle invests in sectors ranging from telecommunications to technology, though its reputation today stems largely from its buyouts of aerospace and defense companies. (It is usually listed as one of the top fifteen defense contracting firms in the United States.) *Fortune* described Carlyle's activities plainly: capitalizing on the absence of restrictions on ex-government officials' soliciting investments (as opposed to "lobbying"), "This is a firm that's been built on the backs of Bush and other big shots who have lent Carlyle their names, their golden networks of friends in high places, and their insights into how government works." Indeed, Carlyle has flourished by enlisting a roster of quintessential political insiders from both sides of the Atlantic, including Reagan's secretary of defense Frank Carlucci; former British prime minister John Major; George H. W. Bush's secretary of state James Baker; and from May 1998 until October 2003, the senior president Bush himself.

After the attacks of September 11, 2001, the revelations of Carlyle's connection with the bin Laden family made the private equity group a household name. Under the firm's auspices, George H. W.

Bush had visited the bin Laden family in Saudi Arabia at least twice in 1998 and 2000, and the bin Ladens had invested several million dollars in a Carlyle fund. That the bin Laden family could profit from America's rapid increase in its war on terrorism produced an intense outcry, and by late October 2001 the bin Laden family's Carlyle investments had been liquidated. (Bush wasn't the only ex-president to associate with the bin Laden clan: before 9/11, Jimmy Carter garnered two hundred thousand dollars for the Carter Center after dining with ten of Osama bin Laden's brothers.)

At Carlyle, George H. W. Bush wasn't rewarded as monumentally as his close friend James Baker, who became a full partner in the company. But as a senior advisor on Asia, whose chief function was to open doors and sway investor audiences, Bush did very well both from his speeches at investment gatherings and through his ability to reinvest his compensation as equity stakes in Carlyle funds. Just how well he did we may never know, since Carlyle is under no obligation to disclose its wages and earnings. (Carlyle cofounder David Rubenstein says only that Bush was paid "in line with market rates.") Responding to the questionable blurring of politics and finance, the Carlyle Group contends that Bush merely addressed audiences, and then a Carlyle principal asked for the money. In other words, Bush steered clear of all financial transactions. The former president eventually stepped down, seven months after the bombing of Baghdad began under his son's administration. Even before Carlyle enlisted him to help woo its overseas clients, Bush was estimated to be worth in the neighborhood of $20 million.

As profitable as Bush's work for Carlyle probably was, his single largest postpresidential financial coup may have come as a result of his involvement with the short-lived telecom start-up Global Crossing. Invited to speak in Japan on the firm's behalf (its cochair was a friend), Bush was allowed to invest his eighty-thousand-dollar speaking fee as equity in the firm. In the bamboozling years of the dot-com gold rush, Bush's stake soon ballooned to $14 million. The company never posted a penny of earnings, and went bust within a few years, becoming a pathetic poster child for the Internet bubble. How much Bush unloaded before its collapse is unknown.

Though Bush's postpresidential income history has hardly been transparent, it seems clear that Bill Clinton's remuneration has outdone that of his predecessor in his first years out of office. The staggering amount of money Clinton has amassed from speaking fees alone—more than $50 million between 2001 and 2007—puts the celebrity ex-president in a special category. Though he left the White House in the midst of ongoing litigation and scandal and more than $11 million in the red thanks to legal fees, the former president and his wife roared back with book deals valued at $10 million and $8 million, respectively, thrusting him quickly into the ranks of the very rich.

The bulk of Clinton's funds was earned straightforwardly—giving speeches for wealthy individuals and institutions, many for more than two hundred thousand dollars a shot. In selecting his clients, Clinton hardly discriminated: he spoke to biotech firms, religious groups, country clubs, life insurance companies, universities, and banks. He even charged the Boys and Girls Club of America a hundred and fifty thousand for his troubles. All told, two-thirds of Clinton's speaking fees from this period came from outside the United States, including six hundred thousand for two speeches to a Saudi investment company. At times, those Clinton addressed were also prominent donors to his wife's Senate and presidential runs, including Goldman Sachs and Citigroup. The public is privy to these coincidences only because, as a senator, Hillary Clinton is bound to financial disclosure requirements on her family's personal earnings.

Clinton's gift of oratory has served him well and, with a few notable exceptions, allowed him to pass up the customary corporate relationships of his Republican predecessors. The one astonishing example where Clinton's consulting paid off handsomely is with his close personal friend Ron Burkle. A California billionaire who made his money in supermarkets, Burkle is a major Clinton fund-raiser and contributor to the former president's philanthropic activities and presidential library. From 2002 to 2007, Clinton signed on to participate as a senior adviser to two of Burkle's Yucaipa Companies' private equity investment funds, complete with a stake in the profits. His charge was simply to suss out good investment opportunities, lend legitimacy to the efforts, and, naturally, act as rainmaker extraordinaire. While Clinton's actual earnings are difficult to estimate—he established his own limited liability company to handle his side of things—it has been reported that his overall payout through 2007 was somewhere between $12 million and $15 million.

Clinton even made news with his choice of office space. After leaving office, he first set his sights on a suite in one of the world's most expensive commercial blocks, on West Fifty-seventh Street in midtown Manhattan. But the going rate for the space was eight hundred thousand dollars a year, and Clinton was soon shamed into dropping the idea. Instead, the man who Toni Morrison dubbed "the first black president" moved uptown to Harlem, leasing a fourteenth-floor penthouse suite. Though Clinton's Harlem digs cost a lot less than a midtown redoubt, at half a million dollars it was still the highest taxpayer-supported rent any former president had ever demanded.

PRESIDENTIAL LIBRARIES AND THE POLITICS OF LEGACY

~

Does [the presidential library] have flaws? Sure, just like America has flaws. But you can't get to Churchill's papers, or de Gaulle's, like you can get at FDR's. Hirohito, I think one guy's been allowed to see his diaries.

Stephen Ambrose

The images [at the John F. Kennedy library] are so powerful, so compelling—it's hard even for me to be objective.

Robert Dallek

History will bear me out, particularly as I shall write that history myself.

Winston Churchill

· · · · · ·

THROUGHOUT HISTORY, MONUMENTAL STRUCTURES HAVE BEEN built to evince grandeur and memorialize leaders: Egypt had its pyramids, Greece its temples, India its Taj Mahal. In the United States, the presidential library provides its own official setting for hero worship. In a country bereft of emperors, monarchs, or pharaohs, America's most powerful elected officials have embraced libraries as their personal shrines.

From their modest origins in Franklin Delano Roosevelt's voluntary handover of his papers, presidential libraries have become big business in the modern era, housed in outsized edifices glorifying those who have held the Oval Office. Yet unlike the subjects of most ancient monuments, presidents are active participants in their own consecration, sharing in everything from conception to execution—including design, fund-raising, construction, and historical interpretation. Architectural expressions of an imperial presidency, these elaborate repositories for documents and exhibits are now a signature feature of a former president's legacy.

Presidential libraries are a growth industry—literally—with most new examples eclipsing their predecessors in volume and cost. Under development at Southern Methodist University in Dallas, George W. Bush's presidential library, reportedly budgeted at an astounding $500 million, is the latest instance of postpresidential gigantism. Together with his projected public affairs institute, Bush's library may end up costing triple the amount of Bill Clinton's complex in Little Rock, Arkansas; six times that of his father's, located three hours south in College Station, Texas; and (accounting for inflation) fifty times that of Harry Truman's in Independence, Missouri.

These ever grander libraries also serve as a showcase for their de rigueur counterpart, the presidential museum (the term *presidential library* now generally refers to both). Boosting and burnishing their subjects' reputations through often partisan exhibits, presidential museums have become a key instrument in each new ex-president's campaign to revise history. Since most visitors to library complexes are tourists and not scholars—recent figures show only ten thousand researchers among 2 million attendees—the treatment given to a president's life and career in his official museum can potentially shape public opinion.

A painstaking collector of documents and memorabilia, Franklin Roosevelt was influential in establishing the public museum function of libraries. Envisioning his library as a popular tourist destination, Roosevelt compiled a prodigious cross section of his belongings, presented both to entertain and to educate. Following his lead, many former presidents and their families have taken such a hand in orchestrating their libraries' development that many are now informal curators themselves.

The curatorial aspects of presidential libraries are no different from those of any museum where narratives are constructed and arguments are made. But these institutions aren't your garden-variety museum; they are high-stakes, taxpayer-supported bodies with the capacity to influence popular thinking on American history. Historical events with checkered reputations inevitably receive short shrift: the Iran-Contra scandal gets barely a mention in the Ronald Reagan library; the Lewinsky follies are an afterthought in Clinton's Little Rock carapace; most famously, even the crimes of Watergate were originally passed over in Nixon's once-private facility. Sharon Fawcett, assistant archivist for presidential libraries at the National Archives—the senior supervisor of the presidential library system—couldn't be more explicit: "A presidential exhibit is an artifact of history. It's a view of how the president viewed his administration." In that light, George H. W. Bush's claim at his library's inaugural that "whether we got things right or could have done things better, the beautiful thing about this library . . . is that history can make that determination" is earnest if naive. No force as abstract as "history," after all, can *determine* any such thing—at least not until human beings, including not just journalists and historians but the president and his team themselves, begin the process.

ORIGINS OF THE PRESIDENTIAL LIBRARY SYSTEM

The presidential library is of relatively recent vintage. After Franklin Roosevelt announced in December 1938 that he was creating a public archive for his papers, seventeen years passed before the U.S.

Congress legislated order into the system. The Presidential Libraries Act of 1955 established a private-public partnership whereby the president raises funds for his building, deeds his papers to the government (while retaining legal ownership), and in return receives the government's commitment to the building's upkeep. The Hyde Park house that Roosevelt built catalyzed this quid pro quo relationship; sensitive to history, FDR urged that "material of this kind . . . ought not be broken up. It ought to be kept intact. It ought not be sold at auction. It ought not be scattered among descendants."

Prior to the legislation, anarchy reigned in the handling of presidential materials. The presidents' papers were considered private property; upon leaving office, presidents carted their documents off with them, becoming (along with their families) the final arbiters of their disposition. Sometimes the papers were destroyed through the inattention of careless heirs, lost to the world by fire and mildew; sometimes the market ruled and they were sold to the highest bidder. Important documents were purged, neglected, secreted, or forgotten. Twenty-three of our former presidents' papers did make their way to the Library of Congress, but these collections were always incomplete, stripped like termite damage of vital elements. This unsystematized free-for-all led to incalculable loss.

The strange career of presidential papers is all the more surprising since even the first president recognized their historical significance. "A species of public property, sacred in my hands," George Washington somewhat affectedly called them; he had hoped to erect a structure to house his, but passed away before he could. The Library of Congress gladly accepted Washington's papers, as well as those of the other early Virginians. Upon transferal, the collection of Washington's papers included sixty-five thousand documents, but the Jefferson collection had only twenty-five thousand, Madison's twelve thousand five hundred, and Monroe's a paltry four thousand. (By contrast, William Howard Taft's single term yielded seven hundred thousand documents.)

Whereas public access to presidential papers is now guided by law, until not long ago presidents and their families had the final say over when such collections would be opened to the public. Abraham Lincoln's son Robert Todd Lincoln handed his father's papers to the Library of Congress after discarding what he deemed insignificant and with the provision that they remain unopened until 1947, twenty-one years after his own death. The papers of Adams père and fils, jealously guarded for more than a century, were made available only in 1950 at the behest of the Massachusetts Historical Society.

Things could have been worse. Fire consumed a major part of the written record of Andrew Jackson's and John Tyler's administrations. Martin Van Buren destroyed a large number of his papers while still in office. On his deathbed, Chester Alan Arthur supervised the torching of most of his private materials. And Florence Harding, Warren Harding's long-suffering widow, set fire to perhaps half the documents of her serial-philandering husband. Only one president, Rutherford B. Hayes, had his papers providently deposited in a private library—the very first presidential library built exclusively for that purpose. It was a visionary act.

Apprehensive perhaps at the founding of Hayes's institution in 1916, former president William Howard Taft worried openly that private ownership of presidential documents could deprive the public record of "some of the most interesting documents of governmental origin bearing on the history of an administration." But Taft's anxiety didn't translate into action. It took the dizzyingly progressive New Deal period, with its faith in the productive potential of government and the positive benefits of public access, to help inspire Franklin Roosevelt's farsighted project. Cognizant of the disarray and chaos that bedeviled his predecessors' materials, Roosevelt sought a single site where the public could easily access all his papers.

The presidential documents of Roosevelt's successor, Harry Truman, were the first to be subject to the Presidential Libraries Act. The federal cost of upkeep at the time was a shade more than sixty thousand dollars, a small investment for securing the materials' open access and guarding their safety. Eisenhower, who had signed the PLA, dedicated his own library in 1962, which was followed three months later by Herbert Hoover's facility in West Branch, Iowa. With a quartet of libraries under its wing, the National Archives established an Office of Presidential Libraries in 1964 to watch over future acquisitions and expansions. The office placed no restraints on the size of future facilities—but few could have imagined the astronomical growth that was to come.

The Lyndon Baines Johnson Library and Museum at the University of Texas–Austin was the first to depart from the relative modesty of the earlier ventures. Dedicated in 1971, Johnson's library was as grandiose as the man himself. Warehousing 31 million documents, from Johnson's congressional career through his presidency, the collection far surpassed the holdings of any previous presidential archive. Although social critic Robert Hughes suggested, a bit excessively, that the only function of LBJ's library would be "pharaonic commemoration," by calling it "a reductio ad absurdum of the presidential library system," Hughes presciently recognized Johnson's monument as a prototype for the years ahead.

Two years later, the auto-da-fé of Watergate signaled a turning point for presidential libraries. Not only did Richard Nixon avoid certain impeachment and likely conviction by resigning his office, he conveniently brokered a sweetheart deal with the General Services Administration the month of his infamous pardon. By depositing his papers with the GSA, rather than deeding his papers to them, Nixon ensured that after three years he could regain control over all his documents.

The public was appalled. In the wake of Watergate, Congress responded quickly, directing the National Archives to retake control of Nixon's writings, tapes, and other paraphernalia, and mandating that the materials be stored in the District of Columbia metropolitan area. Although the government had custody rather than ownership, this step preserved the materials from potential destruction, subverting Nixon's eleventh-hour ploy.

The convulsions of Watergate, and the backlash against the burgeoning of the imperial presidency in the Nixon years, compelled the government to address the question of the ownership of presidential papers. The Supreme Court took a first step in 1977, ruling that the congressional seizure of Nixon's papers and tapes was constitutional, though it left open the question of their legal title. The next year Congress finished the job with the milestone Presidential Records Act, which determined that "the United States shall reserve and retain complete ownership, possession, and control of Presidential records." Presidential records would now be public property. Most papers were to become accessible five years after a president left office, with confidential communications sealed for another seven years.

For Nixon, however, the battle to retain rights over his papers was only beginning. After losing one count, he quickly filed suit to keep the papers sealed on the grounds of privacy, launching two decades of protracted litigation over his presidential materials. Optimistic that a settlement could be reached, he attempted to set up his library at Duke University in the 1980s. When that effort failed, a private Nixon library, the Richard Nixon Library and Birthplace in Yorba Linda, California, was established in 1991. The Nixon library stood outside the jurisdiction of the National Archives and Records Administration; bereft of his presidential papers, it housed only Nixon's pre- and post-presidential documents.

The Nixon family did get the last laugh. In 2000, six years after Nixon's death, the U.S. Justice Department awarded $18 million to his estate as compensation for "taking" property a quarter century earlier that it now conceded was properly his. (The appeals court had ruled in his favor on the issue in 1992.) Aghast, Peter Kornbluh of the National Security Archives flipped the pronoun: "It is unfortunate," he said, "that taxpayers have to pay for what is already rightfully *theirs*."

More than two decades of litigation now behind them, the former president's daughters, Tricia Nixon Cox and Julie Nixon Eisenhower, could now focus on uniting their private library facility with the Federal Archives and transferring their father's presidential materials to Yorba Linda. But a few hurdles remained. The sisters, who had feuded over a $19 million library bequest from Nixon's great pal Bebe Robozo in 1998, now battled over proper oversight of their father's library. Tricia wanted an insider family management scheme; Julie pushed for a more representative board. This would be the last obstacle before the long-awaited breakthrough: in 2007 the Nixon library formally became a part of the National Archives. After more than three decades, Nixon's presidential materials are switching coasts, moving from a warehouse in College Park, Maryland, to the now federally administered Nixon library in Yorba Linda, California, a badly needed corrective to the library's gaping hole.

THE GROWING SIZE AND COST OF LIBRARIES

The drawn-out Nixon saga was far from the only problem to beset the federally managed presidential libraries. The runaway costs of these institutions have also invited increasing attention. Florida senator Lawton Chiles led the legislative crusade against postpresidential perks and the library system's galloping price tag. His colleague Arkansas senator David Pryor, who later became the first dean of Bill Clinton's School of Public Service at the University of Arkansas, joined Chiles's efforts, underscoring "the increasing dollar consciousness of the American people . . . and the Presidential library system [being no] exception to that concern."

The original Presidential Libraries Act of 1955, written when expenditures were still small and presidential libraries few, had studiously avoided imposing any fiscal or aesthetic restrictions on the facilities. Three decades later, however, a $15 million annual budget led to an outcry from reformers to rein in costs. For six years, Chiles fought to wean the government off what he considered the presidential library drug.

The product of Chiles's advocacy, the Presidential Libraries Act of 1986, was signed into law by Ronald Reagan. The new law created financial and size limitations for future libraries and required an endowment to defray the government's upkeep costs. Going forward, educational and other programming would be mostly sourced from these funds. But the idea that endowments could cover rising expenditures proved illusory; in practice, they rarely covered even general operating expenses. In 2004 the George H. W. Bush library at Texas A&M, the first to fall under the law's jurisdiction, raised a $4.5 million endowment that generated approximately two hundred thousand dollars in annual income, which hardly offset the library's $3 million annual operating costs. Under the legislation's restrictions, libraries larger than seventy thousand square feet would have to pony up even more—a provision that prompted creative evasions. The Clinton Foundation, for example, built a one-hundred-fifty-two-thousand-square-foot structure, but used more than half the space for other purposes, leaving sixty-nine thousand square feet to house the archives and library. George H. W. Bush's library occupies precisely sixty-nine thousand five hundred square feet.

Taxpayers today are faced with an almost $60 million price tag to maintain the presidential libraries. Part of this includes storage fees for the vast increase in the number of documents. The Roosevelt library holds 17 million documents; Clinton's library stores more than four times that number. In recent years, the libraries have also been required to hold on to all electronic communications, only adding to the costs: no simple process—Clinton alone had 48 million pages of e-mail.

While critics worry about the growth of the archives, document preservation and access are still viewed as the core of the presidential library enterprise. Other components of the library complex—retail stores selling Ronald Reagan golf balls, bald eagle wind chimes, or reproductions of Nixon's photo op with Elvis—are viewed more skeptically. Why should taxpayers assume the burden of funding the marketing of schlock? As noted, efforts to limit the excessiveness of presidential complexes have seen only limited success. If anything, since the 1986 Presidential Libraries Act these private-public ventures have only ballooned further. Are there remedies that might achieve greater sobriety and moderation in the future?

For years there has been talk of centralizing the presidential libraries, moving them from the various museum facilities to Washington, D.C., and placing them under one roof in the National Archives or the Library of Congress, providing one-stop shopping for history buffs and researchers. Though geographically isolated scholars might make the inevitable arguments against the East Coast bias of such a scheme, it's hard to deny that a move like this would create enormous cost savings. (For one thing, it would eliminate the need to create endless replicas of the Oval Office.) Unified management would also encourage scholarly consistency. As former Truman library director Larry Hackman argues, "you would likely have much more balance if [the libraries] were not separate." The 1986 Presidential Libraries Act actually suggested a "Museum of the Presidents," though, perhaps unsurprisingly, the dreary-sounding idea went nowhere.

Of course the complexity of the existing libraries—and the money, commitment, and marketing that went into creating them—makes any suggestion of wholesale relocation and transformation impractical at best. Instead, some have called for a new model of restraint going forward, encouraging future presidents to "just say no" to building their own ego temples and to place their records with the National Archives in Washington, along with a modest space to display their wares and memorabilia. Those who desire a separate bells-and-whistles museum should arrange for it to be privately financed. Archivist-advocate Richard Cox says it will take an "enlightened president" to make this a reality, one who is prepared to buck the powerful legacy-shaping route of his predecessors and campaign to start a "Center for the Study of the Presidency."

Nonetheless, there have been prominent defenders of decentralization. Historian Arthur M. Schlesinger Jr. was a persistent champion of keeping the regional outposts, which he considered an "unqualified good." Departing from his customary New Deal prism, he argued that the public was better served when libraries were fanned out across the country rather than "swallowed up in the oceanic depositories of Washington." For Schlesinger, presidential libraries represented Jacksonian democracy at work. But even sharp critics of the presidential library system don't rule out further internal reform. "Mend it, don't end it," urges presidential library scholar Benjamin Hufbauer. Legislating further restrictions on a library's overall girth is one idea; offering a more complex reading of a president's time in office, without guaranteeing final cut to the former president and family, another. And to be sure, the longer a president is out of office, the easier it is to move past hagiography toward a more dispassionate historical interpretation.

Paying for Influence

Of all the suggestions for reform, perhaps the most pressing is the need to institute greater transparency by requiring that donor contributions be revealed to the public. As it is always easier to fund-raise when in power, the specter of accepting library donations in exchange for influence has raised serious concerns about conflict of interest. *Washington Post* columnist Richard Cohen's cutting assertion that "an American president's museum is a direct reflection of nothing more than his ability to make friends with rich people while in office" is extreme, but as libraries swell in size and cost, the fund-raising imperative has become a creeping burden during each new president's tenure.

Unlike American campaign finance laws, which bind donors to a very strict set of reporting guidelines and forbid corporations and foreign entities from giving funds to a candidate, presidential library giving is subject to very few restrictions or disclosure requirements. As such, presidential libraries represent an excellent vehicle for foreign governments or multinational corporations seeking to convey their affection for a U.S. president. The presidential foundations that spearhead the fund-raising can also accept unlimited tax-deductible contributions from domestic donors. Gold plaques with donor names may adorn library entranceways, but without any transparency obligations they inevitably tell only part of the story.

Library advocates like Skip Rutherford, former head of the William J. Clinton Foundation, and Sharon Fawcett of the Office of Presidential Libraries at the National Archives and Records Administration both insist that greater disclosure requirements would have a "chilling effect" on giving. Many donors prefer to stay in the shadows, they suggest, for fear of being trampled by a stampede of fund-raisers and development officers. Lifting the veil, it is argued, would unfairly compromise the environment for financing library complexes.

Richard Cox, who advocates for greater transparency, finds that claim spurious. "I'm an archivist, but I'm a citizen and taxpayer first. The idea of a chilling effect is the silliest thing I've ever heard. Archives are not just about memory and history, they are about accountability." Charles Lewis, formerly of the Center for Public Integrity, goes further. "If a donor is giving millions of dollars to the president to enhance his immortality, and doing it while the chief executive is still in the Oval Office, the amount of power that donor has acquired is off the charts." With a reasonably short window of time to raise the funds—as well as all the other planning needs, whether acquiring land, negotiating with municipalities, dealing with the National Archives, or gauging economic development— tax-exempt private foundations are usually established while a president is still in power. Hardwired into this process are unavoidable conflicts of interest and an "invitation for potentially serious influence on the political process."

In recent years, corporate donors have often taken a backseat to the largesse of foreign governments, particularly from the Middle East, where American party affiliation matters little in the decision-making calculus for giving. One former Clinton fund-raiser explains that foreign states will give to both Democratic and Republican libraries alike for one simple reason: spreading wealth is a win-win game. By giving money to a president today, you signal your availability for support to the next president tomorrow. The governments of Saudia Arabia and Kuwait, for example, gave generously to both the George H. W. Bush and the Bill Clinton libraries, with the Saudis contributing around $10 million to each. It's reasonable to assume they will do the same for Bush 43.

Transparency in such library contributions would help citizens assess whether corporate donations or sovereign governments' gifts influence a president's policies. A detailed federal budget exists for what taxpayers are providing to presidential libraries across America. Why not demand the same for private contributions? It's hard to see why the public interest wouldn't be better served if we knew who gives what.

THE ANTINOMIES OF 9/11

Public access to presidential materials raises a different set of transparency questions. In the aftermath of September 11, 2001, new regulations were passed to legitimize secrecy on national security grounds—and access to presidential records became one victim of the new secrecy measures. On the counsel of Attorney General Alberto Gonzales, George W. Bush signed an executive order extending the twelve-year waiting period on classified documents. Violating the letter and spirit of the Presidential Records Act, Executive Order 13233 gives the sitting president, and all former presidents, authority to withhold sensitive materials even after the waiting period has lapsed. Most controversially, it permits an appointed representative of a deceased president to do the same. While presidential archivist Sharon Fawcett contends that the volume of withheld materials has been minuscule, she acknowledges that for scholars the most problematic element is the extension of privilege to family members after a president's death. Others say that what's at stake is the public ownership of the papers. "They may be public property," says Benjamin Hufbauer, "but if no one can see them, are they really publicly owned?" Researchers complain that the necessary extra review time adds at least six months to certain requests. The House of Representatives voted overwhelmingly to override the Executive Order, but by the end of 2008 the full Senate had still not brought it to a vote.

The post-9/11 period was not the first time such restrictions had been placed on access to presidential papers. Bush's father attempted his own end run around the federal regulations. The day before he left office in 1993, Bush's lawyers cut a deal with the National Archives—later backed by Clinton's Justice Department—to obtain full control of all his computerized records. Helpfully, the head of the National Archives, Don Wilson, was appointed director of the Bush Library at Texas A&M. Despite the favorable conditions, a federal judge ruled in 1996 that the archives had no right to surrender the records and that the deal had contravened the Presidential Records Act. The PRA stood vindicated—at least until the younger Bush's executive order flouted it once again.

THE FIRST LIBRARIES: FDR, TRUMAN, EISENHOWER

The presidential library system has its roots in the far-reaching vision—and compulsive collector's mentality—of Franklin Roosevelt. Dedicated five months before the United States entered World War

II, the Roosevelt library drew a stark contrast with the contraction of open society around the world. "This latest addition to the archives of America," Roosevelt himself declared, "is dedicated at a moment when government of the people by themselves is being attacked everywhere." FDR's decision was a victory for the historically minded, and he has long been hailed as a hero by many in the archival field. Of course, there were more pedestrian motivations for the move— Roosevelt wanted a space to bring his papers together in preparation for writing his memoirs—but they hardly undercut the significance of his act.

An amateur architect, FDR himself drew up the plans for his library, a single-story Dutch colonial facility to be constructed of local fieldstone. Roosevelt was evidently more progressive in his politics than in his architectural taste: his library drew less on the streamlined modernist motifs of leading-edge design in his day than on the historical revival movement that marked much domestic architecture between the wars. Roosevelt also drew inspiration from the traditionalism of his predecessor Thomas Jefferson.

Although Roosevelt laid the first fieldstone, Truman's library was the earliest established under the terms of the Presidential Libraries Act of 1955. Compared with the ever more grand and commercialized libraries of recent presidents, Truman's humble structure seems like a library from another planet. Originally intended for his family's property, it was ultimately constructed on another site a mile away ("Ain't no use wastin' good farmland on any dang library," Truman's brother observed).

For Truman, visits to his library became part of his daily routine. Until health problems set him back in the mid-1960s, he spent every weekday there, serving as a kind of civics impresario—providing tours, instructing high school students, and giving his impressions of history and the world. ("Korea," he responded consistently, when asked what was the most difficult decision he ever made.) Filled with the former president's bric-a-brac, the library allowed Truman to spend his retirement living among the artifacts of his public past. Many of his private papers, meanwhile, remained sealed until after his death, frustrating scholars for decades.

The Harry S. Truman Library Inc. was responsible for raising the necessary funds—just under $2 million—to build the library. Reflecting the power dynamics of the time, the larger donations came from labor leaders and organizations—the United Steel Workers, the Amalgamated Clothing Workers, labor giant John L. Lewis himself—rather than the oil magnates of the Persian Gulf. No amateur architect, Truman had hoped that his library would have a simple facade, something like FDR's neocolonial structure—or, even better, something resembling his grandfather's home. But the library's final design was a spare, contemporary edifice that to some recalled the work of Frank Lloyd Wright. "It's got too much of that fellow in it to suit me," Truman grumbled.

The library was dedicated in July 1957, during Dwight Eisenhower's second term, and given the two presidents' bitter relations, journalist Richard Rovere suggested that the occasion could offer a forum for "one of the great hatchet-buryings in American history." Yet it was not to be: Despite the cross section of worthies who attended—including Eleanor Roosevelt, Earl Warren, Lyndon Johnson, Averell Harriman, and Dean Acheson—Eisenhower merely sent an impersonal note of regret. "Only if [Ike] had sent the GSA employee who is up for night watchman at the library" in his stead, one wag commented, "could Mr. Eisenhower have expressed his cold detachment more pointedly." The only other living ex-president, Herbert Hoover, pledged that "except for acts of God or evil persons" he would participate. He kept his word.

Eisenhower's own library dedication followed five years later, in May 1962. Housing roughly 12 million papers—and costing nearly twice what Truman's had—Ike's facility was built on property adjacent to his Abilene, Kansas, childhood home, far from his postpresidential residence in Gettysburg, Pennsylvania. He would visit the facility sparingly, but he is buried in a chapel on the grounds, making his presence a permanent one.

The dedication ceremony for the Eisenhower library was the largest gathering in Abilene's history. With the cultural revolutions of the 1960s only beginning to waft through the air, Eisenhower used the occasion to lament his country's ebbing morality. "I wonder if our pioneer forefathers came back and saw us doing the Twist instead of the minuet, what they would think," he pondered. Modern art, too, came in for Ike's scorn: "Today, art looks like a canvas of dripping paint that has been run over by a Tin Lizzy." By missing the festivities, Herbert Hoover, Harry Truman, and President John F. Kennedy were spared the sermon.

Politics Enters: Herbert Hoover's Library

Only three months after Eisenhower's morality plea, Herbert Hoover dedicated his own library, near his boyhood home in West Branch, Iowa. Unlike its predecessors, however, Hoover's complex soon became enveloped in politics and intrigue.

Hoover himself had never assumed that West Branch, where he had spent his first eleven years, would be the repository of his presidential papers. Rather, he had expected to grant them to the Hoover Institution, the think tank he had established on the campus of Stanford University. In 1895 Hoover had graduated from Stanford in its very first class; a quarter century later, he had given the university a fifty-thousand-dollar start-up contribution to establish the Hoover War Collection (later renamed the Hoover Institution on War, Revolution and Peace) to analyze the root causes of war and revolution. Guided by Hoover's political convictions, the Hoover Institution long maintained a conservative cast to its research and policy (his mission statement commanded the institution "to demonstrate the evils of the doctrines of Karl Marx"), with right-leaning luminaries including Friedrich Hayek and Milton Friedman helping Hoover realize his ambition.

Yet by the 1950s, when the Presidential Libraries Act was passed, tensions had developed between the Hoover Institution and its founder, who had grown concerned that some staff members were straying from Hoover's anti-Communist line. Moreover, Stanford's history faculty had taken issue with the institution's fund-raising materials, which highlighted Hoover's express objective to counter the teachings of Marx. No institution should prejudge any historical issue, the professors complained; objectivity should be their only standard.

Hoover had a librarian's yen for acquisition. Soon after Joseph McCarthy's death in 1957, he sought to obtain the papers of the Wisconsin senator, with whom he'd become friendly. By then, however, he so distrusted the Hoover Institution faculty that he mandated that the McCarthy papers be deposited elsewhere. They "can be put in my personal archives," he bellowed. "There are no left-wingers on that staff." Before long, Stanford's encroachment on the treasured autonomy of his institution motivated Hoover to look elsewhere for a permanent home for his presidential papers. Ironically, this paragon of conservatism eventually turned to the federal government to solve the problem. After almost thirty years of residence in Palo Alto, Hoover's presidential papers were removed to his boyhood home of West Branch, the site of the newly established Herbert Hoover Birthplace Foundation.

At the Hoover library's dedication in August 1962, Hoover was joined by Harry Truman, whose own library he had helped usher in five years earlier. The eighty-eight-year-old Hoover braved the sweltering August heat before a crowd of forty-five thousand onlookers. By then the political waters had calmed somewhat. During negotiations with the West Branch, Iowa Foundation, W. Glenn Campbell—an outspoken conservative who would later figure prominently in the

Reagan library controversy—took the helm of the Hoover Institution and managed to appease Hoover's concerns about political drift. At length the former president's anger at Stanford subsided enough that he accepted the honorary chairmanship of the university's $100 million fund-raising campaign.

Whatever the historical value of his library and its collections, Herbert Hoover's indelible association with the Great Depression continues to limit its public profile. Though in recent years his home state of Iowa has assumed a dominant role in the presidential primary process, no contemporary campaign would welcome a chance to associate its candidate with the disgraced former engineer. During the 2008 presidential campaign, a number of candidates stumped at a nursing home directly across the street, yet preferred passing up the federal memorial to a former president just steps away.

The Second Wave: Lyndon Baines Johnson

After John F. Kennedy's assassination, the Kennedy library should have followed Hoover's, but the Kennedy facility was mired for years in debates over its location. The Kennedy family had hoped to see a Harvard-affiliated Kennedy library in Cambridge, Massachusetts, but residents fought back, fearful of a "tourist invasion," with "the Goths overwhelming the intelligentsia." The battle pushed back the library's opening to 1979, when architect I. M. Pei completed his towering $14 million white concrete-and-glass edifice—not in Cambridge, but overlooking Dorchester Bay in Boston proper.

It would be Kennedy's understudy, Lyndon Johnson, whose library unleashed a second wave of presidential shrines. Sharply diverging from its predecessors in size, expectation, cost, and purpose, Johnson's presidential library and school of public affairs recast the debate about the role and function of presidential libraries.

Lyndon Johnson's daily existence was transformed after the presidency. He would spend the remainder of his life—one day shy of four years—in a period of reflection, detoxification (save a return to smoking), and hopeful redemption. Famously letting his hair grow long, Johnson seemed to have "resigned from life itself," as his old friend John Connally put it. Apart from working on his memoirs, Johnson's only other serious commitment was to watch closely over the establishment of his library.

During his presidency, Johnson had surveyed several potential locales. His hometown of Johnson City, named for a forebear, was an obvious candidate, as was Southwest Texas College in San Marcos, his undergraduate stomping grounds. Yet both sites would have required Johnson to hit the pavement and raise funds. In contrast, the University of Texas, the alma mater of his wife and daughters, was prepared to finance the bulk of the facility. It was an offer he could not refuse: by 1965, Johnson and UT had come to terms.

Those who remember how faculty outcry helped scuttle plans to bring the Nixon and Reagan libraries to the Duke and Stanford campuses respectively may be surprised to learn that the UT faculty was not even consulted on the decision to bring LBJ's library to the University of Texas. According to library director Betty Sue Flowers, for the university's board of regents the decision "was overdetermined from the beginning." By early 1968, ground had been broken for both the library and the associated LBJ School of Public Affairs on a thirty-acre parcel originally occupied by low-income housing and dirt paths. In the spring, when Johnson announced that he would not seek reelection, work on the library redoubled.

Consumed by his legacy—especially on civil rights—LBJ wanted to put his record on the line. Seeking to promote free exchange, Johnson told his vice president, Hubert Humphrey, "I'm going to invite [black leaders] Stokely Carmichael and Rap Brown and we're going to have a free-for-all debate. I'm going to show 'em what free speech really is." Beyond attracting black power's A-list, Johnson also hoped to be appointed "statesman-in-residence," finally exorcising his anxiety toward academic elites with an academic title at his own institution. Yet this dream was dashed: UT offered Johnson a mere honorary professorship, an honor he turned down.

The Vietnam War was still raging when the Johnson complex was dedicated in May 1971. Presidential propriety, not rational choice, made Richard Nixon the keynote speaker. Although some demonstrations were expected, "the *Texas Observer*, the underground press and several hundred long-haired protestors" were kept at bay. Most Texans had no idea that their tax dollars had even paid for the complex. At the opening, Johnson had praised the objectivity of the museum, declaring "it's all here with the bark off." One skeptical observer, journalist Molly Ivins, set out to test the claim, searching the library in vain for any criticism of the Vietnam War. The roughest example she found was a mild-mannered slap on Johnson's wrist from the classical conductor Leopold Stokowski.

Whereas earlier presidents had resisted the incursion of modernist design into their libraries, Lyndon Johnson jumped at the opportunity. Gordon Bunshaft of the then überchic Chicago firm Skidmore, Owings and Merrill was the chief architect. (Disciples of the Bauhaus master Mies Van der Rohe, SOM was acidly dubbed "three blind Mies" by dissenters.) Bunshaft set out to capture a virile LBJ in the lines of his library: "He's very strong, you know. . . . There's nothing 'chicken' about him," he said. Johnson biographer Robert Caro later contemptuously agreed, noting that the "huge, monolithic, windowless structure . . . says quite a bit about the man." To architecture critic Ada Louise Huxtable, the library depicted a "pharaonic pomposity." Indeed, the political cartoonist Herblock sketched LBJ seated as pharaoh, titling his work "Opening of the Great Pyramid of Austin." Dressed in eight floors of cream travertine—a porous limestone in great favor with modernists of the era—the edifice looked modish at the time, but like so much architecture of the period aged quickly.

Johnson was neurotic about drawing tourists to his library, even suggesting opening the facilities at 7 A.M. and offering free doughnuts to fuel admission. In ill health in December 1972, Johnson participated in a civil rights symposium, his last event at the library and his final major public appearance. Although physically weakened—close adviser Jack Valenti recalled that "in full view of the audience . . . [LBJ] popped a nitroglycerine pill into his mouth"—he was still long on eloquence. "To be black in a white society," he instructed, "is not to stand on level and equal ground." And "let me make it plain that when I say 'black' . . . I also mean brown and yellow and red and all the other people who suffer discrimination because of their color or their heritage." In an echo of his nationally televised words after the Selma crisis of 1965, Johnson ended by declaring, "I am confident we shall overcome." Six weeks later he was dead.

THE SAGA OF RICHARD M. NIXON

Johnson's library was still under construction when Richard Nixon, months after his squeaker defeat over Hubert Humphrey and George Wallace, established his presidential library foundation. The move was unprecedented so early in one's term. Anticipating the shape of things to come, the *New York Times* sounded the tocsin. "The pervasive power of Federal regulatory agencies and the volume of Government contracts make it particularly unseemly for wealthy businessmen and other private individuals to contribute money to a foundation for this Presidential purpose." By raising the troubling relationship between money and influence, especially with a sitting president, the paper of record put the problem of presidential library donations on the map.

Despite the early criticism, a foundation chaired by industrial giant Leonard K. Firestone began scouting sites for the Nixon library. The following summer the city of Whittier, California, came forward with the first bid for the library, offering Nixon up to one hundred and twenty acres of free city land. Since Nixon graduated from Whittier High School and Whittier College, and the Nixon Foundation had recently selected his alma mater to put together an oral history of his early years, Whittier struck the foundation as a good bet.

A thousand days later, however, no formal decision had been made. In the heady days of the Watergate storm, more than half of Whittier's student body signed a petition advocating the library's placement there. Asserting that Nixon's contribution "as a major leader of his country and especially as its President has been beneficial," the students defended Nixon against his naysayers. "You have been severely maligned in the past by a notoriously vocal, but small minority of the students from your college," the petition read, and "in this time of duress, we the representatives of the Student Body of Whittier College wish to extend our concern and support to you."

Despite the students' backing, Whittier's proposal remained in limbo until later that year, when scandal hit. With construction on the facility yet to begin, California state authorities began wondering where the monies from Nixon's tax-exempt foundation had gone. The foundation's board included the Watergate troika of John D. Ehrlichman, H. R. Haldeman, and John Mitchell—all of whom had left the administration and would soon be behind bars—and Herbert W. Kalmbach, who had already been jailed for accepting illegal campaign funds. Foundation documents revealed that Nixon's kid brother Edward Nixon, a consultant outside Seattle, Washington, had been paid twenty-one thousand dollars to review six prospective sites, a sum unrecorded in the foundation's tax records. Firestone said that the president's brother had been contracted to assess the "emotional or aesthetic side" of possible library locations. Edward Nixon's wife, Gay, was less taken with her husband's role: "While he's off being paid to do nothing, I'm here alone . . . trying to teach school, and I've got two kids. Let me tell you, it's tough." Nixon had another mess on his hands.

Firestone pledged that the effort to establish a Richard Nixon presidential library would go forward unimpeded, but that was wishful thinking. By the end of 1974, he and the other trustees were contemplating the foundation's closure, with tacit support from Nixon himself; in April 1975, eight months after Nixon's resignation, the foundation formally dissolved. The following week, the University of Southern California announced plans to establish a Nixon library on its central campus. With the fate of the Nixon papers nowhere near sure, USC's offer was improbable at best.

Nixon's resignation prompted a series of events that reconfigured the landscape for archives and preservation. After Congress seized his presidential papers, records, and tapes, they were deposited in the National Archives and the Federal Archives and Record Center, protected by the hastily passed Presidential Recordings and Materials Preservation Act of 1974, designed to ensure that the former president could not (further) destroy any public papers. The act placed thirty-seven hundred hours of recordings and some 40 million pages of documents in the federal government's custody.

It would take a Democrat to relaunch the discussion over a new home for Nixon's papers. Duke University president and former North Carolina governor (later senator) Terry Sanford, together with Duke's board of trustees, agreed to donate land near the university to a future Nixon library. "No collection of presidential papers is likely to be studied more over the next 100 years," Sanford posited. Sanford had been a devout Kennedy man during JFK's run against Nixon in 1960, but he saw acquiring the Nixon papers as a shortcut to international prominence for the university, where Nixon had received his J.D. in 1937. Sanford's quest to enhance Duke's reputation would ignite one of the nastiest conflagrations the Durham campus had ever seen.

Duke's faculty had long been conflicted about Nixon. In 1954, when Nixon was vice president, the university's faculty rescinded an invitation to award him an honorary doctorate—after Nixon had already accepted the offer. In 1971 the faculty blocked a second attempt to grant Nixon an honorary degree. In 1981 many faculty members hoped to make it a hat trick.

It would be an uphill battle for Duke to raise $25 million in private funds for the Nixon library, especially with the National Archives records question unresolved and lawsuits over the materials still under way. And the gestures of rejection continued: One emeritus trustee, former Truman adviser Charles S. Murphy, stepped down in protest, concerned that accepting the library would suggest that the university condoned Nixon's policies. The history department's acting chair, Richard Watson, was receptive to the prospect of housing a Nixon library but not a museum, reasoning that Duke would be receptive to the Al Capone papers, but not an Al Capone museum. Watson was unwilling to accept a facility that told Nixon's story through his own personal prism.

But the museum was a precondition for the Nixon team. Negotiators recommended a one-hundred-fifty-thousand-square-foot facility, though they needed only thirty thousand square feet for his materials. The remaining 80 percent of the space would house a museum that many feared would sugarcoat the reputation of the thirty-seventh president. A scholarly repository for the Nixon materials was one thing; erecting a companion institution designed to rehabilitate a dishonorable president was something else.

Duke's faculty imparted its views to the university's academic council. In a formal vote, the council voted to reject the library by 35 to 34. Their vote was symbolic, but nothing more: decision-making authority lay not with the academic council but with the board of trustees, whose executive committee sided with President Sanford's desire to proceed. "This is a sad day for Duke University," lamented one Duke historian. "The faculty is deeply divided on the question and today's decision to proceed with the Nixon library—in the face of a faculty resolution to stop all negotiations—is likely to continue the acrimony."

English professor George Williams recalled the hypothetical questions that the fury on campus incited: "Would you turn down Caligula's papers? Attila the Hun's? Adolf Hitler's? Where do you draw the line?" Labeling himself "a member of the immoral minority," Williams maintained that the Nixon papers recorded "a period unique, one must hope, in its corruption," containing "horrors and abominations yet unknown." Nevertheless, "it is not helpful to say the collection is valuable but should be housed somewhere else. Whether we like it or not, this place is Mr. Nixon's as well as ours." Williams's colleague Edwin H. Cady went further: "To those professors who do not grasp what access to a great documentary center means to a university, I am afraid it is not possible to explain." One newspaper even snidely proposed that Duke accept the papers "if for no other reason than to prove that scoundrels provide more lively history than saints."

Though the talks with Nixon's team continued, the plans were unraveling. The faculty vote—"one of the most important moments in Duke's history," remembered one historian—energized Duke's university community, and by the end of 1981 the Duke trustees had decided to abandon the museum. Months later, citing a bad economy and political pressure, Duke University waved good-bye to Richard Nixon and his "library cum apologeum," as one critic dubbed it.

Nixon, characteristically, bounced back. Within a year, the former president was in negotiations with Chapman College in Orange, California, to be the academic affiliate for a library built in San Clemente, the locale of Nixon's "Western White House." A San Clemente banker pushing the location said, "I've traveled all over Europe, and whenever I mention San Clemente, the first thing people say is Nixon. He helped put this town on the map. . . . Even during Watergate, they let him come here and forget his troubles. I think he has a warm spot in his heart for this town." Warm spot notwithstanding, local officials remained at loggerheads over whether to provide a formal license for the library and museum. As in Whittier, several years of struggle passed before the Nixon family threw up their hands once again.

After years of failure to place his library—first at his undergraduate body, then at his law school university, finally by his beloved

California redoubt—Nixon finally found it a home in sleepy Yorba Linda, California, where Frank and Hannah Nixon had conceived the future president in a white clapboard home in a former lemon grove. Although Nixon was ensconced in Saddle River, New Jersey, over two thousand miles away, having his library in the Orange County hamlet where he spent his first nine years represented a homecoming.

Inaugurated in July 1990 at a cost of $21 million, and located minutes from Disneyland, the Richard Nixon Library and Birthplace was a privately run facility administered by the Nixon family that housed Nixon's pre- and postpresidential papers. Some found the library "too simple and tasteful" in light of the grievous offenses of Nixon's presidency; others were comforted that taxpayers hadn't contributed to its upkeep.

On opening day, Presidents Ford, Bush, and Reagan were in attendance. Only Jimmy Carter from the presidential fraternity declined the invitation. Nixon had skipped Carter's library dedication five years earlier, yet the Republican bristled at the snub: "I can't believe Carter didn't show up at our library opening. Is that the pettiest damn thing you ever heard of?" With thirty thousand in attendance, Nixon spoke candidly, admitting that he had "many memories, some of them good, some of them not so good."

In the fall of 2006, after years of litigation and bitterness, the Richard Nixon Presidential Library and Museum finally became part of the National Archives and Records Administration. Timothy Naftali, a respected Cold War historian, became the library's first federally appointed director after its decade and a half of existence as a private institution. The yawning omissions and distortions in the museum's treatment of history—which attributed the notorious eighteen-and-a-half-minute gap in Nixon's Oval Office tapes to "mechanical malfunction," among other things—were ripe for revision. "I'm an empiricist," Naftali said. "I have no attachment to Richard Nixon either way." Sharon Fawcett of the Library of Congress pledged that work on the library would involve "starting from scratch."

Alexander Butterfield, momentarily famous for his startling revelation that Nixon had taped his Oval Office conversations, once told the Watergate committee that "There was no doubt in my mind that the taping equipment was installed to record things for posterity—for the Nixon library." Thirty-five years later, Butterfield reaffirms that "there was no sinister purpose to those tapes," that they were simply intended to create a documentary record. Sinister or otherwise, that documentary record is at long last becoming a part of the Nixon library.

PRESIDENTIAL LIBRARIES OF THE 1980S: FORD AND CARTER

Compared with the tumultuous saga of the Nixon library, the establishment of Gerald Ford's presidential library and museum was a piece of cake. Ford became the only president to divide his library from his museum, dedicating his library at the University of Michigan in April 1981 and opening his museum across the state in his boyhood home of Grand Rapids five months later. Despite their separate locations, both bodies constitute a single institution and share one director.

The University of Michigan had originally bid to house Ford's congressional papers shortly after Ford replaced Spiro Agnew as Richard Nixon's vice president. After his defeat in the 1976 election, Ford formally announced that all his papers—congressional, vice presidential, and presidential—would head to Ann Arbor, and a museum would be established in his hometown. According to a Ford library archivist, by splitting them up, the twin institutions may have been shielded from attacks about the excessive growth of presidential libraries. Still, Ford's buildings contain 50 percent more space than Roosevelt's—though he served a mere one-sixth of FDR's time in office.

The dedication of Ford's museum was attended by neither Ford's predecessor nor his successor. "We wanted to focus on my presidency," Ford said, "and I think if we had either one or both here, it would have . . . diverted public attention from the presidency of Gerald Ford." Nevertheless, at the library's inaugural, Nixon's presence was referenced at least implicitly, though never by name. Ford was careful not to let the formal launching of his legacy be darkened by Nixon's shadow, as the 1976 election had been.

If Ford's museum had been dedicated even a short time later, Jimmy Carter would almost certainly have been invited. The two former presidents struck up an unlikely rapport just three weeks after the opening, when they boarded Air Force One together en route to Anwar Sadat's funeral. By the time Carter's library was ready for prime time in 1986, their postpresidential friendship was in full bloom.

Carter was never interested in having his presidential library serve as "a monument to me." He wanted, instead, an "active" institution, and his presidential library is unique in taking a backseat to its far more prominent neighbor, the Carter Center. The graduate policy schools established by LBJ, Bush, and Clinton, though all dynamic institutions, in no way overshadow their associated libraries in the way the Carter Center dominates the Carter presidential complex. With its $300 million endowment, the Carter Center is "the big gorilla," as the Carter library's director concedes. Indeed, the Carter library is the only presidential library without a private fund-raising foundation. The federal government is its sole sponsor. Simply put, the passions and interests of Jimmy and Rosalynn Carter make the library an afterthought.

Housed two miles from Atlanta, in one of four buff-colored interlocking cylindrical buildings next to a Japanese garden and man-made lake, the $25 million Jimmy Carter Library and Museum derived roughly a quarter of its funding from foreign donors and around half from residents of Georgia. The development of the site was not problem free. The major stumbling block concerned a four-lane, two-and-a-half-mile-long parkway off the interstate that would tear through fields of Georgia magnolias to approach Carter's complex. Carter's aides believed the access roads were necessary because of the expected number of visitors, and Carter himself threatened to take his library elsewhere if he didn't get his way. Protestors derisively dubbed the library the "Peanut papers" and the highway the Ex-Prezway, and locals fought hard to block the cutting up of their neighborhood. (Ironically, Carter had successfully fought to stop a similar highway proposal in a nearby area when he was Georgia's governor.)

The Carter library was dedicated on October 1, 1986, long before the parkway issue was resolved (that would take until 1993). At the opening, Carter's sixty-first birthday, Reagan generously saluted the president whose reelection bid he had crushed six years earlier. Carter's reaction was characteristically humble: "I think I now understand more clearly than I ever had before why you won in November 1980, and I lost."

The Reagan Library: From Stanford to Simi Valley

Where Jimmy Carter had seen his library as a mere footnote to more active pursuits, Ronald Reagan considered the establishment of a proper library complex as a principal objective. Not only did Reagan aspire to become the first president to establish a library during his time in office, he also hoped to be the first to organize a think tank to accompany it—placing ideology front and center in the formation of his legacy.

The patron saint of post-Goldwater conservatism, Ronald Reagan took the helm of a reanimated right wing in 1980s America. His espousal of Cold War aggression, small government, and deregulation effected a paradigm shift in political discourse, overpowering liberal Republicans and Democrats alike. Reagan's ideas owed considerably to those generated in the hothouse environment of Stanford's Hoover Institution, "the brightest star," as he called it, "in the constellation of think tanks." The admiration was mutual. Hoover's 1981 annual report was unabashed in its delight, writing that "the high point of the past year was the election of . . . Ronald W. Reagan as President of the United States."

The Hoover Institution, already the repository of twenty-five tons of Reagan's gubernatorial and campaign papers, had named him an honorary fellow in 1975. Some of Reagan's closest advisers, including Martin Anderson, Michael Deaver, and Richard Allen, had long-standing ties with the think tank when they joined Reagan's first-term administration. Soon after Reagan took office, Glenn Campbell, Hoover's director since 1960, sent the president a letter querying his interest in making Hoover the home for his library. Few were surprised when Reagan's team quickly assented to the invitation.

Campbell had long smarted over his institution's losing stewardship of Herbert Hoover's presidential papers to the facility in West Branch, Iowa, and securing Reagan's library for Stanford became a personal crusade. A free-market economist widely known for his truculent personality and virulent anti-Communism, Campbell became close to Reagan in the 1960s when the then governor appointed him to the University of California's board of regents. From that perch Campbell loudly backed Reagan's crackdown on Vietnam War protestors.

With Reagan now president, the synergies between the Hoover Institution and the Reagan administration reached new heights. Twenty-nine Reagan administration officials had ties to Hoover. Campbell joined Reagan's Foreign Intelligence Advisory Board and eventually became the chair of his library foundation. At an event honoring Hoover's board, Reagan thanked Campbell for sending more people to "my campaign than from any other institution." Ex cathedra, Campbell was ideally positioned to shepherd Reagan's desired institute and presidential papers to his think tank. No one doubted that "The President and Mrs. Reagan," as Campbell later recounted, "were particularly enthusiastic about a center for public affairs . . . run by Hoover."

The tight nexus between the government and the campus-based policy institute raised hackles within the Stanford community. In late 1983, the Hoover Institution became the target of a fierce faculty and student petition drive decrying the relationship. "We have no objections to individuals serving in the Reagan administration," a Stanford political scientist said. "What troubles us is that . . . there is at least *prima facie* evidence of a problem . . . of partisan politics by the institution as a whole." Students soon formed the Stanford Community against Reagan University, an outfit with the deliberately insinuating acronym SCARU.

On the other side, seven U.S. senators, including three Democratic Stanford graduates, weighed in to support the library coming to the university. The *Wall Street Journal* branded campus dissenters' actions "academic terrorism," aghast that "a small band of malcontents has spawned a power grab against a venerable . . . think tank." And, naturally, some questioned whether there was any difference between Kennedy's Camelot administration, with its many Harvard mandarins, and the Hoover-inflected Reagan team.

Notwithstanding the conflict, Glenn Campbell delivered Reagan's positive response for formal approval to Stanford's president, Donald Kennedy. (Hoover is a semiautonomous body but technically accountable to Stanford's board of trustees.) Kennedy quickly set up a faculty committee to look into whether both a library and a public policy center would be of benefit to the university. After working for almost a year and soliciting the opinions of the faculty and the broader university community, the committee reported that the library was of certain benefit to Stanford, but that a policy institute must fall under "normal academic governance." In other words, if the Reagan Foundation wanted to establish a think tank at Hoover, it must be governed not by Hoover's policies, but under the standard appointment and operational guidelines of the university. Appointments would have to be approved by academic committees and run through accepted hiring procedures.

Putting it mildly, Glenn Campbell wasn't thrilled. Neither was Reagan's counselor Ed Meese (later his attorney general), who was spearheading the negotiations for Reagan. "If it were not for the Hoover Institution," Meese declared, "Stanford would not be considered" for the honor of housing Reagan's papers. Campbell and Meese grudgingly dropped the proposed policy institute's Hoover connection, counteroffering that the institute remain at Stanford independent from both Hoover and the university.

Stanford's trustees voted overwhelmingly against the idea, but did endorse the library and an affiliated (small) museum—recognizing that even if Hoover had a role in its development, a library and museum would ultimately fall under federal jurisdiction. Unlike a policy institute under Hoover's aegis, Hoover's responsibilities with a federal library would be circumscribed. The Reagan team then reluctantly decided to establish its think tank off-campus.

Donald Kennedy set up a second committee to focus on the details, including the land, site, and overall interface with the university. The committee suggested three different locales. Soon thereafter, the Reagan Foundation selected one of them: a stunning site in the grassy foothills overlooking the campus. Stanford's trustees gave their endorsement, and Reagan himself signed off. Hugh Stubbins, the architect of New York's Citicorp Tower and Philadelphia's Veterans Stadium, was hired to design a structure in the Spanish mission style.

Then, just as the Reagan library was about to forge ahead, a new stumbling block surfaced. To the mushrooming questions about Hoover's propinquity with the Reagan administration was added concern about the library's prominent siting and general design. An ad hoc committee formed that laid down new guidelines for the Reagan library. The complex, it said, had to be "minimally visible" from the campus, and a proposed two-story "presidential suite" made that impossible. Making matters worse, Hugh Stubbins blundered by suggesting that he would employ "superior" materials to the "very ugly" sandstone used on Stanford's campus. Recalling the Kennedy and Carter controversies, community groups rose up to complain about traffic implications, especially for those residing on the access road to the library.

The Reagan library plan was coming undone. The faculty now passed a resolution insisting that the roofline of the proposed library must be modified; this was followed by an overwhelming faculty senate vote not to site the library in the foothills. According to Stanford historian David Abernethy, symbolism was also a factor: the tallest building on campus was Hoover's tower, and now the Reagan library was proposed to be number two.

Reagan was about to throw in the towel. His term would be over in less than two years and he was anxious to move ahead. He turned to his Hollywood Rolodex, recruiting Jimmy Stewart to lend a hand. But the outspoken Republican actor's homespun advocacy proved too little too late, and the Stanford library proposal fell apart. The final blow was the faculty senate's unanimous vote condemning Glenn Campbell for opining that Stanford should "boast" of its "Reagan connection." Despite his Democratic background, future Clinton secretary of state Warren Christopher, then chairing Stanford's board of trustees, was chagrined by the final decision: "I was much in favor of having the Reagan Library on the Stanford campus and disappointed that it did not work out." By May 1987, the Reagan Foundation had abandoned Stanford and begun to look elsewhere.

According to Ed Meese, Reagan himself made the decision to abandon the Stanford plan, concluding that too many people had lined up against it. As Martin Anderson recalled, Reagan shrugged his shoulders and said, "Life is too short." Donald Kennedy learned of the Reagan team's exit "not by a thoughtful letter, but from the press," a whimpering ending to a bang that lasted several years. Two decades later, the subject remained acrimonious. "The attorney general of the United States [Ed Meese] should not have conducted personal business for the president until once he had left office," Kennedy asserted. He retained special scorn for Glenn Campbell: "One of the most dyspeptic and disagreeable people I have ever met. Even Nancy Reagan found him hard to abide."

In search of greener pastures, Reagan's library foundation soon turned to Simi Valley in Southern California's Ventura County, a locale that boasts more cars per household than any city in the United States. One hundred acres of free land in an area of rolling hills generously donated by a local real estate firm sweetened the pot and helped close the deal. Despite some land-use hurdles, this would be no repeat of the Stanford debacle. By 1988, ground was broken on the Simi Valley property.

Three years later, the $60 million, one-hundred-fifty-three-thousand-square-foot Ronald Reagan Presidential Foundation and Library—the largest and most expensive built to that point—was formally dedicated. Hugh Stubbins's mission-style design, originally planned for the Stanford campus, was carbon-copied for the Simi Valley location. The occasion inspired an extraordinary photo opportunity: for the first time in history, five presidents appeared together at the same time—former presidents Richard Nixon, Gerald Ford, Jimmy Carter, and Ronald Reagan, and President George H. W. Bush.

Simi Valley was an appropriate venue for the staging of the Reagan library. As Ralph C. Bledsoe, the library's first director, pointed out, not only was the area's population largely conservative, but countless classic Hollywood Westerns had been filmed nearby. The location also put Reagan himself physically closer to his library, allowing him to participate in events there more easily. And there was another benefit: Stanford would never have had the space to house the hugely popular $30 million Air Force One Pavilion that opened in 2005. Finally, since the Reagans had decided to be buried on the grounds of their library, they would doubtless be more comfortable spending eternity in authentic Reagan country rather than in the liberal precincts up north in Palo Alto.

TEXAS A&M WELCOMES GEORGE H. W. BUSH

Where Reagan's dreams of establishing a think tank were dashed, his successor, George H. W. Bush, never considered the idea in the first place. Whether out of humility or a lack of ideological drive, Bush took a more moderate approach to the development of his presidential library, making it a less complicated enterprise.

Bush showed an early interest in placing his library at his alma mater, Yale University, but the idea never really got off the ground. As his press secretary, Marlin Fitzwater, recalls, Yale was never especially friendly to the president or his Bush Foundation proposal. "They snubbed him during his presidency, booed him, and never welcomed him from the beginning," Fitzwater says. "They just couldn't wrap themselves around a Republican." As the *Economist* mordantly observed, "It was better to have a library in a place where the students would not be tempted to burn it down."

Bush moved on quickly. By the spring of 1991, after a joint bid from Rice University and the University of Houston fell through, his team inked a deal with Texas A&M, the state's first public institution of higher education. The College Station university had many things in its favor: a lot of land (it offered Bush a ninety-six-acre former hog farm, once the home of the Swine Research Center); a willingness to help in raising money (the university is known for oil men with very big pockets); a philosophical alignment with Bush himself (Texas A&M has one of the largest college Republican organizations in the country); and a personal friend of Bush as the university's president. With its graduates widely represented in the oil and ranching industry and the campus only ninety miles from Bush's home in Houston, Texas A&M turned out to be an inspired choice.

At $83 million, the three-building limestone complex bested its Reagan library predecessor in cost. The price tag included the second Texas-based public policy school affiliated with a former president, the George H. W. Bush School of Government and Public Service. (The library cost $40 million, the school another $43 million.) The expenses were shared among Texas A&M and ten thousand other donors—including the former president of the United Arab Emirates, Sheik Zayed bin Sultan al-Nahayan; the Kuwaiti Foundation for the Advancement of Sciences; and sixteen others who gave more than a $1 million apiece. The longtime Saudi ambassador to the United States, Prince Bandar, an old friend of the Bush family, was another seven-figure donor and showed up at the opening ceremonies. Even the followers of Sun Myung Moon, in the cloak of the Washington Times Foundation, generously opened their wallet to provide an additional million.

Some twenty thousand people attended the November 1997 dedication ceremonies, including former presidents Ford, Carter, and Clinton and former first lady Nancy Reagan. The exhibits included Bush's 1947 Studebaker, which he drove upon relocation from Greenwich, Connecticut, to Texas; a restored TBM Avenger he'd flown during the war; and a sculpted quartet of horses in the library's front plaza; one journalist cracked that the library might well be called the "George Bush War, Auto, and Horse Museum."

President Bill Clinton, not yet as friendly with the elder President Bush as he would become after leaving office in 2001, said in his remarks that in George H. W. Bush "America has had a good man whose decency and emotions served our country well and this is the story this library will tell for generations to come." There were other stories, too. Eleven months after Bush left office, his library had received a gift of between one hundred thousand and two hundred and fifty thousand dollars from Edwin L. Cox, the father of a man Bush pardoned. Years later, when Clinton received a library contribution *before* issuing a pardon, the story would become front-page news. In Bush's case, any allegations of quid pro quo quickly faded from view.

William J. Clinton's Bridge to the Future

Costing twice as much as George H. W. Bush's complex, Bill Clinton's library was massive in size and dramatic in the boost it offered to the economic fortunes of Little Rock, Arkansas. Sited on a onetime no-man's-land of forgotten warehouses in the city's River Market section, the Clinton library rose like a phoenix along twenty-seven acres of the Arkansas River. Clinton urged the project on, full steam ahead: "Whatever it costs, when people come to it 100 years from now . . . we will be very glad we made this investment." Known officially as the William J. Clinton Presidential Library, the library was the largest development project in Little Rock's history.

Clinton announced his plans to house his library complex at the University of Arkansas shortly after the start of his second term. Though the city of Little Rock donated the land, construction would be costly, and Clinton followed precedent by beginning the long-haul fund-raising effort while still in office. His pal Terry McAuliffe officially oversaw the fund drive, but another sweet-talking friend of Bill's, James "Skip" Rutherford, emerged as the key protagonist. A friend since the 1970s, Rutherford had an executive background in public relations, strategic communications, and advertising. (He would later teach a university course called Communicating, Rainmaking and Networking.) In 1997 Rutherford became CEO of the William Jefferson Clinton Foundation and quickly got to work lining up donors.

From 1997 to 2002, the foundation's sole objective was to procure funds for Clinton's library. Only afterward did it receive its current mandate to support global health and development. Clinton's surfeit of closely cultivated friends and associates around the world were called upon to help, but the task was nonetheless immense. Raising $165 million to build, in Clinton's pet phrase, "a bridge to the future" would be a mammoth undertaking.

By the end of Clinton's second term, the foundation had almost $14 million in assets. A huge sum of money still needed to be raised, but few doubted Clinton's ability to pull it off. Despite the annus horribilis he weathered in 1998, capped by its reckless impeachment hearings, Clinton remained a political magician with an extraordinary capacity for reinvention. The coda of his second term, however, saw a new round of scandals. Several of the midnight pardons Clinton made just before leaving office led to nightmarish consequences he didn't foresee, momentarily imperiling his fund-raising potential.

Among the one hundred and forty pardons Clinton issued was one to the fugitive commodities trader Marc Rich, who had fled the United States for Switzerland seventeen years earlier during an investigation that led to his indictment for tax evasion and racketeering. Soon it was revealed that Rich's former wife, Denise Rich, had contributed four hundred and fifty thousand dollars to Clinton's library foundation only months before—making the pardon seem as false as a three-dollar bill. Infuriating even the most ardent Clinton defenders, the error in judgment blew the opportunity to exploit the immediate postpresidential afterglow. All contributions and pledges larger than five thousand dollars were promptly subpoenaed, casting a pall over the Clinton library fund-raising machine.

How to explain such a badly timed, self-inflicted wound? One close friend of the Clintons thought the answer might be traceable to their roots in the freewheeling environment of Arkansas politics. No matter how entrenched in Washington the Clintons became, this friend suggested, they had learned their tricks of the trade in Little Rock, an anything-goes atmosphere rife with conflicts of interest.

Clinton came to his own defense, publishing an op-ed in the *New York Times* that read like a lawyer's brief. Clinton insisted that "there was no quid pro quo" and that the pardon had been supported by even "distinguished Republican attorneys" like I. Lewis Libby—Mark Rich's lawyer for fifteen years, and later Dick Cheney's convicted chief of staff. The next year Clinton publicly acknowledged the error, though he framed it in political terms. "It was terrible politics," he wrote. "It wasn't worth the damage to my reputation."

Ever the upbeat Clinton booster, Skip Rutherford had a hard time swallowing the pardon. As a person with primary responsibility to raise funds for the library, Rutherford felt the setback keenly. "No big donors jumped ship, but no big ones came aboard, either," he recalled years later. Clinton's first year out of office was to be the real kickoff period, but the bad news kept coming: further pardon-related scandals involving Bill Clinton's half brother, Roger Clinton, and Hillary's brother, Hugh Rodham, broke at the same time, keeping the pardon issue in the news for months.

The pardon scandals were red meat to a Republican Congress unwilling to abandon their attacks on a president they loathed. The House Government Reform Committee, chaired by Indiana Republican Dan Burton—a longtime Clinton nemesis—couldn't launch hearings fast enough. Beth Dozoretz, a chum of both Clinton and Denise Rich, who'd raised scads of money for the Democratic Party as DNC finance director, was fingered as the person who pursued Denise Rich's millions. (Dozoretz took the Fifth Amendment when called to testify.) Burton's committee was primarily concerned with whether Denise Rich's donations could be traced back to her former husband, since it is unlawful for a fugitive to give funds to political causes. Though Burton's committee ultimately found no illegalities in Denise Rich's conduct, in a lengthy March 2001 report, "Justice Undone: Clemency Decisions in the Clinton White House," it did establish that Denise Rich had played a key role in lobbying for her husband's pardon.

The Rich scandal cost the Clinton Foundation a year's worth of fund-raising. With the library's opening scheduled for the fall of 2004, the pressure was on to procure some very large donations quickly. Foreign governments took the lead. One former fund-raiser remembered the astonishing magnanimity of the emirs in Dubai, who mailed in two checks totaling $30 million. Close Clinton friend Casey Wasserman arranged for his eponymous Los Angeles Foundation to give between $6 million and $7 million. Carlos Slim, the Mexican telecom titan, was in for another million, and Joe Ford of the Alltell Corporation in Little Rock gave $1.25 million.

Skip Rutherford was clear about the Clinton library's economic potential for Little Rock. The eightieth largest metropolitan area in the country—a city whose only other major claim on U.S. history was the protection of black students by national guardsmen in 1957—Little Rock was a place short on destiny. Clinton's legacy institution began to change all that. Rutherford promised that the venture, a bona fide twenty-first-century private-public urban renewal project, would anchor the redevelopment of the city's downtown and waterfront. By the end of 2005, a year after the library's opening, a billion investment dollars had flowed into the city. Situated off Interstate 30, one of the most traveled highways in America, two hours from Memphis and just ten minutes from the airport, the library attracted more than three hundred thousand visitors in 2006—second only to the Reagan library's drawing power that year.

Designed by New York's Polshek Partners, a signature architectural firm, the Clinton library features an interior exhibition area modeled on the library at Trinity College, Dublin. From the outside, the building was designed to evoke Clinton's vaunted bridge to the future, in an edifice of cantilevered steel and glass. "It is our arch," Rutherford says, referencing architect Eero Saarinen's Gateway Arch in Saint Louis. In a period when architecture has joined other art forms as potential marketing venues, one critic has called the Clinton library "architecture as politics, played skillfully to please a large constituency and accommodate a range of perspectives." (Others were not as kind, trashing Clinton's building as a "trailer on stilts.")

Clinton had expressed a hope to spend a week to ten days every month in his all-glass, two-thousand-square-foot penthouse atop the library, but as yet those plans have not panned out. In recent years he has visited the library once or twice a month for a few days at a time, largely to relax and play golf. Together with the library and museum, the former president established the Clinton School of Public Service, housed in an 1899 railroad station on the site. Skip Rutherford would take the reins as the school's dean after former Arkansas senator David Pryor, its first dean, stepped down. Like George H. W. Bush, Clinton chose to develop a graduate program rather than establish a policy institute to further his agenda. For the forty-second president, Reagan's disastrous Stanford experience may have been a lesson learned.

Clinton was joined at the library's November 2004 opening by two former presidents, Jimmy Carter and George H. W. Bush, and by President George W. Bush. Hillary Clinton, now the junior senator from New York, declared that "the exhibits tell the story of someone who loves his fellow man." Bono and The Edge of the Irish pop group U2, substituting for an ailing Jerry Ford, gave an acoustic performance of "Sunday Bloody Sunday." Even John Kerry appeared, only a fortnight after his loss in that year's Tuesday Bloody Tuesday presidential contest.

A THIRD LIBRARY COMPLEX GROWS IN TEXAS: GEORGE W. BUSH

Like his hero Ronald Reagan, George W. Bush believes that his administration's legacy will be best served through a full-fledged policy institute alongside his future library, "a place," he says, "for people to talk about freedom and liberty, and the de Tocqueville model, what de Tocqueville saw in America."

Bush's intent to establish a policy institute became evident after his second term began. In 2005, when Texas A&M expressed an interest in hosting the library, the president's youngest brother, Marvin, and Donald Evans, Bush's former commerce secretary and the head of his library site selection team, responded with a letter that made the president's plans clear: "Part of [the] Institute's mission will be to further the domestic and international goals of the Bush Administration—including needed program reforms, compassionate conservatism, the spread of freedom and democracy throughout the world, and defeating terrorism." In the throes of war, the Bush team was busily organizing the administration's future legacy.

With one Bush presidential complex under its belt, however, Texas A&M was never a serious contender. Other universities submitted bids, accompanied by the usual behind-the-scenes negotiations and public relations campaigns. One group, calling itself the West Texas Coalition for the George W. Bush Presidential Library, was formed to make the case for joint sponsorship by Texas Tech, Midland College, and several local governments. The West Texas Coalition put together an eight-minute video narrated by Texas's "cowboy poet," Red Steagall, but its chances were slim. As a nonsectarian university, Texas Tech was at a disadvantage compared with the other three Texas finalists: Baptist-affiliated University of Dallas, Catholic Baylor University, and Southern Methodist University. David Miller, the coalition's chair, pledged that they had "bathed [their] project in prayer," but their prayers went unanswered.

Determined to have a think tank as part of his library complex, Bush paid a visit to the crown jewel of conservative think tank establishments, the Hoover Institution, in April 2006, during the Bush team's *tour d'horizon*. At a dinner at Hoover, long-term Hoover fellow Martin Anderson, a chastened warrior from the Reagan library controversy of the 1980s, offered the president explicit counsel: "Don't put your library at a university." Still smarting from Reagan's debacle at Stanford, Anderson pointed to the acknowledged success of the Reagan library's ultimate Simi Valley site and tried to steer the forty-third president to an off-campus location. He also cautioned Bush against entanglement in another college battle, warning that "there are too many constraints" in a university setting.

Despite Anderson's advice, SMU soon became the odds-on favorite. Located in a tree-lined part of North Dallas not far from the tony suburb where the Bushes plan to reside, the school had the inside track—not least because it was the first lady's alma mater. A 1968 library science graduate, Laura Bush sits on SMU's board of trustees, and shortly before he became president, George W. Bush gave the university two hundred and fifty thousand dollars to create a walkway named the Laura Bush Promenade. A fellow trustee, SMU alumnus, and Bush family friend, Dallas oil magnate billionaire Ray Hunt contributed tens of millions of dollars to the university and played a powerful behind-the-scenes role in the Bush library negotiations. With fellow Methodist and SMU trustee Dick Cheney and SMU graduates Karen Hughes and Harriet Miers playing prominent roles in the Bush administration, the selection of SMU was, if anything, overdetermined from the start.

In addition to the archives and museum, SMU's original proposal for the library complex included a graduate policy school akin to the George Bush School of Government and Public Service at Texas A&M. But according to James Hollifield, a political science faculty member and part of the original planning committee, the Bush team rejected SMU's concept out of hand. Not only was there already a Bush school in Texas, they argued, but the relationship between his father's school and the library had been fraught with tension from the start. No one anticipated that the Bush committee would seek a policy institute instead, Hollifield added. Yet by the time bids were submitted, the policy institute concept was gospel.

In the fall of 2006, SMU's bid for the library finally attracted campus debate when two faculty members at its Perkins School of Theology published a short opinion piece in the campus newspaper entitled "The George W. Bush Library: Asset or Albatross?" The piece questioned the absence of open deliberation around SMU's bid and appealed for greater transparency going forward. It also took issue with the Bush project as a whole: "Given the secrecy of the Bush administration and its virtual refusal to engage with those holding contrary opinions," it asked "what confidence could be had in the selection of presidential papers made available to the library?" The commentary was the opening salvo in a fierce exchange within the SMU community and ignited a firestorm of discussion in the media. Sleepy SMU was suddenly national news.

By December 2006, the Bush team was in exclusive negotiations with SMU. Their proposed policy center, dubbed the "Freedom Institute" by Bush insiders, was designed to be governed outside SMU's standard procedures, and this became a flashpoint for controversy that echoed the Stanford imbroglio over the Reagan library. While some faculty members were opposed to the prospect of their university implicitly legitimizing the president, more were distressed at the notion of harboring a think tank that would fall outside university governance practices. One objector, SMU political scientist Cal Jillson, accepted the concept of a Bush library, viewing the Bush materials as a certain research bonanza for the small private institution, but he opposed the idea of an independent think tank on principle. Any effort to use a policy center to place the Bush legacy in the best possible light, he said, would be a "recipe for long-term difficulties and dispute and embarrassment. Universities are about open exchange, but the Bush institute is about promoting the president's agenda."

For the Bush team, keeping the future public affairs body independent from SMU's governance was imperative for its viability. Bush had no desire to establish an institute as a degree-granting body that would then be forced to accept university policy. Giving SMU's deans control over its direction would provide Bush's team far less latitude to design its agenda. One example of a potential future conflict arose even as negotiations with SMU were under way: in the fall of 2007, Stanford's president and provost learned, only after Hoover issued its press release, that former defense secretary Donald Rumsfeld had been appointed a distinguished visiting fellow at the Hoover Institution. Any faculty member observing this backdoor appointment process would have a sobering sense of what was in store for SMU.

To document the saga and offer a venue for complaints about

hosting a partisan institute on a university campus, an untenured SMU historian, Ben Johnson, started a Bush Library Blog. "I don't think anyone would lie down on the tracks to stop the library," he said, "but clearly there are a lot of us who would lie down on the tracks to stop the institute." Johnson also worried about the financing of the colossal venture. Although SMU president R. Gerald Turner promised that fund-raising for the library and think tank would be separate from the university, Johnson was unconvinced. "With overlapping donor pools," he argued, "at some point it becomes an academic distinction."

Johnson and others called for a faculty referendum on the governance of the proposed institute. Although one hundred and seventy academics signed a statement supporting the idea, SMU's faculty senate voted it down. Two months later, the same body overwhelmingly endorsed a resolution to omit SMU's name from any future Bush institute title and charter. While faculty members were unwilling to make demands on the think tank's general governance, it did not want the body acting in the name of the university. Although housed on SMU's campus, the Bush institute would be separate in both name and law. As one SMU historian suggested, "It will rise or fall on its own merits, and, I suspect, as at the Hoover Institution, the record will be a mixed one. But the Institute will not be 'the Bush Institute at SMU.' It will stand alone and be judged appropriately."

James Hollifield is confident about the prospects. "If you have a strong university with good values," he says, "you will be okay." As for the concern that the Bush policy institute would be ungovernable, Hollifield is skeptical. "If [Bush's team members] wish it to be a strong institution, they will need the university more than the university needs them." Hollifield offers a unique perspective on the predicament. As a Duke University graduate student in the early 1980s, he had witnessed the Nixon controversy firsthand. Enduring those inflammatory months convinced him that Duke ended up the real loser in not accepting the Nixon library. "If Nixon's library had come to Duke . . . it probably would have been integrated into the federal presidential-library system much more quickly," Hollifield suggests. It was "the high-minded opposition at Duke that actually wound up injuring the cause of scholarship." He was determined not to have a repeat performance at SMU.

Hollifield's colleague in political science Matthew Wilson takes a more defiant stance in defense of the policy institute. Instead of shying away from partisan politics out of fear of polluting the campus, Wilson views the institute concept as a natural concomitant to the hurly-burly of the learning process. Unfazed by accusations of partisanship, he deems "ideological orientation" to be a constituent aspect of any think tank, whether it be the Hoover Institution, the American Enterprise Institute, or the Brookings Institution. "Regardless of one's perspective," he argues, "having such people on campus to give guest lectures, participate in panel discussions, and even teach classes . . . will be a boon to SMU students."

Not surprisingly, Carl Sewell, chair of SMU's board of trustees, is equally bullish on the library complex: "It will be one of the most studied presidencies in our history," he claims, "and SMU will attract intellectuals from all over the world to study the Bush presidency." Skip Rutherford, dean of Bill Clinton's School of Public Service, seconds Sewell's optimism. "I just think it a plus," Rutherford says. "Obviously, people at SMU have real concerns about the [Iraq] war, but I've urged them to take a broader view."

By spring 2007, opposition among SMU faculty had petered out as it became clear that the library and institute were destined to become a reality. In roughly the same time it had taken Duke's faculty to foment opposition to the Nixon library—six months—the Bush complex at SMU became a slam-dunk (though its official announcement would not come until February 2008). Ambivalence on the part of many faculty members was a major factor, suggests SMU historian Alexis McCrossen. To Cal Jillson, the faculty was simply "lacking the self-confidence" to mobilize effectively. Having been through a similar battle once before, James Hollifield naturally took a longer perspective.

Considering university life, which trades in ideas, as inherently rough-and-tumble, he considered it regrettable "if you can't stand a little politics and partisanship on a university campus."

A final perspective on the controversy came from James Hopkins, chair of the university's history faculty, the department that was most intensely engaged with the question. "As a graduate student at the University of Texas at Austin, and an Army veteran, with a visceral reason to condemn the Vietnam War, I saw the vilification of Lyndon Johnson and the Johnson Library at close hand. It was a classic example of anti-intellectualism. Today, after going through a generation of change, it is one of the crown jewels of the University of Texas. I would hope that in time this will also be true of the Bush Library at SMU." And when asked specifically how the proposed Bush complex might stack up against Lyndon Johnson's library, two hundred miles to its south, LBJ library director Dr. Betty Sue Flowers said slyly, "I really like our model, if you can read between the lines."

3

WAR, CONFLICT, AND
THE EX-PRESIDENCY

~

When I was president it was said of me that I spoke softly and carried a
big stick. It can be said of Wilson that he speaks bombastically and
wields a dish rag.

Theodore Roosevelt

The lessons of World War I teach us one thing. We cannot slay an idea
or ideology with machine guns. . . . They live until they have proved
themselves right or wrong.

Herbert Hoover

· · · · · ·

DURING HIS WHITE HOUSE YEARS GEORGE W. BUSH WAS ENVIABLY
immune from criticism from at least one living ex-president: his
father. Although several of George H. W. Bush's former advisers spoke
out against the Iraq War, the forty-first president stood by his son's
administration, registering no public disapproval of the defining conflict of his eight-year tenure.

Save for blood ties, it's hard to fathom the elder Bush adopting
such a guarded position. Many of his once colleagues were proponents
of a "realist" approach to international relations and voiced unabashed

opposition to George W. Bush's missionary ardor, with its emphasis on "democracy promotion" as a cornerstone of foreign policy. Unsurprisingly, the former president resisted publicly second-guessing his son's motives or political choices, preferring silence to conflict. On the rare occasions when he made his opinions known, it was typically to harangue those maligning his boy: "Do they want to bring back Saddam Hussein, these critics?" he sneered in a November 2007 interview. "Do they want to go back to the status quo ante . . . ? Do they think life would be better in the Middle East if Saddam were still there?"

Before the war, Bill Clinton also endorsed George W. Bush's March 2003 decision to invade Iraq. By 2005, however, the former president had come to see the war as "a big mistake." "We never sent enough troops and didn't have enough troops to control or seal the borders," he said. In Clinton's view, the Bush administration had also thoughtlessly erred by pushing for "the total dismantlement of the authority structure of Iraq." Like Bush père, Clinton's recalibration was compelled by family ties. During his wife's 2008 presidential campaign, the former president defended Hillary Clinton's decision to authorize war by swiftly reframing the issue: "It's just not fair to say," he said, "that people who voted for the [congressional resolution authorizing military action] wanted war." Clinton also attempted to revise his own personal history, now proclaiming that he "opposed Iraq from the beginning."

By contrast, the Iraq War was met with little equivocation from Jimmy Carter. As early as the fall of 2002, several months before the conflagration's onset, Carter thundered against the idea of a preemptive strike in his speech accepting the Nobel Peace Prize (an obvious venue to assail the drumbeats of war). And he never let up. Carter's criticism of the Bush administration's policies, from detention in Guantánamo to wiretapping at home, was consistent with his vigilant antiwar stance. Calling the fighting "a quagmire very similar to what we experienced in Vietnam," he vocalized the growing public recognition that Bush's Iraq policy not only squandered the international support the United States had enjoyed after 9/11, but also opened a dangerous chasm between America and the world. The man remembered for making human rights a constituent part of U.S. foreign policy acknowledged dejectedly that "since 2001, the U.S. government has abandoned its role as champion of human rights."

Carter's positions on Bush 43's foreign policies found a soft echo in those of Gerald Ford, though the latter's were embargoed until his death in December 2006. Even under the posthumous circumstances, Ford's disapproving comments were a powerful rebuke coming from an ex-president and fellow Republican during wartime. "I don't think I would have gone to war," Ford said. "I would have maximized our effort through sanctions, through restrictions, whatever, to find another answer." Ford singled out the militant detour of his former White House chief of staff, Dick Cheney, and his former secretary of defense, Donald Rumsfeld, whom he now derided as "pugnacious." Ford's position was simpatico with mainline Republican realism: "I just don't think we should go hellfire damnation around the globe freeing people unless it is directly related to our own national security."

In waiting until his death to have his remarks published, Gerald Ford was following the unofficial tradition of withholding criticism of any sitting president's policy decisions during wartime. But not every former president has maintained that standard; indeed, some have even undertaken their own counterdiplomacy initiatives. Although some have unquestionably supported the president, others have acted as free agents, unbeholden to constituents or other politicians. Yet any former president is by nature more than simply a "private citizen," and some have become visible public opinion leaders whose influence lingered for years, even decades, after they left the White House. Particularly during periods of war and conflict, ex-presidents have provided strategic advice, counsel, and even criticism to their successors.

The First Years of the Republic
⊶⊷

The Founding Fathers placed a premium on stability. After seven years of a grueling anticolonial war for independence, followed by the struggle to design a constitutional framework acceptable to competing social forces, the new republic was a fragile creature, its survival a source of constant anxiety. For the earliest ex-presidents, France was one root cause of that unease.

France had been an important ally during the American Revolution. By the time George Washington left office in 1797, however, he had become increasingly agitated about its potential interference in American politics and society. The XYZ Affair, in which unnamed French diplomats requested bribes as a prerequisite to receiving American envoys, badly damaged U.S. relations with France later that year and helped provoke a two-year undeclared conflict between the countries. Already at war with England, France was irate with America for signing the Jay Treaty during Washington's second term, establishing trading privileges between the United States and Great Britain, and responded by seizing a number of U.S. commercial ships.

Reacting to France's hostility on the seas, Washington espoused a more extreme Federalist line than he voiced while president. In the summer of 1798 he wrote decisively that "the Agents and Partizans of France" were endeavoring "to promote divisions among us," and that "to blind, and irritate the People against the Government (to effect a change in it) is their sole aim." Paranoia regarding French domination prompted Washington to give rhetorical support to John Adams's notorious Alien and Sedition Acts, measures sparked by fears of fifth columnists aligned with France. Unconstitutional and autocratic, the Acts established criminal charges for forms of public criticism of the president and Congress. Denounced and mostly repealed during Jefferson's presidency, they were a black spot on the Federalists' historical reputation and on early American history.

It's unlikely that Washington would have signed such transparently undemocratic decrees during his own time in office. A supporter of "patriotic assimilation," he wrote to his vice president, John Adams, that immigrants should be integrated into American life so that "by an intermixture with our people, they, or their descendants, get assimilated to our customs, measures, laws: in a word soon become one people." With the French contretemps at its apex, however, Washington's head swirled with conspiracy theories, and his growing fear that immigrants were being dispatched to his new country "for the express purpose of poisoning the minds of our people" overcame him.

Increasingly wary of a possible French invasion, Washington was approached by John Adams and Secretary of War James McHenry about the possibility of leading an army if necessary. Washington was as reluctant about this engagement as he was to return to political office; he enjoyed repeating that he hoped to stay "seated in the shade of my own vine and fig tree." Yet he saw the mission as unavoidable and agreed to serve "if a crisis should arrive . . . as to leave me no choice."

The call soon came. Empowered by Congress to establish a provisional army in the summer of 1798, John Adams eagerly recalled Washington from retirement to serve as lieutenant general of the military, without consulting even his own ministers on the matter. After a military hibernation of fifteen years, Washington was recruited both as a consummate tactician and for the symbolic power he continued to wield. Directing the army, the former president clashed with Adams and threatened to resign his position if Adams did not allow him to select his generals. Washington also demanded that his subordinate officers be Federalists, concerned that no one share any "predilection to French measures." And most unsettling for Adams, Washington insisted that Alexander Hamilton be given the number two military slot. Ultimately, all the fraught negotiating and politicking was for naught; the 1798–1800 Quasi War with France would be fought entirely on the seas.

In the earliest years of the nineteenth century, the new nation was plagued with smaller conflicts such as the Barbary Wars of 1801–05 and 1815. But it was the War of 1812, "Madison's War," that allowed America to establish its international profile, giving the nation the credibility it craved. In a break with his Federalist compatriots, who opposed the fighting for fear of a French alliance (and believed that concessions could be wrangled by diplomatic means), former president John Adams supported the war. After U.S. soldiers were conscripted into service in the British navy, and the British imposed a series of restrictions on U.S. trade (in an effort to cripple France's economy), Adams's resolve was only strengthened.

Adams also considered the war a vindication of the judiciousness of his policies as president and a rebuke of Thomas Jefferson's. Many of America's failings in the first year of fighting were attributed to the country's lack of preparedness. Adams had made improving the small and inadequate U.S. Navy a cornerstone of his administration, but Jefferson abruptly changed course, curtailing shipbuilding and selling off vessels. When Madison promised to reanimate the country's enfeebled naval institutions during the War of 1812, Adams reacted with faux praise: "Oh! the wisdom! the foresight and the hindsight and the rightsight and the leftsight; the northsight and the southsight; the eastsight and the westsight that appeared in that august assembly." As for Jefferson, in 1812—the year they launched their lengthy and spirited postpresidential correspondence—he conceded to Adams that his decision to gut the navy was far from prudent. An advocate of the war himself, Jefferson applauded Adams for appreciating the navy's determining role.

Dedicated to the preservation of a strong union, Adams was never able to abide those New England Federalists who not only opposed the war but continued to trade with Britain and even threatened secession. He considered America's ability to survive the conflict a testament to the country's strength. That its first major conflict as an independent nation was mismanaged, poorly funded, highly unpopular, and not particularly successful seemed to matter less.

From the Mexican War to the Civil War

The War of 1812 may have broadened America's presence in the world, but it was James Polk's expansionist Mexican War that stretched America's borders, increasing its territory by 50 percent and adding what would become a bevy of new western states. Polk seized on an 1846 Mexico-Texas border skirmish as a pretext for declaring war, and the resulting conflict was largely supported in Congress, with most Democrats and southerners squarely supporting the president's continentalist stance. But the war did have its opponents, among them many Whigs and northerners who saw it as part and parcel of the expansion of slavery.

Though weak and disorganized, this antiwar movement—led by prominent New England thinkers including Ralph Waldo Emerson, Henry David Thoreau, and William Lloyd Garrison—had a willing champion in former president turned congressman John Quincy Adams. Joined by fellow Whig representative Abraham Lincoln, Adams remained a staunch opponent of the 1846–48 conflict, fulminating against what he deemed "a most unrighteous war" and Polk's acceptance of slavery. Adams delivered his last major address, a denunciation of the war, right before voting against granting the medal of honor to eight generals of the conflict. He then collapsed on the House floor and passed away in the Speaker's chamber days later.

Even some expansionists took issue with the war. Former president John Tyler kept his opinions off the record so as not to impugn his successor publicly, but among friends he spoke openly against Polk's strategy of violence and empire-building through imperial landgrabs. "While he welcomed the spoils of conquest," Tyler's biographer writes, "he deplored [Polk's] method of acquisition." In the end, Polk helped fulfill what had long been Tyler's own aspiration: taking the boundaries of the United States to the Pacific.

The Mexican-American War offered a first taste of battle to many

American soldiers who would later fight in the Civil War. But Polk's war could not truly prepare the citizenry for the hardened political fault lines that would lead to the "irrepressible conflict." At the onset of the nation's bloodiest struggle, an unprecedented five former presidents stood witness.

Hoping to stave off war, members of the ex-presidential class launched two early efforts to preserve the Union. Aspiring to hammer out a blueprint for peace, John Tyler proposed to the Virginia legislature a meeting of the twelve border states, both slave and free. The scheme eventually morphed into a more general invitation in which twenty-one states, fourteen free and seven slave, agreed to send representatives to Washington for a peace conference.

The seventy-one-year-old Tyler was selected to chair the convention, to be held at Washington's Willard Hotel. With one hundred and thirty-one delegates in attendance, the conference convened on February 4, 1861. For the next three weeks, until its conclusion, it would afford Tyler an unexpected outpouring of attention. The former president strove to make the gathering meaningful; what "our god-like fathers created," he entreated his colleagues, "we have to preserve." It was soon obvious, however, that no region was interested in genuine compromise, and the conference's middle-of-the-road resolution was promptly rejected by Congress. Though Tyler was undecided when he arrived for the conference, he gradually turned toward secessionism—especially after a revealing meeting with President-elect Lincoln at the hotel (where the Illinois Republican resided for several weeks before his March 4 inauguration). Lincoln made clear to Tyler and other delegates that he would use the provisions of the Constitution to immobilize the forward march of slavery. "In a choice of evils war may not always be the worst," Lincoln warned; to Tyler the sentiment came as a lightning bolt.

Twenty-four hours after the convention's adjournment, Tyler called for his Virginia to secede; soon thereafter he was elected to the Confederate Congress. Northern delegates were suspicious of the former president's motives from the outset, calling him a "tottering ashen ruin," a figure "more cordially despised" than any person "who ever occupied the Presidential chair." Their mistrust could only have redoubled upon learning that, even as the convention was assembling, seven southern states that had already formally seceded were gathering in Montgomery, Alabama, to establish the Confederacy formally. Tyler's own nineteen-year-old granddaughter, who had been born in the White House, hoisted the new Confederate flag.

Encouraged by influential private citizens, Franklin Pierce, the downtrodden, alcohol-infused former Democratic president, attempted in May 1861 to gather his ex-presidential colleagues to investigate peaceful alternatives to the fighting, which was now in its second month. Pierce attributed a larger share of the blame for the eventual strife to northern abolitionists—no surprise, since his former secretary of war and good friend Jefferson Davis was now president of the Confederacy. But Pierce remained willing to use the symbolic office of the ex-presidency to save the union. In a letter to his ex-presidential colleague Martin Van Buren, he asked, "Is there any human power which can avert the conflict of arms . . . between the two sections of the Union?" Suggesting that all five living ex-presidents meet in the constitutional city of Philadelphia, he appealed to Van Buren, the most senior former president, to convene the proceedings: "No man can with propriety summon such a meeting but yourself." Van Buren, who had voted for Stephen Douglas in 1860, was beginning to recognize the need to support Lincoln in the intensifying national conflict and would have considered attending had Pierce first obtained Lincoln's consent for the meeting and its aims. (Van Buren's vocal opposition to the secessionists, and his efforts to galvanize New York elites behind Lincoln, may have been penance for cynically appeasing the South earlier in his career.)

But there was little chance of Pierce approaching Abraham Lincoln to sanction such a meeting. Among the ex-presidents, Pierce and Tyler were the most decidedly antagonistic to Lincoln and his wartime objectives. While Pierce, unlike Tyler, would not approve of secession as a viable alternative, he did recommend that Lincoln negotiate with the renegade Confederacy to bring an end to the war. Pierce also voiced his opposition to Lincoln's Emancipation Proclamation, interpreting it as an abrogation of states' rights and indicating that for abolitionists the president had become "their willing instrument for all the woe which [had] thus far been brought upon the Country and for all the degradation, all the atrocity, all the desolation and ruin."

Like Pierce, James Buchanan—now retired to his home in Wheatland, Pennsylvania—was often labeled a dough-face: a northerner in sympathy with the South. Indeed, a majority of Buchanan's cabinet had been slaveholders. Though Buchanan himself was a strict unionist who attacked secession as unconstitutional, he pinned much of the blame for the sectional crisis squarely on the North's supposed uncompromising stance on the slavery issue, and joined Pierce in rejecting the Emancipation Proclamation. To some, Buchanan's inept decision-making had been the proximate cause for war, and he was flooded with threatening letters. Some Republican newspapers alleged that he could have prevented the conflict if he had sent troops to South Carolina during the secession crisis of 1860–61. Life at Wheatland was sometimes precarious, and Buchanan allowed committed Masons to guard his home to fend off possible violence. He spent his last years justifying his actions and trying to vindicate his administration's attempts to save the Union with his exculpatory memoir, *Mr. Buchanan's Administration on the Eve of the Rebellion*. Published the year after the Civil War ended, the memoir took pains to spotlight "the malign influence of the Republican Party" and the malevolence of antislavery partisans.

For another former president, the years after the war were also marked by conflict. Though Millard Fillmore had championed the Confederacy's defeat, he had spoken out in favor of restoring Southern rights once the war ended. "When we have conquered the Rebel armies, and disposed of their leaders," Fillmore noted, "let us show our magnanimity and generosity . . . by extending to them every act of kindness in our power and restoring to them all their rights under the Constitution." Fillmore was never a secessionist, but such conciliatory comments caused many to stigmatize him as a copperhead—a northerner in support of the Confederacy—a charge ardent unionists in his native Buffalo and elsewhere never let him live down.

AMERICAN IMPERIALISM

The post-Reconstruction Gilded Age found big business and burgeoning American industry craving new resources and the opportunity to affirm America's power in world affairs. These pressures culminated in the Spanish-American War, sparked by tensions over Cuban independence from Spain and the growing erosion of Spanish colonial control in the Philippines, Puerto Rico, and Guam. The Spanish-American War marked the dawn of a newly aggressive era in American foreign policy, but even at this moment of brash expansionism, America's imperial forays had their detractors. Some considered the expansionism both unconstitutional and immoral, and found the notion of liberating Cubans from their Spanish overlords simply a pretext to conquer Spanish lands. Others, Andrew Carnegie among them, decried the annexed territorial gains, judging the islands' inhabitants both inferior and bereft of the know-how to participate in the U.S. political system effectively.

Ambivalent about America's role abroad, former president Benjamin Harrison was among those troubled by President William McKinley's dalliances in the Caribbean. Though Harrison was a fellow Republican, and sympathetic to Cuba's plight, he was hardly convinced that the United States had secured "God's commission to deliver the oppressed the world around" and considered its control of the Philippines a blatant violation of the Monroe Doctrine's promise to "leave the rest of the world alone."

McKinley's immediate predecessor, Democrat Grover Cleveland, shared Harrison's skepticism. An isolationist *avant la lettre*, Cleveland was aghast at the rumblings toward war and the manipulation of public sentiment by William Randolph Hearst's *New York World*. Even after the U.S.S. *Maine* exploded in Havana Harbor, killing two hundred and sixty-six passengers and crew, Cleveland believed "it would be an outrage to declare war" and wondered why the United States would partner with the Cubans—whom he warmly described as "the most inhuman and barbarous cutthroats in the world." Eventually, Cleveland's aspiration to keep the United States out of war blurred his vision: "I cannot rid myself of the belief that war will be averted," he wrote, anticipating Herbert Hoover's misguided doubts about the prospect of a second world war decades later.

Cleveland warned that the American death toll would result in a "general and ominous inquiry as to the justification and necessity of this war." But he underestimated the cultural impact of one particular rough-riding former New York City police commissioner: Teddy Roosevelt. Roosevelt's charisma and genuine heroics, and the resulting wave of overblown jingoism, blunted the Democratic Party's (and the Left's) critique of America's slide toward imperialism, though Cleveland himself never backed off from his reservations about the war.

A decade and a half later, Teddy Roosevelt, now a restless former president, was quick to push for America to clarify its position in conflicts among its neighbors. After his tumultuous second-place finish in the 1912 election, Roosevelt openly questioned the choices made in Latin America by the newly elected Woodrow Wilson. He took a particular interest in the Mexican Revolution, especially once American soldiers were being routinely captured and killed. Roosevelt took issue with Wilson's decision not to recognize the thuggish government of Victoriano Huerta following a coup in which President Francisco Madero (who had earlier ousted the dictator Porfirio Diaz) was assassinated. Unlike many of America's allies, Wilson refused to confer legitimacy on the Huerta government and pressured Britain to reduce aid to Mexico, believing it would force Huerta to hold free elections. But Roosevelt claimed that Wilson's refusal to support Huerta only aided the revolutionary forces, leading to sustained border raids against Americans and other injustices. Not even Wilson's eventual bombardment and occupation of the port of Veracruz pacified TR. As he wrote in the *New York Times*, "President Wilson interfered in such feeble fashion as to accomplish the maximum of evil to us and to other foreigners and the Mexicans, and the minimum of good to anybody. He hit; but he hit softly. Now, no-one should ever hit if it can be avoided, but never should any one hit soft."

Roosevelt's criticism struck a nerve. Wilson's hope to see self-government and the will of the people expressed in Mexico was certainly defensible, but he hardly wished to see the revolutionary forces rise up violently against Huerta. Uneasily, Wilson asked TR himself to serve as arbitrator for the conflict. Not surprisingly, Roosevelt refused: he clearly preferred being in the opposition camp—where he could keep Wilson accountable during the hostilities with Mexico and, later, the catastrophe of the First World War.

THE GREAT WAR

It was World War I that ignited all of Roosevelt's rhetorical cylinders. After Germany's attack on Belgium in 1914—which Roosevelt considered the conflict's first outright act of war—the former president's position on U.S. involvement began to take form. His thinking was shaped by a number of well-regarded figures from politics and culture who sought his influence. From one camp, Hugo Munsterberg, a pioneering Harvard psychologist and staunch defender of Germany, bombarded TR with his version of reality. From another, Rudyard

Kipling wrote to Roosevelt from England, assessing in gory detail the tragic condition of the Belgians after the German invasion. (Kipling's only son died in the Battle of Loos.) Even the British foreign secretary, Sir Edward Grey, contacted the former president to insist on Britain's righteousness.

Roosevelt soon became convinced of the horrors of German belligerence (while vowing "I am no anti-German"), and began promoting what soon became called the policy of "preparedness." The former naval secretary called for the immediate enlargement and improvement of America's military, and called upon the American public to prepare for the possibility of war. Through speeches, articles, a book (*America and the World War*), and even his behind-the-scenes contributions to a film, *The Battle Cry of Peace,* that examined the consequences of an America unprepared for fighting—Roosevelt skewered Wilson for what he considered the president's cowardice and spineless response to German hostility.

Though he was out of step with public opinion, which championed Wilson for keeping America free of war, Roosevelt nonetheless made a compelling case for intervention. Roaring against Wilson's neutrality, TR stressed that if he had been at the helm he would have interceded to protect Belgium from the Germans. His claim was doubtless fueled by resentment that Wilson, not he, was president during the crisis; his attacks on Wilson only grew in the ensuing years.

Less manic than his mentor, onetime Roosevelt protégé William Howard Taft also took a great interest in the war as it unfolded. Taft cofounded and became first president of the League to Enforce Peace, a forerunner to the League of Nations and an outfit united around a common premise: that only a powerful international organization could ensure the avoidance of war. The league's guiding principle stated that "the signatory powers shall jointly use their economic and military forces against any one of their number that goes to war or commits acts of hostility against another of the signatories."

Active for roughly three years, the league had its share of critics. Roosevelt and his good friend Senator Henry Cabot Lodge were outraged when league members backed Wilson's plan for a negotiated peace settlement to end the war in 1916. (The United States wouldn't enter until the following year.) They objected to the league's intervening in peace negotiations, convinced that it should only operate in peacetime environments. But though he quarreled over the league's proper function, Roosevelt never strictly opposed the idea of a global alliance of nations. During his Nobel Peace Prize acceptance speech several years earlier (he had been awarded the prize in 1906 but didn't make his appearance to accept it until 1910), he called for the strengthening of the tribunal at the Hague (Roosevelt had sent the first case there) and proposed that a world organization be created to stop the outbreak of war.

After Wilson declared war in 1917, Roosevelt dissected his actions almost obsessively. He found Wilson's conduct of the war reprehensible, in particular his inadequate efforts at preparedness and his snail-like pace in supplying aid to the allies. Roosevelt's savage rebukes—he came perilously close to calling the wartime president a traitor—netted him enemies who admonished him to quit "heckling the Commander-in-chief when we [are] at war." Roosevelt's response was simple and direct: it was "unpatriotic not to criticize."

During the war's early years, Taft and Roosevelt were also at odds. Taft took issue with Roosevelt's alarmist pronouncements, claiming that "they misrepresent conditions" and "only serve to discourage the feeling of people that should be high and enthusiastic." And Taft worried that his own efforts to get Congress and the White House to approve compulsory military service were sidetracked by Roosevelt's oddly self-regarding plea to be dispatched to France to command a volunteer mounted infantry—a kind of Rough Riders redux.

Mutual dissatisfaction with Wilson ultimately brought the two former chief executives together. After years of contempt and mistrust, they enjoyed a reconciliation of sorts in May 1918 when they found themselves at Chicago's Blackstone Hotel, Roosevelt stumping for congressional candidates and Taft touring on behalf of the National War Labor Board. Taft approached Roosevelt, who was dining alone, and after a warm greeting (acknowledged by the applause of fellow diners), the two former presidents sat and conversed for half an hour. Summing up their encounter, TR stated that their views on Wilson's mishandling of the war were perfectly aligned. Both Taft and Roosevelt pledged to deliver a Republican victory in the midterm elections, but despite their détente they never stumped together, and Roosevelt died just months after the election.

In the ensuing years, Taft shifted his attention to the fight for Woodrow Wilson's brainchild, the League of Nations. A dedicated sponsor of the league, Taft was pained that Wilson failed to appoint him to the Peace Commission at the Paris Peace Conference of January 1919, where the league's proposal was up for debate. But the slight didn't dampen his enthusiasm, and Taft redirected his energies to securing passage in the Senate. Addressing the many misperceptions surrounding the international organization, Taft offered a two-hour address to separate fact from fiction, clarifying that the league "did not assume any of the powers of the respective nations," was not "super-sovereign," and that it "proposes, not commands" international policy. Insisting that "you violate your duty as patriotic American citizens if you judge the League of Nations . . . on whether President Wilson or his party may gain credit for it," he implored senators to rise above partisan discord and support the league. "If George Washington were alive today and was confronted with the situation we face," he said, "he would favor the League of Nations."

Indeed, Taft's support for the league was guided less by any political compass than by his orientation as a jurist. Despite the evolution of his war position from neutrality to intervention, Taft was always partial to nonviolent judicial settlement of international conflicts. It was this commitment that allowed the Republican Taft to serve as Wilson's activist foot soldier despite his personal aversion to the

Democratic president, whom he colorfully described as "that mulish enigma, that mountain of egotism and selfishness who lives in the White House."

Though his original Fourteen Points were whittled down in the process, Wilson managed to secure approval for the League of Nations at the Peace Conference. On the domestic front, however, the plan met with stiff opposition. The Senate balked at the inclusion of Article 10, refusing to commit the United States to guaranteeing the safety of the other signatory nations against aggression. Though some advocated compromise, calling for the covenant to be ratified "with reservations," Wilson encouraged Democrats to vote against such indiscriminately watered-down proposals. His intransigence, likely exacerbated by a debilitating stroke in 1919, contributed to the league's ultimate defeat in Congress.

Seeing that Wilson was incapable of fighting on, Taft rallied behind his fellow Republican Warren Harding for president in the next election, convinced that the Ohioan might pursue a more measured approach to ratification. Yet Taft's hopes were dashed; Harding turned his attention elsewhere, and the league's moment was lost.

World War II

Two decades later, as Europe's heavens began to darken with the storm clouds of a second world war, Herbert Hoover was America's only living ex-president. And it was Hoover who came closest to offering Americans a firsthand glimpse of fascism—through a winter 1938 sojourn in Europe when he met privately with Adolf Hitler at the German Chancellery and partook in a festive evening with Hermann Goering at his estate outside Berlin.

On March 8, a mere seventy-two hours before the Anschluss, Austria's annexation into greater Germany, Hitler greeted Hoover and the American ambassador to Germany, Hugh R. Wilson, in "black breeches, varnished boots and a khaki-colored jacket emblazoned with a swastika." In an hour-long meeting, Hoover and Hitler reviewed their respective countries' economic and social achievements, with Hoover "expressing his admiration" for the "very hopeful, live atmosphere everywhere in Germany." When the conversation turned to more troubling subjects—among them democracy, Communism, and the Jews—Hitler offered the usual National Socialist boilerplate. Hoover's fierce antileftism led the two men to common ground on the subject of Communism, and his unbending isolationism compelled him to inform the German chancellor that "America was politically very different from Europe and by no means desired to interfere in European political questions." Edward Rickard, Hoover's assistant and good friend, later transcribed the former president's recollections of the meeting, noting that Hoover left the session convinced that Germany was unprepared for war and that if war came it would be "not West but East and South," with "no harm for general peace."

Hoover's meeting with the führer was followed by festivities at the Carl Schurz Society, named for the prominent German-American leader. Hoover was feted by the president of the Reichsbank, Hjalmar Schacht, who told the guests that "it is in a certain sense tragic that Mr. Hoover has not been able to carry out personally the work he conceived from so humane and so idealistic a standpoint," and that "we may expect great things yet from the man who is our guest." Such encomia may in part be attributed to the fact that as president Hoover had instituted a debt moratorium during Germany's financial free fall. Hoover was gracious and conveyed his satisfaction that he was able to help Germany in its time of need.

The next day, Hoover had a more leisurely get-together with Hermann Goering, exchanging opinions on industry and military might with Hitler's deputy at his opulent hunting lodge. Hoover and guests were regaled by "sixteen trumpeters, dressed in elaborate costumes and performing the hunting song from *Siegfried* with servants dressed in uniforms used by Frederick the Great's foot soldiers [serving] sherry and port." And on the main lunch table he found "a jewel-encrusted bust of solid gold . . . a memorial to [Goering's] first wife," on which "pushing a button . . . turned the profile to different angles."

After returning to the United States, Hoover strove to reinvigorate his party, which had been eclipsed by the rollout of Franklin Roosevelt's New Deal. Though Hoover hadn't styled himself a Republican loyalist in the past, in his postpresidential years he toured the country speaking on behalf of his party, donating large sums of money to the GOP, and holding forth during occasional press conferences—seizing a platform for his views even as the enduring taint of the Great Depression impaired his credibility.

As the situation in Europe grew worse, Hoover rallied against American intervention. Despite his tête-à-tête with the German leadership, and his direct observance of the Nazis' mistreatment of Polish Jews, Hoover was convinced that an alliance with Britain, France, or most problematically Russia was a wrongheaded approach to stemming the Fascist tide. Several days after his return from Europe, the former president made it clear that in establishing defensive alliances "we would be fostering the worst thing that can happen to a civilization . . . the building up of a war between government faiths and ideologies." Live and let live, Hoover counseled: "The forms of government which other people pass through in working out their destinies is not our business. We can never herd the world into the paths of righteousness with the dogs of war." A year before Pearl Harbor, Hoover declared with passionate certainty that America was in no present danger but was "far more likely" to be dragged into war by Roosevelt than by the Republican presidential nominee, Wendell Willkie.

Hoover never stopped cautioning against American entrance into the European theater. Thundering against FDR's March 1941 Lend-Lease Act, which allowed the president to supply war materials to allied nations, Hoover lobbied strenuously to weaken its provisions and pressed prominent Republican noninterventionists such as Robert Taft and Thomas Dewey to follow suit. After Pearl Harbor, he did offer at least rhetorical backing for the United States' entry into World War II, but at least in philosophical terms he never deviated from his own isolationism. Though in public he accepted that war had been forced on America, Hoover also believed that if the United States had pursued a less belligerent economic relationship with Japan instead of freezing its assets, the attack on Pearl Harbor just may have been averted.

HERBERT HOOVER AND THE POSTWAR WORLD

Over the years, Hoover's positions were subject to seemingly contradictory interpretations and netted him unlikely bedfellows. His withering criticism of U.S. military adventurism made him an icon of sorts to some New Left historians, though others were skeptical of his credentials as a classic isolationist, citing his overriding desire to maintain a secure and balanced world order. Hoover himself rejected such labels altogether, dismissing them as unhelpful distractions that occluded the larger issues. Advocating for a policy of deterrence during the Korean War, he was adamant that "sane policies cannot be made amid college yells of 'isolationist' or 'internationalist,' nor by smears and slanted news which are the ugly instruments of those who would dictate." However his arguments were later construed, one thing is certain: Hoover's own statements never suffered from opacity.

After World War II, the new principle known as "containment" came to dominate the debate over U.S. foreign policy. And by the early 1950s, Hoover was pushing for the scaling back of American military engagements overseas and the reinforcing of its defenses in the Western Hemisphere. While he believed that America's security must be its first priority, he recommended rectifying the imbalance of military strength abroad. European nations were not pulling their weight in conflict spots, he argued, and the United States was shouldering a disproportionate amount of the burden. (He raised similar objections to the Marshall Plan, proposing that the World Bank finance and oversee the process, with involvement from a number of countries, instead of the United States handling the task alone.) Hoover's critique was timely; reversals in the Korean War were giving Americans pause about the legitimacy of their country's commitments in Asia, and Hoover attacked Truman for going to war "under the most specious reasoning." "If he accomplished nothing else," a *Los Angeles Times* editorial reflected, "Mr. Hoover forced the Truman administration to attempt a coherent understanding of its meandering foreign policy."

The Cold War

Harry Truman saw things differently from Hoover. As president, he backed a dramatic buildup of America's armed forces—its airpower in particular—increasing its defense budget to more than $50 billion. Truman played hardball against Republican efforts to make the Democrats seem "soft on Communism," going so far as to create a loyalty program to root out so-called subversive influences within the federal government. After leaving office in 1953, Truman grew dubious about Eisenhower's conduct of the fight against Communism and slammed Ike's administration for reductions in America's overall military might. "The General doesn't know any more about politics than a pig knows about Sunday," Truman scoffed. Eisenhower explained his actions coolly: "Once you spend a dollar beyond adequacy, you are weakening yourself," he said—a preview of sentiments he later expressed in his warnings about the "military-industrial complex" upon leaving office.

Historians have richly debated Eisenhower's legacy as president: whether he was largely an ineffective and unengaged head of state or a behind-the-scenes master, carefully delegating responsibility and purposefully appearing uninvolved in order to minimize partisanship. Popularized by Fred Greenstein's 1982 study, *The Hidden-Hand Presidency: Eisenhower as Leader*, the revisionist take on Ike as politically adroit was posited by journalist Murray Kempton as early as 1967. (In reviewing Ike's memoirs for *Esquire*, Kempton wrote that "We never knew the cunning beneath the shell.") Whether Eisenhower's successors John F. Kennedy or Lyndon Johnson considered him a somnambulist leader or a wily tactician, they both turned to him during salient moments of military and diplomatic conflict. Obviously not a chief counselor, Eisenhower was nonetheless an influential informal adviser to both men, and helped shape the policies they eventually pursued.

During Kennedy's transition to the White House, he and Ike had a now famous discussion on U.S. policy in Cuba and Southeast Asia. Thereafter, JFK kept his immediate predecessor in the foreign policy loop throughout his presidency, and thus Kennedy not only had Eisenhower's advice but his reaction to policies to consider. "Kennedy thought there was something frightening about Eisenhower," one historian has suggested. "There was also something politically intimidating about succeeding a man of such great popularity. . . . Ike's approval was not necessary, but his public disapproval could be devastating." Eisenhower's gravitas and symbolic power weighed on Kennedy for the duration of his thousand days.

Once the American-supported Cuban refugees were captured off the Bay of Pigs inlet in April 1961, Kennedy immediately sought Ike's advice, inviting him to Camp David for a meeting on strategy. After Kennedy conceded that the landing of the refugees was an unmitigated fiasco and that he had relied upon inadequate intelligence,

Eisenhower skewered the president on several points: his failure to pull together a full meeting of the National Security Council to debate the merits of the mission; the lack of air cover during the invasion; and his illusory belief that it could be carried out in such a way as to mask the U.S. role. Wary of Kennedy's limited foreign policy expertise before the election, Eisenhower was hardly surprised by the young president's rudimentary mistakes. For his part, Kennedy received Ike's words as an unsentimental education.

During the Camp David meeting, some on Kennedy's staff claimed that planning for the invasion had actually commenced on Eisenhower's watch. Ike denied the charge vigorously. With the aid of former adviser Gordon Gray, he retrieved classified documents from his administration relating to Cuba. While Gray's notes indicated that there had been discussions about military planning, Ike flatly contradicted Gray's interpretation, claiming that no actual "planning" had been discussed. Eisenhower even moved to alter the language of the documents, saying, "I'm going to have this page rewritten to reflect the facts."

Although it was true that Cuban exiles were trained and a coup to remove Fidel Castro was considered while Eisenhower was still in power, Ike had never authorized such an invasion, unconvinced that conditions were ripe for it. Nor did he believe that they were right under Kennedy—in large part because no opposition leader strong enough to supplant Castro had emerged to take the reins if a coup were carried out. Yet Eisenhower's reservations about Kennedy and the Bay of Pigs didn't prevent him from continuing to consult with the younger man on both domestic and foreign policy issues, even at times lobbying members of Congress on Kennedy's behalf to support certain legislative initiatives.

Eisenhower's military acumen made him one of the persons to whom Kennedy turned as the Cuban missile crisis unfolded. Behind the scenes, through CIA director John McCone, Eisenhower gave Kennedy tactical advice on how to negotiate with Khrushchev, recommending that American plans should involve "a blockade, intense surveillance, and announcing the intention of taking military action" if the Soviets should refuse to remove the missiles.

Kennedy's team kept Eisenhower closely informed, consulting with him repeatedly even in the hours before they revealed the existence of Soviet missiles in Cuba to the American public. Beyond gaining Ike's perspective on the matter, the briefings were also defensive in nature; by keeping the former president up to speed, Kennedy hoped to induce Eisenhower to buy into his Cuba policy, thus heading off the possibility of future partisan attacks. In response to Kennedy's concern that the crisis would be used as a political football during the midterm congressional contests, Eisenhower even went on record during an ABC television interview as saying that the Cuban missile crisis should not become an election issue. Though he never advocated a wholesale embargo on criticizing future administrations—in fact, Ike himself spoke out against some of Kennedy's policies on the campaign trail—Eisenhower did encourage his party to focus on the administration's past actions and not on the current crisis facing the government.

From the other two living ex-presidents, Herbert Hoover and Harry Truman, Kennedy received reassuring words during the dark moments of the missile crisis. In his customarily unfiltered fashion, Truman told Kennedy that "The Russians have always backed up when we met them with force." Hoover was more circumspect: "There is only one course for the American people in this crisis of communist aggression. That is to stand by the President."

Though Kennedy heeded much of Eisenhower's advice during the missile crisis and its aftermath, Ike thought the deal he struck with Khrushchev—that the United States would agree not to invade Cuba in exchange for the removal of the launchers—unrealistic. Still, Kennedy continued to engage Eisenhower on other foreign policy concerns—from negotiations on the Limited Test Ban Treaty to U.S. involvement in Vietnam.

Vietnam

The Vietnam War, begun during Eisenhower's administration, continued through those of his three immediate successors, and Kennedy, Johnson, and Nixon each deepened American involvement in the region. The same might be said for Truman, since his support for French colonialism in Indochina and promise of resources to South Vietnam earn him a share of responsibility for the conflict.

Spurred on by Cold War imperatives and mindful of the "loss of China" to the Communists, Eisenhower began sending American advisers to Vietnam in 1954. He was at the helm during the creation of the Southeast Asia Treaty Organization (SEATO), which established a system of "mutual defense" between America and the non-Communist Southeast Asian countries.

Magnifying the strategic importance of South Vietnam, John F. Kennedy upped the number of advisers in Saigon to more than sixteen thousand and was party to the coup that removed South Vietnamese president Ngo Dinh Diem on November 1, 1963. Inheriting the presidency and the war only weeks later, Johnson took no responsibility for the conflict's origins. ("I didn't get you into Vietnam," he told an audience sometime later. "You have been in Vietnam for ten years.") Initially continuing his predecessors' strategy of limited involvement, in 1965 Johnson moved toward an open-ended commitment to South Vietnam, backed by a major escalation of the ground war.

Johnson regularly recruited advice from a coterie of experts on how best to manage the conflagration in Vietnam, and Dwight Eisenhower was part of this pool. In particular, Johnson was keen to draw Ike out on how he had ended the Korean War, in hopes of deriving lessons that would help in his own troubling situation. Acutely aware that the former president's imprimatur on their Vietnam policy would resonate with the American public, members of Johnson's administration carefully orchestrated Ike's role. Eventually, Ike would become almost an adjunct member of Johnson's war cabinet.

Truman, of course, was another story. Although he had prosecuted the greater part of the Korean conflict when president, Truman stayed outside the corridors of power and offered just a handful of public statements in support of Johnson. Resisting the natural parallels with Korea, Truman asserted that "Johnson did the right thing" by retaliating against North Vietnamese attacks on U.S. warships, but was quick to point out that he was "not making any comparisons with what [he] would have done when . . . president." The eighty-year-old Truman later added that "Johnson knows what needs to be done, and he knows what should be avoided. . . . In this situation he deserves, and should have, the confidence of everyone."

While Eisenhower seemed to be in concert with Johnson on the escalation of force in 1965—indeed, he was generally at least as hawkish as the president—his perspective was distinguished by nuances, subtleties accumulated during his long military experience that Johnson knew he could not match. "I need your wisdom and your judgment in these decisions which the President must make," he told Ike in 1966, "and whose depth and solemn agony only you can really understand."

Though hardly a fan of Lyndon Johnson personally—he once said LBJ had "no moral courage whatsoever"—Eisenhower was nonetheless pleased to offer his strategic perspective. In so doing he chided Johnson for his singular reliance on force, explaining that military strikes were "only part of the story . . . a preliminary to pacification." Stressing the inevitable postwar difficulties of state-building and the complexities involved in developing stable institutions, Eisenhower counseled, "We should keep constant pressure on bringing the South Vietnamese to the point where they will be strong enough, both in Saigon and the countryside, to govern themselves effectively." Eisenhower also emphasized that the president had an obligation to raise not just the morale of the South Vietnamese but that of Americans as well, by keeping the public carefully informed about what was transpiring in Vietnam. Overlooking the duty to explain and justify an overseas war, Eisenhower foresaw, was a recipe for domestic disaster.

Ike's early reluctance to speak out publicly against Johnson may have been a form of reciprocity: during Ike's time in the White House, LBJ's Senate support had been invaluable. When it came to setting the record straight, however, Ike had no qualms about sharing his reading of history. Just as he had denied to Kennedy that the Bay of Pigs plan had been formulated on his watch, the former president was eager to clarify that Johnson's military policy in Vietnam did not originate with him. At a press conference in August 1965, Eisenhower disputed the Johnson administration's assertion that as president he had guaranteed military support to the South Vietnamese outside the limits of SEATO, explaining that in the 1950s "we were not talking about military programs but foreign aid." Johnson's staff went to great lengths to find evidence that Ike had been ready to offer military support to South Vietnam, but none ever reached the public.

As the decade wore on, Eisenhower became increasingly skeptical about Johnson's Vietnam policy. Ike believed that LBJ was misguidedly fighting a war of gradualism rather than committing to the escalation necessary to win, and made his position explicit to the president. "When you once appeal to force in an international situation involving military help to a nation, you have to go all out!" Reminding him that "this is a war," he warned the president to "do what you have to do!" Ike repeatedly encouraged Johnson to rely more on his military commanders in the field, who could assess the situation firsthand, and less on armchair tacticians. Finally, and most provocatively for Johnson, Eisenhower counseled LBJ to sideline blue-chip domestic policy endeavors like the War on Poverty and the race to the moon and divert the necessary energy and resources to defeat the Vietcong.

Predictably, Ike had little time for the antiwar crowd. "The current raucous confrontation goes far beyond honorable dissent . . . it is rebellion, and it verges on treason." When Johnson seemed to succumb to the growing antiwar sentiment and announced that he was getting out of the 1968 race and freezing most of the bombing of North Vietnam, Eisenhower was enraged. Yet despite Ike's impatience, Johnson continued to seek him out; as he told Richard Nixon in 1968, "No person has been more help to me as president than President Eisenhower."

NIXON REDIVIVUS

As the United States wound down its involvement in the Vietnam War, Americans shifted their gaze back to the domestic arena. Changes in the broader cultural fabric after the rambunctious 1960s, the calamitous fallout from the Watergate nightmare, and increasingly serious economic dislocation dominated public attention. Yet such preoccupations were soon accompanied by the recognition that America remained vulnerable on the international stage, as U.S. citizens were taken hostage in Iran, and Americans at home warily followed the postdétente political dance with the Soviet Union.

A battle-tested veteran of international affairs, ex-president Richard Nixon saw an opportunity to begin slowly reinstating himself in the eyes of his Republican compatriots. Especially with reference to the so-called second world, namely China and the Soviet Union, Nixon's hard-boiled pragmatism had its steady devotees. But his arduous journey to reestablish respectability took time. Two years after resigning his office in disgrace, Nixon made a highly touted fourth anniversary trip to Beijing—a coming out of sorts, including an "almost presidential tour" of the country and an audience with Chairman Mao. (The visit didn't sit very well with the Ford administration, which preferred to conduct its own foreign policy.) Nixon then went on the offensive, trafficking his geopolitical expertise in a stream of essays, interviews, volumes of foreign policy theory and argument, and strategic memos to those in power, recognizing that leveraging his foreign affairs bona fides was his only real hope for a legitimate comeback.

Nixon made it clear that he would resist being muzzled. "I am going to speak out on issues," he insisted, "and maybe I'll lose some and people will tell me to shut up. But when you believe in something, as I do . . . you must speak up. And that's what I am going to do." The always determined former president made good on his pledge. During the Carter administration, Nixon knocked the president's ambition to establish international norms of civil and political conduct as empty "rhetoric on human rights" and hammered him for what he perceived as a values-based foreign policy. Pinning the blame on Carter for the fall of the Shah, Nixon belittled the Democratic administration as rife with weak-willed "moral imperialists." (In reality, the Shah actually got a pass from Carter's otherwise principled human rights record.) "Did anybody suggest," Nixon said breathlessly, "that Saudi Arabia is not an absolute monarchy and that we are going to say to King Khalid or Prince Fahd, 'Look, boys, until you unveil the women . . . we won't buy your oil?' Hell no! Where are the human rights in China? Are we going to change our policy on China because they don't have human rights? Hell no!"

Carter rose above Nixon's scorching words, even extending him an invitation to a White House state dinner honoring Deng Xiaoping. Carter was quick to explain that Watergate was now a part of history and that to invite Nixon was "a fair and proper thing." And, in any case, it was the Chinese delegation that had asked to meet with the former president.

During the denouement of the Cold War, Nixon used his knowledge of international politics to maneuver into a consultative role with Ronald Reagan. Fortunately for Nixon, of the three ex-presidents still alive during Reagan's tenure, his was the only advice Reagan actively pursued. Reagan made it clear early on that he wanted nothing to do with Carter, never inviting him to a state dinner, not even asking him and Rosalynn to the White House when their portraits were hung. Reagan's relationship with Ford was not much warmer; the Michigan Republican was largely cast aside during the 1980s. (Little love was lost on Ford's side, either; he always resented Reagan for challenging him—a sitting Republican president—in the 1976 primaries and for offering only meager support once Ford captured the Republican nomination.)

In October 1981, Reagan invited Nixon to accompany Carter and Ford to Anwar Sadat's funeral—a move that cleared the way for Nixon to assert himself further in the political sphere. Journalists openly questioned the appropriateness of Nixon's presence at the event, but for Mary McGrory of the *Washington Post*, the trip landed Nixon "a round-trip ticket to respectability"; her colleague Haynes Johnson called it a possible "way back from Elba."

Carter's Shadow Diplomacy of the 1980s

Sadat's funeral set the stage for one of the most peculiar, yet fruitful, postpresidential relationships—that of Jimmy Carter and Gerald Ford. It was during the return trip on Air Force One (Nixon carried on to Saudi Arabia for private reasons) that the two ex-presidents forged a political partnership and personal friendship that endured until Ford's passing in 2006. While Ford and Carter had made common cause in the past (Ford, for instance, had helped rally Senate Republicans to ratify Carter's hard-won Panama Canal Treaty), their new alliance had a more far-reaching agenda. In a meeting with select journalists on the flight back to the States, Ford suggested that dialogue with and recognition of the Palestinian Liberation Organization, then an outlaw outfit in the eyes of the U.S. State Department, was inevitable and that it would be better to push things along that course now than to wait for another tragic moment down the road. Carter concurred, adding that "there is no way for Israel ever to have an assured permanent peace without resolving the Palestinian issue."

It's true that, in this conversation, Carter and Ford did not substantively depart from Henry Kissinger's 1975 script prohibiting talks with the PLO until the organization formally recognized Israel's right to exist. The new and indisputably bold move implied by the Ford-Carter conversation was the symbolic resonance behind their call to open talks. Both Carter and Ford seemed to believe that the tragic fate of Anwar Sadat should lead to increased understanding among the nations of the Middle East, not to continued isolation. The PLO, they implied, was the only legitimate representative of the Palestinians. After all, who else could be a credible negotiating partner? "We thought it was wrong to label Palestinians as terrorists," Ford explained. "We would have to start negotiations with the PLO if peace was going to be achieved."

A little over a year later, Carter and Ford published a jointly written article in *Reader's Digest* arguing that Israel was not meeting its obligations under the 1978 Camp David Accords, instead continuing to build settlements and confiscate Palestinian property in the Occupied Territories. Beyond his public commentary, Jimmy Carter continued to travel to the Middle East to meet with Arab and Israeli leaders alike. When Reagan learned that Carter was entertaining the possibility of a meeting with Arafat on his March 1983 trip (Carter had floated the idea in an interview with *Penthouse*), the president quickly pressured Carter to forgo any appointment with the PLO leadership. Carter agreed and ended up meeting with lower-level PLO representatives. "I won't see Arafat," Carter told the press. "I think it would be improper for me to speak to Arafat unless the PLO is willing to recognize Israel's right to exist. But I will see other Palestinian leaders in Gaza and the West Bank." The former president's willingness to accept White House marching orders on Middle East policy would grow less flexible in the years ahead.

Effectively locked out of Washington during the Reagan era (with one notable exception, when Reagan explicitly requested and received Carter's support to lobby Congress on behalf of AWAC missile sales to Saudi Arabia), Carter spent much of the 1980s developing the Carter Center and practicing his self-styled diplomacy and electoral monitoring around the globe. To put it mildly, the Reagan administration didn't take kindly to the ex-president's activities. To them, Carter was little short of a rabble-rousing menace, bent on operating a shadow government in regions like Central America and the Middle East where the administration was strategically focused.

Carter never denied the animus from Reagan's side: "Quite often, my image and goals would be in conflict with those of President Reagan," he said, "and I didn't get any support from his ambassadors. In fact, sometimes they would deliberately put impediments in my way." In one instance, Carter explained how Reagan's State Department, which opposed his 1983 travels to South and Central America, pressed him to scotch his plans, claiming that the trip would be a security risk and that "governments would be embarrassed." Arriving in Costa Rica, Carter learned that "the [U.S.] Ambassador had canceled all my appointments, all the appointments we had laboriously made, unbeknownst to me."

When Carter planned a 1987 visit to the Middle East and North Africa to identify further apertures for the peace process, the Reagan administration learned that Syria was being considered for the itinerary. As the U.S. government had banned high-level meetings between U.S. and Syrian officials, the administration pressured Carter, though obviously no longer a public official, not to visit Damascus. When their efforts failed, and Reagan's staff recognized that it had little influence over Carter's diplomatic rendezvous, the administration adopted a realistic line, actually considering whether to ask Carter to deliver an official message to Syrian leaders regarding the hostages in Lebanon.

As it turned out, the Syrian visit was a red herring. The real embarrassment for the Reagan administration was Carter's stopover in Egypt. In Cairo, despite informing reporters that "I am not here to criticize my own government," Carter slammed the "missing leadership" in Washington, and said that "President Reagan has not been inclined to use negotiation and diplomacy as a means to achieve our nation's goals nearly so much as have his Democratic and Republican predecessors. He's more inclined to exert America's military strength, either the actual use of it or the threat of it." This level of censure from a former president abroad was rare and spoke to the frustration Carter felt in seeing his vaunted Middle East diplomacy scrapped in favor of Reagan's anti-Communist crusades in Central America and elsewhere.

The Reagan administration bristled at Carter's rhetorical invective, which broke the informal rule of not undermining a sitting president when abroad, and asked that he abstain from any further denunciations of White House policy. Carter responded that he wasn't a representative of the government, rather someone who could "say what I please." Upon his return, Carter debriefed Foggy Bottom officials, including Secretary of State George Shultz; despite his estrangement from a conservative establishment, the former president always remained willing to impart his findings.

Nixon and Reagan

While Ronald Reagan was keeping tabs on Carter's wanderings, he turned to Richard Nixon for guidance on international affairs. And like Carter, at least in this one respect, Nixon was eager to speak his mind. Playing down his otherwise security-minded tendencies, Nixon struck the pose of Cold Warrior with a human face when it came to diplomacy on Russia. During the debate over Reagan's proposal for the Strategic Defense Initiative, the missile-defense shield popularly known as "Star Wars," Nixon asserted that "When [the Russians] have 10,000 of these damn things there is no defense." Understanding the perils of defensive superiority, Nixon suggested sharing research as a way to obviate first-strike considerations.

Disagreements aside, Reagan relied on Nixon in preparing for his November 1985 summit with the Soviets in Geneva. (Reagan would have had one earlier, he quipped, but the Russian leaders "kept dying on me.") He even cited verbatim Nixon's summation of the state of play between the superpowers: "We want peace. The Soviet Union needs peace." By then it had also become public knowledge that Reagan had secretly consulted with Nixon during his initial diplomatic foray with a leading Soviet official, Foreign Minister Andrei Gromyko, a year earlier.

Having turned his administration into a kind of rolling mutual seminar on balance-of-power politics with his national security advisor and secretary of state Henry Kissinger, Nixon considered himself a master at the nuances of great power diplomacy. He urged Reagan to manage America's relationship with China carefully, and warned him against provoking the Soviet Union, which feared a military relationship between China and the United States. Addressing Chinese social and political realities, Nixon assailed the cultural notion of "playing the China card," casting it as a "put-down" of the Chinese people. "Nobody wants to be a card," he asserted. "Let them understand that we would want a relationship even if there were no Russia."

Perhaps more than his advice on world affairs, Nixon's support was crucial during the Iran-Contra scandal in the second half of the 1980s. In the first phase of the controversy, the Reagan administration was accused of covertly selling arms to Iran in exchange for the freeing of hostages from pro-Iranian Hezbollah forces in Lebanon in 1986. Former presidents Ford and Carter reproached the administration for what they saw as Reagan's effort to "buy back" the hostages. Their outrage only grew when Lieutenant Colonel Oliver North revealed that revenues from the Iran arms sales, eventually totaling $14 million, were diverted to train Nicaraguan Contra rebels.

In clear contrast, Richard Nixon played GOP loyalist, helping to shore up support for Reagan nearly half a year before the Iran-Contra hearings got under way. In a closed session speech to the Republican faithful, Nixon demanded steadfast support: "Defend the President for trying to seek his goals. . . . Don't, don't weaken the man. And don't let Republicans go on with their favorite sport of cannibalism." As for the diversion of funds to Nicaraguan rebels, Nixon admitted, "That was illegal, apparently. But President Reagan didn't know [about the scheme]. I know that because he just was not involved in details. He has told me so. I believe him." And in addressing the obvious elephant-in-the-room historical analogy, Nixon vowed, "It is not going to be another Watergate, as long as you stay ahead of the curve."

Though Reagan's approval rating plummeted to 50 percent after the details of the Iran-Contra affair were broadcast in congressional hearings, he still managed to leave office in 1989 as a personally popular figure. A little over a year after his exit, he was finally forced to testify in the criminal trial of his former aide John Poindexter. As expected, Reagan pleaded ignorance of any illegal arms trading deals or financial diversions and said repeatedly that he was unable to recall facts and episodes, though he took his share of responsibility for the overall plan. "It was a covert action that was taken at my behest," he said, but, "I, to this day, do not recall ever hearing that there was a diversion." It was the first time a former president or sitting president ever testified in a criminal trial concerning his time in power.

After leaving office, Reagan was far more comfortable running through his favorite platitudes about the inevitable collapse of Communism. In his first postpresidential address, "The Triumph of Freedom," delivered in London's Guildhall in June 1989, Reagan predicted that a communications revolution would sound the death knell of autocracy. Suggesting that the "Goliath of totalitarianism will be brought down by the David of the microchip," Reagan proved at least partially prophetic. That fall, state socialist edifices, taking their cue from the social movements in Hungary and Poland and the democratizing possibilities unleashed by Gorbachev, began to combust throughout Central and Eastern Europe.

In addition to the revolutionary events in Europe, Reagan also spoke to the tragedy that had earlier unfolded in Beijing's Tiananmen Square, where hundreds of students, labor activists, and other demonstrators were killed. "You cannot massacre an idea," he said. "You cannot run tanks over hope. You cannot riddle a people's yearning with bullets. Those heroic Chinese students who gave their lives have released the spirit of democracy and it cannot be called back." Yet on a trip to Japan later that year, he strayed from such idealist rhetoric, offering a more sober appraisal of the Tiananmen situation: "I love those young people, and I agree with what their feelings are, but did they handicap people who were quietly trying to do what they want?"

Even as Reagan was wondering whether the Chinese students had acted rashly, Richard Nixon became the best-known American to visit the People's Republic of China after the crackdown. Following his standard realpolitik-cum-coexistence line, Nixon appealed to the United States and China to recommence their cooperative relationship and urged that China avoid a "return to its isolation." Speaking with Chinese premier Li Peng, Nixon acknowledged that "The cultural, political and ideological differences between us . . . you a Chinese Communist who believes in Leninist rule, I an American conservative who believes in capitalism and democracy, are too great to permit a common understanding of this tragedy." But he suggested that the two nations "rise above the acrimony of the moment and resume the progress and cooperation that are worthy of two great peoples."

Nixon on Russia

Following the Soviet Union's quiet death in late 1991, Nixon spent much of his final years speculating about the future of Russia. During the 1992 presidential campaign, he insisted that the United States must assist Russia in its tentative moves toward democratic rule, calling Russia's transition one of the most critical international questions of our time. To press his case, he disseminated a memo to a number of prominent political leaders, the contents of which were leaked to the *New York Times*. "The hot-button issue in the 1950s was, 'Who lost China?,'" it began. "If Yeltsin goes down, the question of 'Who lost Russia?' will be an infinitely more devastating issue in the 1990s." Interpreted as an attack on what Nixon considered President Bush's passive Russia policy—he labeled it "pathetically inadequate" and "penny-ante"—the memo fueled a powerful debate on Russia's future and even pushed Bush to offer a degree of guarantees, including his signature on the Freedom Support Act, legislation that mandated the United States to pass on a "peace dividend" to countries within the former Soviet Union at a cost of $417 million.

Nonetheless, Nixon remained dissatisfied with Bush's commitment to Yeltsin and labeled the president one of "those who overcommitted themselves to Gorbachev." Nixon felt that Bush had made a serious strategic blunder in the 1992 election by not addressing head-on with Bill Clinton the fragility of the Russian democratic experiment and choosing instead to focus on domestic policy. Exploring what he would have done differently in Bush's shoes, Nixon boasted, "I would have hit the Russian-aid thing hard by saying, 'I know it's not popular, but it must be done.'"

Shortly after Clinton's electoral victory, Nixon raised the red flag in an op-ed piece. Fearing that the Yeltsin government was in "mortal danger" and that the country faced a possible restoration, he advised the United States to offer a major aid package—to reschedule Russia's debt, extend financial support, and encourage private investment. In view of Clinton's plan to focus his honeymoon-period political capital on the domestic side, Nixon persuasively laid out the potential drain on the U.S. economy should the response to a more threatening Russian leadership demand an arms buildup.

Clinton met with Nixon shortly after he came into office. Though even as late as 1993 he felt it unwise to be photographed with the former president (he would wait until Nixon's funeral the following year to let the cameras roll), he did value the utility of Nixon's recommendations on Russia. And by inviting him for a policy discussion in the White House, Clinton conferred upon Nixon another leap of legitimacy. Watching their interaction, Thomas Friedman suggested that "Mr. Nixon is not only rehabilitating [Yeltsin], but also himself." Clinton, too, benefited from the association: Nixon promised to mobilize skeptical GOP Congress members to support greater Russian financial aid.

Nixon's final trip to the former Soviet Union in 1993 was eye-opening. He spent a grueling fortnight in Russia during a fraught period when Boris Yeltsin's ham-fisted authoritarian maneuvers were inspiring a backlash, spurring angry mobs and culminating in an attempted coup. Nixon now took a less glamorized view of Yeltsin, who refused to meet with the former president and said he "should be supported not idolized." By romanticizing Yeltsin's government, Nixon wrote, "the West runs the risk of personalizing its Russia policy and creating a potential trap for itself." Nixon's feedback to the Clinton administration was also a personalized mea culpa. Heeding the advice of Henry Kissinger, who implored the United States to reach out to other parts of the former empire rather than coddling Russia, Nixon did travel to other newly independent former Soviet states on the trip, and in his final months moved away from an exclusive embrace of Yeltsin and Russia. In perhaps his last philosophical contribution to American foreign policy—one that spoke volumes a decade later during the era of Vladimir Putin—Nixon pointed out that "The cold war is only half over. Communism has been defeated, but freedom is not yet won."

Jimmy Carter's Opening

After being shut out of the Reagan White House, Jimmy Carter encountered a comparatively more receptive audience under his successors, Bush and Clinton. "It's a totally different attitude to the Presidency," Carter observed. Reagan thought "everything that happened was either my fault, or Ford's fault, or Nixon's fault or Congress's fault or some foreigner's." Maintaining a rigorous schedule of election monitoring and international diplomacy in the post-Reagan era, Carter entered a new era of possibility for his ex-presidency on the world stage.

During the first period of George H. W. Bush's tenure, Carter was granted far greater leeway to pursue his "diplo-evangelist" conflict-resolution approach in tandem with the White House. Bush's receptivity to Carter spoke to the new administration's reliance on pragmatism over ideology and its growing recognition that Carter might actually be useful in advancing policy. Integral to the former president's entree was Bush's secretary of state, James Baker; even before his boss was sworn in, Baker approached Carter to help frame the new administration's policy toward Nicaragua in the wake of the Iran-Contra debacle. The Bush team's distancing from the insurgent Contras, and its bipartisan overtures toward democracy promotion in Central America, grew out of these discussions. Carter was a key beneficiary: not only did the Bush administration begin to rely on his efforts, it also viewed his Carter Center as a neutral site for constructive diplomatic engagement.

What soon became arguably Carter's greatest strength—electoral monitoring and observation—was still in its nascent stages and just beginning to emerge as a discipline. The Carter Center's significant strides not only helped legitimize newly created government-funded outfits such as the National Democratic Institute, but also helped answer a common complaint that organizations like NDI and its parent body, the National Endowment for Democracy, were pawns of the CIA. It was during two Central American elections, in Panama and Nicaragua, that electoral monitoring gained significant international exposure, paving the way for the practice's enhanced credibility.

During the May 1989 election in Panama, from which despot Manuel Noriega expected his handpicked successor to emerge victorious, Carter led an international delegation to watch over the country's polls and counting stations. Once Noriega realized that his chosen candidate would lose the election without his intervention, he dispatched armed gangs to switch the voting tally sheets. Panama's favorite American son—the man who repatriated the Panama Canal to its people—Carter was on hand to observe the contest. In a press conference outside the vote count headquarters, he swiftly denounced Noriega's attempts at obstruction as "totally fraudulent." In a moment of high drama, the bilingual Carter jumped on a platform and hollered in two languages to the gathered crowd: *"Son ustedes honestos, o ladrones?* Are you honest people, or thieves?"

Carter's "guerilla diplomacy," as his former speechwriter Hendrik Hertzberg dubbed it, made the difference. George H. W. Bush formally authorized Carter to offer Noriega the right to seek exile in Spain in exchange for accepting the election's true results. After years of support, "El Norte" was now turning on Noriega—but the dictator would not leave easily. It took twenty-seven thousand U.S. troops to sweep him from power that December.

That same year, Carter traveled south once again, to monitor elections in Nicaragua. The United States had never accepted the Sandinistas' previous electoral victory in 1984, and for the 1990 contest Carter wanted to ensure a universally accepted outcome. (Between the elections, the Reagan administration had continued its concerted efforts to undermine the FSLN by any means necessary.) Nicaraguan president Daniel Ortega refused visas to official U.S. observers because of America's long-standing funding of the Contras. But Carter's delegation was welcomed by the Nicaraguan government, the opposition, and international organizations like the United Nations and the Organization of American States alike. It was left to Carter to invite a bipartisan group of U.S. congressional representatives to join his delegation, which then became the Bush administration's default monitoring vehicle.

Carter's diplomatic skills were on full display once it was determined that Ortega and the Sandinistas had lost. He met late into the night with the outgoing and incoming leaders to help smooth the transition and ensure that the FSLN abided by the vote's outcome. He shared with Ortega his personally humbling experience of losing the 1980 election, explaining to the Sandinista veteran that the freedom of his postpresidential years had allowed him to scale the heights of success. The nonviolent transfer of power was a key transitional moment for the long-suffering country; according to Robert Pastor, who directed the Carter Center's Latin America program, Carter "put Nicaragua on the course of democracy, no matter how fragile." Thanks to Carter's widely acknowledged "scrupulous neutrality," and despite America's seven-year-long sponsorship of a counterrevolutionary force and subtle support for the Nicaraguan opposition—even during the election itself—the Sandinistas let the outcome stand.

Between his monitoring expeditions to Panama and Nicaragua, the former president offered the help of the Carter Center to provide a supradiplomatic venue for mediation between the Ethiopian government and Eritrean rebels in an effort to halt their long-standing civil war. Recognizing its own limitations, and desperate for regional stability in Africa's horn, the Bush administration welcomed Carter's efforts to "wage peace," as he put it. One State Department official explained, "The United States government isn't in any position to mediate the Eritrean conflict. So what Mr. Carter is trying to do . . . suits our interest just fine." Carter himself had a simple functional explanation for his work: "We don't want to duplicate what others can do. But there's a vacuum we are attempting to fill."

Soon thereafter came Iraq. After Saddam Hussein's armed forces invaded Kuwait in August 1990 on the partial pretext that Kuwait was stealing its oil and driving down world prices, a UN-authorized resolution backed by the United States gave Iraq an ultimatum to withdraw or face military action. Carter responded by sending off letters to the permanent members of the Security Council and to President Bush, urging diplomatic alternatives to ensure Iraq's withdrawal from Kuwait before considering military options. Carter also penned articles outlining areas for negotiation between the UN and Iraq, cautioning world leaders to weigh carefully their participation in a war that could have limited public support and potentially result in excessive casualties. Less than a week before the ultimatum expired, Carter wrote to the heads of Egypt, Saudi Arabia, and Syria, asking them to oppose military action and come to a peaceful resolution on their own. "I urge you to call publicly for a delay in the use of force while Arab leaders seek a peaceful solution to the crisis," he pleaded. "You may have to forego approval from the White House, but you will find the French, Soviets, and others fully supportive. Also, most Americans will welcome such a move." In the annals of postpresidential diplomacy, Carter's intervention was nothing short of astonishing.

Carter's unilateral diplomacy, especially his letter-writing campaign to international leaders, was met with furious criticism. Some claimed that his actions were tantamount to treason. Accusing Carter of advancing an unsanctioned foreign policy of his own, Brent Scowcroft, Bush's national security advisor, said, "It seemed to me that if there was ever a violation of the Logan Act prohibiting diplomacy by private citizens, this was it." As the Gulf War raged, Carter defended his support of peace negotiations with Iraq, asserting that "negotiation is not capitulation." Challenged on his actions several years later, Carter suggested that he now had second thoughts. While the world community should have remained dedicated to a diplomatic solution, he admitted that his own lobbying technique of quietly addressing letters to Security Council members was "not appropriate, perhaps." "Such is the pretentious effrontery," Murray Kempton cuttingly remarked, "inescapable for anyone who sets himself up to persuade the voters that they were wrong not to reelect a saint." The *Washington Post*'s Jim Hoagland was more to the point: "Carter did not simply write op-ed pieces or give speeches to sway public opinion and get the American electorate to demand changes in policy. He actively promoted an alternative policy."

Former officials in Carter's administration defended the ex-president's actions, insisting that his remarks to Security Council members were no different from those he made to President Bush. But their defense did little to counter the arrogant, even unseemly impression left by Carter's actions.

Carter During the Clinton Years

Bill Clinton may have been the first Democratic president in the White House since Jimmy Carter, but the two southerners had their difficulties. Much to the Georgian's dismay, the Clinton administration did everything to rebuff his involvement in its foreign policy activities. There were real and symbolic concerns: a desire to disassociate from a Carter administration that was widely considered ineffective at best and disastrous at worst, and a reluctance to link up with an ex-president who was still perceived as headstrong and uncontrollable. (Clinton had also hired many former Carter staffers; in seeking to distance the Carter administration from their new perch, they may also have been trying to confirm their status as Clinton loyalists.)

Despite his best efforts to keep Carter at bay, Clinton's first years in the White House were dogged by the former president's repeated involvement in peacekeeping matters. But the two leaders, at least on a personal level, found a degree of common ground. After Yasser Arafat and Yitzhak Rabin signed a peace declaration in September 1993, Carter's relationship with Clinton took a turn for the better. Invited with George H. W. Bush to spend the night at the White House, Carter stayed up late debating policy and ideas with the president. (Bush turned in early.) Carter's photo op with Clinton the following day (along with Ford and Bush) in support of Clinton's North American Free Trade Agreement probably only bolstered the political relationship—as did Carter's slamming of Ross Perot as "a demagogue with unlimited financial resources who is extremely careless with the truth."

In that same week, even as Carter was swapping war stories with Clinton, he also helped the new president's administration disengage from the disaster unfolding in Somalia. Clinton had inherited from Bush a plan known as Operation Restore Hope, a U.S.-led military effort under the auspices of the United Nations whose goal was to safeguard humanitarian aid planned for shipment to Somalia. (Much of the aid previously sent to the region was being diverted by warring Somali forces and often sold for munitions.) But what began as a humanitarian mission soon became militarized after UN peacekeeping forces were killed while inspecting a weapons storage site. In retaliation, the United States and the UN sent in soldiers to target General Mohammad Farah Aidid, the warlord assumed to bear responsibility for the killings. The bloodiest skirmish, the battle of Mogadishu, was a mismanaged U.S. effort to hunt down Aidid; eighteen U.S. soldiers and an untold number of Somalis were killed in the process. Televised images of dead American soldiers being dragged through the Mogadishu streets sent shock waves, and the United States removed its troops shortly thereafter.

Carter was prudent about the role he agreed to play in the conflict. Despite being asked by Aidid to mediate the conflict directly, he limited his engagement to promoting an Aidid-proposed UN investigative panel that would assess wrongdoing—in particular, charges that

Aidid was responsible for the murder of UN soldiers. Carter also committed to seeking a safe haven for Aidid outside Somalia while he awaited the commission's findings. Arguing that the UN's priority should be humanitarian efforts to assist the Somali people, Carter said, "I think the sustained effort to kill or capture Aidid, which is resulting in the deaths of many Somali civilians, should be terminated." (It was later reported that U.S. forces in Mogadishu seeking to arrest Aidid were unaware of Carter's simultaneous overtures to the warlord.) Chastened perhaps by concerns that he was embracing another despot, Carter made it clear that he wouldn't vouch for Aidid's sincerity in offering to work with the UN: "I don't know him. I've never met him. I don't know if he's lying or just trying to create good public relations or stop the violence."

Carter played a more instrumental role defusing crisis situations in North Korea and Haiti. While Carter's involvement in Haiti was formally sanctioned by Clinton's strategy to reinstate the deposed Jean-Bertrand Aristide, his vanguard diplomatic efforts in North Korea forced the hand of the Clinton administration. In the spring of 1994, Bill Clinton was working with the United Nations to pressure North Korea into full compliance with the Nuclear Nonproliferation Act. North Korea's decision to expel inspectors examining its nuclear sites and withdraw from the International Atomic Energy Agency signified the country's readiness to confront the international community head-on. While Clinton discussed with world leaders possible sanctions against North Korea and contemplated preemptively striking against the reactors in Yongbyon, Jimmy and Rosalynn Carter were visiting North Korea as private citizens—not to serve as formal administration representatives, but to discuss, with Clinton's approval, "some of the important issues of the day with leaders in the area." Although his Pyongyang visit with North Korean president Kim Il-Sung was first believed to have breathed new life into U.S.–North Korean diplomacy, critics soon feared that Kim was doing little more than repackaging old proposals. Following their talks, Carter advocated that the UN terminate its sanctions, contending that North Korea would find acceptable ways to comply with U.S. and UN demands and satisfy international weapons inspectors.

As a self-appointed mediator, Carter's North Korean expedition put the Clinton administration in a bind. Without Clinton's own diplomatic corps participating in the negotiations, any decision to follow the former president's recommendations too closely made top government officials uneasy. (One disgruntled Clinton cabinet member even referred to Carter as a "treasonous prick.") Carter was also speared for his freelancing, and for his allegedly naive assessment of the complexities of the situation. He was even accused of misleading the North Koreans by telling them, erroneously, that the UN had ended its sanctions. Again Murray Kempton: "Jimmy Carter, private citizen, took wing to Pyongyang, alighted to Kim Il-Sung's courtesies, and emerged to describe him as 'charming,' Carter's favored adjective for statesmen otherwise ill-famed. He was persuaded that Kim would be reasonable and agreeable and the President welcomed the assurance, since agreeability is his pole star. North Korea was thereafter consigned to the cemetery of forgotten menaces."

But when it appeared just weeks later that North Korea was ready to meet U.S. preconditions for talks and to suspend its nuclear program temporarily, Clinton saluted Carter's triumph. "It is the beginning of a new stage in our efforts to pursue a non-nuclear Korean peninsula," Clinton said. Months later, the North Koreans signed a framework agreement freezing all reactor activity at Yongbyon. Clinton's second-term head of policy planning, Morton Halperin, called the neutralization of North Korea's nuclear program in exchange for a resumed policy dialogue with the United States Carter's "most important achievement." After all, Halperin said, "we were on the verge of going to war." It would take the administration of George W. Bush to make things come undone.

As a direct envoy to Haiti on behalf of the Clinton government that same year, Carter met with less skepticism from the administration.

The United States was seeking to reinstate the exiled president, Jean-Bertrand Aristide, following his ousting by General Raoul Cedras in a 1991 military coup. Despite Aristide's occasional authoritarian tendencies, he remained a popular leader, and the coup was not supported by the Haitian people. In President Clinton's last-ditch effort at negotiation before unleashing the U.S. military to remove the Cedras regime, he dispatched Carter, along with Colin Powell and Senator Sam Nunn, to cajole Cedras into stepping down and allowing Aristide to return.

In Haiti, however, Carter's negotiations were received more problematically. With anti-Carter graffiti filling the walls of Port-au-Prince, the former president assumed a "classic negotiating stance," in which both sides inhabit a level playing field, according to Paul Farmer of the nonprofit public health organization Partners in Health. In reality, however, the standoff was "never [a matter of] two equal and unopposed sides as Carter assumed." After meeting with the Cedras family, Carter persuaded the general to relinquish control, though his evenhanded treatment appalled human rights activists and right-wing critics alike. Carter's diplomacy did resolve the stalemate: Aristide was returned to power, an invasion was averted, and the restoration was made complete. Who knows whether his unexpected praise of Mrs. Cedras—he called her "slim and attractive" and said she was key to Cedras's decision to stand down—contributed to the outcome. Whatever the case, Carter called the mission "the most important and urgent visit I have ever made."

With his triumphs in Pyongyang and Port-au-Prince, 1994 was shaping up to be the former president's annus mirabilis. At year's end, however, Carter risked sullying his record by privately negotiating with Bosnian Serb leaders in the former Yugoslavia. Hoping to mediate an end to the thirty-two-month war, Carter traveled to Bosnia at the invitation of Bosnian Serb leader Radovan Karadzic. He pledged not to take sides in the conflict between the Muslim-led Bosnian government and the Serb insurgents, an approach that veered sharply from the Clinton administration's backing of the Bosnian government and its labeling of the Serbs as the chief war crimes perpetrators. Carter accepted Karadzic's offer for talks, with the precondition that the Serbs would allow the movement of UN aid convoys and troops, whose freedom had been restricted for several weeks. Carter never asked for Clinton's endorsement of his trip, though he kept him abreast of his dealings. For his part, Clinton publicly stated that while he was skeptical that Karadzic would fulfill Carter's preconditions for their meeting, he would not prevent the former president from visiting the region.

Carter's venture into Bosnia's murky diplomatic waters raised many of the same questions as his North Korean trip: Was the former president being used to push the U.S. government into a more accommodating relationship with insurgent forces? (*Time* even used the notorious term *appeasement*, most often associated with Neville Chamberlain's Munich pact with Hitler, in describing Carter's mission.) Did the Bosnian Serb leaders invite Carter in order to confer legitimacy on their proposal to end the violence—a proposal that offered fewer concessions than the United States was seeking? While some in the Clinton administration were optimistic that Carter could negotiate a short-term cease-fire between the warring factions, most were uneasy about his involvement—a sentiment shared by many others who were working their own channels to resolve the conflict, including the UN leadership, France's foreign minister, and England's foreign secretary. And following his rendezvous with Kim Il Sung, Carter's diplomatic exchanges with the architects of "ethnic cleansing" gave further fuel to his critics, who blanched at negotiating with war criminals.

Carter claimed success in securing a four-month cease-fire from the Bosnian government and Bosnian Serb leaders, expecting them to use the cooling-off period to hammer out the details of a comprehensive peace plan. And while objecting to Carter's position that equal pressure had to be applied to both parties, the Clinton administration warmly accepted the pause in fighting. A human rights champion but no human rights absolutist, Carter defends his methods with an almost biblical injunction: If the goal is to end people's suffering, finding a resolution to a conflict should not be held back by judgments about which party is guiltier of wrongdoing. Carter bemoans the notion that "We select a favorite side in a dispute and [the other] side becomes satanic. This all-white or all-black orientation is usually not true. In most cases, both parties are guilty of atrocities."

Carter continued his postpresidential diplomacy throughout Clinton's second term, though with less direct White House involvement. With the next administration Carter was sidelined further from executive power, as George W. Bush avoided any diplomatic collaboration with the former president. But Carter's high-profile 2002 mission to Cuba finally forced the Bush White House to take a stand.

In May of that year, Carter became the first president (current or former) to visit Cuba since its 1959 revolution. Fidel Castro had invited him when they had met at Pierre Trudeau's funeral in the fall of 2001. The invitation came at a time when Castro was trying to build support for the lifting of American trade sanctions against his country. Given Carter's quiet efforts during his presidency to ease relations between the United States and Cuba, he was a natural invitee.

Bush's State Department gave Carter the go-ahead, despite concerns that his visit could bolster the efforts of U.S. legislators who were urging an end to the sanctions. But the State Department's official assurances were soon contradicted by a none-too-subtle attempt to subvert Carter. Days before the former president's departure, John Bolton, then under secretary of state for arms control, alleged that Cuba had advanced "at least a limited offensive biological warfare research and development effort" and "provided dual-use biotechnology to other rogue states." Speaking days later to a Cuban audience that included Castro himself, Carter expressed surprise at Bolton's eleventh-hour assertions and explained that he had already vetted the concern with U.S. intelligence and learned that "there were absolutely no such allegations made . . ." "I asked them myself on more than one occasion," Carter went on, "if there was any evidence that Cuba has been involved in sharing any information with any country on earth that could be used for terrorist purposes. And the answer from our experts on intelligence was no."

Carter openly speculated about whether Bolton's curiously timed comments were made to undermine his visit—a suspicion that could only have been supported by an address George W. Bush gave in Miami a short time later, which called for a tightening of U.S. sanctions against Cuba. Bush's speech neatly coincided with Carter's own nationally televised Spanish-language address calling for the United States to lift its travel restrictions and economic embargo against Cuba. Though Carter also used his Cuban airtime to slam Castro's regime for its lack of openness and its constraints on free speech, the Bush administration was determined to ensure that its Cuba policy, not Carter's, led the evening news.

Carter's Middle East

Ground zero for Carter's diplomatic efforts over the course of his public life is the land long dearest to his born-again roots: the Middle East. Since his presidency's most memorable success story, the signing of the 1978 Camp David Accords, Carter has made myriad trips to the region, monitored several elections, and authored books examining the area's thorny history.

Throughout Carter's Middle East travails, the wrenching issue of Israeli-Palestinian relations has naturally been a central concern. While he has both acquired and lost admirers because of his unflagging dedication to the question, it wasn't until the late 2006 publication of his book *Palestine: Peace Not Apartheid* that many drew clear lines in the sand. Excoriating the Palestinian leadership for its ongoing corruption and general incompetence, Carter used much of the book to condemn the divisive practices of the Israeli government. Its policies in the occupied territories, Carter argued, constituted "a system of apartheid, with two peoples occupying the same land, but completely separated from each other, with Israelis totally dominant and suppressing violence by depriving Palestinians of their basic human rights."

Well aware that the "A-word" in his title would likely inspire a firestorm of protest, Carter neither shrank from the controversy nor assigned blame to his publisher when it did. "I chose that title knowing it would be provocative," he confirmed. And, indeed, the title and its contents incited immediate reaction. At the book's publication, fourteen members of the Carter Center's board of councilors, an advisory body of more than a hundred persons, resigned en masse, infuriated at what they characterized as Carter's one-sided accusations. Melvin Konner, an Emory anthropologist who helped lead the procession, set the tone in a letter to the Carter Center's executive director, John Hardman. "[Carter] seems to me no longer capable of dialogue," Konner wrote. He has become "an apologist for terrorists and places my children, along with all Jews everywhere, in greater danger."

"Terrorist apologist" was but one of many epithets hurled at the former president, whose book had touched one of the third rails of American political discourse. Emory's Deborah Lipstadt claimed that Carter's prose gave "refuge to scoundrels"; Harvard's Alan Dershowitz alleged it was "obvious that Mr. Carter just doesn't like Israel or Israelis." And seeking an explanation for Carter's commentary, Melvin Konner suggested that the former president must have "a screw loose somewhere." For a medical anthropologist like Konner, this was no idle statement. Konner went so far as to ask two of his former students, Stuart Seidman and Misha Pless, the latter a neuroophthalmologist at Harvard Medical School, to conduct an informal study of Carter by watching him on television to discern whether he was displaying any signs of senility. The nonscientific studies were inconclusive.

Others offered less agitated readings of Carter's exposition. Political scientist and former diplomat William Quandt observed that "from the storm generated by . . . Carter's book . . . one might have thought that the former president had developed some radical new views that had rarely been heard before. That is not the case." And writing in *The American Conservative,* Philip Weiss dangled a provocative thesis about the incendiary reaction: "For the first time since the State of Israel was created in 1948," Weiss argued, "a prominent American politician has publicly taken up the cause of the Arabs."

Carter himself readily admits that he made at least one grave error in the book by asserting that the Palestinians must cease suicide bombing after statehood, rather than at once. It was a dreadful misstep and the ex-president paid the price. (Carter apologized vehemently and pledged to retract the statement from all future editions.) This did little to satisfy critics such as *New Republic* owner Martin Peretz, who eagerly tarred Carter with the bitter brush of anti-Semitism, or neoconservative commentator Joshua Muravchik, who called Carter's comments "wildly inappropriate" and worse.

Carter was openly distressed at the reaction. "This is the first time," he lamented, "that I've ever been called a liar and a bigot and an anti-Semite and a coward and a plagiarist." Carter had doubtless been maligned with some of those labels before, but probably never in extenso. Despite the fraught nature of the debate, Carter's remarks on television and in public were nothing if not judicious. Still, in withstanding the ambush, he rushed to establish his pro-Israel bona fides: "I was taught by my father every Sunday about the special status of the Jewish people," he said, reminding listeners that he had "visited Yad Vashem [the Holocaust memorial] three times." Carter—a man journalist Richard Cohen once said had "bulletproof self-confidence"—was not unaffected by the fallout.

While detractors like Deborah Lipstadt feel that the *Palestine* debacle obliterated his capacity to act as an honest broker for Middle East peace, Carter's professional work in the region has not diminished in the wake of the controversy, and contributions to the Carter Center have actually increased since the book's release. (The book itself was a smash hit, selling three hundred thousand copies within several months.) The spring of 2008 found the former president in Syria, meeting with the exiled leader of the Islamist organization and party Hamas. In response to critics who pounced on him for meeting with the militant group, Carter reiterated his traditional position that peace requires the widest roundtable. "The problem is not that I met with Hamas in Syria," he said. "The problem is that Israel and the United States refuse to meet with someone who must be involved."

Israel's foreign policy was hardly the only object of Carter's derision. His attacks on George W. Bush's overseas interventions have also been notable for their severity. In a 2007 interview Carter summed up Bush's years in office: "I think as far as the adverse impact on the nation around the world, this administration has been the worst in history." Curiously, Carter has not dismissed out of hand the possibility of a constructive Bush postpresidency. When asked by *The Guardian* to predict what Bush's standing as an ex-president might be internationally, Carter hypothesized, "I think it'll be hard among human rights activists to forget that we have declared that the Geneva Conventions on treatment of prisoners was inapplicable, or that we have done things that are universally construed as torture and publicly endorsed them. Or that we have seen the embarrassments of our mistreatment of prisoners in Abu Ghraib and Guantánamo. That'll be difficult to overcome. But if [Bush] decides after leaving the White House . . . to adopt human rights promotion and the enhancement of democracy around the world, I think that would be a very good opportunity for him to contribute."

4

ON THE ROAD AGAIN

Ex-Presidents on the Hustings

They can use my name in any way they may think proper.

Andrew Jackson

I would greatly welcome total eclipse from dealing with the contemporary world. But so long as my voice will be heard I shall do the best with it that I can.

Herbert Hoover

In 1984, I was very unpopular with the Democratic Party. I had committed the unforgivable sin of losing. In 1988 there was a little more warmth. And this year [1992], I've been more or less reconstituted as a positive figure . . .

Jimmy Carter

· · · · · ·

THROUGH THE YEARS, FORMER PRESIDENTS HAVE OFTEN ENGAGED in political races on behalf of candidates they considered worthy of their support. Whether as quiet counselors, stumping partisans, revenue generators, or convention keynoters, America's retired leaders have long exploited their status to boost favored candidates during presidential campaigns.

In postrevolutionary America, overt electoral politicking was considered undignified. The Founders' stated antipathy to party politics, even if illusory in practice, forced ex-presidents to campaign circumspectly. By the second quarter of the nineteenth century, however, Andrew Jackson—sometimes dubbed "the people's tribune" for his defense of the common man—helped widen the space for popular participation, and campaigns evolved as an effective instrument for appealing to voters directly. This decisive change in the political landscape opened a legitimate opportunity for past presidents to canvass for their preferred candidate.

After the Civil War, the American presidential campaign had become a political spectacle—a theatrical staging for a presidential run. In this environment, former presidents naturally emerged as headliners for the parades and mass rallies that marked early efforts to get out the vote. At the parties' national conventions, ex-presidents were celebrated figures, titular party heads who added gravitas to the proceedings. With the rise of electronic communication in the twentieth century, these former heads-of-state extended their reach further, their images piped into the living rooms of the electorate to drum up support. For some ex-presidents, going on the campaign trail during election season became a full-time job, and for good reason: their desire to protect their party's core mission was motivation enough to send them out campaigning for others.

BEHIND THE SCENES

George Washington, Thomas Jefferson, and especially James Madison all struggled to divert their brethren from the divisive world of party politics. Reared on republican ideas of virtue these Founders believed that political polarization could be the undoing of the fragile new nation, and that the maelstrom of politics must be kept at a healthy distance if America were to preserve its stability. The dangers of factionalism were stressed in the Federalist Papers, and even the concept of political parties fails to appear in the Constitution—proof positive of the Founders' common faith in unified government.

George Washington never abandoned his tightly held belief that political parties were menacing creations. Yet it wasn't long after his presidency that the grim reality of party politics materialized on the American scene. By urging John Marshall to consider a run for Congress, and conveying "infinite pleasure" upon hearing of his victory, Washington undercut his own solemn pledge not to interfere in political contests. The first ex-president also felt little compunction about cajoling the retired Patrick Henry to reenter local Virginia politics. Though Henry himself protested that he was "too old and infirm ever again to undertake public concerns," Washington's entreaties proved impossible to rebuff, and Henry accepted his "earnest wish."

In his brief postpresidency, Washington not only singled out favorites, he also began to align himself with a genuine political faction—the ascendant Federalist wing, led by his former treasury secretary, Alexander Hamilton. Apprehensive of creeping Jeffersonian control in his native Virginia and with mounting recognition of parties as the vehicle for achieving political power, Washington was quickly drawn into a Faustian bargain.

JOHN ADAMS: THE VIEW FROM QUINCY

Washington died in 1799, and it wasn't until 1804 that a former president—his successor, John Adams—would live through a presidential election. By that year, two factions, the Democratic-Republicans and the Federalists, had squared off as the dueling components of America's first party system—replete with all its worrisome manifestations. After losing to Jefferson in 1800—in an election he believed to have been stolen—Adams left office enraged. "I shudder at the calamities which I fear [Jefferson's] conduct is preparing for his country," he wrote, accusing his successor of "a mean thirst for popularity, an inordinate ambition and a want of sincerity." Though he made those comments in a private letter, Adams thought his scorching words might nevertheless prove useful in undermining Jefferson. (For his part, during the 1804 election season, Jefferson maligned the opposition Federalist Party as a "prigarchy," or aristocracy of prigs—a none too subtle dig at Adams himself.) The poison-pen letter surfaced two decades later, but by then Jefferson and Adams had long established one of history's greatest letter-writing exchanges, and the mean-spirited barbs failed to damage it.

From his quiet perch in Quincy, Massachusetts, Adams observed the slow dissolution of his Federalist Party and the two-decade-long dominance of Democratic-Republican presidential leadership under the Virginia dynasty of Jefferson, Madison, and Monroe. During those years, Adams's interest in electoral politics was piqued mostly by the rapid rise of his son John Quincy Adams through the diplomatic corps. In particular, the elder Adams watched James Monroe's triumphant 1816 and 1820 elections keenly. In the summer of 1816, newspapers were suggesting that a future president Monroe might name Adams's son as secretary of state (an appointment that came to pass the next year, after Monroe took office). Stationed in London as minister to the Court of Saint James's, John Quincy Adams had lived outside America since leaving for Russia in 1809. Upon learning that his son had returned to the United States in August 1817 to take up his new post, John Adams exulted, "Yesterday was one of the most uniformly happy days of my whole long life."

John Quincy Adams's appointment signaled the last phase of a transformation in the long and strained relationship between John Adams and James Monroe. The two had fought bitterly over Monroe's affinity with France, his friendship with Tom Paine (whom Adams detested), and his attacks on the pro-British Jay Treaty during Adams's administration. Monroe even once briefly contemplated challenging Adams to a duel. But relations between the two men had begun to warm during John Quincy Adams's appointment as minister to Russia, which came when Monroe was secretary of state, and Adams began to court Monroe with an eye toward the care and advancement of his son. At the same time, Adams developed a slow but steady tilt toward Republicanism—a shift that was confirmed when the former president became a Massachusetts elector for Monroe during his 1820 bid for a second term. When Monroe left office—succeeded by John Quincy—Adams père wrote to the departing president, "I cannot pass this opportunity of Congratulating you on the singular felicity of your Administration, which as far as I know has been without fault." Family ties had helped transform the once staunch Federalist's field of vision.

If there was one presidential contest in which John Adams took more interest than any other during his postpresidency, it was almost certainly the 1824 race featuring his son. Not unlike Adams's own 1800 election, the 1824 contest was marked by backroom machinations—a "corrupt bargain," according to Andrew Jackson's partisans, that was decided in the House of Representatives—which put John Quincy Adams over the top despite the fact that Jackson received more popular and electoral votes. Old age prevented the former president from doing more than watching the events unfold, but when it was all over his emotions ran high: "The multitude of my thoughts, and the intensity of my feelings, are too much for a mind like mine, in its ninetieth year," he said; they inspire "ineffable feelings in the breast of a father." He died sixteen months into his son's presidency.

JEFFERSON, MADISON, AND MONROE

Adams's great epistolary partner, Thomas Jefferson, never took to Adams's son, and withheld his support in the 1824 contest. Writing to his old comrade the Marquis de Lafayette, Jefferson predicted that Monroe's successor would "be ultimately reduced to the northern-most and southernmost candidate." In that race, which pitted John Quincy Adams, Andrew Jackson, Henry Clay, and William H. Craw-ford against one another, Jefferson swung his support behind the "southernmost," Crawford, a Georgian and former Virginian. For Jef-ferson, Crawford (Monroe's treasury secretary) represented the true heir to his "1800 revolution" and shared the former president's in-creasingly strident states' rights perspective. It would be the only time Jefferson backed a loser in a presidential election.

James Madison pledged early on to take a disinterested stance with regard to candidate endorsements. With his unassuming person-ality, Madison preferred to declare his positions only on issues of fun-damental principle, such as slavery or nullification, rather than becoming mired in political races. Nonetheless, his friends tried to push their luck. During the 1828 race that brought Andrew Jackson to power (after Jackson had spent the previous four years trumpeting the injustice of his 1824 loss to John Quincy Adams), Madison's compatri-ots entreated him to speak out against the crude demagoguery of the Tennessean and his followers. Madison's revered Constitution itself was at risk in the contest, they argued. The former president politely declined, preserving his commitment "to keep aloof from the politi-cal agitations of the period."

Hoping like Madison to stay above the fray, through no fault of his own James Monroe was nearly drawn into the heated contest of 1828, the only national election he would witness after leaving the White House. During the election season, Adams's naval secretary remarked

repeatedly that Monroe, the secretary of war during the War of 1812, deserved credit for the conflict's crowning victory at New Orleans— rather than Andrew Jackson, the wartime general. Jackson, who heard the remarks thirdhand, came to believe they traced back to Monroe himself. After the notorious 1824 election that denied him the presidency, Jackson was anxious to challenge any perceived falsehoods. Monroe, however, had no interest in the matter. Similar to Madison, he believed strongly that former presidents should remain outside the political realm unless called upon to address national emergencies. But there were also practical reasons for his abstention: Monroe was preoccupied with securing congressional approval of the long-standing financial claims he had accumulated during his time as minister to France. So he clung to a line of strict neutrality—convinced that political involvement would only complicate his chances of getting repaid.

THE TRANSFORMATIONS OF THE JACKSONIAN PERIOD

Andrew Jackson's election in 1828 was transformative. It upended the first party system and unleashed the new Jacksonian era, which saw the growing incorporation of working men into political life. As the right to vote was extended to all white adult males (still leaving behind most African Americans and all women), the landscape for American political participation was dramatically reshaped. The huge turnout that year also marked the result of the first full-fledged U.S. presidential campaign, with organized, legitimate partisanship and professional politicians stumping for votes. Soon a new party system would emerge, dominated by two key political organizations: the Democrats and the Whigs. In sharp contrast with the Founders' antipathy to party politics, Jackson's lieutenant and second-term vice president, Martin Van Buren, hailed the new period of partisanship as a positive example of democracy's consolidation.

John Quincy Adams, who was defeated by Jackson in his bid for reelection in 1828, represented the last gasp of the Founding Father generation. He considered the Jacksonians' new means to mobilize voters—town meetings, popular songs, pamphlets, broadsides, parades—to be dangerous departures from the familiar parameters of political engagement. It goes without saying that Adams found Andrew Jackson's 1832 reelection objectionable. Bearing little goodwill toward "Old Hickory," whom he viewed as a crude and vulgar rabble-rouser, Adams felt the Jacksonian movement was nothing short of politics debased. When Harvard conferred an honorary degree on Jackson the following year, a petulant Adams boycotted the ceremony. "My darling Harvard disgraced herself by conferring a Doctor's degree upon a barbarian and savage who could scarcely spell his own name," he fumed.

In the election year of 1836, Adams, now a congressman, began a momentous struggle to fight the institution of slavery, using the right of petition as his legislative cudgel. Adams was infuriated that Martin Van Buren, the leading Democratic presidential candidate and Jackson's anointed successor, refused to attack slavery for fear of damaging his precarious alliance of southern and northern Democrats. Adams was hardly more excited about the Whig candidate, William Henry Harrison, who struck him as one of "the golden calves of the people . . . their dull sayings . . . repeated for wit, and their grave inanity . . . passed off for wisdom."

Four years later, the 1840 race was a low point to Adams, a vivid illustration of everything the former president found wanting in American political discourse. Chiefly remembered by the campaign slogan and song "Tippecanoe and Tyler Too," referring to the winning ticket of William Henry Harrison and John Tyler, it was a campaign of cheap oratory and raw symbolism (hard cider, log cabins, coonskin caps) in which empty bromides replaced the passionate rhetoric of the Founding Fathers generation. Adams scorned the "immense assemblages of people . . . of twenty, thirty, fifty thousand souls where the first orators of the nation address the multitude, not one in ten of whom can hear them," convinced that large campaign rallies only bred violence. As for the new party conventions, which replaced the caucus system, Adams found them "unwieldy mass[es] of political machinery to accomplish nothing." Where the Jacksonians saw democracy on the march, John Quincy Adams saw only a mob-rule threat to traditional institutions.

Although Adams was probably thrilled to see Van Buren's 1840 reelection bid thwarted—Van Buren had helped Jackson defeat Adams in 1828—he had no great love for William Henry Harrison. Harrison may have served Adams as minister to Colombia, but the former general struck Adams as a "shallow mind, a political adventurer . . . self-sufficient, vain, and indiscreet." It came as no surprise when Adams turned down the invitation to his inauguration.

Whereas John Quincy Adams embraced few political candidates during his long postpresidency, Andrew Jackson lent support to a number of favorite sons from his plantation outside Nashville, Tennessee. From behind the scenes, Jackson played éminence grise during the 1840 and 1844 campaigns, offering advice and consultation as the day's monumental political question, the annexation of Texas, hung in the balance.

In 1840 Andrew Jackson worked hard to reelect Van Buren, his former protégé. Only one prominent stumbling block stood in the way: Jackson wanted Van Buren to abandon his dismal vice president, Richard Mentor Johnson, whose relationship with a former slave caused disquiet in the Democratic ranks. Eventually, Jackson won out: the Democratic National Convention refused to renominate Johnson, and Van Buren ended up running alone. Despite being in poor health during the fall campaign, Jackson undertook a speaking tour for Van Buren—a first for a former president on behalf of a presidential candidate. Distressed to witness the elite William Henry Harrison being spun as a common man while Van Buren was lampooned as an out-of-touch easterner, Jackson drew a stark contrast between them: "The election of Mr. Van Buren is essential to the preservation of our republican principles," he intoned. If Harrison were to triumph, "every feature of our democratic system would be trampled under foot." Jackson's pleas weren't enough to change the outcome. The Whigs chanted "Van, Van, the used-up man," and Harrison won handily.

Andrew Jackson had hoped that Van Buren would select his fellow Tennessean James Polk for vice president in 1840. In the next election, Jackson made a radical decision: he dropped Van Buren outright and swung his full support behind Polk for president. It was all because of Texas. Led by General Sam Houston, Texas had declared its independence from Mexico in 1836, styling itself the Republic of Texas and adopting a constitution legalizing slavery. But within a few years its citizens recognized the challenges of trying to survive as an independent republic, and a majority started campaigning to join the United States. With sectionalism and the battle over slavery's extension already a lightning-rod issue, the future status of Texas galvanized American political debate in the early to mid-1840s.

Once again seeking his party's nomination, Martin Van Buren shared one critical position with his Whig rival Henry Clay: they both opposed statehood for Texas. Outraging expansionists and southern Democrats alike, and deeply agitating his former patron Jackson, Van Buren lost the nomination over the issue. James Polk was Jackson's preferred Democrat (Herman Melville's brother dubbed him "Young Hickory"), and with Old Hickory's backing he became the first "dark-horse" candidate, going on to defeat Clay in the fall. (According to one historian, Andrew Jackson's withdrawal of support for Van Buren was probably far more decisive than his actual support of Polk.) Curiously, Polk was less concerned with expanding the bounds for slavery; his priority was ensuring that there would be land available for independent, nonwage farming. His indifference on the question of annexation helped sew up even Van Buren's endorsement. To friends who had threatened to boycott the election, the ex-president sent letters reassuring them of Polk's character, and "Young Hickory" carried the day.

Civil War Elections

In the years before the carnage of the Civil War, Martin Van Buren and Millard Fillmore both attempted quixotic third-party runs: Van Buren on the Free Soil line in 1848 and Fillmore with the quasi-nativist Know-Nothings in 1856. Only Fillmore took any states, Maryland going the way of the Know-Nothings the year James Buchanan took the presidency. By 1860, the nomination of Republican attorney and former one-term congressman Abraham Lincoln moved the nation one step closer to what would become the deadliest conflict in American history. In the shadow of war, the campaign positions of the former presidents would assume a decidedly politicized cast.

In 1860, four years after the Democratic Party convincingly rejected his quest for a second term, Franklin Pierce was pressed by various figures—not least his former secretary of war, Jefferson Davis—to consider another run for the presidency. Pierce had modestly reentered politics in the late 1850s, lending support to the pro-Union movement, a group of largely northern Democrats including his former attorney general, Caleb Cushing, and secretary of state, Edward Everett. Keen to promote harmony, Pierce was prepared to address the dangers of sectionalism, but he had not "a single lingering desire" to be a candidate himself. Pierce's own preferred candidate was Jefferson Davis, who he thought could unite the northern and southern wings of the Democratic Party. This fanciful suggestion deepened the ex-president's unpopularity and dogged him negatively for the rest of his life.

The Democratic nomination eventually went to Stephen A. Douglas (whom Davis, in a letter to Pierce, called a "grog-drinking, electioneering Demagogue"). Douglas's selection prompted many southerners to bolt their party and establish a splinter Democratic ticket with John Breckenridge at its helm. Breckenridge, James Buchanan's vice president and later a leading Confederate Army general, was the candidate of choice for ex-president John Tyler, who believed that the Union's preservation was inextricably hinged to territorial expansion and that Breckenridge would ensure its development. Out of power since 1845 and soon to be elected to the Confederate Congress, Tyler promised to do battle with abolitionists who stood in the way of Breckenridge's notion of progress, unambiguously promising "live or die, survive or perish." Tyler was even briefly under the delusion that he could be a Democratic Party compromise candidate—that his broad popularity in Virginia might translate nationally and help break a deadlocked convention. "The whole South would rally with a shout," Tyler thought dreamily. They rallied, to be sure, but not for him. When Lincoln won the election, Tyler was terrified: "We have fallen on evil times," he said, "the day of doom for the great model Republic is at hand."

Pierce played the role of party man during the Democrats' factional infighting, deriding his party only for subjecting themselves to such an unhealthy rupture. "Integrity of the Union," he said, need not result in the "blind control of passion." Probably casting his vote for Breckenridge, as Tyler did, Pierce despaired that Lincoln's victory presaged a "distinct and unequivocal denial of the coequal rights." Other former presidents also lined up against Lincoln. Despite his Free Soil Party run twelve years earlier, Martin Van Buren remained faithful to the Democratic Party, backing Douglas. So, too, did Millard Fillmore, who phlegmatically commented that he voted Democratic "not because I was a Democrat, but because I was not a Republican."

Lincoln's reelection victory four years later, during the throes of the Civil War, was by no means preordained. Nearly 2 million Americans voted against him in that race, and although he won impressively, the Democratic candidate, Civil War major general George McClellan, received 45 percent of the popular vote. Three of those votes came from the roster of surviving ex-presidents: Millard Fillmore, Franklin Pierce, and James Buchanan (Tyler and Van Buren had died in 1862). No former president ever cast a vote for Abraham Lincoln for president of the United States.

The fact that Pierce, Buchanan, Tyler, and Van Buren all voted against Lincoln was unsurprising, as they were Democrats. Millard Fillmore, on the other hand, came out of the Whig tradition, with a detour to Know-Nothingness, and his leanings were less certain. After voting Democratic in 1860, he threw his support behind Lincoln once the Civil War began. Fillmore told a rally in his native Buffalo, "It is no time for any man to shirk from the responsibilities which events have cast upon him." Yet by the presidential contest of 1864, Fillmore had become appalled at Lincoln's handling of both politics and the war, and claimed that the country was now facing "national bankruptcy and military despotism." Only a different administration, he warned, could ensure a "restored Union, and an honorable peace." Fillmore supported McClellan in the 1864 race, writing that "as a general rule I am not in favor of electing military chieftains to the Presidency," but that "this is a crisis in the affairs of the nation when a truly patriotic and skillful military man of disinterested devotion . . . can do more than save it from ruin than any other."

With the country enmeshed in a horrific civil war, it was a singular achievement that the 1864 election was even pulled off. The Democratic Party platform called steadfastly for an end to the war (even though McClellan was in favor of continuing to victory) and a negotiated peace with the South. James Buchanan, who had presided over the lead-up to the conflict as president and strongly backed McClellan, remained a committed Democrat and offered counsel to his party. Like his earlier proposal to participate in Pennsylvania's 1862 congressional elections if "my interference should promise any good," Buchanan's proposition went unheeded. Skeptical that the Democrats could defeat Lincoln, he believed that victory would only plunge the party into disaster. "Have you ever reflected upon . . . the embarrassments of a Democratic administration," he asked, "should it succeed to power with the war still existing and the finances in their present unhappy condition?" Like John Tyler, Buchanan greeted the news of Lincoln's reelection in dark spirits: "They have won the elephant; & they will find difficulty in deciding what to do with him. . . . Now would be the time for conciliation. . . . A frank and manly offer to the Confederates that they might return to the Union just as they were before . . . might possibly be accepted." Ex-president Buchanan wanted nothing more than to return to the status quo ante.

After the war, Fillmore shared Buchanan's approach to reconciliation. Hostile to the idea of many northerners to "exterminate the South, or hold it by military subjugation," he defended Andrew Johnson's southern appeasement policy and endorsed Johnson's reconstruction plans against the radical Republicans. (Fillmore also neglected to drape his house for mourning after Lincoln's assassination, prompting a mob to splatter it with ink.)

POSTBELLUM PRESIDENTIAL POLITICS

Andrew Johnson, a leading war Democrat and an obstinate foe of radical Reconstruction, also maintained an ambivalent relationship with Republicans, even during his time as Lincoln's vice president. After the war, Johnson attempted to undermine Ulysses S. Grant, failing to appear at his 1869 inauguration—making him the third and last president to take such a stand (only his irascible predecessors John Adams and John Quincy Adams did the same). Johnson had nothing but contempt for the prospect of President Grant: "The little fellow has nothing in him. He hasn't a single idea. He has no policy, no conception of what the country requires. . . . He is mendacious, cunning, and treacherous." Lambasting the sitting president for graft, deficit spending, and monarchical drift, in 1872 Johnson threw his support behind Horace Greeley, the nominee on the Democratic line, whose dissident candidacy emerged from a split in the Republican ranks (Greeley was part of the "Liberal Republican" faction).

Horace Greeley was an unlikely choice for Johnson's affection. The longtime reformist editor of the Republican *New York Tribune*, Greeley had railed unremittingly against the iniquities of the Slave Power, and after the war advocated successfully for Johnson's impeachment. Yet Greeley grew antagonistic to the bloated corruption of Grant's administration and made an unexpectedly sharp turn thereafter by endorsing bail for Confederate icon Jefferson Davis. By the time Grant pursued reelection in 1872, Greeley's heated opposition had won him Johnson's backing, while Greeley's Liberal Republican Party's endorsement of home rule and amnesty for the South secured him broader Democratic support. Although Johnson may have been more anti-Grant than pro-Greeley, historian James McPherson has concluded that Johnson was impressed by Greeley's contention that "no reconstruction can be successful without the voluntary cooperation of 'the better class' of southern whites." Put simply, Johnson thought a Greeley win might forestall national catastrophe.

Johnson's loathing notwithstanding, Grant crushed Horace Greeley in 1872. Eight years later, Grant was hoping to be nominated a third time—and once Rutherford B. Hayes kept his pledge and declined to run for a second term, the 1880 Republican field was wide open. Beset again by intraparty factionalism, Republicans squared off into two opposing patronage-seeking wings: the Stalwarts, led by New York senator and party boss Roscoe Conkling, who watched vigilantly over the spoils system and backed the idea of a third Grant term; and the Half-Breeds, directed by Maine senator James Blaine, who pushed for civil service reform and eventually endorsed James Garfield. After falling short on a late ballot at the convention, Grant promised to back Garfield, the eventual nominee, and got busy making campaign stops for the ticket. (Conkling's Stalwarts got Chester Arthur installed as vice president as a consolation prize.)

That autumn, Grant's patron, Roscoe Conkling, traveled with him to New York and the Midwest making speeches for the Garfield-Arthur ticket. Conkling often spoke for up to four hours; Grant kept things brief. To one wildly cheering audience of thirty-five thousand in Warren, Ohio, the former president gave a short stump speech about why he was a Republican and the damage to the country a Democratic victory would deliver. A party man who felt "a very deep interest in the success of the Republican ticket," he reminded his good friend and fellow general John A. Logan that he would "gladly attend any meeting intended to further [its] success."

The most extravagant moment of the campaign came when Grant led a Republican reception in his own honor—a six-mile parade down New York's Broadway, with sixty thousand party activists and veterans in attendance and three hundred thousand others watching from the sidelines (a "monster demonstration," one newspaper dubbed it). By the Gilded Age, such political party gatherings had become massive affairs, and Grant was happy to lend his support. "Probably a more brilliant spectacle . . . was never witnessed on Manhattan island, if, indeed, in any other city in this country," the *New York Times* gushed. Grant's party activities paid off: Garfield defeated Winfield Scott Hancock, the Democratic nominee—though by fewer than two thousand votes, making it the closest popular vote margin in American presidential history.

Struck down by throat cancer, Grant played little public role during the 1884 campaign. "I have not taken any active part in politics," he responded to a reporter's question, "I have been shut up in a sick-room." Though physically subdued, Grant still let his preferences be known: "I have never made any concealment of the fact that I should prefer John Logan [then Illinois senator] to all the other candidates," who included President Arthur and the eventual Republican nominee, James Blaine. Grant was less than thrilled when the nod went to Blaine, who he thought represented the wrong wing of the party, but his unease was tempered when Logan was tapped as Blaine's running mate. By the early fall, Grant was sufficiently comfortable that he paid Blaine a public visit.

QUESTIONS OF PARTY LOYALTY

Grant's successor, Rutherford B. Hayes, preferred to spend his days immersed in progressive social causes rather than mired in political struggle. Yet Hayes did keep abreast of the shifting prospects of the Republican Party over the dozen years of his postpresidential life, even if his participation was meager. In 1884, during the first presidential contest after he left power, Hayes grew weary of the Republicans' interminable missteps and feared the party would lose the election. The Democrats had been bereft of the presidency for more than a quarter century, and the time seemed ripe for them to take back the White House. Like Grant, Hayes was uncomfortable with his party's nominee, James Blaine, calling him "a scheming demagogue, selfish and reckless." But he endorsed Blaine out of party loyalty, worried that his Democratic opponent, Grover Cleveland, would siphon off votes from independent Republicans. After Cleveland's win, Hayes fretted about the implications for his two beloved causes, civil service reform and civil rights. "I dread," he wrote, "the turning back of the hands of the clock."

Four years later Hayes remained despondent with the policies of the Cleveland administration. Hayes thought Cleveland might do himself in by making tariffs a central issue in the 1888 election. "For more than twenty years," Hayes said, "existing legislation has enticed capital and labor into manufactur[ing]. . . . To strike them down now . . . looks like cruelty and bad faith." Accordingly, though he would have preferred a different candidate—such as his own former treasury secretary, John Sherman—Hayes was pleased with Benjamin Harrison's Republican victory. But the former president's real interest was in promoting his pet issue: replacing the four-year election cycle with a single six-year term. Having already laid the groundwork years earlier during his own inaugural address, Hayes had become intimately associated with the idea and hoped in vain that it would catch on in 1888.

The last presidential contest Hayes witnessed as a former head of state was the 1892 election. While this time the ideal candidate was his protégé, Ohio governor William McKinley, he accepted the governor's readiness to step aside to ensure Benjamin Harrison's renomination. Calling McKinley "the man with the purest fame and the most brilliant record of any statesman in our political history," Hayes correctly, if hyperbolically, forecast a bright future for his fellow Ohioan.

Even when he had no real affection for his party's nominee, former president Hayes always maintained the appearance of moderation. Others were less adept at concealing their aversions. Grover Cleveland, for example, had a miserable time with William Jennings Bryan, his thirty-six-year-old successor, as party standard-bearer. The late nineteenth century could hardly have produced two Democrats who differed more starkly. Cleveland was the archetypal conservative Democrat—friendly to business, unfriendly to labor, and a resolute defender of the gold standard. Bryan, an "unsound money" man bidding for the coinage of silver, enraged Cleveland with his full-throated populist grandstanding at the 1896 Chicago convention. Bryan's "Cross of Gold" address at that convention—one of the pivotal speeches in American political history—encapsulated much of what Cleveland loathed.

Cleveland could not bring himself to vote for Bryan that year and bolted with most of his cabinet to rally behind the breakaway "Gold Party." (The party wanted Cleveland himself to run, but he ceded to the duo of John M. Palmer and Simon B. Bruckner, who gained a whopping 1 percent of the popular vote.) Delighting in the Democrats' fissures, ex-president Benjamin Harrison happily offered his support to Bryan's opponent, William McKinley. Trumpeting a protective tariff, Harrison made forty speeches in Indiana alone on McKinley's behalf. Democratic disarray helped McKinley easily take the 1896 election.

Four years later, during a repeat face-off between Bryan and McKinley, Cleveland once again made known his revulsion for Bryan, professing to be "in a constant state of wonderment, when I am not in a state of nausea." Yet he recognized that he would have to back Bryan if the Democrats were to stand a chance in the fall—especially since McKinley had sewed up the big moneymen from the eastern establishment. Cleveland was unwelcome at the annual Fourth of July Tammany Hall gathering in New York that summer because of apparent concern that he would attack Bryan. When the Democratic convention rolled around (it was held in Kansas City where a sixteen-year-old boy from Independence named Harry Truman served as a page), Cleveland stayed home. By the end of the race, however, Cleveland swallowed his pride, offering weak assurances that Bryan would triumph. (As his running mate, Bryan chose Adlai Stevenson, the grandfather of the 1950s Democrat and Cleveland's own second vice president, which may have softened the blow.) The ex-president told one reporter, "My young man, you will see a landslide for Bryan the morning after election. Of this I am confident." In private, however, Cleveland thought differently, cynically hoping Bryanism would hasten the party's implosion—that "sanity will succeed insanity and the Democratic masses will cry out for deliverance from Bryanism and a resurrection of true Democratic faith."

As New York governor in the early 1880s, Grover Cleveland had close ties with Theodore Roosevelt, then an upcoming reformist state legislator. Two decades later Roosevelt, now president, hailed Cleveland's antisilver tenacity: "I think now we have definitely won out on the free-silver business, and therefore I think you are entitled to thanks and congratulations." Despite the plaudits, Cleveland had little in common with Roosevelt's progressivism or military adventurism, and by 1904 espoused "clearing out" Roosevelt's administration. Some Democrats even urged Cleveland to throw his hat in the ring, as did some influential Republicans who hated TR, including J. P. Morgan and Mark Hanna. Before the Saint Louis convention, Democratic delegates began to fear that their likely nominee, Alton B. Parker, chief justice of the New York Court of Appeals, wouldn't stand a chance against Roosevelt in the general election. Only Grover Cleveland, the person who had won three national elections via the popular vote, could credibly compete. After enduring several years of intense postpresidential unpopularity, Cleveland was now viewed by many as the sage who had it right all along, especially on the gold issue. Cleveland gave what he could during the fall campaign, making speeches close to home in New York and New Jersey and writing a series of articles on the issues for mass publications. But he was through with national politics: out of office for seven years, he had neither the ambition nor the craving for a final hurrah. This was to be Roosevelt's election, and he defeated Parker handily.

TR and Taft

Cleveland died in 1908, leaving no former presidents on hand to witness Teddy Roosevelt's orchestrated campaign that year to install William Howard Taft as his successor. Taft could never have imagined that by 1912 his patron would first turn on him and then run against him, instigating one of the greatest presidential contests in American political history. (Dismayed by his inability to garner sufficient support among Republicans, Roosevelt created a breakaway political entity, the Progressive Party, that ran against both Taft and the Democrat Woodrow Wilson.) Following that acidulous race, which was eventually won by Wilson, Taft thought it best to withdraw from the fray in the 1916 contest. Comfortably ensconced in his law school appointment at Yale, Taft announced that he was "out of politics" already in the fall of 1915. But he was scarcely divorced from the oncoming campaign. In fact, there was one prominent Republican Taft hoped to champion.

The man Taft saw fit to defeat Wilson in 1916 was Elihu Root. The prototype for the twentieth-century "wise man" who shuttled from Wall Street to Washington's corridors of power, Root had been a Republican senator, secretary of war, secretary of state, and winner of the Nobel Peace Prize in 1912. Taft praised Root as "one of the greatest living Americans," calling him "a statesman in the same class as Alexander Hamilton." The two political conservatives were in solidarity over key issues during the 1916 campaign: both opposed the confirmation of the more liberal Louis Brandeis to the Supreme Court, even signing a petition calling Brandeis "not a fit person" for the post, and both felt America was in considerable need of budgetary and judicial procedural reform. Taft's support of Root was understandable: Root represented old-line Republicanism, Taft's own political stripe, and, no less important, both men had fallen out with the mercurial Roosevelt. Regardless of Taft's backing, however, Root was always a long shot—many felt his nomination would split the Republican Party yet again—and Taft's favored candidate peaked on the convention's first ballot. Taft himself skipped the Chicago convention, opting instead to give a forgettable commencement speech at Peddie Institute in Hightstown, New Jersey.

With Roosevelt's Bull Moose Party enfeebled (there were no Progressive senators and just seventeen representatives in the new Congress), TR dissuaded the Progressive Party from nominating him again in 1916 and threw his support behind Supreme Court Justice Charles Evans Hughes (no easy thing, as he was never an admirer). Roosevelt's physical condition may also have contributed to his decision not to run again; after his 1913–14 Brazilian adventure, he was partially crippled, overweight, and hampered by poor vision. With Root no longer a viable candidate, the outstanding question was whether the passion to defeat Wilson might at last bring an end to the acrid feud between the two former presidents. Roosevelt had been unsparing in his assault on Taft since the latter's presidency, and they had met only once since the 1912 election, exchanging pleasantries at an April 1915 funeral for a Yale professor. ("It was a bit stiff but it was all right," Taft remarked at the time.) Would they stump together for Hughes in 1916?

When queried after the June convention about what he would do were he on the same pro-Hughes dais as Roosevelt, Taft replied that it would not "make a particle of difference to me. . . . I would not be so little as to let my personal feelings interfere." Taft played the loyal foot soldier and pledged to do "anything in my power to elect Mr. Hughes." Promises of joint appearances by Taft and TR continued throughout the summer. By early fall, Roosevelt grew tired of the hubbub. At a stop in Battle Creek, Michigan, Roosevelt growled that buttons were being prepared with the group faces of him, Taft, and Hughes. Mentioning a forthcoming reception at the Union League Club in which he and Taft were to be present, Roosevelt was explicit: "I will make no advances to shake hands with Mr. Taft. . . . This attempt to make it a reconciliation meeting between myself and Mr. Taft is all wrong." At the October reception, where Root was master of ceremonies, the two weather-beaten ex-presidential foes shook hands and exchanged a simple "How do you do?" Taft summarized: "We shook hands just like any gentlemen would shake hands."

Hughes ended up losing the 1916 race to Wilson by a narrow electoral margin. The conventional wisdom holds that Hughes fell short because he didn't reach out to California Progressive governor Hiram Johnson, Roosevelt's 1912 running mate. (Hughes had reportedly failed to pay his respects to Johnson when the two crossed paths at a Long Beach, California, hotel one day, a probable oversight that was received as a snub.) Observers at the time believed the gaffe might have cost Hughes California's thirteen electoral votes, which would have put him over the top. Even without Hiram Johnson's backing, if Roosevelt and Taft had campaigned enthusiastically for Hughes as a team, it might have tipped the exceptionally close race in his favor.

With Roosevelt's death in 1919, Taft became the only surviving ex-president to observe the 1920 race. This election was particularly meaningful for him because its victor would hold the key to his long-standing ambition—to be nominated to the Supreme Court. Taft never hid his infatuation with the federal bench, frequently commenting that his desire to join the court always trumped any interest he had in the presidency. Whether or not Taft's active campaigning for Harding was heartfelt, his labors paid off. When Chief Justice Edward Douglass White died only months after Harding was elected the country's twenty-ninth president, Harding promptly nominated Taft to replace him. Taft's dream was now a reality.

WILSON AND COOLIDGE

Following a devastating stroke in 1919, Woodrow Wilson's physical frailty prevented him from assuming any meaningful electioneering role after the White House. His limited commentary on the congressional races of 1922 consisted of put-downs—maligning the Democratic candidate for senate in Massachusetts, Sherman Whipple, as being "not of our intellectual breed," and "just about as much interested in human progress . . . as a hog in the grand opera." (Whipple lost.) Yet Wilson's death in February 1924 did not still his influence. His electoral "participation" was instead transmuted to the plane of political ideas: the Democratic platforms of 1924 and 1928 included support for his two treasured projects, the globalist dream of the League of Nations and the domestic agenda he called the New Freedom.

Like Wilson, Calvin Coolidge remained largely quiescent after his retirement, living up to his sobriquet Silent Cal. Saying that "Ten

years in Washington is longer than any other man has had it—too long!"
Coolidge decided against renomination in 1928. Though he refrained
from active campaigning, Coolidge did quietly back Hoover's reelection
effort in 1932, writing three supportive articles during the race. The
most important was an apologia he published in the *Saturday Evening
Post*, where he painted the Great Depression as a worldwide conflagration beyond Hoover's control. "When men in public office have to meet
a crisis which they themselves did not in any way create," he suggested,
"the measure of credit or blame which should attach to such officehold-
ers is not the intensity of the crisis, nor the danger or damage that results
from it, but the manner in which they may meet it and the remedies
which they apply to it." Hoover must have been pleased that the only
surviving ex-president was standing by him.

Coolidge was invisible at that June's Chicago convention. Though
there were rumors that he might be drafted to run as Hoover's vice
president, shortly before the convention began he took himself out of
contention, and a distinctly minor "Coolidge for President" movement also faded. During the autumn campaign, Coolidge made one
major address from Madison Square Garden, where he railed against
FDR and in a peculiar flash of optimism noted that the "economic
recovery is beginning." Such prognostication illustrated his blinders
to the day's realities: America was indeed changing, and Calvin Coolidge was incapable of moving with it. Two months after Hoover's
defeat, Coolidge was dead.

The Ideology of Herbert Hoover

Until Harry Truman joined him in March 1953, Herbert Hoover was
the country's only living ex-president. The 1930s and 1940s were
charged years for Hoover, as he continued to push his ideological cer-
tainties in the hope that they might inform his party's platforms. With

the country facing "the greatest struggle which we have seen in two generations," Hoover worried that Roosevelt's New Deal was creating a "fountain of fear" among Americans; and as a former president and private citizen, he set out on a personal quest to overturn it.

After the wreckage of the 1934 midterm elections, Hoover grew concerned that a vulnerable Republican Party might betray its core principles in order to win back power. The former president began a crusade to resuscitate his party and amplify its differences from the dreaded New Dealers. Like Cleveland and Taft, who also took pains to rein in their parties in times of ideological drift, Hoover was eager to move the GOP back onto a rightward course. In Hoover's mind, Roosevelt's enterprise was veering treacherously toward a "Fascist-Nazi state," and Hoover promised to reverse the "five horsemen" of the New Deal: "Profligacy, Propaganda, Patronage, Politics, and Power." (For those who liked their alliteration more caustic, he proffered an alternative set of Ps: "Pork-barrel, Poppy-cock, Privileges, Panaceas, and Poverty.")

Desperate to unseat Roosevelt, in 1936 Hoover was eager to impart his wisdom to whoever became the Republican standard-bearer (though he remained quietly hopeful that a groundswell of support might garner him the nomination). Ultimately, he was distressed with the party's nominee, Alf Landon of Kansas. To Hoover, Landon was deficient in key respects: more than once the nominee had voiced charitable words for the New Deal (heresy of heresies); he was supported by the Liberty League, a group Hoover loathed; and he was endorsed by Hoover's arch-nemesis, William Randolph Hearst, who had once called the former president "selfish and stupid" and who was barred from the White House during Hoover's tenure. Generally oblivious to his standing within the party, Hoover remained unaware of the GOP's lack of interest in his services. His political glory was limited to a rousing speech at the Cleveland convention, where he warned that "The New Deal may be a revolutionary design to replace the American system with despotism." And with a literary flourish, he added, "It may be the dream stuff of a false liberalism. It may be the valor of muddle. Their relationship to each other, however, is exactly the sistership of the witches who brewed the cauldron of powerful trouble for Macbeth. Their product is the poisoning of Americanism." For his explicit comparisons of the New Deal with ascending European autocracies, Hoover received a thirty-minute ovation.

There was a subtext to Hoover's eloquent Sturm und Drang. While he was keen on smashing the Popular Front shibboleths of the day, he had become a punching bag for the country's ills and an "enemy of the people" to the many millions suffering from the Great Depression. To countless Americans, Hoover was the man who had shot down veterans seeking a fair bonus to their salaries; who forced working Americans to set up camp in "Hoovervilles"; and who brought higher tariffs to a land whose economy was in danger of total collapse. "When you have a good story, run it every once in awhile," an editor of the *New York Sun* once suggested, and in the worst days of the Depression, "Hoover Ruining America" was just that kind of story. The former president was actively determined to change the headline.

Landon kept Hoover at arm's length, his campaign considering him a bumptious loser who could offer little positive value to his fellow Republicans in 1936. The party was only beginning its slow march toward a more pragmatic politics, with candidates like Landon and later Willkie, Dewey, and Eisenhower gradually casting off Hoover's ideological mantle. By the time the race was over, the ex-president could take solace in one thing: FDR outmatched Landon by even more than he'd beaten Hoover four years earlier.

Exploding the hallowed tradition inaugurated by George Washington's voluntary retirement after two terms, FDR's ambition to run again in 1940 accelerated Hoover's anti–New Deal rhetoric. At the time, some viewed Roosevelt's move as hubristic, a viewpoint largely dispelled over time. Despite the war raging in Europe, the Republican field was populated by isolationists: Ohio senator Robert Taft, Michigan senator Arthur Vandenburg, and New York district attorney

Thomas E. Dewey—who were anxious to avoid entanglement over-seas. (One rumor even briefly had Hoover leading an isolationist ticket with Charles Lindbergh.)

Hoover watched the convention from the bleachers of the Phila-delphia Auditorium, naively hopeful that the delegates might turn to him in a late ballot. During the nomination process his close ally, Robert Taft, entreated the former president to give him his delegates. Though he had only a handful to offer—he maxed out at thirty-two on the third ballot—Hoover refused, imagining fantastically that his long-shot candidacy might snake through a deadlocked convention. During his speech, Hoover struck a clear isolationist chord, emphasiz-ing that "the three thousand miles of ocean is still protection" and that "the immense task now is to shape our foreign policies to protect us from the conflagration in Europe and Asia." Journalist Drew Pear-son interpreted the former president's position as basic realpolitik: Hitler would prove victorious and the West would have to deal with him. In other words, far better to prepare for the imperatives of diplo-macy, no matter how dismal, than sound the drumbeats of war.

The only prominent Republican voice to depart from the chorus of isolationism was an outsider to the thicket of Washington politics: Wendell Willkie. A former Democrat (he had been a delegate for FDR in 1932) and current Wall Street industrialist, Willkie tactically advanced a soft interventionist line, calling for the United States to adopt a policy of preparedness. Willkie's internationalism coincided with the Nazis' savage tour of European capitals, which buoyed his candidacy. Where Hoover and others were content to insist that the European democracies could hold their own, Willkie took a broader perspective—and won the formal nod to oppose FDR.

In support of the party, and given his antipathy to FDR, Hoover offered to make speeches around the country on Willkie's behalf. But the former president's acute foreign policy differences with Willkie made the offer unconvincing. At the onset of the fall campaign Hoover repeated his belief that the "actual dangers" to America were at their lowest ebb, and that "it is evident that the people are firmly and vigorously opposed to our involvement" in the war. Hoover never warmed to Willkie, and the feeling was mutual. "I shall do any proper thing they want me to do," he said curtly. "I don't think it will be very much." For his part, Willkie went out of his way to avoid Hoover in the two states, California and New York, where the former president resided.

By 1944, the United States was deeply entrenched in World War II, and Herbert Hoover was no longer under any illusion that the GOP might turn to him as a possible dark horse. Yet preventing FDR from winning yet another term remained his obsession. He even developed a tactical friendship with Alf Landon, someone he had disparaged eight years before. The Hoover-Landon alliance coalesced around one point: Willkie must not be the candidate again in 1944. Fortunately for them, Willkie dropped out early after a weak primary showing (the result of "a public revulsion from Hollywood demagoguery," Hoover snickered). Landon backed Thomas Dewey, now the governor of New York, and though Hoover was partial to a simpatico conservative, Ohio governor John Bricker (for whom Hoover edited some speeches), by the fall he was ready to support the nominee.

Like Landon and Willkie in 1936 and 1940, Dewey was publicly detached from the seventy-year old ex-president. Discreetly he solicited Hoover's advice and eventually his help recruiting John Bricker for the number two spot. Yet the Dewey camp worried that labor leaders would tar him by his association with Hoover, and enlisted Herbert Brownell, Dewey's central strategist and later Eisenhower's attorney general, to keep Hoover sidelined. Brownell went so far as to ask Hoover to deny that he'd met with Dewey after the convention. ("He's afraid that association with me will be brought up against him by the Democrats," Hoover lamented.) By this point, as one historian noted, Hoover was the "nation's leading political leper." Brownell managed to keep the association largely under wraps, but ultimately it didn't matter: FDR triumphed again in November, winning a record fourth term.

By the first postwar presidential election, Hoover had started to shed his leper spots. After being persona non grata at FDR's White House, Hoover managed to establish cordial relations with Harry Truman, a relationship that surprised many. Truman asked the former president to reprise his acclaimed international relief efforts for Europe and Asia. A year later, he also put Hoover in charge of an eponymous commission to recommend reforms of the executive branch. The old political order was changing: the New Deal had run its course, the war years were over, the Republicans controlled Congress, and Roosevelt was dead. Few realistically wagered that Harry Truman could hold on to power.

Republicans in 1948 felt less anxious over the presence of Herbert Hoover. After enduring four terms of Democratic near invincibility, the solitary former president at last entertained real hope of witnessing victory for the Grand Old Party. Undaunted by the prospect of a Dewey candidacy, Hoover nonetheless urged his party to choose his preferred conservative, Robert Taft, as the 1948 nominee, but Dewey carried the day. At the Philadelphia convention, Hoover gave a rip-roaring speech denouncing the Soviet menace, calling it an existential threat by "the hordes from the European steppes who would ruin Western civilization." And addressing his companion bête noire, the malevolence of collectivism at home, he suggested that "our difficulty lies not so much with obnoxious communists in our midst as with the fuzzy-minded people who think we can have totalitarian economics in the hands of bureaucracy."

Despite their professional cooperation, as Election Day drew near, Harry Truman couldn't resist raising the specter of a Hoover resurgent, brandishing the former president's name no less than sixteen times in one speech. Always the pragmatist, Dewey didn't risk coming to Hoover's defense. ("The governor held to the opinion I was still political poison," Hoover griped.) Instead the former president occupied himself with his commission responsibilities, watching from the sidelines as Truman stunned the world by pulling out his unexpected victory.

Although the press satirized Hoover's physical condition—"the once plump bull-terrier cheeks now sag mastiff-like," one magazine cracked—Hoover was unfazed by his decades in the political wilderness, insisting "they're not going to shut me up." Traditionally refusing to endorse candidates before the nomination, in 1952 the former president reversed practice and pledged for Taft. According to Hoover, the Ohio conservative "provided the Republican party with a fighting opposition to the current of collectivism in our country," and might be the one to end the Republican Party's two-decade-long losing streak. But it was not to be: this was Dwight Eisenhower's year. Not a great Ike advocate, Hoover delivered a rambling television address weeks before the election, expressing muted support for the ticket. "I have tonight come out of what I had hoped was final retirement from political activities," he began. "I have done so at General Eisenhower's request." Hoover concluded with a self-regarding peroration defending his own administration's policies, twenty years after that administration was ushered out of Washington.

Truman Makes Two (and Goes Negative)

Following Ike's victory, Hoover was joined by an ex-presidential counterpart for the first time: Harry Truman. Though he declined to run for a second full term in 1952, the cantankerous Democrat did not wish simply to drift away after leaving office. Returning to Independence, Missouri, to occupy himself with his library's development, Harry Truman envisioned involvement in future campaigns as one way to remain relevant. And in his postpresidential debut, with a popular Eisenhower seeking reelection in 1956, Harry Truman was ready to brawl. Spitefully shut out of Ike's White House, Truman had waged a personal cold war with Eisenhower, and scarcely controlled his venom toward Ike's red-baiting vice president, Richard Nixon. He brought a taste of slash-and-burn to the 1956 race. "Remember this and remember it well," he warned, "you cannot elect Ike without electing Tricky Dicky."

Truman's antipathies to the reigning Republicans were in no way matched by any passion for the Democratic ticket. In 1952 Truman had solidly backed the Democratic candidate, Illinois governor Adlai Stevenson, assured that he would continue Truman's policies. But Stevenson's anemic showing that year depressed Truman, and by 1956 the former president was convinced that the party needed another man to unseat Eisenhower. There were personality issues, too: an urbane patrician admired as much for his wit and sophistication as for his principles, Stevenson had a smart-set following that Truman distrusted. Indeed, to some Stevenson must have seemed like the anti-Truman.

During the spring of 1956 Truman acted as a close adviser to New York governor Averell Harriman, who had served as his secretary of commerce and ambassador to Russia. Truman was as quick to shower praise on Harriman as he was to attack Stevenson. Slamming Stevenson's suggestion that the Democrats adopt a "time for moderation," Truman countered, "If you're referring to drink then moderation is a good thing. However in political campaigns, I have always gone on the theory that it is best to go after the opposition hammer and tong." Disdainful of such attack-dog politics, Stevenson fell further afoul of the former president.

Truman resisted making any formal announcement of support. "I did not promise to support anyone before the convention," he said. "It is not my place or business to tell the Democratic Party what to do." Coyness aside—"I like them both" was his public refrain—Truman continued to extol Harriman, saying that there was no one he thought of "more highly." By the time of the Chicago convention, the party was awash with rumors that Truman was preparing to run Stevenson down and ally formally with Harriman. On the convention's eve, Truman "exploded an H-bomb," in the savage words of the *Tribune*'s

Walter Trohan, naming Harriman as his choice for the nomination. Assuming the air of a power broker, Truman withheld Harriman's name until the very end of his prepared speech, then for good measure reread his statement in full to reporters. This was Truman's post-presidential moment in the sun, and he was basking in it.

By endorsing Harriman, Truman hoped to derail an easy first ballot nomination and ensure that the race was two-way: Stevenson versus Harriman. But other party stalwarts found his grandstanding divisive and irritating. Eleanor Roosevelt, a solid Stevenson backer, was peeved by Truman's antics yet resisted going on record about her husband's successor. In private she reminded Truman that they were both seventy-two and that it was time to hand over power to a younger generation. Truman's bravura endorsement could hardly put Harriman over the top—even if Harriman's backers had sewed up more than three hundred delegates, as they claimed. In a last-ditch effort to sway votes to Harriman, Truman assailed Stevenson for being "too defeatist" and called his inability to "carry any more states than he did in 1952" a recipe for Democratic failure.

With Harriman's nomination appearing out of reach, Truman began to flail wildly. The former president attacked Stevenson for tying himself to "conservatives and reactionaries" (and taking a page from Joe McCarthy, he failed to clarify precisely who such people were). Finally, in a moment of weakness, Truman provided more nuanced insight into his stubborn support for Harriman's long-shot bid. Declaring that he was "shocked that any liberal Democrat would encourage the abandonment of the New Deal and the Fair Deal as out of date," Truman grieved openly that his treasured public policies were no longer in fashion. The ex-president was a victim of the forward march of time.

Arthur Krock, the dean of Washington newsmen, a man who had covered eleven presidents, was convinced that Truman "is determined to use his great influence at the convention constructively and without conscious personal motive." Yet most felt the opposite:

Truman's self-destructive behavior risked dividing his party over the eventual nominee. Confusing popularity for power, Truman's audition for kingmaker was undone by hubris. The journalist James Reston put it best: "Harry Truman, the Goliath who set out to slay David, has succeeded only in knocking out himself."

Though he played a tamer role during the overall campaign, Herbert Hoover, now eighty-two, continued his tradition of addressing the Republican National Convention. Hoover's speech and his autumn broadcast appearances were standard fare, giving him a forum to drive home many of his pet themes: the malignance of encroaching government; the evils of Communism ("human slavery"); military preparedness; and maximum employment (Keynes was not yet passé). Ike's campaign people even recruited Hoover to appear on the president's behalf in Philadelphia, where they needed votes. Pleased to be sought out, Hoover was nonetheless uneasy over the GOP's trajectory. Eisenhower's circle was far too eager to win over liberal and moderate Republicans, he thought, and dead wrong to presume that they'd locked in the party's conservative base. Chalking up the Republicans' congressional losses in 1954 to the notion that "Republican radicalism can get nowhere" rather than to typical midterm losses and the ongoing recession, Hoover insisted again on a rightward tack. In its current incarnation, he explained, the GOP failed "to comprehend that the only way they can live as a vital party is on the conservative side."

1960

By the election of 1960, some thought that the party might move to the right, under the guidance of its new standard-bearer, Vice President Richard Nixon. While he had been championed by Hoover years earlier, Nixon largely snubbed the former president during the fall campaign. Hoover groused about the oversight to reporters: "How do you think I feel? I'm among those who persuaded him to run for Congress in the first place." Participating in his final convention— "Unless some miracle comes to me from the good Lord, this is finally it," he told the Chicago-gathered delegates—Hoover called for a spiritual rebirth in society. Americans were facing a "frightening moral slump," and only by summoning those forces "embedded in the soul of America" could the country do proper battle with its manifold ills.

On the Democratic side, Truman's fall from grace in 1956 may have cost him a measure of legitimacy, but it hardly deterred him from hazarding further fissures in the party. The campaign for the 1960 Democratic nomination presented another opportunity for Truman's political indiscretions. Provoked by John F. Kennedy's spirited idealism, Truman once more challenged a candidate who departed from the former president's playbook. But this time, instead of waiting for the convention to unfold, Truman anointed his preferred candidate in the spring. His choice was Senator Stuart Symington, a protégé from his home state who had been Truman's secretary of the air force and served seven consecutive assignments under him.

Truman's temper ran high that summer. Believing that Kennedy's coronation had been unfairly predetermined, he resigned as a delegate and boycotted that year's Los Angeles convention. As in 1956, Truman took a confrontational tone. At one point, with television cameras rolling, he pointedly queried Kennedy: "Senator, are you certain that you're quite ready for the country or the country is ready for you?" Embarassingly for Truman, his 1956 favorite Averell Harriman came quickly to Kennedy's defense, praising his "poise and maturity."

Kennedy clearly was never a favorite of Truman's, but it was Kennedy's father whom the former president found truly repugnant. Though he claimed indifference to JFK's Catholicism, Truman was explicit about his dislike of the father. "It's not the pope that worries me," he memorably put it, "it's the pop." At the convention, Symington had hoped to use a pincer strategy, winning the hearts of fleeing delegates as a compromise candidate. He never stood a chance; Kennedy triumphed easily. Clark Clifford, Truman's confidant and Symington's lead adviser, brokered a meeting between Kennedy and Truman to help mend fences, and by the time of the general election campaign all was forgiven.

Truman was in fine form that fall, touring the country for the Kennedy-Johnson ticket and offering his characteristically salty slogans. ("If you vote for Nixon, you ought to go to hell," he told the crowds. "If he ever told the truth politically it was by accident.") With Fidel Castro newly ascendant in Cuba, Truman pounced on the issue, blaming Ike for improper enforcement of the Monroe Doctrine. Fed up with Truman's loose-cannon speechifying, the *Washington Post* scolded the former president: "The fact is that when Mr. Truman puts on his political hat the country no longer takes him seriously," and "some . . . are again talking about the possibility of muzzling or exiling ex-Presidents during election campaigns." As in 1956, James Reston cogently summed matters up: "In human and historic terms this is a tragic story."

Ironically, it would fall to Herbert Hoover to return a measure of dignity to the ex-presidential class. In a peculiar coincidence, after the election both Kennedy and Nixon decided to get some rest and relaxation in southern Florida—Nixon in Key Biscayne with his chum Bebe Rebozo, Kennedy with his family in Palm Springs. Joe Kennedy, a friend of Hoover's (he sat on the second Hoover Commission), asked the former president to broker a meeting between Nixon and his son to help heal the country after the hotly fought election. (The spectacle of Joe Kennedy working constructively with Herbert Hoover was another slap to Truman: after the election, Truman called the new president's father "as big a crook as we've got anywhere in this country, and I don't like that he bought his son the nomination for the presidency.") The resulting November 14 meeting between Kennedy and Nixon at the Key Biscayne Hotel was anticlimactic, except for one detail that would become interesting in retrospect: Nixon's insistence that Kennedy never recognize China, nor allow it to join the United Nations.

EISENHOWER'S NEUTRALITY

Barry Goldwater, the Republican standard-bearer four years later against Lyndon Johnson, came closer than any previous GOP presidential nominee to fulfilling Herbert Hoover's ideological idyll. Then in his ninetieth year, Hoover said little during the 1964 campaign, but he must have been pleased that the outspoken Arizonan got the nod. Goldwater's best-selling *The Conscience of a Conservative* and his riveting convention speech declaration—"extremism in the defense of liberty is no vice, moderation in the pursuit of justice is no virtue"— were signature moments for the modern conservative movement and anticipated Richard Nixon's notorious backlash politics several years later. After three postpresidential decades of nominees he found wanting, Hoover died just three weeks before the election, missing his chance to vote for a model conservative at last.

Dwight Eisenhower was far less thrilled at the prospect of a Goldwater nomination. During his first presidential race out of power, the former general wore his military-style pledge to maintain a detached neutrality until the convention like a badge of honor. Though his preferences were hardly mysterious—he leaned toward middle-of-the-roaders like Pennsylvania governor William Scranton—Ike was silent until San Francisco.

Barry Goldwater's new conservative vision alienated the centrist from Abilene, but the former president's alternatives were few. He could sit out the election and remain uncommitted, as he had during the primaries, or cast his lot with Lyndon Johnson—both remote possibilities at best. Dedicated to his party, Eisenhower promised to do whatever he could to further its ends. The decision would leave him not without regret. As he watched the fire-breathing Arizonan impugn his steady-as-you-go administration, Eisenhower agonized why he hadn't pushed harder for someone like Scranton. Without Ike's endorsement, Scranton's candidacy never had legs. Eisenhower later explained his inaction with some contrition: "It is pretty hard to go back and say what might have been. I did what I thought my conscience dictated and . . . I think I would probably assume the same role again, but probably I would try to do it better."

Right-wing scribe and Goldwater acolyte William F. Buckley Jr. urged his candidate to steer clear of gutless moderates like Eisenhower, unleashing a flurry of rhetorical questions: "Would Goldwater have sat frozen in indecision when the tanks marched into Budapest? Would he have concluded a peace treaty over Korea that denied us the goals which even the United Nations had legitimized? Would Goldwater have sat back at Suez and allowed a bellicose neutralist to take control of the windpipe of the Near East to further his rabid pan Arabism?" Goldwater himself was equally ardent, but still pleased when he eventually received Eisenhower's backing, however reserved it may have been. He quickly exploited the former president's endorsement, promising to enlist him to travel to South Vietnam once elected. The Republican nominee framed things carefully: "I intend to come to grips with this vital question. And at that time I want the very best and soundest advice available."

IKE AND TRUMAN ON THE SIDELINES

Four years later, the ground had changed precipitously. By then war was raging in Vietnam, the sitting president was bowing out, and Richard Nixon was mounting a stunning comeback as the likely Republican nominee. Despite Eisenhower's frailty—he was holed up for several months at Walter Reed Army Medical Center after two heart attacks—he declared himself for Nixon three weeks before 1968's Miami Beach convention. (Nixon pressed his old boss to announce before the event, not during it, as Ike originally planned.) In a statement from his hospital bed, Ike stressed the personal over the political: "He's a man of great reading, a man of great intelligence, and a man of great decisiveness." Nixon was convinced that "a number of delegates [who were] waiting to see which way to go" would be swayed by Ike's words. For Eisenhower, his endorsement was at least in part a tactical move to distance himself from Nelson Rockefeller, whom he thoroughly disliked. He may also have been moved by remorse. More than once, Ike had regretted his quiescence during Nixon's 1960 campaign, capped by his cutting reply when a reporter asked him to name any ideas Nixon had contributed to his administration: "If you give me a week I might think of one." By 1968, there were also family ties affecting the equation. Nixon's daughter Julie was engaged to marry David Eisenhower, Ike's grandson, in a ceremony scheduled for shortly after the November elections.

Ike did address the Miami convention, via a television hookup from his hospital room at Walter Reed, giving a spirited Cold War speech alerting viewers that "the Communists reach ruthlessly for domination over Southeast Asia and are trying to break our will to foil the attempt." The next day he was struck down by another heart attack and spent the rest of the year in bed. On his back, Eisenhower marshaled a last-minute plea for voters to ignore Johnson and Humphrey's allegedly calculated halt to the bombing in Vietnam. Coming two days before the November vote, the plea exorcised the ghost of elections past, when he failed to rise to his vice president's defense. Nixon's razor-thin victory over Humphrey and Wallace benefited by the words of support from his old master.

Truman's role in the 1968 campaign was slight, his timing poor.

The ex-president spoke convincingly of Johnson's chances: "It doesn't make any difference what the rest of them do. . . . The present man in the White House is the man we'll vote for. And he's the one to be elected and he ought to be." Unfortunately, this vote of confidence came only eleven days before LBJ announced he was dropping out of the race. Despite Truman's optimism, the meager victory Johnson eked out in the March New Hampshire primary prompted his exit from the campaign. With Johnson's egress, Truman rallied behind Humphrey, becoming honorary chair of a committee to push the vice president's candidacy. Humphrey later made a pilgrimage to Independence, Missouri, where he hoped a little of Truman's 1948 mystique might rub off. Humphrey needed the boost and even joked self-deprecatingly, "Let's be candid. My campaign . . . has not peaked too soon."

LBJ Retreats to the Ranch

By 1972 there were two former presidents, Harry Truman and Lyndon Johnson, but general infirmity (in the former) and severe exhaustion (in the latter) prevented both men from participating. Not that the eventual nominee, George McGovern, seriously solicited the services of either; the policies of both men stood in marked contrast to McGovern's progressive platform. Truman sat out the campaign entirely—the heart of the primary season coincided with his eighty-eighth birthday celebration—but he was able to make his views known to others. After a private visit with Truman in April, Averell Harriman told the press that Truman believed "the most important thing now is to make sure Mr. Nixon is a one-term president." Truman died in December, before Nixon was sworn in for his abortive second term.

LBJ's public role narrowed to near nonexistence after he left the White House; he retreated to his ranch, and into an insular world pierced only by those closest to him. With the Vietnam War still ongoing, the Democratic establishment was certainly keeping its distance. Johnson wasn't welcome at the Miami Beach convention; his photograph was absent from the usual gallery of former Democratic presidents; and it was not until Ted Kennedy's late convention speech that his name was even mentioned. Jack Valenti, LBJ's former adviser, bridled at the omission: "President Johnson was a non-person, expunged from the Democratic Party with the same kind of scouring effectiveness that Marxist revisionists used to rewrite Communist history." McGovern and his party were running away from Johnson as hard as they were running against Nixon.

Then, seemingly out of the blue, McGovern made a volte-face and paid a visit to Johnson's ranch. That LBJ accepted McGovern's request for a meeting was an event in itself. Perhaps McGovern assumed that he had the anti-Johnson Democrats' vote securely locked up, and that those who'd turned to Nixon in 1968 would turn back if he played his cards right. Maybe he was trying to regain some legitimacy after a series of blunders—from the imbroglio over the vice presidency, when he was forced to drop Thomas Eagleton for Sargent Shriver, to his contention that South Vietnam would go Communist immediately following the November election. Whatever the case, after months of relentless attacks on the former president, McGovern emerged from a three-hour steak dinner with Johnson to declare the visit "one of the most treasured moments of my life."

It's hard to fathom who could have been fooled by such an admission. But Johnson must have taken some comfort in the fact that McGovern, who had laid into him so venomously, now saw fit to treat him "with affection and respect." He responded by offering the nominee counsel on key issues, advising him not to slash the defense budget and to shelve any plans of raising taxes.

NIXON RETURNS

In America's bicentennial year, the only living former president, Richard Nixon, was in the early stages of his arduous rehabilitation. His highly touted return trip to China that winter eclipsed Gerald Ford's unsuccessful sojourn to the PRC several months before. Ford's campaign to remain president of the United States was complicated by his ex-boss. During the summer convention season, Ronald Reagan, the insurgent candidate of the '76 campaign, deliberately floated the Nixon liability issue. The specter of the former president was inescapable, and Ford was boxed into defending something he would have preferred to avoid. Nixon's absence from the riveting Kansas City convention—the last Republican summit in which the primaries did not determine the candidate—was conspicuous, if understandable (Pat Nixon had suffered a debilitating stroke in July, which would have kept Nixon away in any event). An early draft of the GOP platform praised Nixon's China diplomacy, but that was quickly excised. A Ford spokesman gave the party line: "We're trying to forget Richard Nixon, not memorialize him." The man who four years earlier led the GOP to its largest victory ever was now a nonentity.

Throughout the fall, Nixon's name was verboten in Ford's campaign. (Across the political aisle, Jimmy Carter was happy to remind people.) Unless cornered, Ford described Nixon simply as "my predecessor," or worse, "Lyndon Johnson's successor." Then, weeks before the election, in a paid broadcast interview with the sports personality Joe Garagiola, Ford let loose. Responding to a question about the difference between the Nixon and Ford presidencies, Ford answered sharply, "Joe, there's one very fundamental difference. Under President Ford there's not any imperial White House, which means there's no pomp, there's no ceremony, there's no dictatorial authority." It was a calculated risk: if he wanted any chance at victory, Ford knew he had to confront the Nixon issue head-on. Yet too little time had passed since Watergate, and Ford fell short.

Richard Nixon's calculated climb back to respectability was on exhibit during the 1980 campaign. In February, he moved into a twelve-room, six-fireplace town house on New York's East Sixty-fifth Street that had formerly been owned by Judge Learned Hand. That spring he published *The Real War*, one of his many tracts on foreign policy. Teeming with Nixonian nostrums clearly intended for Jimmy Carter—"You can never reject the use of force," "You can never let a terrorist think you don't have any other recourse except diplomatic protest"—Nixon blasted the president for his failures with Afghanistan and Iran. Nixon also predicted that by 1985, Russia would have "unquestioned nuclear superiority, overwhelming superiority on the ground, and at least equality at sea." (As it happened, 1985 was the year Gorbachev came to power.)

That year's Republican candidate, Ronald Reagan, admired the book's tough-minded détente policies. Although he rarely saw Reagan in person, Nixon exerted an influence on his campaign via a number of Reagan aides who had worked in the Nixon administration, among them Richard Allen, Lyn Nofziger, William Casey, and John Sears. Brimming with self-confidence, Nixon was ready to intercede on behalf of partisan interests. After the independent candidate in 1980, John Anderson, slighted Reagan for his absence of foreign affairs credentials, Nixon jumped to Reagan's defense; and when the *New York Times* questioned Reagan's travel experience abroad, Nixon penned his first-ever letter to the editor to correct the paper.

Despite Nixon's foreign policy–based overtures, he remained conspicuously banished from July's nominating convention. One journalist reported that "Nixon's name is never mentioned. His poster adorns no wall. His acts are never recalled. His campaign buttons are not for sale." Even Pat Buchanan, Nixon's former speechwriter, held his nose and conceded, "This is a forward-looking party now." The consensus that Nixon had cost Ford the 1976 election stanched all public references to the former president.

At the summer convention in Detroit, few expected the exhilarating times that were to come. In a unique moment, a former president—Gerald Ford—engaged in a heady negotiation about becoming his party's vice-presidential nominee. Though some Republicans considered a Reagan-Ford ticket a "dream team," the deal was scotched when Ford apparently demanded a kind of copresidency arrangement. Once the delicate negotiations fell through, Ford actively campaigned for Reagan—despite the fact that Reagan had done him no favors in the tight election four years earlier. Taking a page from Carter's 1976 playbook, Ford cited the misery index (a combination of inflation and unemployment rates), which Carter had employed to great effect against him. "If twelve percent was good enough to get Jerry Ford out of the White House," Ford said, "then twenty percent is plenty reason to do the same to Jimmy Carter now."

By 1984, Richard Nixon's lost years were approaching their terminus. Seventy-one years old, a full decade beyond his pained resignation, Nixon was now a wealthy man and a recognized voice in foreign affairs. Aware of his success and yet sensitive to the needs of his party, he readily assumed the role of éminence grise, giving off-camera counsel and guidance to all comers. Resigned to his lightning-rod status, Nixon voluntarily skipped that year's Dallas convention, saving the party the chore of failing to invite him. Nixon may have installed himself as a senior statesman, but his visage still didn't play well on national television.

Gerald Ford was also keeping a low profile. The former president was enlisted to provide primary support to some Senate candidates—notably his former commerce secretary, Elliot Richardson, who ran an unsuccessful campaign in Massachusetts—but Ford did little more. Arguably, his greatest contribution to the party in 1984 was to announce that it "would be in the best interest" of the Republicans if Nixon were to apologize for Watergate. Astutely shying away from his substantive differences with the GOP on social issues, Ford focused instead on bread-and-butter concerns, hailing President Reagan for his "fairness" and his success in reducing inflation and the prime interest rate. Ford also got in some uncharacteristically mean-spirited digs, remarking that the Democratic nominee, Walter Mondale, and his party believed "America's future belongs to the wishers, the wasters, the wanters, the whiners and the weak." It was all gravy, of course; that year Ronald Reagan needed little help in gaining a second term.

CARTER FALLS, THEN RISES

At the 1982 Democratic midterm convention in Philadelphia, two years after his defeat at the hands of Reagan, Jimmy Carter was snarkily described as receiving "about as much respect as a Toyota dealer in Detroit." Two years later, his name still calling up images of defeat and dithering impotence, he played only a minor part in the '84 campaign. Democrats debated how to employ Carter gingerly during that July's San Francisco convention without banishing him entirely. Carter, too, was sheepish about the prospect. "I would hope I would not be a detriment to anybody," he said, "particularly the ticket." After first offering him a humiliating extra-early time slot, the organizers arranged to move the former president to prime time. Carter obliged with a speech that was short on minutes but long on human rights. Shunned during the autumn campaign, Carter immersed himself in his newest project—helping Habitat for Humanity build houses on New York's Lower East Side and elsewhere.

By the end of the decade, Jimmy Carter's stock had begun to rise perceptibly. Indeed, almost all the Democratic candidates in 1988—the "seven dwarfs," as they were dubbed—paid their respects to him. Carter was even drafted to perform his signature mediational work to repair preconvention fissures between Michael Dukakis and that year's runner-up for the nomination, Jesse Jackson. Carter's capacity to bring people to the table was critical to getting the Democrats to fall in line. Though even he admitted that "I still have a ways to go," Carter had returned to the fold.

The 1988 convention was held in Atlanta, Georgia, giving the former president a symbolic boost and ensuring him of a choice speaking slot before his hometown fans. Exploiting the opportunity, Carter was only too eager to play to the audience and slam President Reagan's record. During those heady days of Gorbachev fever, Carter suggested that "It is a sad situation when a Soviet leader has a better image around the world than the President of the United States." But though buoyed by polls suggesting that primary voters had a favorable impression of him, Carter was still reluctant to stump for Dukakis. Claiming that former presidents should avoid active campaigning, Carter said it was better to look toward the future "and not go back eight or ten years to a previous president and resurrect old issues."

For the GOP, Carter's redemption had no bearing on its calculations; tarring the ex-president remained a staple of the party's playbook. Carter's nasty swipe at George H. W. Bush's masculinity (he called him "kind of effeminate" and "silly") amplified the Republicans' thunder. To hit-man political consultant Lee Atwater, Democratic nominee Michael Dukakis was dismissed as a "northern-fried Jimmy Carter." Carter's own convention speech included a joke that referenced both his own 1976 campaign slogan and George Bush's jibes: "My name is Jimmy Carter and I'm not running for President. Did you hear that, George?"

While Republicans pounded away at Carter, one Republican ex-president took the high road. During the 1988 contest, Gerald Ford and Jimmy Carter established the American Agenda, a forum designed to advance a policy dialogue about the most pressing needs for the next administration. In one of his many postpresidential appeals across the aisle, Ford put the long-term interest of resolving intractable problems over the short-term gain of simple party stumping. "For the first time in the nation's history," Carter said, "we'll have a bipar-

tisan effort to help heal the political divisions of our election process."
Though Ford's and Carter's efforts would have little influence on the
George H. W. Bush administration, their cooperation spoke volumes
about the former presidents' capacity to transcend party identity.

A Splintering GOP

Richard Nixon was never particularly happy with George Bush as a
candidate. He considered the former CIA director effete and unin-
spired, lacking "independence" and "drive" and "trapped by the establishment." But once Bob Dole dropped out and there was no one
else to throw his support behind, Nixon backed Bush by default. At
the summer's GOP convention in the New Orleans Superdome, Bush
delivered his "thousand points of light" speech, with its hollow pledge:
"Read my lips—no new taxes." Yet again, Richard Nixon was absent.
Fourteen years after Nixon's resignation, the party continued to keep
its distance. Nixon himself was finally back on the Sunday news programs after a twenty-year hiatus, but he remained unwelcome at the
party's main event. Still, not everyone had Nixonitis: the former president fielded two dozen requests from congressional and other political candidates seeking his presence, and the American Society of
Newspaper Editors—an organization he'd once fought bitterly—
invited him to their annual gathering.

The presidential contest of 1992 was a swan song for both Nixon
(who died in 1994) and Reagan (who carried on another dozen years).
In a contest that spotlighted a shaken Republican Party, GOP candidate Pat Buchanan stirred up angry conservatives by decrying the
alleged wantonness of American culture and firing away at both Japanese investment in the United States and free trade. Independent
candidate Ross Perot, a down-home-speaking Texas billionaire trafficking in a similar economic populism, spent $80 million to garner

19 percent of the vote. With the Cold War formally over and the Reagan era nearly concluded, new fault lines began to appear in a splintering Republican Party.

Ronald Reagan endorsed his former vice president early on, a week before the New Hampshire primary. But Reagan's gravitas was barely enough to still the Buchanan challenge: Bush eked out a narrow victory against Buchanan in the Granite State. The next month, Reagan made headlines by dismissing Bush's chances in California in the general election, reportedly saying, "He doesn't seem to stand for anything." Bush didn't believe his former boss could have said such a thing, but the story ran. Recalling Ike's remarks about Nixon in 1960, Reagan's comment pointed to an emptiness in his long-serving foot soldier, and his words threw ice water on the incumbent's campaign.

After a summer spent white-water rafting in Wyoming and receiving thumbs-up at his Mayo Clinic physical, Reagan gave what would be his final major public address at August's Republican convention in Houston. Thanks partially to the ongoing Iran-Contra investigation, Reagan's overall popularity was at a low ebb, but the former president retained godlike status among his fellow conservatives. His convention speech was vintage Reagan: homespun, cliché-laden, and factually imprecise. Refering to a celebrated campaign barb four years earlier, Reagan joked about Bill Clinton: "This fellow they've nominated claims he's the new Thomas Jefferson. Well, let me tell you something. I knew Thomas Jefferson . . . and Governor, you're no Thomas Jefferson." Rallying the troops, he stressed that "We need George Bush," and "I warmly, genuinely, wholeheartedly, support [his] re-election." And when he told the crowd in closing, "Goodbye and God bless each and every one of you," the *Washington Post* presciently wrote that the "goodbye" suggested "a haunting aura of finality."

Marring Reagan's address was one embarrassing factual error. The former president cited a sermonizing Abraham Lincoln saying, "You cannot help the wage earner by pulling down the wage payer. You cannot help the poor by destroying the rich. You cannot help permanently by doing for them what they could and should do for themselves." The passage evoked effectively the Algeresque bootstrap-pulling of the Reagan era. The only problem is that Lincoln never said it. Lincoln scholars quickly pointed out the quote's spuriousness; the words actually belonged to a Pennsylvania minister, John Henry Boetcker, born seven years after Lincoln's assassination.

Despite the mistake, Reagan's speech had its ennobling moments: "Whether we come from poverty or wealth; whether we are Afro-American or Irish-American; Christian or Jewish . . . we are all equal in the eyes of God," he said. "But as Americans, that is not enough. We must be equal in the eyes of each other." Confronting head-on the cultural-warfare rage behind Pat Buchanan's campaign, which had excited isolationist, America-first devotees—"There is a religious war going on in our country for the soul of America," Buchanan crowed—Reagan's words stood as a peace offering. Buchanan's long and over-the-top address ("the speech probably sounded better in the original German," Molly Ivins famously cracked) bumped the eighty-one-year-old Great Communicator out of prime-time viewing on the East Coast.

Holding true to his moderate convictions and recommending caution to Buchanan's fire-eaters, Gerald Ford also addressed the convention, questioning the political wisdom behind the far-right backlash. The most conservative Republicans "are losing a chance to continue policies that have been reasonably close to their goal," Ford said. "And they ought to understand that a Clinton election is going to roadblock ninety percent of what they believe in. . . . For them to be so critical and threaten to sit out the election is very, very shortsighted." Blasting media attitudes that assumed Bush was "done" or "kaput" at the convention, Ford's convention speech offered nothing groundbreaking. His sole public advice during the campaign was given a month earlier, when he recommended that Bush wipe his economic advisers' slate clean—the economy in that year's second quarter had grown by an anemic 1.4 percent—to confront the fallout directly. Bush ignored the former president's counsel.

After being rebuffed at four conventions, Richard Nixon finally received an invitation to come to Houston. He opted instead to vacation in Montauk, New York. In a race he called "the dullest of them all, with the most vapid candidates," Nixon reserved his harshest words for his former speechwriter Pat Buchanan: "He's so extreme; he's over there with the nuts. Attacking the gays was wrong, wrong, wrong. Besides, they vote too." A week before the general elections, Ronald Reagan assailed Democrats for their alleged pessimism: "Today we hear the voice of the Doomsday Democrats who gave us the turmoil of the 1960s and the malaise of the 1970s. To hear the Democratic politicians, things are so bad that down at McDonald's even the Happy Meals are depressed."

Unlike the northerners Walter Mondale and Michael Dukakis who ran on the Democratic ticket in the 1980s, southerner Bill Clinton in 1992 wasn't discomfited by Jimmy Carter's stumping for him. After a dalliance with Paul Tsongas in March, Carter endorsed Clinton in April, giving the Arkansas governor a lift. With integrity lapses dogging his public profile, Clinton needed the credibility boost, and Carter's perceived honesty proved helpful. At the summer's convention, Carter gave a well-received address that focused on the domestic ills plaguing American society: poverty, homelessness, violent crime, and unemployment. Using his native city of Atlanta as an example of the dramatic polarization between haves and have-nots, he stirred the audience: "This is a great city in America and not the slums of Haiti, Bangladesh or Uganda. And this has got to change."

AGAIN CLINTON

Seeking reelection in 1996, Bill Clinton couldn't count on another electrifying Carter speech. After his less than inspired relationship with the president during Clinton's first term in office, Carter blew off the convention, relaxing instead with Ted Turner and Jane Fonda on their Montana ranch. In a strangely emotionless statement, Carter explained, "I have participated in the last three conventions when we did not have an incumbent president to reelect, but will now follow the custom established during the past forty years by other Democratic Presidents, including Harry Truman, who only attended the first convention after he left office." Many attributed Carter and Clinton's lukewarm relationship to Carter's foreign policy adventurism and high-end moralism. (One former Clinton State Department official summarized the former president's doings thusly: "Carter was a major pain in the ass.")

With Nixon dead and Reagan incapacitated by Alzheimer's disease, in 1996 the Republican ex-presidential baton was passed to George H. W. Bush (though Jerry Ford was still on call where necessary). Bush remained largely invisible during the Clinton-Dole face-off, perhaps already thinking ahead to the possible nomination of his son in the 2000 race. (At that point it was Florida governor Jeb Bush, not his older brother, George, who was most often cited as presidential timber.) The elder Bush made a passing appearance at the convention, which nevertheless helped blunt the residual traces of Buchananite dogma that had punctured GOP unity the last time around. In an obvious gibe against the elements in his own party that had worked to undo him four years earlier, Bush declared that "leadership means standing against the voices of isolation and protectionism." And in a thinly veiled attack on the Clintons, he added, "It breaks my heart when the White House is demeaned," introducing his wife, Barbara, as "a woman who unquestionably upheld the honor of the White House." But Bush's low blows were not enough to sway conservative voters to Dole; the forty-first president's bold letter to the NRA, announcing that he was quitting the lobbying group, put a screeching halt to the very notion.

FATHER AND SON

Like the elderly John Adams, who rooted for John Quincy Adams with paternal adulation from his Massachusetts home, one hundred and seventy-six years later George H. W. Bush played a modest role in his son's first presidential campaign. The former president was generally cautious in speaking to the press during the campaign, but occasionally his close-to-the-surface resentment got the best of him. Early in the 2000 contest, when reporters mused that the Bush family could become a Kennedy-like dynasty, the former president fumed, "That really irks me. We're not like them. We don't do press about everything, and we certainly don't see ourselves as a dynasty. . . . We don't feel entitled to anything." The ex-president preferred to compare his son with the younger President Adams. "What kind of fellow was Quincy?" Bush asked. "Was he an aristocrat, or was he as good a guy as George?"

Weeks before the Philadelphia GOP convention, Bush senior offered some pointed remarks about George W.'s campaign in a Kennebunkport interview. On the subject of foreign policy, he claimed that his son "knows every bit as much about it as Clinton did," but quickly resisted commenting further on George W.'s plans: "I literally don't go into the analysis of these issues. . . . I don't give a damn. I'm out of it. I'm out of it. And I don't do television and I don't do interviews." This was, of course, a stretch: the former president agreed to several strategically timed interviews, including Larry King, using them to prick George W.'s opponent. In one example, Bush disingenuously suggested that "I'm not here to attack George's opponent at all," then proceeded to point out that Al Gore had claimed he remembered a union song from childhood that had actually been written many years later. Bush chalked up Gore's mistake to a failure in character.

George H. W. Bush made at least two key contributions to the 2000 race in the early autumn: the selection of his secretary of defense, Dick Cheney, as his son's running mate, and the massaging of the overall structure for debates (the ex-president largely looked down on debates as "show business"). Yet these efforts don't hold a candle to the support he and his allies offered during America's most severe modern electoral crisis. James Baker, one of George H. W. Bush's closest political associates, was the obvious choice to become the younger Bush's chief legal adviser and public spokesperson during the fallout over the Florida votes, and was critical in helping to ensure that the Supreme Court intervened in the recount. No less important was Jeb Bush's on-the-ground presence as governor of the state at the storm's center. When the press attacked Jeb in the midst of the fallout, his father exhaled, "I tell you as a dad: some of what has been said about him, questioning him, just kills me."

The convulsive events of September 11, 2001, less than eight months after George W. Bush took office, led to a decisive shift away from the comparatively pragmatic politics and ideas of Bush père to an aggressively pursued right-wing agenda. George H. W. Bush's influence diminished in the face of his son's neoconservative reaction to the attacks. During the 2004 New York City GOP convention, the first President Bush declined a speaking role, preferring to leave matters to his granddaughters and daughter-in-law, but was present to cheer on his son's reelection nomination.

The elder Bush did stumble his way through an interview with Jim Lehrer of the PBS *NewsHour*. When asked whether the Iraqi people were better off when Saddam Hussein was in office, he heatedly replied, "Do you really think that's what we ought to have? And I went to do a show yesterday and I said you know, somebody ought to ask this awful Michael Moore, this—you know who I'm talking about, horrible guy—and ought to ask him. . . . So they went and asked him and he kind of hedged around; he didn't say, no, we ought to have Saddam Hussein back. So I think if you phrased the question that way, there's plenty of support for the president, but if, you know, are you troubled by the way things are; there are these divisions."

Jimmy Carter spoke with greater clarity in addressing what he saw as the abysmal failures in the ongoing war in Iraq. "I never have believed that Saddam Hussein was a direct threat to the security of the United States or Great Britain or China or Japan or Australia," Carter said. "You could list fifty countries in the world that don't have democracies, and it would be better if they all had democracies. But to attack a country almost unilaterally and waste away the almost universal global support and friendship and alliances that we had after the tragedy of 9/11 is what has been done."

At the 2004 Democratic convention's opening night, Bill Clinton tried to prop up nominee John Kerry's military bona fides: "During the Vietnam War, many young men, including the current president, the vice president and me, could have gone to Vietnam and didn't," Clinton said. "John Kerry came from a privileged background. He could have avoided going too. But instead he said, 'Send me.'" Speaking the same night as Clinton, Jimmy Carter piled it on. John Kerry, he affirmed, "showed up when assigned to duty. With our allies disunited, the world resenting us, and the Middle East ablaze, we need John Kerry to restore life to the global war against terrorism." And, riffing once again on his famous tagline, Carter said, "My name is Jimmy Carter, and I'm not running for president. But here's what I will be doing: everything I can to put John Kerry in the White House with John Edwards right there beside him."

In the fall campaign, Carter urged Kerry to press home the message of a failed war: "I think that's the issue that Kerry has to pursue, because, in my opinion, President Bush has not been honest with the American people." Clinton was sidelined by probably the only thing outside of deliberate snubbing that would preclude him from participating in a Democratic political contest: open heart surgery. But even a September quadruple bypass didn't keep him down for long. Toward the end of October, Clinton willingly took to the hustings for Kerry, planting himself in key battleground spots like Arkansas that Gore had lost four years earlier. Trading on his down-home image,

Clinton said, "Let's just shell down the corn here and talk about some things no other Democrat can talk about, but heck, I ain't running for anything." He then asked the rhetorical question "How come we're not winning in Arkansas by the same margin I did?"

HILLARY CLINTON AND THE 2008 RACE

Clinton's eleventh-hour barnstorming for the stiff John Kerry proved too little too late. But ultimately it was a mere dry run for his most significant ex-presidential political engagement: becoming the front-and-center impresario for his wife's campaign in the 2008 national contest, following her hugely successful pit-stop reelection as the U.S. senator from New York.

The sometimes acrimonious, occasionally venomous, and always fraught primary season found Clinton at his best—and worst. To be sure, Clinton's presence in several key states provided a galvanizing boost to his wife's political standing. But the would-be first husband also made a series of incendiary comments that got him relegated to a backstage presence from time to time during the campaign. One of the low points came after Barack Obama beat Senator Clinton in the South Carolina primary, when Clinton insensitively compared Obama's showing to that of an earlier era's civil rights leader: "Jesse Jackson won South Carolina in '84 and '88. Jackson ran a good campaign. And Obama ran a good campaign here." Such tin-eared comments spread like brushfire on new viral media like YouTube, making the 2008 race substantively different even from its immediate predecessor.

Clinton's flubs were shocking, especially coming from a man long touted as America's consummate politician. The former president had earned any number of criticisms over the years, but racism was never one of them. The unexpectedly challenging primary season his wife encountered seemed to have flared Bill Clinton's temper and unleashed one of his signature behavioral flaws: finger-wagging. All who dared buck Hillary Clinton's campaign—former devotee Bill Richardson among them—found themselves receiving a tongue-lashing from the former president.

Clinton's example raises the question of whether a former president who has scaled the heights of humanitarian righteousness can damage his credibility by reentering the political battlefield—and yet regain his footing in some future venue. As we've seen, American postpresidential history contains plenty of fall-from-grace and rehabilitation narratives—but one is hard-pressed to think of another ex-president who has had to make so many comebacks as Bill Clinton. At the end of the 2008 primary season, Clinton declared that this "may be the last day I'm ever involved in a campaign of this kind." Only time will tell.

As for George H. W. Bush, once John McCain became the party's presumptive nominee, the forty-first president stood shoulder to shoulder with him at a Houston airport hangar photo op and offered his unqualified endorsement. "No one is better prepared to lead our nation at these trying times than Senator John McCain," he said, perhaps forgetting that his own son was still responsible for leading the nation as he spoke.

Early on, in the winter of 2007, Jimmy Carter had expressed a desire to support another member of the Nobel Prize fraternity: former vice president Al Gore. "If Al should decide to run—which I'm afraid he won't—I would support [him]. His burning issue now is global warming and preventing it. He can do infinitely more to accomplish that goal as the incumbent in the White House than he can making even movies that get—you know, that get Oscars." Carter's faith in the powers of the office was not enough to convince Gore to take the plunge. Carter—who once candidly told *Playboy* that he had lusted in his heart—had a strangely ardent reaction to Barack Obama's candidacy, saying that observing Obama's success had been "extraordinary and titillating for me and my family." Carter endorsed Obama the day he went over the top in delegates.

A RETURN TO POLITICS

~

There is a lure in power. It can get into a man's blood just as gambling and lust for money have been known to do.

Harry S. Truman

My hat's in the ring. The fight is on and I'm stripped to the buff.

Theodore Roosevelt

Perhaps it is the comfort and dignity and power without worry I like.

William Howard Taft on the Supreme Court

· · · · · ·

ALTHOUGH IT HASN'T HAPPENED IN NEARLY A CENTURY, AMERICAN history offers striking examples of former heads of state seeking another shot at the Oval Office. Several of America's past presidents viewed a return to politics as the surest way to regain influence. Among these, the most significant must be Teddy Roosevelt's intoxicating Bull Moose third-party run of 1912. Impressive for its challenge to the Republican establishment and its intensifying effect on the nexus between ideas and public policy, TR's intervention set the stage for the most thrilling contest in American presidential history.

Other, less well-remembered third-party attempts, including Martin Van Buren's Free Soil and Millard Fillmore's Know-Nothing campaigns, are reminders of the troubled social currents of antebellum America. And the one successful repeat effort has made Grover Cleveland, the sole president to garner two nonconsecutive terms of office, a staple of latter-day presidential trivia.

Today, the prospect of a modern ex-president returning to the White House, Cleveland style, seems unlikely enough; even more challenging, though, is the idea that a former president might set his sights on another political office. Having held the most powerful position in the country, how could an ex-president have any interest in a less influential post? Yet America's postpresidential history is studded with instances of presidents looking elsewhere—to Congress, the judiciary, even to local politics—to satisfy their continuing yen for politics or power.

A THIRD BITE AT THE APPLE

For a century and a half, the prospect of any president running for a third term was a thorny issue in American politics. Though it was mandated nowhere in the Constitution, George Washington's momentous decision to step down voluntarily after two terms would have immense influence going forward. Yet Washington never intended to make a broader statement by his departure: when he returned to Virginia in 1797, it was largely because he was distressed by the rapid politicization and factionalism he was witnessing around him, and felt he could no longer function as a truly national leader. But Washington's exit struck a deeper chord in a young republic that still harbored a deep fear of monarchy, and cast an enormous symbolic precedent.

Although Washington made a decisive farewell address, some Federalist leaders urged him to reconsider. A year before the 1800 election,

Connecticut governor John Trumbull tried to draft the former president to return to office. Trumbull voiced the anxieties of many of his colleagues, panicked that a Jefferson triumph would result in "a French President" coming to power. Hardened by the political realities of the day, Washington was skeptical that he could be seen as a unifying leader. "I am thoroughly convinced," he wrote, that "I should not draw a single vote from the anti-federal side." He refused to give the suggestion serious consideration. "It would be criminal," he told Trumbull, "to accept an office under this conviction." The opposition was so fiercely determined to regain power, he judged, that even if it should "set up a broomstick and call it a true son of liberty, a democrat, or give it any other epithet that will suit their purpose . . . it will command their votes in toto." Were he even to entertain the notion, Washington was convinced, "I should be charged not only with irresolution, but with concealed ambition which waits only an occasion to blaze out; and, in short, with dotage and imbecility." His mind was made up.

Eight decades passed before a former U.S. president would contemplate a third-term run. U. S. Grant might well have accepted renomination for a third term in 1876, but his party was unable to unify behind his candidacy. (Grant tried to play it cool, saying, "I do not want it any more than I did the first.") After a two-and-a-half year worldwide journey, however, Grant arrived home in September 1879 to a rousing groundswell of support for another run. Finding Rutherford B. Hayes's civil service reforms intolerable, a so-called Stalwart faction within the GOP emerged to call for another Grant administration. But not all Republicans were enthusiastic. Grant's eight years as president had polluted his heroic Civil War reputation, and his detractors were determined to block his return to Pennsylvania Avenue, going so far as to introduce constitutional amendments prohibiting a third term for any president.

Grant was attracted to the notion, but remained circumspect, preferring others to put out feelers for him. His wife, Julia Dent Grant, tried to persuade her unwilling spouse to make the trip to Chicago for the Republican convention. "How I entreated him to go on

Sunday night and appear on the floor at the convention on Monday morning—but no! He said he would rather cut off his right hand," she recalled. "I said: 'Do you not desire success?' 'Well, yes, of course,' he said, 'since my name is up, I would rather be nominated, but I will do nothing to further that end.'"

The idea of a Grant candidacy troubled and divided Republican Party loyalists. They debated the legacy of his first two terms as president: Should he be remembered for two terms of graft and misrule or for resolutely preserving party unity and safeguarding Reconstruction? Helpfully for Grant's advocates, the former president's cosmopolitan travels throughout Europe, the Far East, South Asia, and the Middle East were covered in thrilling fashion by the *New York Herald*, and the public devoured the dispatches, renewing their fascination with him. Grant's longtime aide Adam Badeau argued that the ex-president's trip abroad had made him a more capable and attractive candidate for another presidential run, as it had increased his mastery of the world and his skills at diplomacy. And Grant's great patron, Senator Roscoe Conkling, expressed his confidence that "nothing but an act of God could prevent Grant's nomination."

But other Grant supporters believed that the former president had ended his travels too soon, that instead of arriving home nine months before the Republican convention, he should have extended his trip until the last moment to preserve his allure. The months that followed saw a resurgence of criticism of his graft-addled administration, diluting the favorable feedback he'd received during his time away. Despite the obstacles, however, Grant came closer to winning a third-term major-party nomination than any other ex-president in history. At the June Chicago convention, his supporters hung on until the thirty-sixth ballot, when the deadlock between him and Maine senator James Blaine was broken by the selection of James Garfield as a compromise candidate. If Grant had attended the convention, it could have made the difference, but the former president refused to appear, despite passing through Chicago en route to Milwaukee to address a gathering of the Grand Army of the Republic. Garfield reached the magic number of three hundred seventy-nine votes, but Grant had come as close as three hundred and seven.

Twenty years later, some Democrats—especially those who disliked the antigold Nebraska populist William Jennings Bryan—quietly hoped that the twenty-second and twenty-fourth president, Grover Cleveland, might entertain a third-term nomination and take on Republican incumbent William McKinley in 1900. Comfortably ensconced in his retirement in Princeton, New Jersey, Cleveland was hardly yearning for a third term. Yet some held out hope that his antipathy for Bryan, and his growing aversion for McKinley's policies—the annexation of Hawaii, an increase in tariff rates, and the war with Spain among them—might move Cleveland to reconsider. There were even Democrats who backed Cleveland simply because he was the only Democrat who had made it to the White House since 1856. One letter to the *New York Times* waxed nostalgic about the year of Cleveland's first win: "[Cleveland] is the only statesman we have who would bring order out of chaos; rout the Bryanites, McKinleyites, Populists, Prohibitionists, expansionists, anti-expansionists, and the good Lord only knows what all, and land the old party back to its enviable position of 1884." But Cleveland never really contemplated a return to power; instead, he felt the splintered Democratic Party needed a wholesale shake-up. It would "never be in winning condition," Cleveland declared, "until we have had a regular knock-down fight among ourselves." When Bryan once again became the nominee, Cleveland steeled himself for what he believed to be his party's inevitable fate—running itself into the abyss.

JUMPING SHIP: THE THIRD PARTY

Unlike Grant and Cleveland, who faced the prospect of a third campaign with their established party, three ex-presidents dropped their traditional affiliations to gamble on a third-party run. Third parties have been generally relegated to the margins of the U.S. political system: America's winner-take-all electoral regime and the fund-raising imperatives of running for office have only cemented the role of the prevailing two-party structure in American political life. Yet at junctures in American history when the two dominant parties have failed to accommodate the political or ideological orientations of a particular candidate, third parties have emerged as an alternative. Ironically, the first former president to pursue this route was a disappointed architect of one of those two parties: Martin Van Buren.

LEAVING THE DEMOCRATS

Soundly defeated by William Henry Harrison in his 1840 bid for re-election, Martin Van Buren aspired to return to politics, and modestly informed the public of his "availability for re-nomination if the party wished him to lead it once again." Two years after his exit, Van Buren encountered an unexpected outpouring of affection following a trip spanning seven thousand miles around the American South and West. His hopes raised, the former president was encouraged once more to become the Democratic Party standard-bearer.

The sitting president, John Tyler, posed no significant obstacle. A compromise Democrat who had run as William Henry Harrison's vice president in 1840 to balance the ticket and placate the South, Tyler had ascended to the presidency after Harrison's sudden death and hoped to remain in the White House in 1844, but he had precious few backers from either side. The Whigs found him intolerable—Harrison's entire cabinet, save Daniel Webster, resigned after Tyler became president in 1841—and the Democrats failed to embrace him. He had become a man without a party. Nevertheless, together with his secretary of state, states' rights advocate John C. Calhoun, Tyler was prepared to make a run for the office on the issue du jour, the annexation of Texas and the expansion of slavery.

Van Buren appeared poised to secure the Democratic nomination. But the debate over annexing Texas, which injected the slavery problem decisively into American politics, stood between him and another term. Texas had been an independent republic since its secession from Mexico in 1836. Van Buren came out against its immediate incorporation into the union, though he meekly left open his support "if the people showed they strongly favored it." After serving during the catastrophic panic of 1837, Van Buren worried that annexation could cause profound financial strain on the country, not to mention war with Mexico.

Van Buren's opposition to annexation turned out to be political suicide. The decision frayed his relationship with his mentor and patron, Andrew Jackson, and ultimately cost him Jackson's backing. Jackson soon became the behind-the-scenes power broker of the 1844 race, switching his allegiance to Van Buren's would-be vice-presidential candidate, James K. Polk, a fellow Tennessean who favored annexation. Now, instead of Van Buren leading a ticket with Polk as his number two, Jackson helped put Polk over the top. (The Democratic Party's convention rules helped Jackson's cause: even though Van Buren nailed down a majority of delegates, a two-thirds vote was now required for nomination.) In a bitter postscript to Van Buren's defeat, John Tyler formally annexed the Republic of Texas in late February 1845, in one of his final acts as president.

Assuming that the loss was Van Buren's swan song, the Democratic Party offered him their thanks: "We hereby tender to him in his honorable retirement, the assurance of the deeply seated confidence, affection, and respect of the American Democracy." Yet Van Buren's political career wasn't quite finished. Stung by the indictment of his anti-Texas stance and the loss of those southern Democratic supporters to whom he'd once appealed in the interests of sectional harmony, Van Buren was now alienated by many in his party. Having suffered bracing defeats with the Democrats in 1840 and 1844, he began to question the viability of remaining with the party.

It would be wrong to assume that Van Buren's enlightened position on Texas turned him into a forceful antislavery voice. Abolitionists never ceased questioning the former president's authenticity; after all, Van Buren had opposed eliminating slavery in the District of Columbia and endorsed the "gag rule" squelching debate on it in Congress. But Van Buren's return to politics in his native New York kept him knee-deep in the slavery predicament. He took a politically opportunistic detour when he assumed leadership of the "Barnburners," an antislavery Democratic faction that rejected the acquisition of new slave states (and a rival to the "Hunkers," who soft-pedaled the issue). When the Barnburners bolted from the Democrats at the New York State convention to help found the Free Soil Party, Martin Van Buren became an unlikely protagonist of the new political organization.

The new party's Buffalo convention in August 1848 was attended by twenty thousand, including such luminaries as Frederick Douglass and Walt Whitman. The Free Soilers nominated Van Buren as their presidential candidate, with Charles Francis Adams, son of the sixth president, as his running mate. With its stirring guarantee of "free soil to a free people," and its bold statement that Congress had "no more power to make a slave than to make a king," the Free Soil Party drew considerable support from the antislavery sections of both the Whig and Democratic Parties (though its elevated rhetoric stopped short of extending social or political rights to freed blacks).

Van Buren received just under three hundred thousand votes—around 10 percent of the overall count—not a bad showing for a ticket that was on the ballot only in free states (with the lone exception of Virginia, where he amassed a whopping nine votes). Yet Van Buren did have an important effect on the race. By coming in second in New York and Massachusetts, the Free Soilers likely prevented the Democratic candidate, Michigan's Lewis Cass, from besting Zachary Taylor in the national race. (For this, Van Buren earned the nickname "Free

Spoiler.") Ironically, the Free Soilers had vilified Cass for appeasing the party's southern wing—the same strategy Van Buren had taken a decade earlier. Never truly at home with the antislavery party's full range of positions, Martin Van Buren was merely a transitional leader for the movement; by 1852 he had returned comfortably to his Democratic home—and the Free Soil Party was on its way to being folded into another newborn political body: the Republican Party.

From Whig to Know-Nothing

That same year saw another prominent New Yorker cast aside by his party. Millard Fillmore, who was elected Zachary Taylor's vice president in 1848 and became commander-in-chief at Taylor's death in July 1850, was shunned by the Whigs in 1852, when they nominated General Winfield Scott to oppose Franklin Pierce. Following Van Buren's precedent, Fillmore bolted the party to lead a third-party ticket in the pivotal election of 1856.

The institutional base from which Millard Fillmore would attempt his presidential run was the American Party, a nativist political organization informally called the Know-Nothings. (According to journalists of the time, when members were asked about their party activities, they claimed to "know nothing.") Catalyzed by xenophobic regional secret societies like the Order of the Star Spangled Banner, the Know-Nothing movement was a reaction to the rapid influx of Irish Catholic and German immigrants, nearly 3 million of whom came to the United States from 1845 to 1854, more than during the previous seven decades combined. The Know-Nothing platform included restricting elected office to American-born citizens, requiring all public school teachers to be Protestant, and curtailing immigration, especially from Catholic countries. The party's high-water mark came in 1854, when its membership skyrocketed and Know-Nothing candidates won several major offices, including governorships in Massachusetts, Connecticut, New Hampshire, Rhode Island, and Kentucky.

Even at its pinnacle of national attention, however, the American Party was always a fringe organization, one whose extremist views ran counter to the founding principles of the republic. How did Millard Fillmore, a former president, come to associate himself with its xenophobic excesses? The Know-Nothing Party was not an obvious home for Fillmore, and he never fully shared its ideas. By 1856, however, the party was in decline. It had moderated its rhetoric from an explicitly exclusionary platform to a relatively more acceptable conservatism that claimed "saving the union" as its first priority. At the same time, Fillmore's traditional home, the Whig Party, was splintering, with many members fleeing to enlist with the new Republican Party. With no intention of joining the Republicans—Fillmore associated the party with abolitionism—he was politically homeless and in search of a vehicle to help him regain influence. Personal factors were also in play: after the death of his wife and daughter in the early 1850s, Fillmore relished the tonic of political attention. When the Know-Nothings offered him their party nomination for 1856, he accepted without hesitation.

Although the party's nativist intolerance had softened by 1856, Fillmore still needed to play to its southern base, and some months before the election he joined the Order of the Star Spangled Banner to bolster his credentials. In several dozen election speeches he claimed that "men who come fresh from the monarchies of the old world, are prepared neither by education, habits of thought, or knowledge of our institutions, to govern America," and assailed the "corrupting influence . . . of the foreign vote." More generally, Fillmore campaigned on the intrinsic dangers of a Republican win, threatening that it would fuel discord and likely lead to civil war.

Sharing the ticket with Andrew Jackson's stepson, Andrew Jackson Donelson, Fillmore more than doubled the percentage of Van

Buren's third-party vote eight years earlier, with the bulk of his support coming from southern Whigs. He received 22 percent of the vote and carried the state of Maryland outright, likely taking away enough ballots to prevent Republican candidate James Fremont from defeating James Buchanan. But this would be his final campaign: "I consider my political career at an end," he told a friend, "and [I] have nothing further to ask."

The Bull Moose

The greatest third-party run in American history took place more than half a century later, when Teddy Roosevelt, after several disgruntled if adventure-filled years on the sidelines of power, came roaring back to accept the 1912 nomination for president on the Progressive ticket.

Roosevelt had left office after serving out the bulk of William McKinley's second term (McKinley was gunned down in Buffalo in late summer 1901) and a full term in his own right after a landslide victory in 1904. Declining to run again in 1908, he chose instead to entrust the furtherance of his public policies to his hand-picked successor, William Howard Taft.

Not until a certain Arkansan left the ranks of formal power in the first days of the twenty-first century was there such skepticism about a former chief magistrate fading gently into the postpresidential night. In April 1910 Roosevelt categorically refused to run again—"I most emphatically desire that I shall not be put in the position of having to run for the Presidency, staggering under a load which I cannot carry"—but in retrospect that was so much obvious bluster. By the second half of that year, Roosevelt was traveling by train throughout the South and West, two dozen journalists in tow, broadcasting the burgeoning political philosophy of "New Nationalism" inspired by journalist Herbert Croly's *The Promise of American Life*. In a decisive turn away from the laissez-faire precepts of the Gilded Age, Roosevelt spoke of human welfare over property rights and called on the federal government to ensure equality of opportunity, security, and justice to all. Articulating many of the underlying principles of a welfare state, the New Nationalism soon became a key ideological underpinning of the Progressive Party—and TR's sojourn around America became one extended stump speech, revealing his forward-thinking vision for the country's future.

Roosevelt's broad popularity as a writer gave him further opportunity to share his developing views with the public—including his increasing disaffection with his former protégé, William Howard Taft. TR used his bully pulpit as an occasional columnist with the weekly journal *The Outlook* to attack Taft on issues ranging from arbitration treaties to trust-busting to Taft's stratagems for securing renomination. Theories abound as to what compelled Roosevelt to return to formal political life. He craved power, to be sure, but there were other likely motivations: Roosevelt had real misgivings about the direction that Taft was taking the Republican Party, and may have joined the race out of a sense of duty to the GOP. Roosevelt also felt slighted by Taft's lack of gratitude for TR's prodigious efforts in getting him elected, and was enraged when Taft purged much of TR's former cabinet after taking office. Concluding that he'd made a poor judgment in orchestrating Taft's 1908 victory, TR set out to achieve political absolution.

Afraid that Roosevelt might stand for president again, Taft offered to give him a role in his administration and to strike particular advisers if TR endorsed his reelection bid. When TR refused, Taft brought his institutional power to bear, lobbying to stop Roosevelt from becoming temporary chair of the New York State Republican Committee in 1910, an influential position at the state convention and a useful political launching pad. (Roosevelt laughed last, however, as committee members rejected Taft's personal choice and selected Roosevelt instead.) With his flair for the dramatic, Roosevelt withheld his ultimate intentions about running, watching with delight as speculation mounted.

By the winter of 1912, TR's closest advisers unofficially acknowledged that he was seriously contemplating another presidential bid. Soon thereafter Roosevelt made things official. He arranged to be drafted by a group of governors who affirmed that he would lead the country down the path of New Nationalism, putting his faith in the new primary system to galvanize popular support (though he was less confident of his success at the Republican convention). Although many states continued to select convention delegates via caucuses, the primary process was expected to garner huge press coverage—a fact that Roosevelt gambled would be in his favor.

Roosevelt's awesome popular support catalyzed his triumphs in nine of the fourteen Republican primaries held that year, including in Taft's home state of Ohio. By the end of the primary season, however, no candidate had amassed enough delegates to put anyone over the top. And there was another complicating factor: Taft maintained an incumbent's influence at the convention, especially over the Republican National Committee, whose responsibility it was to apportion contested delegates. The result was a victory for Taft and the Republican establishment. Roosevelt cried foul, thundering against alleged fraud, and stormed out of the Chicago convention with a posse of irate Progressive backers.

Capitalizing on his momentum, Roosevelt promptly set about establishing a new political organization. Dubbed the Bull Moose Party after Roosevelt's boast that he was "as fit as a bull moose," it split from the Republican mainstream, slicing the party in two, and advanced a Progressive program that became the cornerstone of TR's third-party presidential campaign.

At the Bull Moose counterconvention six weeks later—held in the same Chicago Coliseum where the Republican convention was staged—thousands congregated to usher in a new political era. Accepting his party's nomination, Roosevelt sermonized from the mountaintop, telling his followers, "We stand at Armageddon and we battle for the Lord!" The former president had prepared a twenty-thousand-word address, but he was able to deliver only half of it, interrupted a remarkable one hundred forty-five times by a euphoric audience. The Bull Moose platform attracted reformers of varying stripes with its guarantees of pensions, health insurance, a minimum wage, and women's suffrage. (Women actually played a meaningful role in the convention's proceedings.) Yet Roosevelt's refusal to embrace full racial equality—both because he found the issue too controversial and because he believed that certain southern black districts had elected illegally chosen Taft delegates at the convention—lost him the support of some influential black leaders, most notably W. E. B. DuBois, who endorsed Woodrow Wilson on the Democratic ticket.

In an election that served as a mandate on the future of progressivism in America, all four leading candidates in the 1912 contest—Taft, Roosevelt, Wilson, and Socialist Eugene V. Debs—advocated variations on progressive themes. Roosevelt knew he was fighting an uphill battle, but the enthusiasm that met his campaign around the country, and his overwhelming determination to preach the progressive gospel, may have blunted the sting of his second-place finish. Even an assassination attempt in Milwaukee a few weeks before the election kept Roosevelt on point. "I have been shot," he declared, "but it takes more than that to kill a Bull Moose." Wounded, with a bullet less than an inch from his heart, he addressed his audience for over an hour before agreeing to go to a hospital.

As expected, Wilson bested TR with a popular vote margin of 42 percent to 27 percent (Taft and Debs received 23 percent and 6 percent, respectively) and a commanding victory in the Electoral College. Four years later the Progressive Party eagerly approached TR for another run, but this time Roosevelt refused. He swung his support behind Charles Evans Hughes in 1916, "ruthlessly smothering his own party" in the process.

ONE FINAL STAB AT EXECUTIVE POWER

Teddy Roosevelt was the last former president to run for reelection to the White House. Only one ex-president since has come close to even hinting at a return to executive power—in this case a former commander-in-chief lured into discussions about the number two position.

There was never a great deal of warmth between Gerald Ford and Ronald Reagan. One a standard-bearer for mainline moderation, the other the godfather of the post-Goldwater conservative consensus, the two men held substantively contrasting visions for the future of their Grand Old Party. In 1976 their ideological differences were played out in the electoral realm. As the party launched an uphill campaign to liberate itself from the prison house of Watergate, Reagan fought an insurgent battle to wrest the nomination from Ford, the sitting president. Few could have imagined that four years later they would nearly forge an alliance at the party's next convention.

In a behind-the-scenes negotiation at the July 1980 Republican gathering that sent shock waves throughout the American political establishment, Ford and Reagan discussed a power-sharing arrangement that would have made Ford a muscular number two and turned the chief executive office into a kind of copresidency. Ford made a series of lofty demands of the presumptive nominee, including returning Henry Kissinger to the State Department and placing Alan Greenspan at the Treasury. Reagan considered the plan, but when he presented it to his confidant and future national security advisor, Richard Allen, the latter was flabbergasted. "That is the craziest deal I have ever heard of," Allen cried. Still, the delegates at the convention thought it more intense than crazy, and the possibility of a Republican "dream ticket" sent them into a state of high excitement.

That evening Ford began to back down on some of his preconditions, specifically regarding Kissinger. ("Kissinger carries a lot of

baggage," Reagan apparently complained. "I couldn't accept that.")
In their place, Ford's team worked out a rather elaborate and potentially extraconstitutional scheme to maintain veto power over key
presidential appointments. After Ford broached the subject of the
private negotiations in a prime-time interview with Walter Cronkite,
however—infuriating Reagan—the deal fell apart. "I have to say the
answer is no," Reagan disclosed. "All this time, my gut instinct has
been that this is not the right thing." George H. W. Bush, a former rival in the primaries who had derided Reagan's fiscal policies as "voo-
doo economics," agreed to sign on to Reagan's platform, which was far
to the right of his own, and it was he who got the final call of the evening. On that steamy July night in Detroit, Jerry Ford's political career
came to a close.

CONGRESSIONAL DETOUR

The notion of Gerald Ford entering an alliance with Ronald Reagan
was shocking for a variety of reasons, not least the prospect of a former president running for a position lower than the presidency itself.
This was not always so. In the nineteenth century, a number of former presidents turned to the legislature to fulfill their political appe-
tites. While not quite a conventional pathway, the prospect of a former
president serving in Congress was not yet the unimaginable detour it
would surely be today. Easily the most distinguished case is John
Quincy Adams, who made an astounding leap from an ineffective and
beleaguered president to a transformative member of the U.S. House
of Representatives. Adams's achievements may earn him equal standing with Jimmy Carter for the title of our finest former president.

Adams left power in a hurry. Duplicating his father's cut-and-run
example almost three decades earlier, Adams boycotted the March
1829 inauguration of his antagonist, Andrew Jackson, and headed out-

side Washington, where his family had taken up temporary residence. After enduring four years of withering attacks from Jacksonians who believed he had robbed them of the 1824 election in a "corrupt bargain" with Henry Clay, the departing president was depleted and demoralized. He considered that in deciding to skip Jackson's ceremony and to leave the city altogether, he was like "a nun taking the veil"; he expected it to represent his final exit from public life.

Adams's first year out of office, marked by depression and turmoil—exacerbated by the suicide of his eldest son—contributed to a self-described descent "into dejection, despondency, and idleness," although his voluminous reading and occasional writing did provide a salve. He especially enjoyed the commentaries of Cicero, who had once influenced the young revolutionaries of his father's generation, and now guided Adams in interpreting the false steps of his successor.

Then, to his great surprise, the former president's Quincy neighbors and the local *Boston Courier* began bandying his name about as a potential future member of Congress. Having forsaken the White House not more than eighteen months earlier, Adams warned that he had "not the slightest desire to be elected," but he wouldn't rule it out. With that door left open, outgoing representative Joseph Richardson pressed Adams to take his seat. Ambivalent about the prospect, Adams was nonetheless overcome by the goodwill of the gesture and assented to run. After walloping his opposition, Adams found himself in November 1830 elected to the Twenty-second Congress. His lingering resentment toward the parvenu Jacksonians and his anguish at having been "deserted by all mankind" were, at least for a time, assuaged by victory. With renewed spirit—"no election or appointment conferred upon me ever gave me so much pleasure"—sixty-three-year-old John Quincy Adams was about to embark on one of the most remarkable second acts in the annals of the postpresidency.

The slavery question was where Adams would make his most formidable mark. Though he was never the staunchest public opponent of the peculiar institution, he and his father were the only presidents in the country's first half century not to own human property. The younger Adams judged slavery a "great and foul stain," but he remained troubled by abolitionists, who he believed destabilized the union by their sectarian posturing. In this he was no different from his father, or even Abraham Lincoln for much of his life. Adams stood resolute against slavery's expansion but steered clear of openly calling for its eradication. Only when he came to the House did his position begin to shift. Focusing squarely on the constitutional guarantee to petition Congress, Adams immersed himself in the defining question of the day.

In the first half of the nineteenth century, Congress often listened to citizens' written petitions entreating it to address a particular issue. In the early 1830s, with the founding of William Lloyd Garrison's abolitionist journal *The Liberator*, petitions around slavery, calling especially for the termination of the institution in the District of Columbia, started to flood the House. By 1836, unhinged by the increasingly vocal antislavery challenges, southern Democrats passed a "gag rule" tabling any further petitions on the question. It remained in force for eight years. During this period Adams worked tenaciously, and usually alone, using parliamentary maneuvers to circumvent the closure of debate and ensure that the petitions of antislavery advocates were not silenced. The gag rule's repeal became his signature congressional issue.

Though he declined to describe himself as an abolitionist, Adams's efforts turned him into one of abolitionism's greatest champions in Congress. His "adopted cause," wrote one historian, "transformed him into a debater so impassioned, so mischievous, so stubborn, and so radical, that his foes and even some friends wondered at times if he had lost his sanity." After eight years of his brilliant and sustained advocacy, the House in December 1844 voted to overturn the gag rule. South Carolina's Francis Pickens, who opposed Adams's superhuman labors for years and who had motioned to censure him just two years before, offered recognition at Old Nestor's final triumph: "Well, that is the most extraordinary man on God's footstool." Adams had become an abolitionist in spite of himself.

In the midst of his fight over the gag rule, Adams's antislavery bona fides swelled further when he agreed to serve as codefense counsel in the famous *Amistad* trial. The case involved several dozen kidnapped Africans who were being transported on a Portuguese slave ship to different Cuban ports when they mutinied in 1839, killing a captain and cook. Rather than sailing back to Africa, as they had hoped, the schooner was seized off Long Island Sound and the Africans imprisoned in New Haven, Connecticut, on murder charges. The incident ignited a firestorm of protest between the Spanish government, which sought their extradition to Cuba, and abolitionists, who demanded their return to Africa.

After federal and circuit courts ordered their repatriation, an anxious Martin Van Buren, up for reelection in 1840, had his U.S. Attorney appeal the case, sending it to the Supreme Court. Adams agreed to join the esteemed New York abolitionist Lewis Tappan as assistant counsel to Roger Baldwin on the case and spent the final months of 1840 avidly preparing. Not having argued a case before the Court in thirty years, and fearful of its composition—all but two of its justices had been nominated by Jackson and Van Buren—Adams knew he would have his work cut out for him.

In two marathon defense arguments that together lasted more than nine hours, Adams argued that the passengers aboard the *Amistad* were illegally enslaved and should be freed. Celebrated as "old man eloquent" for his passionate advocacy against the gag rule, Adams bested his performance during the hearing. Stressing the violations of the Africans' liberty, Adams implored, "The moment you come to the Declaration of Independence, that every man has a right to life and liberty, as an inalienable right, this case is decided. I ask nothing more on behalf of these unfortunate men, than this Declaration." Adams prevailed: the thirty-eight surviving Africans were liberated and allowed to return home.

As historian Eric McKitrick has noted, John Quincy Adams's nearly decade-long struggle to strike down the gag rule, and his wondrous defense in the *Amistad* case, "made his exertions more than those of any public person responsible for converting the Northern public to the antislavery temper it brought to the choosing of Lincoln in 1860."

EX-PRESIDENTIAL APOSTATE

On most of the key issues of the early nineteenth century—slavery certainly among them—John Quincy Adams's worldview stood light years apart from John Tyler's. The despairing heir to the founding generation, and a man who loathed and valiantly challenged the institution of slavery, Adams had only one thing in common with Tyler: both chose to serve as congressional representatives after leaving the White House. But even there the similarities are faint: where Adams served in the U.S. House of Representatives, Tyler offered his legislative service to a different body: the Confederate States of America.

Tyler's ascension to the presidency, upon the April 1841 death of William Henry Harrison, had by no means been a foregone conclusion. There was not yet a constitutional provision for the vice president to assume power upon the death of the chief executive. Among those who rejected Tyler's rise was John Quincy Adams, who belittled him as the country's "acting president," and more pointedly, "His Accidency." Adams had few charitable words for the new head of state, smearing Tyler as "a political sectarian, of the slave-driving, Virginian, Jeffersonian school."

Upon retiring to Sherwood Forest, his Charles City, Virginia, plantation-estate, in 1845, Tyler assumed the pose of elder statesman, proudly voicing his judgments on the preservation of the Union and the future of slavery. Vocal in his support for territorial expansion and the safeguarding of the peculiar institution, Tyler's private life meshed consistently with his broader vision: not only did the number of slaves he owned apparently increase over time, he also refused to manumit any at the time of his death.

A year after John Brown's famous raid on Harper's Ferry terrified the slaveholding class, Tyler fantasized that he might have a shot at the 1860 Democratic nomination. It was a delusion; Tyler's candidacy never ignited. Instead, his worst fears were realized by Lincoln's electoral triumph. Tyler agonized about the president-elect's intentions, leaving him deeply anxious about Virginia's future.

In the wake of the election, Tyler watched as the Deep South embarked on its secessionist course. In December 1860, in the hope of stemming the secessionist tide, Kentucky senator John Crittenden sponsored a series of amendments that would effectively sanction slavery forever in the South and return the country to the status quo ante of the Missouri Compromise, where slavery was ensured south of the 36° 30' parallel. Tyler backed the so-called Crittenden Compromise, but Lincoln's strict opposition to its amendments, and their eventual defeat in the House and Senate, sealed matters—and brought the nation that much closer to war.

When the Compromise failed, Tyler spearheaded a last-ditch attempt to quell sectional hostilities at the Washington Peace Conference of January 1861. When that, too, fell short, the former president gave up on his quixotic hope to save the Union and joined up with the Virginia State Convention to press the case for secession. Writing to his wife, Tyler braced himself for the upcoming conflict: "Virginia has severed her connection with the Northern hive of abolitionists and takes her stand as a sovereign and independent state. Do dearest, live as frugally as possible . . . trying times are before us."

Following the transfer of the Confederate capital from Montgomery to Richmond in May 1861 (in which he had a hand), Tyler was unanimously selected to the provisional Confederate Congress. He would be no passive bystander. With great fervor, he (unsuccessfully) urged Confederate troops to storm Washington, D.C. To many, Tyler was now an apostate and traitor.

In the fall of 1861, Tyler was elected a member of the Congress of the Confederate States. Before he could take office, however, he died suddenly in his Richmond hotel room. His funeral there was an occasion for public mourning, with a one-hundred-and-fifty-carriage cortege leading the ceremonies. Tyler's passing raised nary a stir in Washington, however: no flags at half-mast, no formal proclamation from Lincoln, none of the spectacle that usually accompanies presidential deaths. The *New York Times* published a frank obituary: "He ended his life suddenly . . . going down to death amid the ruins of his native State. He himself was one of the architects of its ruin; and beneath that melancholy wreck his name will be buried, instead of being inscribed on the Capitol's monumental marble."

A BRIEF RETURN TO THE SENATE

Southerner Andrew Johnson shared with John Tyler several attributes: he was chosen vice president as a means to achieve unity and appease the opposition; he bounded to the presidency following his superior's death; and he was later elected to be a member of Congress, in his case to the U.S. Senate. For Andrew Johnson it was an unlikely transition. During his time as president, Johnson squared off against a Republican Party that scorned him, impeached him, and came within one vote of forcing his resignation. After the war, Johnson's assuagement of lingering rebel anxieties, and his overriding desire to reintegrate the South expeditiously, fell afoul of Radical Republicans who placed a primacy on justice. Failing to consider political equality for freed slaves a meaningful postwar objective, and pardoning all except the Confederacy's top brass, Johnson was never a realistic candidate for the presidential nomination in 1868.

Though he initially pledged to remain a private citizen after his presidency, Johnson's passion for politics never dimmed, and before long he had clearly set his sights on regaining his former seat in the U.S. Senate. "I had rather have the vindication of my state," Johnson said, "by electing me to my old seat in the Senate of the United States than to be monarch of the grandest empire on earth." After losing congressional races in 1870 and 1872, Johnson was at last selected by Tennessee legislators to return to the Senate on the fifty-fifth ballot in 1874, defeating three Confederate generals. Johnson had skillfully balanced the interests of moderate Republicans, former Whigs, and Democratic voters, steadfastly defending the legacy of Lincoln while appeasing conservative sections through the rhetoric of white supremacy. He became the only former president ever to serve in the Senate and was administered his oath by Vice President Henry Wilson, who had once voted for his impeachment. The *New York Herald* opined that "In the Senate [Johnson] will be of greater use to the country than he was in the Presidency."

Many expected the seventy-one-year-old Johnson to storm back and do battle with his dreaded Republican foes, who he believed had humiliated him and derailed his career. By that time, however, only thirteen of the thirty-five senators who had voted to convict him in 1868 were still serving in the upper house. And Johnson himself would serve only a few months in this final run: after using his new office to assail President Grant for fecklessness, he died while traveling back to Nashville that July.

HOOVER IN CONGRESS?

Among the twentieth century's former presidents, only Herbert Hoover gave any meaningful consideration to attaining a congressional seat after his stint on Pennsylvania Avenue. In early 1945, word came that Hiram Johnson, the elderly senator from California, was ailing. A fellow isolationist, and Roosevelt's vice presidential candidate on the Bull Moose line in 1912, Johnson had represented California for three and a half decades. If Johnson should expire, Hoover let it be known, he could be interested in assuming the seat.

When Hiram Johnson died that summer, the *New York Times* came out for Hoover. Suggesting that "his disinterested counsels would be of the highest value in the national capital," the *Times* called for California governor Earl Warren to appoint the former president to Johnson's seat. (Mindful of Hoover's special talents as World War II drew to a close, the paper added that "there is no greater problem facing this country today than that of feeding the world . . . and there is no man who has more to contribute on the subject than Mr. Hoover.")

Herbert Hoover would not have been Hiram Johnson's choice to succeed him. Journalist Drew Pearson reported that an ailing Johnson, "under an oxygen tent in the Naval Hospital," sparked a momentary recovery when he received "word that Governor Warren would appoint . . . Hoover to his Senate seat." But the ex-president was always a long shot. Warren ended up selecting William Knowland, the son of an influential publisher who had aided Warren's career. Hoover tried to disguise his frustration, but Knowland's appointment was a disappointment. Four years later, when New York governor Thomas E. Dewey offered Hoover the chance to finish Robert F. Wagner's Senate term after health concerns caused Wagner to vacate his slot, Hoover declined outright.

The Third Branch of Government

Congress and the White House have not been the only means past presidents have seized to reacquire formal institutional power. William Howard Taft's trajectory in the 1920s offers a unique example of an ex-president taking the helm of another branch of government entirely: the Supreme Court. In Taft's case, it represented the culmination of a lifetime's ambition.

"There is no function more important in our government than that which the Supreme Court performs," Taft once said. During his single term as president, Taft named six justices to the court—a record number—surpassing all presidents before him save George Washington. Knowing his reverence for the court, Teddy Roosevelt offered Taft several opportunities to join the august body. In 1902, when Taft was governor of the Philippines, Roosevelt first advanced Taft's nomination as associate justice, but Taft said he felt morally compelled to decline, asserting that he would be abandoning his responsibilities to the Filipino people by leaving the islands. Four years later, when a second chance arose, TR was once again prepared to offer Taft an associate judgeship. This time, Taft—now returned to Washington as Roosevelt's secretary of war—tendered a special plea to Roosevelt: "I have said to my wife several times that I had become so absorbed in the work that I concluded . . . not [to] seek . . . any appointment to the Bench unless you offered me the Chief Justiceship which is so great an office that I could not resist the temptation." Roosevelt said no. Taft still thought the possibility of his future nomination was not foreclosed, but he began to fret "that this which I am now declining will be my last chance."

There were additional militating factors. Taft's ambitious family didn't share his enthusiasm for the Court; instead, they wished to see him anointed as Roosevelt's heir apparent. A Supreme Court appointment, his wife felt sure, would be a career-ending capstone that would destroy his White House future, and she made clear her disappointment at the idea that he "should be shelved on the bench at [his] age." Even Taft's mother stepped in, reminding her son of Senator Roscoe Conkling's quip that he "preferred some other mode of burial" than relocation to the Supreme Court.

After his presidency, Taft momentarily considered the idea of running for Congress with an eye toward serving on the House Judiciary Committee. Afraid that the move would look like an opening salvo toward a 1916 presidential run, however, he quickly dismissed the idea and settled into his teaching position at Yale Law School.

But Taft's yearning to serve as chief justice never faded. With the Republican triumph in 1920, and the increasingly fragile health of Chief Justice Edward Douglass White, whom Taft had promoted during his own presidency (leading later historians to speculate about his motives), Taft's aspiration appeared within reach. President-elect Warren Harding consulted extensively with Taft on the makeup of the Court, and in 1920 he enticed him with an offer of at least an associate justice position. As he had with Roosevelt, however, Taft held out for the highest rank. When White died, two months into Harding's term, the opportunity finally presented itself. Praising his "progressively conservative and conservatively progressive attitude," after several weeks of consideration Harding nominated Taft to his dream job. Confirmed overwhelmingly by the Senate, the former president spoke humbly and candidly of his personal fulfillment: "It has been the ambition of my life to be Chief Justice, but now that it is gratified I tremble to think whether I can worthily fill the position and be useful to the country."

During his nine-year tenure on the Court, Taft worked vigorously to fortify the judicial branch through streamlining and reorganization. His reforms invested more power in appellate courts, created a uniform approach to judicial procedure, centralized the federal judicial administration, reduced the Court's workload, and set in motion the Court's departure from its crammed quarters in the Capitol building. Taft's progressive program to modernize the Supreme Court was of considerable influence in the years ahead.

The former president's legal philosophy was less surprising. In his two hundred and fifty-three opinions, he proved himself an unambiguously conservative jurist who treated property rights as sacrosanct and put his faith in immutable natural law. Taft was an obvious counterpart to the Court's more liberal justices, such as Louis Brandeis. But the former president's moral rigidity did little to hamper his otherwise freewheeling attempts to influence court appointments. Circuit Court Judge Arthur Denison joked that Taft never allowed a "merely technical canon of propriety [to] prevent him from using his influence in what he thought the right direction." And indeed Taft was eager to insert himself subtly into the judicial selection process, leaning on the three Republican presidents of the decade—Harding, Coolidge, and Hoover—to accept his counsel.

In one of his more dubious moments on the bench, Taft—vacationing in Canada at the time—refused to allow the cause célèbre of working-class Italian anarchists Nicola Sacco and Bartolomeo Vanzetti to be heard by his Court. He even crossed the border into America to block the appeal officially. Sacco and Vanzetti were electrocuted as planned. Though many had criticized their trial as devoid of due process, meager in civil liberties protection, and lacking in empirical evidence, Taft was vocal in his support of the verdict, going so far as to label Sacco and Vanzetti's prominent advocate, Felix Frankfurter, "an expert in attempting to save murderous anarchists from the gallows or the electric chair." After their deaths, John dos Passos offered his poignant lament: "All right, we are two nations."

Taft retired from the Court just a month before his death in March 1930. Toward the end of his life, when asked about his accomplishments, he mused, "I don't remember that I ever was President."

LOCAL POLITICS

Not every former president who endeavored to reengage in the political world sought a high-stakes position at the federal level. Several found satisfaction working without fanfare to influence politics locally. At the advanced age of eighty-four, the senior John Adams became a delegate to the 1820 Massachusetts convention, where he helped revise the state's constitution—which he had written forty years before. At the convention Adams proposed an amendment to repeal the state's limitations on religious freedom. Though it failed to pass, the move did win him the kind words of Thomas Jefferson, who commended his old comrade on his struggle for the "advance of liberalism." At his life's end, Adams's views on religion and liberty had grown ever closer to Jefferson's.

James Madison and James Monroe participated as delegates to their own constitutional convention in Virginia in 1829, held in the Jefferson-designed capitol building in Richmond, with Monroe serving as its official chair. At the respective ages of seventy-eight and seventy-one, Madison and Monroe tried to broker a compromise between Tidewater slaveholders and those from the state's western counties who were bent on fairer representation. (The slaveholding Tidewater region was greatly overrepresented, a reflection of the South's general overrepresentation in Congress.) Madison's trip there was perhaps the longest distance he traveled outside of Montpelier during his years out of office. In his sole address, he stood by his belief in the constitutional mandate that each slave should be counted as three-fifths of a citizen. It would be his last political appearance.

THE GREATER GOOD

Public Service and Humanitarianism

Being a politician is a poor profession. Being a public servant is a noble one.

Herbert Hoover

You can sit there and feel sorry that you're not president anymore, or you can find some way to use what you know, and who you know, and what you know about how to do things, and go out there and do all the good you can.

Bill Clinton

Unless you're Shirley MacLaine, you only get one shot at this life.

George H. W. Bush

· · · · · ·

IN JANUARY 2005, PRESIDENT GEORGE W. BUSH ASKED HIS FATHER, George H. W. Bush, and Bill Clinton to travel to Southeast Asia as goodwill ambassadors after the region was devastated by a tsunami. In doing so, he helped revive the underexploited tradition of recruiting former presidents to engage in public service. On frosty terms since Clinton's thumping of Bush in the 1992 election, the two former presidents soon fashioned an unlikely postpresidential partnership, and acquired a reputation for working together in the aftermath of large-scale natural disasters.

There is "something refreshingly American about watching old foes . . . put down their political swords to forge a friendship and find a common purpose," one newspaper suggested at the time. That claim may be open to debate—for every hatchet buried in American politics, it's easy to think of dozens that were brandished until death—but the collaboration between Clinton and Bush sparked new hope for bipartisan postpresidential humanitarian contributions. On the first leg of their trip, the elder Bush mustered only modest, typically staccato comments about his traveling companion: "When it comes to helping people, politics is aside. . . . We were political adversaries. The current president [Bush 43] and he [also] don't always see eye-to eye on issues. But that is not what's important here." By the time of their return, however, the "odd couple," as Barbara Bush amiably described them, had become downright chummy. Sigmund Freud even played a cameo role. Describing Clinton, twenty-two years his junior and raised without a biological father, Bush suggested that "maybe I'm the father he never had."

For Bill Clinton, his Southeast Asia activities were only beginning. Capitalizing on Clinton's special ability to raise consciousness and cash for a cause, Kofi Annan named him the UN's special envoy for tsunami relief. Then, in late August 2005, as Clinton was pursuing his UN assignment, Hurricane Katrina struck the U.S. Gulf Coast. Though the Bush administration received ferocious criticism for its inept handling of the crisis and recovery, it did receive praise for calling the Clinton–Bush 41 team back into action.

Clinton and Bush's most significant achievement lay in their astonishing fund-raising performance on behalf of the storm victims. The former presidents had originally set out to encourage giving to established aid organizations, but soon vast sums of money began streaming into their offices, and they recognized the tactical advantage of creating charities in their own names. "Bush and Clinton have created a new post-presidential brand," one magazine trumpeted, "and put it to work sealing the cracks between public need and public aid." The joint fund they assembled for the tsunami disaster, the Bush-Clinton Tsunami Relief Fund, was relatively small; most of the more than $1 billion they helped raise went directly to mainline groups. In the aftermath of Hurricane Katrina, however, the past presidents established a fund in their names from the outset, and the Bush-Clinton Katrina Fund brought in an estimated haul of more than $130 million for schools, state governments, and religious institutions on the Gulf Coast, assuming third place in Katrina fund-raising behind only the Red Cross and the Salvation Army.

Inevitably, some questioned both Clinton's and Bush's motives in taking on the shared responsibility of relief czar. Bush's participation in such high-profile public service activity did allow him to lend a lifeline to his son during one of the lowest points of Bush 43's second term; his involvement with the righteous cause doubtless also burnished a postpresidential legacy that had largely revolved around the Carlyle Group. The collaboration with Clinton may have additionally discouraged the still popular Democrat from making withering attacks on his son.

On Bill Clinton's part, some assumed that his wife's presidential ambitions factored into his calculations. Clinton's new friendship with the Bush clan—he took photo opportunities with the Bushes, who even dubbed him "42" in a nod to his place in the presidential sequence—helped to soften the wellspring of aversion many in the GOP still felt for the Clintons. At a Philadelphia award ceremony for the two ex-presidents, Clinton offered a gushing tribute to his new companion: "I always liked and I always admired I can now tell you, and may all the Democrats forgive me this close to the election, I love George Bush, I do."

Clinton's deputy in his tsunami work, Eric Schwartz, dismissed those who saw Clinton's activities as related to his wife's political future and his own personal legacy. The tsunami work "came at some sacrifice to other objectives that Clinton had," Schwartz said, "and took time away from further high-visibility efforts. And when you look at what Clinton achieved—playing a significant role leading the multiple players in the recovery effort—it was hardly the work of someone guided purely by self-interest."

Despite their improbable comradeship, Clinton and Bush never lost sight of their personal and political objectives. Former president Bush made it clear that, just as Bill Clinton's "not going to tiptoe about his differences with the president, I wouldn't tiptoe with my differences with Hillary." When Bill mused that Hillary's earliest priority as president would be "to send me and former President Bush . . . around the world to tell them that America is open for business and cooperation again," Bush's office responded sharply that he had "never discussed an 'around-the-world-mission' with either former President Bill Clinton or Senator Clinton, nor does he think such a mission is warranted. . . ."

Forgotten Reformers

Rutherford B. Hayes: Education For All

Whenever a conversation turns to postpresidential public service or humanitarian activity, the name that gets top billing is inevitably that of Jimmy Carter. And for good reason: Carter's example is inspiring. Yet his achievements form only one piece of the historical record; a host of other ex-presidents have turned to charitable work, often with an unassuming attitude and momentous results.

A passionate advocate for the underprivileged, Rutherford B. Hayes would undoubtedly wish to be remembered for his forward-thinking reforms involving universal education and social justice. Instead, the nineteenth president's legacy is inextricably tied to his scandalous win in the election of 1876, in which a backroom deal elevated him to power under a compromise that removed the remaining federal troops occupying the post–Civil War South. A gash on his reputation, the devastating results of Reconstruction's formal termination largely obscure Hayes's courageous and munificent postpresidential record.

Upon returning to his home in Fremont, Ohio, Hayes shared with friends his views on the proper role of an ex-president: "Let him . . . promote the welfare and the happiness of his family, his town, his State, and his country." Such work, he prophesied, would yield "more individual contentment and gratification" than public life. Hayes soon began devoting much of his energy to what would become his signature issue—universal public education, in the first instance for African Americans. Affirming that "the American people have a grave and indispensable duty to perform with respect to the millions of men and women among our countrymen whose ancestors our fathers brought forth from Africa to be held in bondage," Hayes viewed education as the nation's great equalizer. Only by expanding educational opportunities, he believed, could the social disenfranchisement of black Americans be effectively remedied.

Hayes deemed the public school a core institution, one that should instill in freed slaves "the thrift, the education, the morality, and the religion required to make a prosperous and intelligent citizenship." Identifying tangible ways to press the issue that he modestly described as his "hobby," Hayes agreed to serve as president of the board of the Slater Fund and trustee of the Peabody Fund, two organizations dedicated to broadening access to higher education (the former for southern blacks, the latter for both blacks and whites). Like Hayes, the agents behind Slater and Peabody recognized that the South itself had inadequate resources to provide the necessary technical educational skills to its populace, and saw a need for capital infusions from other sectors. Though Hayes's name brought a certain cachet to the two institutions, the former president was no figurehead.

He took an active role in decision-making and traveled throughout the South visiting schools that received foundation grants to evaluate their levels of success. W. E. B. Dubois, the great educator and historian, was one beneficiary of such funds.

Hayes's ethics derived principally from a Victorian paternalism, whose overriding societal objective was the improvement of individual morality. Uplift was the leitmotif of his calls for reform. "These millions who have been so cruelly degraded must be lifted up," Hayes emphasized, "or we ourselves will be dragged down." Hayes may have been "a bit too aware of his own rectitude," as historian Stanley Elkins once suggested, but the former president was hardly unique in that respect. Other Gilded Age educational reformers sounded the same notes—including the Slater Fund's founder, who said that the fund's mission was the "uplifting of the lately emancipated population of the Southern States." In Hayes's view, social change lay not in the passing of legislation and laws, but in the strengthening of a person's character; individuals could always change for the better. Of course, Hayes's good intentions were not always realistic; his faith that improved educational mobility would result in increased social harmony was utopian at best—racist violence and Jim Crow waved good-bye to all that.

Education may have been Hayes's greatest interest, but he also filled his time with other pressing social concerns. Observing the abysmal state of America's prisons, Hayes saw penal reform as a natural complement to vocational education. Committed to the ideas that only manual skills could deter recidivism and that prisons themselves were breeding grounds for crime, Hayes became president of the National Prison Reform Association, a network of advocates dedicated to fundamental change in the deplorable conditions of the incarcerated. (The group also boasted Teddy Roosevelt as its treasurer.) Hayes's attention to prisoner welfare, hardly a subject with mass public appeal, was courageous.

In an 1888 address to the Prison Congress in Boston, Hayes linked crime to conditions of poverty and to the consolidation of wealth in the hands of the few. He came to see that an explicit focus on individual character was inadequate for addressing structural disparities, particularly when so many lacked economic opportunity. Indeed, the last years of his life were animated by a "protoprogressive" spirit and a deepening critique of the vast divide between rich and poor. His grievances against the Gilded Age establishment—in which "government of the people, by the people, and for the people" had become "government of corporations, by corporations, and for corporations"— spoke to a broader disenchantment with callous, unfettered capitalism. The former president began to view rapid capital accumulation as the bane of American society and urged the curbing of its malevolent excesses. While he declined to embrace the collectivism championed by later progressives, Hayes did support state regulation of business, particularly corporations, and restrictions in areas such as inheritance. Never seeing himself among the ranks of modern reformers, he admired their work from afar and understood their aspirations.

One area in which Hayes did distinguish himself as a reformer was the crusade against government patronage, which he made a centerpiece of his White House term and carried on into his postpresidency. In his first months out of power, Hayes kept close watch over successor James Garfield's civil service program, critiquing the new president's weakness for giving legislators sway over political appointments. Fearful that Garfield was disavowing the civil service policy he once struggled to introduce, Hayes stressed that "the capital mistake is to attempt to build up the administration or a party by the use of the offices as patronage. The offices should be filled for the good of the service. Country first and party afterwards."

Hayes's concerns over Garfield's early policies were nothing compared with the dread he felt at Chester Arthur's ascension to power. As president, Hayes had fired Arthur from his position as customs collector for the Port of New York in 1878. After Garfield's death, Arthur—a compromise vice presidential candidate championed by patronage-happy Republicans such as Roscoe Conkling—was a troubling prospect as commander-in-chief. Hayes could hardly have imagined that within two years Arthur would sign the Pendleton Act, sweeping away the spoils system and establishing a merit basis for most federal employees.

Without Fanfare

Some former heads of state tapped for public service did so under the radar. Two examples have their roots in labor disputes of the early twentieth century. In the midst of an acrimonious coal miners' strike in 1902, President Teddy Roosevelt received a letter from Grover Cleveland proposing a way to end the standoff. Surprisingly, Cleveland cautioned against the use of force, chastened perhaps by his own notorious breaking of the Pullman strike eight years earlier, when he had sent in twelve thousand U.S. Army troops on the premise that the strike interfered with U.S. mail delivery. Eyeing an opportunity to employ the former president, Roosevelt quickly appointed Cleveland to chair a commission to mediate the conflict. Cleveland agreed to investigate the situation, though not to arbitrate, but his willingness was soon moot: the management side of the conflict proclaimed Cleveland too radical and refused to participate if the former president were involved. Roosevelt acquiesced and created a Cleveland-less panel to meet the mine owners' demands.

William Howard Taft had greater success as an ex-president on the industrial relations front. Before his Supreme Court appointment, Taft served as joint chairman of the National War Labor Board, created by Woodrow Wilson in April 1918 to prevent possible strikes in strategic military-related industries during World War I. Although quelling labor disputes was the board's priority, its principles included upholding workers' rights to organize, to receive a living wage, to adequate health and safety regulations, and to equal pay for equal work.

Wilson appointed Taft at the behest of employers, but the idea of a conservative foe of organized labor assuming a nonpartisan position resolving industrial disputes was troubling. Yet Taft took his dispassionate role seriously and traveled the country meeting with workers and management, enlightening himself on the actual conditions of the American proletariat. (Though not dramatic, Taft's experience with the NWLB did complicate his thinking upon moving to the nation's highest court.) Wilson's respect for Taft's leadership during his fourteen-month tenure, and the board's constructive recommendations, made the NWLB an effective institutional lever through the war's conclusion.

Herbert Hoover: Global Food Relief Czar

Taft and Hayes both profited from the gravitas of the postpresidency to push ahead a reformist agenda after leaving office. Herbert Hoover's humanitarian triumphs had their origins long before his presidency; in fact, it was his reputation as a humanitarian that helped to propel his political career. Raised as a Quaker with a strong commitment to service, Hoover considered his role in wartime food distribution to be his most significant contribution to public life. He began that work in 1914, when the American ambassador to Britain encouraged him to take on the chairmanship of the Commission for Relief in Belgium. The country's reliance on imported food had made mass starvation an appalling possibility, as Belgium stood at the mercy of an invading German army and a British naval blockade. Looking back at his decision to assume leadership, Hoover reflected, "I did not realize it at the moment, but on August 3, 1914, my engineering career was over forever. I was on the slippery road of public life."

Working in concert with the Belgian Comité National, Hoover intimately acquainted himself with the mechanics of food importation and distribution, helping to feed 9 million people in Belgium and northern France over a two-and-a-half-year period. His achievements made him internationally celebrated and led Woodrow Wilson to establish for him the position of Food Administrator during the remaining days of the war. (In that post, Hoover encouraged the patriotic conservation of foodstuffs for soldiers with such protocols as "meatless Tuesdays" and "wheatless Mondays and Wednesdays.") Hoover parlayed his success into becoming chief of postwar relief in Europe, responsible for the continent's overall food distribution and for shoring up the associated transportation and communications infrastructure.

In the next decade, Hoover directed the American Relief Administration's assistance to the Soviet Union during its postrevolution famine, and aided homeless victims from the Mississippi flood of 1927. But the panegyrics for the "Great Humanitarian," a designation he earned specifically because of his wartime relief work, abruptly ended during his years in the White House. As president, Hoover's attempt to support the victims of the great drought of 1930–31 in the American South was harshly criticized because of his reluctance to make it a federal responsibility and his reliance on an unwilling American Red Cross to oversee the work. The resulting effort, decentralized and poorly organized, left thousands destitute and hungry. Hoover's plan for ameliorating the effects of the drought were symptomatic of his broader failing to respond adequately to the oncoming Depression. His rigid attachment to the tenets of individualism and voluntarism—what Richard Hofstadter disparaged as "his loyalty to the American folklore of self-help"—was a dead-wrong strategy for a country in need of strong federal assistance.

The damage to Hoover's reputation did little to blunt his readiness to reengage in international humanitarian work after he left the White House, and the former president made an impressive comeback during a wartime period of exceptional need. When FDR refused to extend food relief to the Poles after the German invasion of September 1939, private citizen Herbert Hoover quickly established his own organization, the Commission for Polish Relief, to oversee food distribution. Hoover's isolationist inclinations in no way affected his commitment to relief activities, and his agency dispatched food and clothing to families living in ghettos as well as to the Polish government-in-exile. The commission was instrumental in feeding hundreds of thousands of Poles under German occupation from 1939 to 1941.

Stopping hunger in Europe remained Hoover's permanent idée fixe, despite political barriers. In a controversial move, Hoover proposed that the National Committee to Feed the Small Democracies, another entity he founded, intervene to protect the domestic food supplies of Norway, Poland, Belgium, Finland, and the Netherlands, to ensure that supplemental provisions reached the respective countries in the face of blockades. Though Hoover's proposal enjoyed considerable congressional and public support, Franklin Roosevelt and Winston Churchill contended that funneling food to civilians in countries occupied by Germany would only prolong the war. Hoover adamantly disagreed. "I do not believe it would make the slightest difference in the military outcome of this war if we assured food to the needy among the whole 40 million democratic children in Europe," he insisted. "Hitler cannot be defeated with armies of starving children." Hoover's plan required the lifting of the British blockade, a proposition Churchill was unwilling to contemplate. The British prime minister challenged the former president's position that ending hunger was the Allies' most significant priority, and the combined resistance of FDR and Churchill carried the day.

With the ascension of Harry S. Truman, Hoover was called back into service to help avert the threat of famine in postwar Europe. Heading up the Famine Emergency Commission at the age of seventy-one, Hoover crisscrossed thirty-eight countries in three months in the spring of 1946 to assess the magnitude of the crisis. Hoover also took his advocacy to the airwaves, appealing to his countrymen by radio:

"If your neighbors and their children were hungry, you would instantly invite them to a seat at the table. These starving women and children are in foreign countries, yet they are hungry human beings—and they are also your neighbors. . . . Will you not take to your table an invisible guest?" He was no fan of euphemism: "We do not want the American flag flying over nationwide Buchenwalds," he told the American public bluntly.

Truman's invitation to run the administration's food relief program ended Hoover's persona non grata period in the U.S., and the former president was grateful for the opportunity to employ his long-standing talents. Two years before his death, Hoover expressed his appreciation to Truman in a letter. "When the attack on Pearl Harbor came, I at once supported [FDR] and offered to serve in any . . . capacity. Because of my various experiences . . . I thought my services might again be useful, however there was no response. . . . When you came to the White House, within a month you opened a door to me to the only profession I know, public service, and you undid some disgraceful action that had been taken in prior years."

THE COMMISSIONS OF HERBERT HOOVER

Beyond food relief, Hoover's public service skills proved valuable in a second area. During his first term, Harry Truman became convinced of the need to streamline the executive branch to ensure greater managerial effectiveness. Yet his repeated proposals were blocked by a Congress that had its own ideas about executive reform. Out of the impasse, Congress authorized the establishment of the Commission for Organization of the Executive Branch of the Government—and, in an inspired stroke, Truman appointed Herbert Hoover its chair. With members hailing from both private and public sectors, Hoover worked tirelessly for twenty months. The Hoover Commission was uniformly hailed as a success: after the commission's findings were reported back to Truman in early 1949, nearly three-quarters of its two hundred and seventy-three proposed recommendations were adopted in some form.

With the rapid acceleration of the Cold War, Red Scare hysterics led Truman to ask Hoover to chair a bipartisan group of a different stripe—investigating the potential infiltration of Communists in government. This time, however, Hoover declined the invitation (several years earlier he had also turned down the opportunity to testify at the House Un-American Activities Committee's maiden session). To be sure, Hoover was a faithful anti-Communist, but he found Truman's approach to the matter all wrong. The former president was less inclined to single out those he thought might be Soviet sympathizers than to challenge the broader permissiveness toward Communism that he believed pervaded the New Deal establishment. Hoover told Truman that he doubted there were "card-carrying" Communists among the mandarins of the U.S. government and assumed that the FBI would know of any who were. Hoover felt certain that any erosion in public confidence stemmed from unthinking leftists in key government positions who "have disastrously advised on policies in relation to Communist Russia," not actual Communists. Truman's proposed commission never came to pass.

In 1953 President Eisenhower tagged Hoover to chair a second Hoover Commission with the same underlying objectives as the first. Although Ike was skeptical that another commission was necessary (he was in the process of authorizing a different working group to look at issues of federalism and thought its research would cover the same ground), several key members of Congress demanded a reprise with Hoover, and Ike relented. He later recalled how the former president sought to stack the deck in his own favor: "The only individuals [he] wanted on the commission were those whom he knew shared his general convictions—convictions that many of our people would consider a trifle on the moth-eaten side." Eisenhower's additional appointments resulted in a more balanced participant list.

Even at eighty, Hoover still put in fourteen-hour days guiding the work of his second commission. Like the first group, this commission was also assigned to ferret out instances of government excess. But Hoover II took on the expanded mission of reviewing policy and managerial issues, gauging not only the effectiveness of government agencies but their overall usefulness. Because of its focus, the second commission evoked greater controversy, specifically from New Dealers who resented Hoover's recommendation to rely on private industry in place of government wherever possible. Yet not all the commission's suggestions promoted governmental streamlining. Hoover II also pushed for an increase of funds for medical and scientific research and for the creation of a cabinet-level Department of Education, Health and Welfare.

Hoover's labors did not go unnoticed. At a dinner in his honor, Senator John F. Kennedy paid tribute to the thirty-first president: "The name of Herbert Hoover has truly become synonymous with efficiency and economy in government." It must have been a sweet vindication: a quarter century after leaving behind a broken government unable to rise to a national crisis, Hoover was now being hailed—by a Democrat, no less—as a champion of governmental efficacy. Working under the auspices of Truman and Eisenhower, the much-maligned former president found his way back to the White House with dignity and on his own terms.

JIMMY CARTER AND WILLIAM JEFFERSON CLINTON

Jimmy Carter and Bill Clinton, in a break from their predecessors' style of humanitarian work, have created their own large-scale institutions to advance philanthropy. Through the Carter Center and the William J. Clinton Foundation, these former presidents have employed their surnames to advantage, stamping their individual approaches on charitable activity and institutionalizing the Carter and Clinton brands.

Bill Clinton's foundation did not set out to ape the Carter Center in its diplomatic ventures—democracy-building, for example, has never been its bailiwick—yet clear parallels in the institutions' far-reaching public health and antipoverty programs suggest a correspondence in their aims. The Carter Center has fought expertly to eradicate parasitic diseases like Guinea worm and river blindness in more than twenty African countries, while the Clinton Foundation has taken strides to advance the diagnosis and treatment of HIV/AIDS throughout southern Africa, South America, and Asia. The Carter Center has programs devoted to agricultural development in sub-Saharan Africa; Clinton's organization is engaged in a sustainable economic growth project in Rwanda and Malawi. Clinton and Carter have also devised targeted health programs in the United States: Clinton has embraced the fight against childhood obesity through his Alliance for a Healthier Generation, and the Carter Center, influenced by Rosalynn Carter's personal interests, has been a champion in fighting for better treatment, services, and parity for people with mental health needs, including early intervention for children.

With their astonishing range of philanthropic and humanitarian endeavors, Bill Clinton and Jimmy Carter have forged an important postpresidential standard. Their modern ex-presidencies have coupled personal wealth accumulation—especially in Clinton's case—with global wealth dissemination. And both men operate from the premise that their status as former presidents is an invaluable tool in furthering their goals, but that the onus is on them to apply their efforts where they can be most successful. "Every former president is just as different as two people that you might meet going down the street," Carter once said. "It's very good to have some element of competition among former presidents, but I think it is also . . . important for each former president not to try to duplicate what the others have done."

Both Jimmy Carter and Bill Clinton are drawing on the capital they amassed while president—on their reserves of international recognition, leadership status, and a complex grasp of global issues—and investing it in a good works platform out of office. Unlike Hoover or Taft, who ultimately deemed their White House years inconsequential compared with their extrapresidential activities, Carter and Clinton have never devalued the significance of their time in office. Jimmy Carter, in particular, has used his postpresidency to pursue many of the same themes that permeated his single term in Washington, including conflict resolution, safeguarding human rights, and advancing antipoverty measures. And Bill Clinton has repeatedly acknowledged that some of his postpresidential ambitions have been influenced by a desire to remedy critical missteps he feels he made in office, seizing opportunities now that he missed then.

THE BIRTH AND LIFE OF THE CARTER CENTER

The historian Douglas Brinkley has likened Jimmy Carter's postpresidency to the masterful congressional achievements of John Quincy Adams. Carter himself prefers a less acclaimed role model: his mother, Lillian Carter. The former president was inspired by his mother's midlife accomplishments. Not only did she reinvent herself at age fifty-nine, after her husband died, but she also joined the Peace Corps at age sixty-eight and made countless speeches about her experiences after returning from her tour in Bombay.

After losing the White House to Ronald Reagan in 1980, Carter needed his own shot of inspiration. Assuming he would have another four years to contemplate his next move, a demoralized Carter returned to his home in Plains "completely exhausted," facing "an altogether new, unwanted, and potentially empty life." While passing time writing his memoirs and planning his presidential library, Carter soon came upon what was to be his calling. Driven out of bed one evening, according to the now familiar anecdote, Carter had an epiphany: "I know what we can do at the library," he excitedly told his wife. "We can have a place to resolve conflicts." His vision would become the seed of the future Carter Center.

Like many institutions, the Carter Center has expanded its mission over time. Originally envisioned as a Camp David–type retreat where warring leaders could congregate in the hopes of forging a peaceful resolution, the center changed focus as the former first couple recognized that a more substantive and comprehensive approach to democracy-building was necessary. They extended their offerings to include programs on promoting free and fair elections, providing governance training for new leaders, and supporting what soon became customarily labeled as "civil society." Moreover, the Carters' broadened understanding of what constitutes human rights—including civil, political, social, and economic rights—grew to encompass "not only the right to live in peace but also to adequate health care, shelter, food and economic opportunity." This additional focus on social-justice concerns was duly reflected in the Carter Center's portfolio as it established multiple public health initiatives, devised projects on sustainable agriculture, provided technical and organizational training for nongovernmental organizations, supported a multilayered community development project for the city of Atlanta, and promoted abolition of the death penalty.

Within its broader mandate, the Carter Center's election reform activities have become a kind of cottage industry. Including monitoring and certifying elections abroad, shepherding foreign observations of domestic elections, and developing educational materials outlining best practices, Carter's vast expertise has led to his participation in two U.S. election reform commissions. In January 2001, Carter and

Gerald Ford were selected to serve as cochairs of the National Commission on Federal Election Reform, charged with improving the electoral process following the unmitigated debacle of the 2000 presidential contest. The blue-ribbon commission unanimously agreed to a series of concrete proposals, including uniform voting procedures and the employment of a standardized nonpartisan commission (or individual) to oversee the process from top to bottom. Exploiting the commission's proposals, Congress passed and George W. Bush signed October 2002's Help America Vote Act. By the next presidential contest, however, Carter was irate that the legislation's recommendations had been only partially implemented, and forecast that the upcoming 2004 election could stand victim to many of the tribulations marring the 2000 poll. Whether Carter's concerns proved prescient is open to debate, although there were substantial allegations of voter fraud in Ohio, a state that played a defining role in determining the outcome.

Carter's dissatisfaction with the implementation of the Help America Vote Act prompted him to join forces with former secretary of state James Baker—the architect of the Bush-Cheney postelection strategy in Florida in 2000—to chair a second reform panel that might restore integrity to the electoral process. But their concluding report was immediately imperiled by one hugely controversial proposal: that voters be required to produce a standard identification card in order to cast their vote. The concept raised troubling concerns about privacy rights, and the possibility of deterring and intimidating certain groups, particularly immigrants, the poor, the young, and the elderly. Other core recommendations were welcomed, including universal voter registration, a paper trail audit for electronic voting machines, and a revamped presidential primary schedule.

Complementing his diverse efforts in electoral reform are Carter's enormous achievements in public health since leaving the White House. The former president has selected a series of specific projects through which his intervention could offer meaningful improvement in people's lives, and his triumphs have been undeniable. As an accompaniment to his 2002 Nobel Peace Prize, awarded for "decades of untiring effort to find peaceful solutions to international conflicts, to advance democracy and human rights, and to promote economic and social development," in 2006 Carter received the Bill and Melinda Gates Foundation Award for Global Health in recognition of his work to eradicate preventable illnesses. The Gates Foundation celebrated the Carter Center for reducing the incidence of Guinea worm disease by 99.5 percent, delivering more than 75 million treatments for river blindness, and establishing more than four thousand community-based prevention programs for trachoma.

The next year, in an encore performance, the Carter Center launched a new malaria initiative to distribute 3 million insecticide-laden bed nets in Ethiopia, where malaria is the leading cause of death. Spearheading the effort with the Ethiopian Health Ministry and other partners to meet the goal of providing 20 million nets and associated health education, the center was able to build on its long-standing infrastructure and community-based organizations already in the country.

Unlike his public policy statements during his ex-presidency, which have had their share of detractors, Carter's public health initiatives have been greeted with general admiration. In contrast to his high-profile negotiations with problematic figures and pointed assessments of sitting presidents, his motivations in pursuing disease prevention and agricultural sustainability projects have occasioned little second-guessing from critics or historians. Carter has sometimes been characterized as a loose cannon on the foreign policy front, unilaterally pursuing an unsanctioned mandate of his own invention, but in implementing his center's health care and poverty reduction initiatives, he has generally been recognized as a figure of dedication and probity. For Carter himself, this dual perception must be puzzling; he has said that he considers his diplomatic and humanitarian work fundamentally interrelated, both aspects of the Carter Center's broader human rights agenda.

With his reputation as self-appointed diplomat, fearless election monitor, global health champion, antipoverty advocate, and recipient of the Nobel Peace Prize, Jimmy Carter has engineered a uniquely multifaceted postpresidential legacy. Even those unfamiliar with the extent of his international involvement are most likely aware of the former president's well-publicized work with Habitat for Humanity (where he and Rosalynn lead a work project one week a year) and his related commitment to affordable housing.

Carter's most recent collaboration is with a group of roughly a dozen internationally renowned figures calling themselves (a bit saccharinely) "The Elders," who have joined forces to combat global suffering. The idea came from musician Peter Gabriel and Virgin CEO Richard Branson, who presented it to an enthusiastic Nelson Mandela and Gracha Machel (and via them to Desmond Tutu); since then, additional members have included Burmese democratic leader Aung San Suu Kyi, former UN secretary general Kofi Annan, former Irish president Mary Robinson, and Bangladeshi entrepreneur Muhammad Yunus. After its formation in July 2007, the Elders' first public act was an autumn mission to Darfur (coinciding with Carter's eighty-third birthday) to promote a resolution to the country's violent conflict.

TWENTY-FIRST-CENTURY EX-PRESIDENT: BILL CLINTON

As Bill Clinton left office in early 2001, he had the example of Jimmy Carter's humanitarian exploits as he reflected on his own future. Only fifty-four, Clinton, like Carter, spent his first year out of power contemplating how to employ his time meaningfully. After close scrutiny of the roads taken by his predecessors, Clinton settled on the public interest mission that Carter had established as an ideal. "I had to re-convene my life when I got out," Clinton explained. "I'd been in one vein for thirty years. I didn't want to go back to elective office. I didn't want to be a judge. And I wanted to be more active than Hoover. That's why I mainly thought [about] Carter." After his problem-laden, impeachment-plagued second term, Clinton was well aware that his legacy remained a work in progress. His turn to Carter's philanthropic model of global outreach was a shrewd gambit. Yet international hu-manitarian work is no uncomplicated realm, and Clinton's success was far from predetermined. Plowing ahead, the newest former president soon made clear his interest in spearheading projects that could make a difference.

Clinton first noticed the scope of his sway within the public ser-vice realm in the winter of 2001, when he helped generate a huge fund-raising windfall for earthquake relief after the death of tens of thousands in Gujarat, India. At a time when he was dogged by multiple scandals in America, Clinton was still welcome in the overseas arena, and his efforts to oversee an international humanitarian program im-bued him with a sense of possibility. As one Clinton adviser pointed out, "Some of the problems that have bedeviled [Clinton] at home and made him controversial don't really exist abroad."

The extant William J. Clinton Foundation was the platform that turned Clinton's aspirations into a sustainable reality, as he trans-formed what was once a fund-raising vehicle for his Little Rock li-brary into a large-scale, charitable body. At the outset, Clinton was not actively sold on any concrete mission; indeed, it appears that the mission found him. Nelson Mandela's plea to the former president to help address the AIDS scourge once Clinton left office catalyzed his foundation's earliest activities. And in the process of exploring the seemingly intractable problems of treatment delivery, Clinton began to test-run his own particular methods for tackling global crises.

HIV/AIDS

In July 2002, Bill Clinton accompanied Nelson Mandela to an AIDS conference in Spain. There he was approached by Dr. Denzil Douglas, prime minister of the Caribbean's Saint Kitts and Nevis, who suggested that his country's problem in resolving its AIDS emergency had little to do with denial or stigma. It was rather a "money and organizational problem." Douglas's frank acknowledgment was a defining moment for Clinton's thinking on the issue. The former president was now compelled to examine precisely how public goods were being distributed—in this case HIV/AIDS treatment, diagnostic options, and education—and to reconceptualize the public goods market using a private market model.

According to Ira Magaziner, chief executive of the foundation's HIV/AIDS Initiative, this rethinking engendered a process designed to "aggregate enough demand [for AIDS drugs] to form what businesses call a buyers' club." With a sufficient volume of drugs sold, pharmaceutical producers could lower their prices, making treatment affordable, and still generate a profit. What began as a small effort in the Bahamas to reduce drug costs later vastly expanded as the Clinton Foundation helped organize sixty-five countries into a procurement consortium so they could access dramatically lower prices on first- and second-line HIV/AIDS drugs, including pediatric retrovirals. Partnering as well with governments in more than twenty countries in Africa, Asia, and the Caribbean, the foundation was soon offering technical assistance and human and financial resources, as well as disseminating information on best treatment practices.

While his alliances with leaders of affected nations have been essential, Clinton's partnerships with the pharmaceutical industry have invariably been decisive in making HIV/AIDS diagnosis and treatment affordable. Clinton Foundation CEO Bruce Lindsey claims that the procurement consortium drove down the price of HIV/AIDS medication from seven hundred to one hundred and forty dollars for a year's supply, while the cost of pediatric AIDS drugs fell from five hundred dollars per child to two hundred. Certainly this commitment to affordability has saved countless lives.

Yet some experts have pointed out that the advances in making HIV/AIDS medications less expensive began long before Clinton came on the scene: generic drugmakers like India's Cipla, one of the companies with which the Clinton Foundation collaborates, had already started challenging Big Pharma's stranglehold on the marketplace by producing cheaper generic AIDS medicines; groups like Doctors Without Borders, Knowledge Ecology International, and Health Action International had loudly protested the astronomical costs of AIDS drugs for years; and even George W. Bush became committed, at least budgetarily, to fighting HIV/AIDS in Africa and the Caribbean.

The Clinton Foundation has also been criticized for its McKinsey-style management-consulting approach and aggressive public relations operations. Some advocates have groused that the foundation doesn't always heed the advice of other AIDS advocacy outfits with a longer track record, and retains a narrow focus when it could expand its operations to, say, providing preventive education or financing vaccines. Entering into the sharply politicized field of pharmaceutical industry reform, where an established cadre of aid organizations was already hard at work, the Clinton Foundation did itself few favors by usurping much of the credit for the dramatic successes in price reductions on AIDS drugs.

Jamie Love, one of the pioneer activists closely involved in the debate, finds the Clinton Foundation's credit-taking inexcusable. For years, he argues, AIDS activists were on the front lines of the issue—canvassing the Hill, presenting rigorous arguments, and determinedly struggling to push down drug prices. Then the Clinton team arrived, he says, and wrapped itself in the glory. "It is a miscarriage of justice," one prominent public health expert asserted, after "a lot of people put their lives on the line to make the first quantum leap." Skeptics say that the Clinton Foundation was simply pushing at an open door: drug prices had already begun coming down dramatically, and while the foundation's pharmaceutical negotiations telescoped that process, cost reduction was inevitable.

Taken aback by the criticism, Magaziner stresses that "while others made sincere progress this does not take away from the fact that we made it possible for very significant additional price reductions to take place on first line AIDS drugs." Magaziner contends that other efforts had "hit a wall" before the Clinton Foundation stepped in. Although Magaziner himself has been a clear target for some of the activists' criticisms, few deny that the Clinton Foundation's innovative approaches and powerful commitment to the issue helped broker distribution deals and brought disparate forces together to make treatment more affordable.

For Clinton himself, one poignant dimension has driven his foundation's investment in AIDS: the former president's stated regret at his administration's stunning abdication of responsibility concerning the pandemic, from its reluctance to challenge the pharmaceutical industry on drug patents to its ban on federal financing for needle exchange programs to its inadequate leadership in fighting AIDS globally. There was understandable skepticism from various quarters at the revelation that, after leaving office, Clinton was finally primed to tackle the AIDS question. The former dean of Harvard's School of Public Health, Howard Hiatt, confronted Clinton in 2002, scornfully asking why the former president felt able "to accomplish now what you didn't undertake in your presidency." The head of Harvard's AIDS Institute, Richard Marlink, expressed similar caution. "Everyone was worried," he recalled. "Is this a campaign with photo-ops and press releases or a long-term commitment?" Predictably, Clinton himself tried to shrug off the inevitable questioning of his motives. "I think it's all a bunch of hokum," he said, adding that "the reason I do this work I do is that I really care about politics and people and public policy."

As abject as Clinton's unwillingness to lead on the global AIDS crisis was, the former president acknowledges that his administration's greatest mistake was its failure to intervene in Rwanda's 1994 genocide. Among others, human rights activist Samantha Power has memorably excoriated Clinton's team as "bystanders to genocide" for their reckless dithering while eight hundred thousand people were killed in a little over three months, and has greeted his postfactum mea maxima culpa with disbelief.

Whatever psychological factors may underlie Clinton's decision to extend his work to Africa, his foundation's programs in Rwanda have been welcomed by both its leadership and its people. After Clinton's several-year effort to woo Paul Farmer, the doyen of international public health activism, Farmer agreed to collaborate in the foundation's programs through his own esteemed organization, Partners in Health. Farmer told Clinton immediately that PIH's approach was different from Clinton's business-model methods, and further pointed out that "we don't do AIDS, we do comprehensive health care." Moreover, Farmer suggests that his thinking is "ideological," in the sense that he is determined to make public health a right, not simply a "pragmatic" goal, as he interprets the guiding philosophy of the Clinton Foundation's programs. Farmer was nonetheless enlisted, and his work to build a sustainable, high-quality rural health system for Rwanda (first piloted in one area and since scaled up) has been nothing short of astounding. Bringing funding and grantees together, rather than simply dispersing funds, Clinton's role in Rwanda as in his foundation's activities writ large has been more as a facilitator than a traditional grant-maker.

THE CLINTON GLOBAL INITIATIVE

At the inaugural gathering in September 2005 of the Clinton Global Initiative, an annual three-day fund-raising event held in New York

City and attended by entrepreneurs, corporate titans, foundation directors, activists, and celebrities, Scottish entrepreneur Sir Thomas Hunter pledged $100 million for sustainable economic growth efforts to fight poverty in Africa. A pathbreaking commitment, Hunter's pledge translated the following year into the Clinton-Hunter Development Initiative, a self-styled new approach to poverty alleviation.

Strategically hosted during the days of the UN General Assembly meetings, the CGI partners individuals and institutions with development projects and focuses its energies on abiding planetary concerns, including climate change, access to education and health care, and poverty. Headmaster/impresario Bill Clinton presides over the gathering, a social networking occasion of sorts for the wealthy, underlining only one necessary condition for all pledges: that they result in a "significant public good." A worthy philanthropic stepsister to the World Economic Forum in Davos (though the casts of characters increasingly overlap), the CGI is a newfangled charitable vehicle that is unsurpassed in its ambition. In its first two years, the gathering of over a thousand donors amassed more than $10 billion in corporate and individual pledges (though an effective penalty to deter deadbeat donors remains to be developed).

Some skeptics have questioned the motivations of CGI donors, suggesting that they are acting only to further their own corporate bottom lines and self-interests. Others grumble that "grantors are incentivized to do good deeds" simply "to bask in the approval of Bill Clinton." For the Clinton Foundation, of course, this is exactly the point. The CGI's guiding ideology—that financial interests must not be sacrificed at the altar of altruism—allows heads of industry not just to rub shoulders with the forty-second president, but to share a knowing wink. At the 2006 gathering, for example, Virgin CEO Sir Richard Branson pledged to plunge his next decade's profits from transportation interests, around $3 billion, into fighting global warming, in particular by investing in new energy sources. Underscoring the capitalist's advantage, Ted Turner explains that "he'll probably make more money off this than he would off the airlines themselves."

The Clinton Global Initiative is part of a developing movement wherein the financial tools traditionally associated with the business world are applied to the ambit of social change. Philanthrocapitalism, as *Economist* editor Matthew Bishop has dubbed it, signifies this intersection of charitable and market-driven approaches. The investors expect that participating nonprofits will assume standard business models of efficiency and long-term viability and will more easily achieve programmatic outcomes through a sustained influx of capital. Philanthrocapitalism has its share of critics, to be sure, one core objection being that market-based philanthropy on its own, without the necessary bulwark of powerful social movements, cannot generate fundamental, transformative change. But that debate is in its infancy, and meanwhile the CGI marches on.

CLIMATE CHANGE INITIATIVE

The Clinton Foundation has also launched the Climate Change Initiative—which finds a rather idiosyncratic group, including Branson (again), Brad Pitt, and Rupert Murdoch, joining forces to confront the global warming crisis—another missed opportunity of the Clinton administration, as some have argued. (As president, Clinton fought a losing battle to pass an energy tax and was roundly criticized for not seeking Senate ratification of the Kyoto Protocol.) In explaining his decision to create a new initiative for climate change, Clinton tells a most likely apocryphal story: unable to locate compact fluorescent bulbs in all the sizes he needed to outfit his new home in Chappaqua, New York, Clinton quickly recognized the challenges involved in spreading environmentally sound practices throughout our culture.

On a macro level, Clinton realized that activists fighting climate change often confronted a woefully limited understanding of economic options, profound undercapitalization, and incomplete markets. The fight against climate change, Clinton has said, "is in my view, for the United States, the greatest opportunity that we've had since we mobilized for World War II."

In 2006 Clinton jump-started a climate change initiative proposed by eighteen leading cities around the world to reduce carbon emissions and increase fuel efficiency. In line with its general ethic, the Clinton Foundation resolved to work collaboratively with the hope of harnessing collective market power to access climate-friendly technologies. In partnership with the Clinton Foundation's Climate Change Initiative, the project generated significant forward momentum and the number of participating cities expanded, leading to the group's new moniker: the C40 Cities.

The Clinton Foundation's methods in assisting the C40 Cities are markedly similar to the efforts of its HIV/AIDS Initiative. The CCI is creating its own procurement consortium by pooling the buying power of an array of international cities to make energy-saving technology more affordable and to promote the expedient development of new technologies. Additionally, the CCI has created a partnership with Microsoft to produce online tools that will allow major cities to "understand and improve their environmental footprint" by tracking their carbon emissions, and established a joint venture with five large banks—including Deutsche Bank AG, JP MorganChase, and Citigroup—with each committing $1 billion to renovate municipal buildings with green technology in fifteen cities.

While encouraging of the CCI's efforts and intentions, some environmental realists feel that the foundation's initiative can ultimately have only a marginal influence on a problem of such meteoric proportions. Ira Magaziner responds that the Clinton Foundation's business approach to the public goods problem and its emphasis on accelerating markets provide a powerful complement to the advocacy and education efforts of Clinton's former partner, Al Gore. (Clinton staffers would be happy to leave behind the gripe that "Gore envy" drives Clinton's Climate Change Initiative.)

Time will tell how effective the Clinton venture will be, but its multicity project is certainly not the first attempt to employ a business model to halt the damage from greenhouse gases. The market-driven policy tool of cap-and-trade, created originally to combat acid rain, is now a standard instrument in some industries to reduce emissions. Economist Paul Krugman has pointed out that "the idea of markets in emission permits [has] long been accepted by economists of all political stripes." Clinton's notion of public-private partnerships to end global warming thus has time-tested precedents.

TARGETING CHILDHOOD OBESITY

Another effort that has gained Bill Clinton much attention is his commitment to reduce childhood obesity in America. Clinton's personal struggle with weight gain as a child, his lifelong fast-food addiction, and his battle with heart disease—culminating in his quadruple bypass surgery in 2004—make him a convincing spokesperson to tackle the damaging social problem. Under the Alliance for a Healthier Generation arm of his foundation, Clinton has joined with the American Heart Association to get soft drinks out of schools, improve overall school nutrition, encourage physical activity for students, and engage health care providers and insurers to promote healthier lifestyle options for children. Preventive cardiologist Dr. Arthur Agatston, creator of the South Beach Diet, says that "the long-term health ramifications of obesity are greatly underappreciated by the great majority of our political leaders," but that Clinton is "an important exception."

To further the cause, Clinton has organized a series of partnerships with corporate entities including the National Basketball Association, the Nickelodeon television network, and TV chef Rachael Ray. Yet the association with Ray stirred unexpected controversy for the foundation's work. Not long before Ray's Yum-O nonprofit organization joined forces with Clinton, the Food Network celebrity signed on as spokesperson for Dunkin' Donuts. Although Ray's appearances only showed her drinking Dunkin' Donuts coffee, not eating donuts ("Everyone always asks me how I manage my schedule, and the answer is coffee"), her alliance with the fast-food chain cost the Clinton Foundation credibility points among nutrition advocates.

Members of the food industry have also signed on to Clinton's antichildhood obesity crusade. Though some might compare their efforts to the spectacle of Philip Morris's dubious antismoking initiative, several snack food companies have endorsed the Alliance's food guidelines. And, in what interested parties have labeled a "landmark agreement," major food conglomerates such as Kraft, Pepsico, Campbell's, and Mars have committed themselves to a set of nutritional standards for food items sold to students throughout the school day. (The exception is the federally assisted National School Lunch Program.) The standards, which are voluntary and nonenforceable, consequently have their share of detractors. While applauding the companies' intention to meet healthier standards, for example, the president of the School Nutrition Association underscored that it was no substitute for federal enforcement of school nutrition guidelines.

As with his AIDS work, Clinton is just one of several players trying to remediate the sorry state of foods developed for and marketed to children. There has been a groundswell of activity from government agencies like Health and Human Services and the Federal Trade Commission, who have considered regulatory changes in advertising, and from individual food companies dedicated to making child-oriented food more natural and less caloric. And just as some criticized Clinton for the priorities he selected in fighting AIDS, some nutrition experts have questioned Clinton's approach to reducing childhood obesity. Joan Gussow, former chair of the Nutrition Education Program at Columbia University's Teachers College and pioneer of the locavore movement, is one skeptic. "[I] notice that he is getting on the bandwagon like everyone else," she says of Clinton. "When someone points out that our whole food supply is a mess and conducive to obesity and we're all eating a lot of mock foods instead of the real thing, then I'll take them seriously . . . but I don't think Clinton is on that bandwagon." Similarly, Toni Liquori, architect of New York City's school meals reform program, has complained that Clinton doesn't "really seem to have a whole picture of food. Part of what is driving some of the major environmental problems today, what is a huge component of what factors into global warming, as well as childhood obesity, relates to how we produce our food—but none of that is questioned."

Clinton's small steps may be no match for the food-related problems facing Americans today—the dearth of high-quality produce in poor neighborhoods, the ease of grabbing meals at fast-food restaurants, the substitution of television and computer time for physical activity, all of which doubtless contribute to the obesity of American children. Whatever its specific effects, however, the former president's call to arms may at the very least stimulate debate about how and what we should eat, fostering the momentum to build a healthier next generation.

CONCLUSION

The Future of the Ex-Presidency

THERE IS NO OVERARCHING THEORY OF THE EX-PRESIDENCY. WHILE SHAR-ing certain common elements such as legacy-building and campaign stumping, ex-presidencies have not followed any singular arc. Rather, throughout American history former U.S. presidents have fashioned diverse narratives of the postpresidential experience. Yet two significant developments in recent decades—the commercialization of the office and the commitment to public service—signal a distinct direction for the future.

Americans have traditionally wrestled with the problem of how to make best use of our former presidents—as there was no designated institutional role once they left office and no clarity as to how their knowledge and insights might be harnessed. But the manifold opportunities the ex-presidency provides rendered moot the need to worry about their next phase. Instead, the concerns today have shifted to postpresidential responsibility and accountability. Namely, what should we expect from our former presidents? And what might be demanded of the ex-presidency?

The philanthropic endeavors of recent ex-presidents have changed the landscape of expectations as the public views firsthand former heads-of-state employing influence and access for salutary ends. The humanitarian assistance proffered by the Clinton Foundation and Carter Center and the envoy work of George H. W. Bush has become synonymous, for many, with the ex-presidency. Will George W. Bush and his successors inevitably fall short if they neglect to engage similarly?

A positive by-product of the charitable work of Carter, Clinton, and Bush Sr. has been their ability to garner international goodwill. But George W. Bush has jeopardized these achievements by his patent disregard of multilateral engagement in his foreign policy leading to the United States' reputational free fall. Will the restraints now set on American power reduce the capacity for postpresidential influence abroad? Will former presidents need to form associations with other world leaders instead of going it alone to make their mark?

Jimmy Carter, the quintessential maverick ex-president, is likely aware of the winds of change. As founding member of the Elders, an outfit established specifically to mobilize ex-leaders and activists to work collectively to solve global problems, Carter understands the usefulness of multilateralism. As noted earlier, working in tandem with such worthies as Nelson Mandela and Mary Robinson, Carter has transferred his presidential gravitas into a broader body. Clinton, too, through his Clinton Global Initiative, has recognized that global problems perforce require transnational solutions. Others might take their cue from the Club of Madrid, a loose organization comprised of seventy former heads-of-state working in support of democratic institutions around the globe. As American hegemony wanes, former U.S. presidents may find collective action a requirement not an elective.

The Exploitation of the Ex-Presidency?

Beyond public service, capital accumulation has also become a feasible, full-time pursuit for exiting presidents. As we have seen, the panoply of economic opportunities didn't always exist, causing some early ex-presidents to die penniless, and eventually inspiring Congress to establish a pension in response to Harry Truman's plight following his White House tenure. In marked contrast, the dramatic increase in wealth now associated with the ex-presidency reveals a heightened exploitation of the office for personal gain.

Today the spectacular windfalls amassed by our ex-presidents and the absence of transparency in the funding of their exorbitant library ventures all raise serious questions about the defiling of the office. These are not novel concerns. The abiding fear of the Founding Fathers' generation, and one that endured through at least the country's first century, was the possibility of the private interests of ex-presidents demeaning the exalted institution. These anxieties were echoed when the presidential pension with its related perks was signed into law; its function was to ensure its recipient a life of dignity and to prevent the pursuit of transactions unbecoming of a former president.

At this juncture, however, when cashing in on the presidency has become routine, it is an opportune moment to consider what the public should expect from former presidents. Following the example of wealthy individuals like Lee Iacocca, Michael Bloomberg, and Arnold Schwarzenegger, who at times have taken a salary of a dollar a year or less, would it not behoove our former presidents who earn millions, tens of millions, even, to decline their taxpayer-funded pensions? Indeed, there are examples of former presidents withdrawing from select benefits: Nixon gave up his Secret Service protection, Carter didn't accept money for his staff's benefits, and Reagan refused his health insurance policy. Ultimately, it will take public pressure to shame our former presidents into action by demanding that they return to the taxpayer that which represents mere gravy to their bulging accounts.

It is also in the public interest for former presidents to transparently disclose their income sources. Those who have stood at the pinnacle of American power have more than a leg up attracting well-remunerated opportunities. Whether it is George H. W. Bush consulting with a private equity concern heavily invested in the defense industry or Bill Clinton offering rainmaker services to Ron Burkle's Yucaipa companies, their financial dealings must be above scrutiny. Due to the enormous reservoir of access and influence that presidents maintain and exert, and that these individuals will forever carry the honorific of president, it is unreasonable for the American people to be kept in the dark as to how they made their money. Using the office for personal enrichment, a matter of course apparently favored by George W. Bush, can hardly be denied. But shining a light on how ex-presidents accumulate their largesse is a necessary accompaniment to maintaining the dignity of the office.

Legacy Considerations

Presidential libraries over time have grown in size and monumentality, and the accompanying costs have required a greater intensity and scope in fundraising. No different than ex-presidential income statements, library donations also lack disclosure requirements and demand greater transparency. When sovereign governments and the superwealthy are able to provide exceptional donations with no obligation to disclose their gifts, the public remains unaware of any possible quid pro quo. Assuming that one single federal repository for all presidential materials is not in the cards, there must be a way going forward to check these increasingly astronomical contributions. Many in the U.S. Congress agree that the donations present potential conflicts of interest and are pushing for disclosure legislation. Louis Brandeis's great adage—sunlight is the best disinfectant—could not then be more relevant.

George W. Bush's proposed policy institute may turn out to be a useful vehicle for spinning his presidency and, in turn, his legacy. Quite possibly, the forty-third president, who commandeered one of the most controversial administrations in American history, will employ his institute to justify his policies and push for their furtherance. With a cadre of researchers and policy practitioners extolling the former president's message through various media, Bush can ensure that his favored convictions remain in play. Like the modish quality of the libraries themselves in which most presidents tried to outshine their predecessors, if Bush's so-called Freedom Institute is effective, the postpresidential think tank may become the wave of the future.

The story of the evolving ex-presidency is far from over. With a general trending toward younger heads-of-state, the transition from commander-in-chief to citizen-in-chief increases in its significance. For some, the ex-presidency will even become a second career. In his final days Lyndon Johnson conceded "I can't provide much go-go at this period of my life." Going forward, Johnson's lament will, no doubt, be more the exception than the rule.

ACKNOWLEDGMENTS

∼

Tackling a project that covers the sweep of American history requires a leap of faith and a lot of help. Fortunately, we encountered no shortage of persons ready to offer guidance, suggestions, wisdom, and critique. For responding to our queries we thank kindly: David Abernethy, Arthur Agatston, Martin Anderson, Christiane Baker, Steve Berman, Michael Birkner, Robert Boorstin, Robert Bryce, Paul Burka, Justin Burke, Alexander Butterfield, Robert Caro, William Chafe, Ellen Chesler, Richard Cohen, Rhodes Cook, Richard Cox, E. J. Dionne, Lou Dubose, Paul Farmer, Sharon Fawcett, Norman Finkelstein, Marlin Fitzwater, Betty Sue Flowers, Joan Gussow, Jay Hakes, Mort Halperin, James Hollifield, Michael Holt, James Hopkins, Benjamin Hufbauer, Cal Jillson, John Judis, Donald Kennedy, Baine Kerr, Melvin Konner, Stephen Kotkin, Gara LaMarche, Phyllis Lee Levin, Mark Levine, Chuck Lewis, Deborah Lipstadt, Toni Liquori, Jamie Love, Ira Magaziner, Alexis McCrossen, William K. McElvaney, Michael McFaul, William McNitt, Ed Meese, Joshua Muravchik, George Nash, Aryeh Neier, Charles Palm, Robert Pastor, William Quandt, Robert Ritchie, Skip Rutherford, Fred Ryan, Mark Schmitt, Nina Schwalbe, Eric Schwartz, Laura Silber, James Symington, Strobe Talbott, John Taylor, Mabel van Oranje, George Vickers, Timothy Walch, Kane Webb, George Williams, and Kenneth Wollack.

One of the pleasures of writing this book was engrossing ourselves in the work of many accomplished historians. We are especially fortunate to have had the opportunity to engage directly with a number of them. Special thanks go to Edward Crapol, Alonzo Hamby, Joan Hoff, Ari Hoogenboom, and Herbert Sloan. We would also like to thank Ben Johnson and Warwick Sabin, who helped deepen our understanding of the politics of presidential libraries.

For his sage counsel and long-standing comradeship we are grateful to Adam Shatz, and for their ingenious suggestions and creative input we offer our appreciation to Lisa Fitzgerald, Ted Kiem, Don Maszle, Jonas Rolett, and Philippe Weiss. We say thanks as well to Lauren Brown, Ben Esner, David Golub, Rebecca Krucoff, Gina Schmeling, and Debbie Stone.

To our families in Chicago—Olga Weiss and George Honig, Stephanie and Shimon Faratci, Philippe and Lynn Weiss, and in New York—Leo and Helene Benardo and Sandy and Kathy Benardo, as well as our fabulous nieces and one fabulous nephew, thank you for encouraging our efforts and for maintaining as much excitement about this project as humanly possible. Especial gratitude goes to Yaakov Faratci, a young man wise beyond his years, for his strategic and well-timed advice. We also respectfully acknowledge the late Gerald Weiss, whose approach to life remains a guiding influence to this day.

Great thanks to our esteemed editor Cal Morgan and his genial and helpful editorial assistant, Brittany Hamblin. Not last, for shepherding this book from idea to reality, we warmly recognize Doug Schoen, our dedicated pro-bono agent.

NOTES

INTRODUCTION. AN EXPLORATION OF THE EX-PRESIDENCY

1   "The American Presidency . . ." John Updike, *Assorted Prose* (New York: Alfred A. Knopf, 1965), 105.

1   "Whatever vestiges of power . . ." Doris Kearns, *Lyndon Johnson and the American Dream* (New York: St. Martin's Press, 1991), 359.

1   "There are things . . ." Jimmy Carter, Jennings Parrott, "Carters Center on a Better World," *Los Angeles Times*, December 3, 1984.

2   "What shall be done . . ." "Grover Speaks in Chicago," *Atlanta Constitution*, February 23, 1907.

2   "They managed things better . . ." James Bryce, *The American Commonwealth* (Indianapolis: Liberty Fund, 1995), 56.

3   "rich man's place . . ." Marie Hecht, "Today President, Tomorrow . . . ?" *Chicago Tribune*, January 15, 1977.

3   "If I must go . . ." Richard Norton Smith and Timothy Walch, eds., *Farewell to the Chief* (Worland, WY: High Plains Publishing, 1990), xi.

3   "the lucubrations of ex-Presidents." Hecht, "Today President, Tomorrow . . . ?"

3   there were numerous . . . "Let Ex-Presidents Sit in Congress," *New York Times*, November 25, 1912.

3   Before the Twenty-second . . . "Ex-Presidents," *Washington Post*, October 9, 1938.

3   "Twenty years ago . . ." Gary Dean Best, *Herbert Hoover: The*

Post-presidential Years, 1933–1964, vol. 2. *1946–1964* (Stanford, CA: Hoover Institution Press, 1983), 415.

3   During the Cold War . . . "Advisor Role Urged for Ex-Presidents," *New York Times*, January 12, 1954.

4   "the structure, expectations . . ." James Fallows, "Post-President for Life," *Atlantic*, March 2003, 62.

5   "Whether we like it or not . . ." Jeannie Kever, "Treasuries of History," *Houston Chronicle*, January 13, 2008.

5   The conventional wisdom says . . . Kai Bird, "The Very Model of an Ex-President," *Nation*, November 12, 1990, 564.

5   Political commentators never tire . . . Elizabeth Kurylo, "Jimmy Carter: His Second Term," *Atlanta Journal Constitution*, November 11, 1990; "His Second Term," *Economist*, September 2, 1989.

5   "Every President has had a different . . ." David Treadwell, "Presidential Center to Be a Forum for Ideas and World Issues," *Los Angeles Times*, September 24, 1986.

6   a résumé of triumphs . . . John Whiteclay Chambers II, "Jimmy Carter's Public Policy Ex-Presidency," *Political Science Quarterly* 113, no. 3 (1998): passim. Bird, "The Very Model of an Ex-President."

6   "I have infinitely . . ." Art Harris, "Citizen Carter: Nicaragua and Beyond: The Peacemaker's Moral Mission," *Washington Post*, February 22, 1990.

6   Joshua Muravchik, "Our Worst Ex-President," *Commentary*, February 2007, 17; author interview with Joshua Muravchik, August 4, 2007.

6   "high profile stunts" . . . "diminishing returns." . . . Robert D. Kaplan, "The Dignity of Ford's Post Presidency," TheAtlantic.com, December 29, 2006.

7   "When you leave . . ." Fallows, "Post-President for Life," 63.

7   "Jimmy Carter had made . . ." Benjamin Hufbauer, *Presidential Temples: How Memorials and Libraries Shape Public Memory* (Lawrence: University Press of Kansas, 2006), 179.

7   "Like me, she believes . . ." David Remnick, "The Wanderer," *New Yorker*, September 18, 2006, 42.

8   Often charging hundreds of thousands . . . Mike McIntire, "Clintons Made $109 Million in Last Eight Years," *New York Times*, April 5, 2008.

8   Clinton also employs . . . Brian Hiatt, "Rolling Stones Shoot Scorsese Film, Party with the Clintons," *Rolling Stone*, November 30, 2006, 17.

9 "the prestige of the presidency" . . . Richard Cohen, "Crass," *Washington Post*, December 27, 1983.

10 "the dreadful calamity . . ." "James Madison's Attitude Toward the Negro," *Journal of Negro History* 6, no. 1 (1921): 96.

11 "one of the great deficiencies . . ." Richard H. Rovere, "Mr. Truman Shows Off His Library," *New York Times*, June 30, 1957.

11 "I'm so poor . . ." Author interview with Alonzo Hamby, August 29, 2007.

13 George W. Bush presidential library . . . David Glenn, "When History Becomes Legacy," *Chronicle of Higher Education*, March 9, 2007.

13 "the least the corporations . . ." Author interview with Warwick Sabin, August 31, 2007.

14 "A lot of conservatives . . ." Author interview with Rhodes Cook, September 4, 2007.

16 "I made up my mind . . ." "Former Presidents Havel and Clinton Issue Advice to Fledgling Democracies at Kraft Event," *Columbia News*, November 16, 2006, http://www.columbia.edu/cu/news/06/11/kraft.html.

16 Instead, he spent . . . Dudley Clendinen, "Bill Clinton: After the White House, What?" *New York Times*, August 30, 1999.

16 Clinton suggested that . . . Marc Ambinder, "Running Mate," *Atlantic*, May 2007, 42.

16 one persistent rumor . . . Wilbert A. Tatum, "Bill Clinton for New York City Mayor," *Amsterdam News*, November 30, 2000; Elisabeth Bumiller, "Ex-President for the Capital of the World?" *New York Times*, December 2, 2000.

17 "I want you to take good care . . ." Irina Belenky, "The Making of the Ex-Presidents, 1797–1993: Six Recurrent Models," *Presidential Studies Quarterly* 29, no. 1 (1999): 151.

17 Most shocking of all . . . Charles Peters, *Five Days in Philadelphia: The Amazing "We Want Willkie!" Convention of 1940 and How It Freed FDR to Save the Western World* (New York: Public Affairs, 2005), 102.

18 Sadly, the former president . . . Myron Magnet, "Monticello's Shadows," *City Journal*, Autumn 2007, http://www.city-journal.org/html/17_4_urbanities-monticello.html.

18 Paternalistic in tone . . . "The Nineteenth-Century United States President Who Was a Strong Advocate of Black Higher Education," *Journal of Blacks in Higher Education*, no. 28 (2000): 34–36.

18   "tireless energy and single-heartedness . . ." David Thelen,
      "Rutherford B. Hayes and the Reform Tradition in the Gilded Age,"
      American Quarterly 22, no. 2, part 1 (1970): 153.

18   No matter the success of the "Hoover-meals" . . . Joan Hoff Wilson,
      Herbert Hoover: Forgotten Progressive (Boston: Little, Brown, 1975),
      256; David Burner, *Herbert Hoover: A Public Life* (Norwalk, CT:
      Easton Press, 1996), 335.

19   Historian Joan Hoff . . . Author interview with Joan Hoff, March 30,
      2007.

19   "the political figure who has been revived . . ." "The Remaking of
      the President," *Newsweek*, June 30, 1990.

19   Small wonder his presidential library . . . Roger Rosenblatt,
      "Underbooked," *New Republic*, December 1, 1997, 16.

19   "May the day of judging . . ." Maureen Dowd, "Clinton Asks Nation
      to Judge Ex-President on His Entire Life," *New York Times*, April 28,
      1994.

21   "replenishing the ol' coffers" . . . Katharine Q. Seelye, "And for My
      Second Act, I'll Make Some Money," *New York Times*, September 9,
      2007.

21   "What strikes me about Bush . . ." Author interviews with Lou
      Dubose, August 31, 2007, and Robert Bryce, August 28, 2007.

21   "I can just envision . . ." Seelye, "And For My Second Act, I'll Make
      Some Money."

21   "He's become a goddamn farmer . . ." Robert Dallek, *LBJ: Portrait of
      a President* (New York: Oxford University Press, 2004), 367.

22   During the McCarthy period . . . James Giglio, "Harry S. Truman and
      the Multifarious Ex-Presidency," *Presidential Studies Quarterly* 12,
      no.2 (1982): 251–52.

22   "I never dreamed . . ." http://www.baseball-almanac.com/prz_qgwb
      .shtml.

23   "Fay, what do you think . . ." Fay Vincent, *The Last Commissioner: A
      Baseball Valentine* (New York: Simon & Schuster, 2002), 225.

23   "I'm afraid Selig . . ." Ibid., 226.

23   in 2006 Selig pulled down . . . http://www.bizjournals.com/milwau-
      kee/stories/2008/03/10/daily/g.html.

23   Moreover, a former president . . . Author interview with Robert Bryce,
      August 28, 2007.

23   "He will have so many choices . . ." Author interview with Marlin
      Fitzwater, September 25, 2007.

Chapter 1. Getting solvent: The Financial Journey of Past Presidents

25 "It is a national disgrace . . ." James C. Clark, *Faded Glory: Presidents Out of Power* (Westport, CT: Praeger, 1985), 59.

25 "I never had a nickel . . ." John Solomon and Matthew Mosk, "For Clinton, New Wealth in Speeches," *Washington Post*, February 23, 2007.

25 "[Gerald Ford] has become . . ." Richard Cohen, "Crass," *Washington Post*, December 27, 1983.

26 Franklin wanted to diminish . . . Forrest McDonald, "A Comment," *Journal of Politics* 42, no. 1 (1980): 32; Gerald Stourzh, "Reason and Power in Benjamin Franklin's Political Thought," *American Political Science Review* 47, no. 4 (1953): 1106.

26 "That we can never find . . ." The Founders' Constitution: Volume 3, Article 2, Section 1, Clause 7, Document 2.

26 Although Congress occasionally allocated. . . . Allan Damon, "Presidential Expenses," *American Heritage,* June 1974, http://www.americanheritage.com/articles/magazine/ah/1974/4/1974_4_64.shtml.

27 Thomas Jefferson found himself . . . Henry Graff, "The Wealth of Presidents," *American Heritage*, October 1966, http://www.americanheritage.com/articles/magazine/ah/1966/6/1966_6_4.shtml.

27 "Puritan America was trying . . ." Graff, "The Wealth of Presidents."

27 "Were it not for occasional supplies . . ." James Thomas Flexner, *Washington: The Indispensable Man* (Boston: Back Bay Books, 1994), 364.

28 Having acquired his first . . . James Thomas Flexner, *George Washington: Anguish and Farewell 1793–1799*, vol. 4 (New York: Little, Brown, 1972), 371.

28 He also bore witness to . . . Ibid., 372.

28 "never [to] undertake anything . . ." Flexner, *Washington*, 364.

28 "shameless, asking government officials . . ." Ibid., 365.

28 planning to rent out parts . . . Paul Johnson, *George Washington: The Founding Father* (New York: HarperCollins, 2005), 118.

28 "a ruinous mode . . ." Douglas Southall Freeman, *Washington* (New York: Scribner, 1995), 738.

29   In his first year out . . . Katherine Winton Evans, "Rebellious Spirits:
      Hard Liquor in Early America," *Washington Post,* December 30, 1979;
      Richard Norton Smith, *Patriarch: George Washington and the New
      American Nation* (Boston: Houghton Mifflin, 1993), 313.

29   At his death, Washington's estate . . . Johnson, *George Washington,* 121.

29   His twenty-seven-page will . . . Robert F. Jones, *George Washington:
      Ordinary Man, Extraordinary Leader* (New York: Fordham University
      Press, 2002), 197; Eric McKitrick, "Washington the Liberator," *New
      York Review of Books,* November 4, 1999.

29   "His greatness, in the last analysis . . ." Graff, "The Wealth of
      Presidents."

29   "prisoners of their own plantations." Susan Dunn, *Dominion of
      Memories: Jefferson, Madison, and the Decline of Virginia* (New York:
      Basic Books, 2007), 26–27.

29   The emergence of a world economy . . . Ibid., 8–9.

30   Suspicions of the commercial . . . Gordon Wood, "The Trials and
      Tribulations of Thomas Jefferson," in *Jeffersonian Legacies,* ed. Peter
      S. Onuf (Charlottesville: University of Virginia Press, 1993), 411.

30   "Instead of the unalloyed happiness . . ." Steven Harold Hochman,
      "Thomas Jefferson: A Personal Financial Biography" (Ph.D diss.,
      University of Virginia, 1987), 249.

30   "I place economy . . ." Francis Neilson, "Taxes Are Devilish Things,"
      American Journal of Economics and Sociology 20, no. 3 (1961): 231.

31   The constant flow . . . Fawn Brodie, *Thomas Jefferson: An Intimate
      History* (New York: W. W. Norton, 1974), 429–30.

31   Selling land . . . Hochman, "Thomas Jefferson," 55–60.

31   Jefferson was also faced . . . David T. Konig, "Thomas Jefferson:
      Legal Wordsmith," in *America's Lawyer-Presidents: From Law Office to
      Oval Office,* ed. Norman Gross (Evanston, IL: Northwestern
      University Press, 2004), 28; Hochman, "Thomas Jefferson," 254–55.

31   The final price Jefferson . . . Dumas Malone, *Jefferson and His Time:
      The Sage of Monticello,* vol. 6 (Boston: Little, Brown, 1981), 171.

31   "the institution that emerged. . . ." Ibid.

31   "I cannot live without books . . ." Brodie, *Thomas Jefferson,* 430–31.

32   "Somehow or other these things . . ." Wood, "The Trials and
      Tribulations of Thomas Jefferson," 413.

32   "an approaching wave . . ." Malone, *Jefferson and His Time,* 34.

32   His status in Virginia . . . Author interview with Herbert Sloan,
      August 23, 2007.

32   Although he was bailed out . . . Herbert Sloan, *Principle and Interest: Thomas Jefferson and the Problem of Debt* (New York: Oxford University Press, 1995), 11.

32   he was forced to pay . . . Hochman, *Thomas Jefferson*, 250.

32   "My application to the legislature . . ." Hal Willard, "Jefferson, $100,000 in Debt, Tried to Raffle Monticello," *Washington Post and Times-Herald*, April, 19, 1973.

32   A public lottery was planned . . . Author interview with Herbert Sloan, August 23, 2007.

32   Though his friends finally . . . Damon, "Presidential Expenses."

33   "the earth belongs to . . ." Eric McKitrick, "Portrait of an Enigma," *New York Review of Books*, April 24, 1997.

33   It was one of history's astringent . . . Willard, "Jefferson, $100,000 in Debt, Tried to Raffle Monticello."

33   Though Madison took a . . . Dunn, *Dominion of Memories*, 28.

33   After a streak of bad luck . . . Drew R. McCoy, *The Last of the Fathers: James Madison and the Republican Legacy* (New York: Cambridge University Press, 1991), 257; Ralph Ketcham, *James Madison: A Biography* (Charlottesville: University of Virginia Press, 1990), 624.

33   By the late 1820s . . . Jack K. Rakove, *James Madison and the Creation of the American Republic* (New York: Longman, 2006), 208.

33   Convinced that the races . . . Ketcham, *James Madison*, 625–26.

34   Saddled with gambling debts . . . McCoy, *The Last of the Fathers*, 259.

34   "He still talks of the last . . ." Ibid.

34   Madison did retain . . . Rakove, *James Madison*, 209.

34   The last of the original Virginians . . . Harry Ammon, *James Monroe: The Quest for National Identity* (New York: McGraw-Hill, 1971), 553.

34   "tottered from the White House . . ." Jane Frederickson, "How Ex-Presidents Have Fared," *Los Angeles Times*, February 21, 1930.

34   a "necessary of life" . . . http://wiki.monticello.org/mediawiki/index .php/wine_is_a_necessary_of_life.

34   "infected by a spirit . . ." Lucius Wilmerding Jr., *James Monroe: Public Claimant* (New Brunswick, NJ: Rutgers University Press, 1960), 127.

34   In general, however, American ministers . . . Ibid., 126.

35   Monroe's duress played out . . . Gary Hart, *James Monroe* (New York: Times Books, 2005), 146.

35   Sensing that the political tides . . . Ammon, *James Monroe*, 546–47.

35   To pay his debts . . . Ibid., 548.

35   The funds helped . . . Hart, *James Monroe*, 147.

35   "Mr. Monroe is a very remarkable . . ." Wilmerding, *James Monroe*, 125.

36   "made a fortune . . ." James Grant, *John Adams: Party of One* (New York: Farrar, Strauss and Giroux, 2005), 433.

36   "all but me very rich . . ." Ibid.

37   "The error of judgment was mine . . ." McCullough, *John Adams*, 576.

37   Although the sixth president . . . Lynn Hudson Parsons, *John Quincy Adams* (Lanham, MD: Rowman & Littlefield, 1999), 220; Clark, *Faded Glory*, 33.

37   Only when his son Charles Frances Adams . . . Parsons, *John Quincy Adams*, 220–21.

37   "I carried five thousand dollars . . ." Robert Remini, *Andrew Jackson and the Course of American Democracy: 1833–1845*, vol. 3 (New York: Harper & Row, 1984), 423.

38   Madison, at least, recognized . . . Ibid., 454–55; H. W. Brands, *Andrew Jackson: His Life and Times* (New York: Doubleday, 2005), 533.

38   "one hundred and fifty odd negroes . . ." Remini, *Andrew Jackson*, 477.

38   He even went so far . . . Brands, *Andrew Jackson: His Life and Times*, 533.

38   Planning a January 1840 trip . . . Ibid.; Remini, *Andrew Jackson*, 454–55.

38   The Whig party gleefully . . . Remini, *Andrew Jackson*, 478.

38   "all the calamities that may befall a nation . . ." Ibid.

39   "Poverty stares us in the face . . . "Ibid., 514.

39   After Jackson's death . . . Ibid., 477.

39   Van Buren arrived . . . Graff, "The Wealth of Presidents."

39   his situation was so fortunate . . . "Demand for Former Presidents," *Washington Post*, December 22, 1912.

39   Virginia slave owner John Tyler . . . Edward Crapol, *John Tyler: The Accidental President* (Chapel Hill: University of North Carolina Press, 2006), 249.

39   Deeply involved in the management . . . Author interview with Edward Crapol, August 14, 2007.

39   "The President" . . . "He thinks a good farm" . . . Crapol, *John Tyler*, 236–37.

40   "my wife will upon each . . ." Ibid., 253–54.

40   One of the earliest proponents . . . Robert J. Scarry, *Millard Fillmore* (Jefferson, NC: McFarland, 2001), 299.

40   After signing a prenuptial . . . Ibid.

40   the former president spent . . . Donald Altschiller, "Ex-Presidents' Golden Years Not Only So," *Los Angeles Times*, January 19, 1981.

40   "After the White House . . ." Cal Jillson, *American Government: Political Change and Institutional Development* (New York: Routledge, 2007), 251.

40   Pierce had wisely stashed . . . Roy Franklin Nichols, *Franklin Pierce* (Newtown, CT: American Political Biography Press, 1998), 507.

41   "Making all reasonable deductions . . ." Philip Klein, *President James Buchanan: A Biography* (Norwalk, CT: Easton Press, 1987), 424.

41   "You have made a mistake . . ." Clark, *Faded Glory*, 68.

41   Cautious and deliberate . . . Elbert Smith, *The Presidency of James Buchanan* (Lawrence: University Press of Kansas, 1975), 196.

41   "Though I could not approve . . ." Asa Martin, *After the White House* (State College, PA: Penns Valley Publishers, 1951), 241–42.

41   This turned out to be an act . . . Crapol, *John Tyler*, 269–70.

41   The first president to leave office . . . Hans Trefousse, *Andrew Johnson: A Biography* (New York: W. W. Norton, 1997), 365.

42   the Grants had saved enough . . . Josiah Bunting III, *Ulysses S. Grant* (New York: Times Books, Henry Holt, 2004), 146.

42   Though hardly impoverished . . . Ibid., 151.

43   "Ward was kiting . . ." Jean Edward Smith, *Grant* (New York: Simon & Schuster, 2001), 619–21.

43   The extraordinary fleecing . . . James McPherson, "The Unheroic Hero," *New York Review of Books*, February 4, 1999; Smith, *Grant,* 621.

43   which he eventually did . . . Sarah Booth Conroy, "Granted, He Had His Faults," *Washington Post*, July 23, 1985.

43   The year before his death . . . McPherson, "The Unheroic Hero."

44   Just minutes before leaving office . . . Zachary Karabell, *Chester Alan Arthur* (New York: Times Books, Henry Holt, 2004), 136.

44   Twain marketed Grant's *Personal Memoirs* . . . Bernard Weisberger, "Expensive Ex-Presidents," *American Heritage*, May/June 1989; Edward Wagenknecht, "US Grant Stands Inspection in All His Glory and Shame," *Chicago Tribune*, March 15, 1981.

44   "I shall leave here in debt . . ." Ari Hoogenboom, *Rutherford B. Hayes: Warrior and President* (Lawrence: University Press of Kansas, 1995), 464.

44   Hayes failed to predict . . . Ibid., 489–90.

45   "moderate fortune" . . . "not rich, but well-to-do" . . . H. Paul Jeffers, *An Honest President: The Life and Presidencies of Grover Cleveland* (New York: William Morrow, 2000), 325; Henry F. Graff, *Grover Cleveland* (New York: Times Books, Henry Holt, 2002), 132.

45   With most of his funds tied up . . . Jeffers, *An Honest President*, 325.

45 Journals as wide-ranging . . . Graff, *Grover Cleveland*, 132.

45 The late nineteenth century was an era . . . Alyn Brodsky, *Grover Cleveland: A Study in Character* (New York: Truman Talley Books, 2000), 435–37; Graff, *Grover Cleveland*, 134–35.

46 As he relaunched his law practice . . . "Gen. Harrison's Big Fees," *New York Times*, December 12, 1896.

46 Venezuela hired the former . . . Allen Sharp, "Presidents as Supreme Court Advocates," *Journal of Supreme Court History* 28, no. 2 (2003): 133–35; Charles W. Calhoun, *Benjamin Harrison* (New York: Times Books, Henry Holt, 2005), 162.

46 By the time of his death . . . Martin, *After the White House*, 352.

46 Popular perception to the contrary . . . Joseph L. Gardner, *Departing Glory: Theodore Roosevelt as Ex-President* (New York: Charles Scribner's Sons, 1973), 201.

46 Soon after leaving the White House . . . Ibid.

46 Offering signed editorials . . . Ibid., 108.

47 Expanding on an already outsized . . . Henry P. Pringle, *Theodore Roosevelt* (San Diego: Harcourt Brace, 1984), 359.

47 In one six-week stretch. . . . Gardner, *Departing Glory*, 123.

47 "the people follow the account . . ." Nathan Miller, *Theodore Roosevelt: A Life* (New York: William Morrow, 1992), 499.

47 a compilation of the *Scribner's* pieces . . . Ibid., 519.

47 Upon hearing of Roosevelt's windfall . . . Pringle, *Theodore Roosevelt*, 366.

47 Roosevelt continued to write . . . Patricia O'Toole, *When Trumpets Call: Theodore Roosevelt After the White House* (New York: Simon & Schuster, 2005), 342.

48 Within a year after leaving . . . Judith Icke Anderson, *William Howard Taft: An Intimate History* (New York: W. W. Norton, 1981), 255.

48 The former president trekked . . . Henry P. Pringle, *The Life and Times of William Howard Taft*, vol. 2 (New York: Farrar and Rinehart, 1939), 856–57.

48 "You will find that Congress . . ." "The Laundry Is Free," *Time*, January 24, 1949.

49 "a very fine piece . . ." . . . "Day after day I sit . . ." Gene Smith, *When the Cheering Stopped: The Last Years of Woodrow Wilson* (New York: William Morrow, 1964), 198.

49 Wilson's weakened health . . . Ibid., 184.

49 "There ain't gonna be none . . ." Ibid.

49   When Wilson grew short . . . Louis Auchincloss, *Woodrow Wilson* (New York: Lipper/Viking, 2000), 123; Phyllis Lee Levin, *Edith and Woodrow: The Wilson White House* (New York: Scribner, 2001), 459.

50   Two years later . . . Levin, *Edith and Woodrow*, 460.

50   Just a day after leaving office . . . Robert Sobel, *Calvin Coolidge: An American Enigma* (Washington, DC: Regnery, 1998), 403.

51   "These people are trying to . . ." Richard Norton Smith, "The Price of the Presidency," *Yankee Magazine*, January 1996.

51   Only the constant exposure . . . Sobel, *Calvin Coolidge*, 402; Smith, "The Price of the Presidency."

51   He had come a long way . . . "The Humanitarian," *Time*, October 30, 1964.

51   His interventions were largely confined . . . Richard Norton Smith, *An Uncommon Man: The Triumph of Herbert Hoover* (Worland, WY: High Plains Publishing, 1984), 231.

52   as a Quaker . . . Smith, *An Uncommon Man*, 291–92, 294.

53   The broad issue of pensions emerged . . . Burton Folson Jr., "Grover Cleveland: The Veto President," *Freeman* 54, no. 3 (2004): 34.

53   Cleveland strongly supported . . . "Care of Ex-Presidents," *Washington Post*, December 31, 1907.

53   "I am not in need of aid . . ." "Mr. Cleveland on Our Ex-Presidents," *Hartford Courant*, December 30, 1907; "Let Nation Keep Ex-Presidents," *Atlanta Constitution*, December 29, 1907.

53   "a certain dignity" . . . "a reciprocal connection" . . . "Ex-Presidents as Wards of Nation," *Chicago Daily Tribune*, December 29, 1907.

54   Was there a way to grant . . . "Howard's Letter," *Boston Daily Globe*, May 23, 1886.

54   The matter fell to Congress . . . "Pensions for Presidents," *Washington Post*, January 16, 1902.

54   "Why shouldn't they earn . . ." "Pay of Presidents and Vice Presidents," *Washington Post*, January 29, 1906.

54   "When [a president] goes out of office . . ." Ibid.

54   Congressional discussion was revived . . . "Washington Briefs," *Boston Daily Globe*, April 6, 1910.

54   "would probably not consider . . ." "Pensioning Presidents."

54   Hoping to set a fire under . . . "Carnegie Pension to Ex-Presidents; Bars Roosevelt," *New York Times*, November 22, 1912.

54   Carnegie was said to have been . . . "Holland's Letter," *Wall Street Journal*, November 26, 1912.

55   Shown up by the industrialist . . . "Washington Against It," *New York Times*, November 22, 1912; "Taft Will Not Take a Pension," *Boston Daily Globe*, November 23, 1912.

55   "it is a piece . . ." "Attack Carnegie's Offer," *Washington Post*, November 22, 1912.

55   "I do not think . . ." Ibid.

55   "Unless it is the policy of Congress . . ." "Washington Against It."

55   But a decade later . . . Alpheus Thomas Mason, *William Howard Taft, Chief Justice* (New York: Simon & Schuster, 1965), 274; John P. Frank, "Conflict of Interest and US Supreme Court Justices," *American Journal of Comparative Law* 18, no. 4 (1970): 744–45.

56   "Mrs. Taft's wishes . . ." Mason, *William Howard Taft: Chief Justice*, 274.

56   "next to my wife . . ." Ibid.

56   At the time of the Carnegie proposal . . . "Mrs. Lincoln Sought Government Pension," *New York Times*, November 29, 1912.

56   less than a fortnight later . . . "Halt Presidential Pension," *New York Times*, December 5, 1912.

56   In the early 1920s, Senator . . . "Pensions for Ex-Presidents," *Chicago Daily Tribune*, March 10, 1921.

56   "It may be un-American to condemn . . ." "Why Ex-Presidents Should Be Pensioned," *Los Angeles Times*, July 31, 1921.

56   In 1945 House Republican leader . . . "GOP Victory Seen by Confident Taft," *Washington Post*, October 6, 1948; "For Presidential Pension," *New York Times*, October 6, 1948.

56   The concept was later . . . "Americana," *Time*, October 18, 1948.

57   House Republican August Johansen . . . John Fisher, "OK Pensions for Former Presidents," *Chicago Daily Tribune*, August 22, 1958.

58   "No man can make any substantial savings . . ." *Time*, September 8, 1958.

58   Within a few years, additional perks . . . "Supporting Ex-Presidents: How It All Began," *U.S. News & World Report*, June 1, 1981.

58   When Congress passed a $1 million . . . Maureen Dowd, "Paying for National Pyramids," *Time*, May 16, 1983.

59   "era of the 'imperial' former presidency . . ." Henry Boyd Hall, "Caring for Ex-Chief Executives," *Wall Street Journal*, July 27, 1984.

59   "To take care of former presidents . . ." Ibid.

59   "We need to send a clear message . . ." Jonathan Eig, "House Votes to Curb Ex-President Funds," *Los Angeles Times*, July 27, 1985.

59 "These guys, with their . . . pensions . . ." Jonathan Karp, "How Ex-Presidents Are Staying in Office," *Washington Post*, August 21, 1986.

60 "They're ornaments, curiosities . . ." Eig, "House Votes to Curb Ex-President Funds."

60 "If anyone hated . . ." Andy Rooney, *Out of My Mind: The Opinions of Andy Rooney* (New York: Public Affairs, 2006), 228.

61 "I could never lend myself . . ." Richard Cohen, "For Sale: A Former President," *Washington Post*, April 25, 1986.

61 "I know what poverty means . . ." Graff, "The Wealth of Presidents."

61 LBJ's accounts were augmented . . . Robert Dallek, *Flawed Giant: Lyndon Johnson and His Times, 1961–1973* (New York: Oxford University Press, 1998), 609.

62 In 1972, however, Johnson was forced . . . Ibid., 613.

62 "God—if he hadn't been president . . ." Ibid.

62 the most affluent former president . . . Irwin Unger and Debi Unger, *LBJ: A Life* (New York: Wiley, 1999), 505–6; Dallek, *Flawed Giant*, 609.

62 such support is provided to . . . "Presidential Transitions," *Congressional Research Service Report for Congress*, updated December 27, 2007, 4–5.

62 Yet time heals . . . "An $800,000 Yearly Tab for Nixon, Ford," *US News & World Report*, April 16, 1979.

63 Marking Nixon's post-Watergate . . . "Nixon and Ford: Staying in Public Eye," *U.S. News & World Report*, July 10, 1978.

63 He even won . . . Conrad Black, *Richard Nixon: A Life in Full* (New York: Public Affairs, 2007), 1,013.

63 He would eventually sign over the whole . . . Jonathan Aitken, *Nixon: A Life* (Washington, DC: Regnery, 1994), 539–40.

63 The $2.5 million advance . . . Ibid., 539.

63 It was a smart bet . . . Ibid., 538.

63 "the lonely figure . . ." Iver Peterson, "As Neighbors, Nixons Proved Easy to Take," *New York Times*, July 11, 1999.

63 "are nutty people around . . ." Susan Heller Anderson and David Bird, "New York Day by Day," *New York Times*, February 7, 1984.

64 "the huckstering of an ex-president . . ." Ronald Brownstein, "The Selling of the Ex-President," *Los Angeles Times*, February 15, 1987.

64 "getting harder and harder to see . . ." Jerald terHorst, "President Ford, Inc.," *Washington Post*, May 29, 1977.

64 Ford now had three homes . . . Benjamin Alexander-Bloch, "Former Presidents Cost US Taxpayers Big Bucks; Tab from 1977 to 2000 Is

Pegged at $370M," *Knight Ridder Tribune Business News,* January 7, 2007.

65 "to pay President Ford . . ." Robert Lindsey, "Busy Gerald Ford Adds Acting to His Repertory," *New York Times,* December 19, 1983.

65 "I'm a private citizen . . ." Douglas Brinkley, *Gerald R. Ford* (New York: Times Books, 2007), 153.

65 "this is what the free enterprise . . ." terHorst, "President Ford, Inc."

65 Ford set a postpresidential record . . . Brinkley, *Gerald R. Ford,* 153; Clark, *Faded Glory,* 158.

65 By 1983, when the former president . . . Lindsey, "Busy Gerald Ford Adds Acting to His Repertory."

65 "He's busy making speeches . . ." Monica Crowley, *Nixon Off the Record: His Candid Commentary on People and Politics* (New York: Random House, 1996), 19.

65 "feel guilty for serving . . ." Kai Bird, "The Very Model of an Ex-President," *Nation,* November 12, 1990, 560.

66 "a naïve and sincere commitment" . . . Sara Rimer, "Enjoying the Ex-Presidency? Never Been Better," *New York Times,* February 16, 2000.

66 "You have carried the dignity . . ." Wayne King, "Carter Redux," *New York Times,* December 10, 1989.

66 "Just as almost two decades . . ." Jimmy and Rosalynn Carter, *Everything to Gain: Making the Most of the Rest of Your Life* (Fayetteville: University of Arkansas Press, 1995), 11.

66 Selling the warehouse . . . King, "Carter Redux"; David Brock, "Jimmy Carter's Return," *American Spectator,* December 1994.

66 To pay down his debts . . . Carter, *Everything to Gain,* 12.

66 Carter allegedly included a clause . . . Joe Brown, "The Carter Memoirs," *Washington Post,* March 14, 1981.

66 "If he and Mrs. Carter . . ." Clark, *Faded Glory,* 163.

66 "How much money I make . . ." Charlotte Curtis, "Carter: 20 Months Later," *New York Times,* August 17, 1982.

67 "I'm a farmer still . . ." Nick Paumgarten, "Jimmy Carter Aloft," *New Yorker,* December 11, 2006, 40.

67 As the honored guest . . . Elisabeth Bumiller, "In Japan Hail to the Reagans," *Washington Post,* October 24, 1989.

67 "I've been telling the press . . ." "Peanuts and Postscripts," *Washington Post,* November 6, 1989.

67   "If America looks . . ." Steven R. Weisman, "Reagan Sees Virtue in Sale of Studio to Sony," *New York Times*, October 26, 1989.

68   "I just have a feeling . . ." Ibid.

68   His prepresidential investments . . . William Green, "All the President's Money," *Money*, July 1999.

68   "I don't know that I'd call it . . ." Weisberger, "Expensive Ex-Presidents."

69   Often charging a hundred . . . Jeffrey Taylor, "As Speechmakers Go, Few Can Say They Are in Bush's League—Former President Commands $100,000 Appearance Fees," *Wall Street Journal*, May 29, 1997.

69   These relationships helped forge . . . Michael Lewis, "The Access Capitalists," *New Republic*, October 18, 1993.

69   "Beltway alchemy . . ." William Powers, "The Call of the Skunk," *National Journal*, May 10, 2003.

69   "This is a firm . . ." Melanie Warner, "What Do George Bush, Arthur Levitt, Jim Baker, Dick Darman, and John Major Have in Common? (They All Work for the Carlyle Group)," *Fortune*, March 18, 2002, 104.

70   That the bin Laden . . . Kurt Eichenwald, "Bin Laden Family Liquidates Holdings with Carlyle Group," *New York Times*, October 26, 2001.

70   Bush wasn't the only . . . Daniel Golden, James Bandler, and Marcus Walker, "Bin Laden Family Is Tied to U.S. Group," *Wall Street Journal*, September 27, 2001.

70   But as a senior advisor . . . Tim Shorrock, "Crony Capitalism Goes Global," *Nation*, April 1, 2002, 14.

70   Bush did very well . . . Craig Unger, *House of Bush, House of Saud: The Secret Relationship between the World's Two Most Powerful Dynasties* (New York: Scribner, 2007), 158.

70   "in line with market . . ." Warner, "What Do George Bush . . . and John Major Have in Common?"

70   Responding to the questionable . . . Ibid.

70   Even before Carlyle. . . . Green, "All the President's Money."

70   As profitable as Bush's work . . . Ibid.

71   The bulk of Clinton's funds . . . Solomon and Mosk, "For Clinton, New Wealth in Speeches."

72   While Clinton's actual earnings . . . Linda Feldmann, "How Voters May React to the Clintons' $109 Million Income," *Christian Science Monitor*, April 7, 2008.

Chapter 2. Presidential Libraries and the Politics of Legacy

73 "Does [the presidential library] have flaws?" . . . Paula Span, "Monumental Ambition," *Washington Post*, February 17, 2002.

73 "The images [at the John F Kennedy library]" . . . Ibid.

73 "History will bear me out . . ." Robert D. Schulzinger, *A Companion to American Foreign Relations* (Malden, MA: Blackwell, 2003), 203.

74 Architectural expressions . . . *Public Historian* 28, no. 3 (2006): inside cover.

74 Since most visitors . . . Jason Lantzer, "The Public History of Presidential Libraries: How the Presidency Is Presented to the People," *Journal of the Association for History and Computing* 6, no. 1 (2003).

74 recent figures show . . . Kenneth Jost, "Presidential Libraries," *Congressional Quarterly Researcher* 17, no. 11 (2007): 243.

74 A painstaking collector . . . Witold Rybczynski, "Presidential Libraries: Curious Shrines," *New York Times*, July 7, 1991.

75 Following his lead . . . Author interview with Benjamin Hufbauer, August 28, 2007.

75 "A presidential exhibit is an artifact . . ." Jost, "Presidential Libraries," 247.

75 "whether we got things right . . ." Sam Howe Verhovek, "Ex-Presidents Gather," *New York Times*, November 9, 1997.

76 The Presidential Libraries Act . . . Lynn Scott Cochrane, "Is There a Presidential Library Subsystem?" *Public Historian* 28, no. 3 (2006): 144.

76 "material of this kind . . ." Charles Hillinger, "Presidential Libraries Now a Tradition," *Los Angeles Times*, October 15, 1978.

76 "A species of public property . . ." Patricia Elizabeth Kelly, "Courting the Presidential Library System: Are President George Walker Bush and Baylor University a Match Made in Heaven?" (Ph.D. diss., Baylor University, 2005), 24.

76 the collection of Washington's papers . . . Charles Hillinger, "Presidential Libraries: U.S. Gold Mines," *Los Angeles Times*, October 5, 1978; Bruce Kirby, Library of Congress, e-mail message to author, January 6, 2008.

77 Abraham Lincoln's son . . . Robert J. Donovan, "The Presidential Library System Hastens Our Access to History," *Los Angeles Times*, August 29, 1974.

77   Fire consumed a major part . . . Cynthia J. Wolff, "Necessary Monu-
      ments: The Making of the Presidential Library System," *Government
      Publications Review* 16, no. 1 (1989): 49.

77   Martin Van Buren destroyed . . . Jennifer R. Williams, "Beyond
      Nixon: The Application of the Takings Clause to the Papers of
      Constitutional Officeholders," *Washington University Law Quarterly*
      71, (1993): 871.

77   On his deathbed . . . Martin E. Mantell, review of *Gentleman Boss: The
      Life of Chester Alan Arthur,* by Thomas C. Reeves, *Journal of Southern
      History* 41, no. 4 (1975): 567–68.

77   And Florence Harding . . . Richard Cox, "America's Pyramids:
      Presidents and Their Libraries," *Government Information Quarterly* 19,
      no. 1 (2002): 45–75.

77   "some of the most interesting documents . . ." Wolff, "Necessary
      Monuments," 48–49.

77   Cognizant of the disarray . . . Lantzer, "The Public History of
      Presidential Libraries."

78   "pharaonic commemoration" . . . "a reductio ad absurdum . . ." Robert
      Hughes, "The New Monuments," *Time,* September 13, 1971.

78   By depositing his papers . . . Jost, "Presidential Libraries"; Cox,
      "America's Pyramids."

78   In the wake of Watergate . . . Clement Vose, "The Nixon Project," *PS*
      16, no. 3 (1983): 512.

79   "the United States shall reserve . . ." Kelly, "Courting the Presidential
      Library System," p. 31.

79   the U.S. Justice Department . . . Cox, "America's Pyramids," 45.

79   "It is unfortunate . . ." Ibid., italics added.

80   who had feuded over . . . James Sterngold, "Nixon's Daughters End
      Rift Over Gift," *San Francisco Chronicle,* August 9, 2002.

80   "the increasing dollar consciousness . . ." United States Congress,
      "Cost of Former Presidents to U.S. Taxpayers: Special Hearing," 1980.

81   Three decades later . . . Fred A. Bernstein, "Who Should Pay for
      Presidential Posterity?" *New York Times,* June 10, 2004.

81   the Presidential Libraries Act of 1986 . . . Ibid.; Jost, "Presidential
      Libraries," 251.

81   Under the legislation's restrictions . . . Bernstein, "Who Should Pay
      for Presidential Posterity?"; Lynn Scott Cochrane, "The Presidential
      Library System: A Quiescent Policy Subsystem" (Ph.D. diss., Virginia
      Polytechnic Institute and State University, December 1998), 221.

81   the libraries have also been required . . . Miriam A. Drake, "Presidential Archives: Hype, Reality, and Limits to Access," *Information Today*, June 2007, 1.

82   "you would likely have much more balance . . ." Jost, "Presidential Libraries," 247.

82   "Museum of the Presidents" . . . Author interview with Benjamin Hufbauer, August 28, 2007.

82   the complexity of the existing libraries . . . "Of Presidents and Pyramids," *New York Times*, January 20, 1977, 36.

82   it will take an "enlightened president" . . . Author interview with Richard Cox, October 22, 2007.

83   "unqualified good . . ." Arthur Schlesinger, "A Historian Stands Up for Presidential Libraries," *New York Times*, November 4, 1973.

83   "swallowed up . . ." Ibid.

83   "Mend it, don't end it." Author interview with Benjamin Hufbauer, August 28, 2007.

83   "an American president's museum . . ." Richard Cohen, "Palaces," *Washington Post*, September 22, 1981.

84   "chilling effect . . ." Author interviews with Skip Rutherford, July 12, 2007, and Sharon Fawcett, August 15, 2007.

84   "I'm an archivist, but I'm a citizen . . ." Author interview with Richard Cox, October 22, 2007.

84   "If a donor is giving . . ." Don Van Atta Jr., "Dinner for a Presidential Library, Contributions Welcome," *New York Times*, June 28, 1999.

85   "invitation for potentially serious . . ." Author interview with Charles Lewis, August 24, 2007.

85   One former Clinton fund-raiser . . . Author interview with Warwick Sabin, August 28, 2007.

85   The governments of Saudi Arabia . . . Don Van Natta Jr., "Going Is Tough for Clinton Library Campaign, Backers Say," *New York Times*, April 29, 2002; John Solomon and Jeffrey H. Birnbaum, "Clinton Library Got Funds from Abroad; Saudis Said to Have Given $10 Million," *Washington Post*, December 15, 2007.

85   On the counsel of . . . Steven L. Hensen, "The President's Papers Are the People's Business," *Washington Post*, December 16, 2001; David Glenn, "Legal Barriers Hamper Scholars' Access to Papers of Recent Presidents," *Chronicle of Higher Education*, March 9, 2007.

86   Sharon Fawcett contends . . . Author interview with Sharon Fawcett, August 15, 2007.

86   "They may be public property . . ." Author interview with Benjamin Hufbauer, August 28, 2007.

86   Researchers complain . . . Glenn, "Legal Barriers Hamper Scholars' Access to Papers of Recent Presidents," 21–22.

86   Bush's lawyers cut a deal . . . "A Special Place in History for Mr. Bush," *New York Times*, March 1, 1995.

87   "This latest addition . . ." http://www.fdrlibrary.marist.edu/php63041.

87   more pedestrian motivations . . . Author interview with Richard Cox, October 22, 2007.

87   An amateur architect . . . Rybczynski, "Presidential Libraries."

87   "Ain't no use wastin' . . ." Robert H. Ferrell, *Harry S. Truman: A Life* (Columbia: University of Missouri, 1994), 387; David McCullough, *Truman* (New York: Simon & Schuster, 1992), 931.

87   "Korea," he responded . . . Richard Rhodes, "Harry's Last Hurrah," *Harper's*, January 1970, 55

88   Many of his private papers . . . Ferrell, *Harry S. Truman*, 389; Alonzo Hamby, *Man of the People* (New York: Oxford University Press, 1995), 630.

88   the larger donations . . . McCullough, *Truman*, 962.

88   "It's got too much of that fellow . . ." Richard H. Rovere, "Mr. Truman Shows Off His Library," *New York Times*, June 30, 1957.

88   "one of the great hatchet-buryings . . ." Rovere, "Mr. Truman Shows Off His Library."

88   the cross section of worthies . . . Hamby, *Man of the People*, 630.

88   "Only if [Ike] had sent . . ." Steve Neal, *Harry and Ike: The Partnership That Remade the Postwar World* (New York: Touchstone, 2001), 301.

88   "except for acts of God . . ." Richard Norton Smith, *An Uncommon Man: The Triumph of Herbert Hoover* (Worland, WY: High Plains Publishing, 1984), 421.

88   Ike's facility was built . . . "Abilene Library Planned for Eisenhower Papers," *New York Times*, March 9, 1955.

89   "I wonder if our pioneer . . ." Austin C. Wehrwein, "Eisenhower Discerns a Decline in Morality," *New York Times*, May 2, 1962; "Ike at Dedication of Library Urges Return to Pioneer Virtues," *Washington Post Times and Herald*, May 2, 1962.

89   "to demonstrate the evils . . ." George H. Nash, *Herbert Hoover and Stanford University* (Stanford, CA: Hoover Institution Press, 1988), 157.

90   tensions had grown . . . Nash, *Herbert Hoover and Stanford University*, 137–43.

90   Stanford's history faculty had taken issue . . . Author interview with Charles Palm, former deputy director of the Hoover Institution, September 5, 2007.

90   "can be put in my personal archives . . ." Nash, *Herbert Hoover and Stanford University*, 143; author interview with George Nash, August 26, 2007.

90   Ironically, this paragon . . . Author interview with George Nash, August 26, 2007.

90   The eighty-eight-year-old Hoover . . . Smith, *An Uncommon Man*, 425.

91   accepted the honorary chairmanship . . . Chesly Manly, "Hoover Flies Home for His 88th Birthday," *Chicago Daily Times*, August 10, 1962.

91   During the 2008 presidential campaign . . . Author interview with Hoover Library and Museum director Timothy Walch, November 18, 2007.

91   a "tourist invasion," with "the Goths . . ." Ada Louise Huxtable, "What's a Tourist Attraction Like the Kennedy Library Doing in a Nice Neighborhood Like This?" *New York Times*, June 16, 1974.

92   "resigned from life itself." Irina Belenky, "The Making of the Ex-Presidents, 1797–1993: Six Recurrent Models," 153.

92   In contrast, the University of Texas . . . Bill Porterfield, "Back Home Again in Johnson City," *New York Times*, March 2, 1969.

92   "was overdetermined . . ." Author interview with Betty Sue Flowers, August 30, 2007.

92   Consumed by his legacy . . . Robert Dallek, *Flawed Giant: Lyndon Johnson and His Times, 1961–1973* (New York: Oxford University Press, 1998), 610.

92   "I'm going to invite . . ." Irwin Unger and Debi Unger, *LBJ: A Life* (New York: Wiley, 1999), 507; Porterfield, "Back Home Again in Johnson City."

93   "statesman in residence" . . . Porterfield, "Back Home Again."

93   UT offered Johnson . . . Ibid.

93   "the *Texas Observer*, the underground press . . ." Gary Cartwright, "The L.B.J. Library: The Life and Times of Lyndon Johnson in Eight Full Stories," *New York Times*, October 17, 1971.

93   "it's all here with the bark off." . . . Ibid.

93   One skeptical observer . . . Molly Ivins, "A Monumental Undertaking," *New York Times*, August 9, 1971.

93   "He's very strong, you know . . ." Unger and Unger, *LBJ*, 506.

93   "huge, monolithic, windowless structure . . ." Paula Span, "Monumental Ambition."

93   "pharaonic pomposity" . . . Huxtable, "What's a Tourist Attraction Like the Kennedy Library . . ."

93   "Opening of the Great Pyramid . . ." Richard Haywood and Haynes Johnson, *Lyndon* (New York: Praeger, 1973), 153.

93   Johnson was neurotic about . . . Benjamin Hufbauer, *Presidential Temples: How Memorials and Libraries Shape Public Memory* (Lawrence: University Press of Kansas, 2006), 176.

94   "in full view of the audience . . ." Jack Valenti, *A Very Human President* (New York: Norton, 1975), 377.

94   "To be black in a white society . . ." Haywood and Johnson, *Lyndon*, 169–70.

94   "The pervasive power . . ." "A Question of Honor," *New York Times*, May 19, 1969.

94   Despite the early criticism . . . "Nixon Library Site Offered," *Los Angeles Times*, August 27, 1970; Charles Hillinger, "With Nixon Papers Seized, Plans for Library Up in Air," *Los Angeles Times*, November 5, 1978.

95   "as a major leader of his country . . ." Ed Meagher, "Whittier College Students Back Nixon, Petition for Library Site," *Los Angeles Times*, May 25, 1973.

95   "You have been severely maligned . . ." Ibid.

95   Foundation documents revealed . . . Robert Fairbanks, "Nixon's Brother Is Paid $21,000 to Aid on Presidential Library," *Los Angeles Times*, December 31, 1973; "U.S. Probes Taxes of Nixon Foundation," *Washington Post*, January 18, 1974.

95   "While he's off being paid . . ." "People," *Time*, January 14, 1974.

96   Firestone pledged . . . "Nixon Library Called 'Unfinished Business,'" *Los Angeles Times*, August 17, 1974.

96   By the end of 1974 . . . "Hope Dim for Nixon Library," *Chicago Tribune*, December 26, 1974.

96   The following week . . . "U. of Southern California to Build a Nixon Library," *New York Times*, April 21, 1975.

96   "No collection of presidential papers . . ." "A Nixon Library? Duke Makes a Move," *U.S. News & World Report*, September 14, 1981, 14.

96   he saw acquiring the Nixon papers . . . Author interview with Duke University historian William Chafe, December 22, 2007.

96   Duke's faculty had long been conflicted . . . "Plan for Nixon Library
      Stirs Duke U. Dispute," *New York Times*, August 16, 1981.

97   The history department's acting chair . . . "Duke U. Dispute Over
      Nixon Library Growing," *New York Times*, August 27, 1981.

97   But the museum was a precondition . . . "Nixon Library Talks to Go
      On at Duke," *Los Angeles Times*, September 4, 1981; author interview
      with William Chafe, December 22, 2007.

97   In a formal vote . . . "Nixon Papers Stir Acrimony at Duke," *New York
      Times*, September 1, 1981.

97   "This is a sad day . . ." "Duke Trustees Back Nixon Library Plan
      Despite Faculty Plea," *New York Times*, September 5, 1981.

97   "Would you turn down Caligula's papers? . . ." Author interview with
      George Williams, December 19, 2007.

98   "a member of the immoral minority . . ." George Lardner Jr., "Duke
      Faculty, By 1 Vote, Disapproves of Nixon Library," *Washington Post*,
      September 4, 1981.

98   "To those professors . . ." "Duke U. Dispute Over Nixon Library
      Growing."

98   "if for no other reason . . ." "The Richard Nixon Library," *Boston
      Globe*, August 22, 1981.

98   "one of the most important moments . . ." Author interview with
      William Chafe, December 22, 2007.

98   citing a bad economy . . . "Duke Drops Nixon Library," *New York
      Times*, February 27, 1982.

98   "library cum apologeum," Cohen, "Palaces."

98   Within a year, the former president . . . "Nixon Library to Be Built in
      San Clemente," *New York Times*, May 1, 1983.

98   "I've traveled all over Europe . . ." Ibid.

99   "too simple and tasteful" . . . "The Remaking of the President,"
      Newsweek, July 30, 1990, 24.

99   "I can't believe Carter . . ." Monica Crowley, *Nixon Off the Record*
      (New York: Random House, 1996), 20.

99   "many memories . . ." Tom Morganthau, "The Rise and Fall and Rise
      and Fall and Rise of Nixon," *Newsweek*, May 2, 1994, 22.

99   "mechanical malfunction" . . . Jost, "Presidential Libraries," 246.

99   "I'm an empiricist . . ." Jennifer Howard, "A Scholarly Salesman
      Takes Over the Nixon Library," *Chronicle of Higher Education*, March
      9, 2007.

99   "starting from scratch." . . . Ibid.

100 "There was no doubt . . ." David Holley, "Race for Nixon Library Enters the Home Stretch," *Los Angeles Times*, April 11, 1983.

100 "there was no sinister . . ." Author interview with Alexander Butterfield, December 17, 2007.

100 The University of Michigan had . . . Charles Hillinger, "Ford Library to Blend into Campus Setting; Former President Specifies Dignified, Gracious Building for Papers," *Los Angeles Times*, November 16, 1978.

100 After his defeat . . . "Ford Offers Papers to U.S. and Michigan," *Los Angeles Times*, December 15, 1976.

100 by splitting them up . . . Author interview with Ford Library archivist William McNitt, August 28, 2007.

100 Still, Ford's buildings contain . . . Maureen Dowd, "Paying for National Pyramids," *Time*, May 16, 1983.

100 "We wanted to focus . . ." Mitchell Locin, "Old Campaign Wounds Healed at Ford's Fete," *Chicago Tribune*, September 19, 1981.

101 at the library's inaugural . . . Edward Walsh, "Ford Hailed at Dedication of Library," *Washington Post*, April 28, 1981.

101 "a monument to me." . . . Wayne King, "Carter Redux," *New York Times*, December 10, 1989.

101 "the big gorilla" . . . Author interview with Jay Hakes, October 9, 2007.

101 the Carter library is the only . . . Lantzer, "The Public History of Presidential Libraries."

101 in one of four buff-colored . . . Peter Applebome, "Carter Center: More Than the Past," *New York Times*, May 30, 1993.

101 a quarter of its funding . . . David Treadwell, "Library a Monument to Carter's Vision," *Los Angeles Times*, September 24, 1986.

101 The major stumbling block . . . Art Harris, "Road to the Carter Library Is Paved with Protests," *Washington Post*, July 6, 1982.

102 "I think I now understand . . ." William E. Schmidt, "President Praises Carter at Library," *New York Times*, October 2, 1986.

102 Reagan's ideas owed considerably . . . Jonathan Wilcox, "Champion for Freedom," National Review Online, December 3, 2001, http://www.nationalreview.com/comment/comment-wilcox120301.shtml.

103 "the high point of the past year . . ." Stephen Chapman, "Stanford and 'Liberal Hypocrisy,'" *Chicago Tribune*, January 26, 1984.

103 The Hoover Institution, already the repository . . . "Reagan Library; Hoover's Gain," *Economist*, February 25, 1984.

103 Soon after Reagan took office . . . Author interview with Charles Palm, September 5, 2007.

103 Campbell had long smarted . . . Author interview with George Nash, August 19, 2007.

103 Twenty-nine Reagan administration officials . . . Wallace Turner, "Reagan Library Debated," *New York Times*, October 25, 1983.

103 "my campaign than from . . ." Anne C. Roark, "Hoover Institution Target of Petitions," *Los Angeles Times*, May 11, 1983.

104 "The President and Mrs. Reagan . . ." Anne C. Roark, "Reagan Library Proposal Sparks Debate at Stanford," *Los Angeles Times*, October 31, 1983.

104 "We have no objections . . ." Roark, "Hoover Institution Target of Petitions."

104 Students soon formed . . . Ibid.

104 On the other side, seven U.S. senators . . . Turner, "Reagan Library Debated."

104 "academic terrorism" . . . "The Best and Brightest," *Wall Street Journal*, September 1, 1983.

104 Glenn Campbell delivered Reagan's positive response . . . Author interview with Charles Palm, September 5, 2007; "Reagan Library; Hoover's Gain."

105 "If it were not for the Hoover Institution . . ." Jay Mathews, "Stanford Advised to Delay Reagan Library Decision," *Washington Post*, October 23, 1983.

105 Campbell and Meese . . . Jay Mathews, "White House, Stanford Reach Agreement on Reagan Library," *Washington Post*, February 15, 1984.

105 Stanford's trustees voting overwhelmingly . . . Jay Mathews, "Trustees Reject Reagan Center at Stanford," *Washington Post*, March 14, 1984.

105 Donald Kennedy then set up . . . Author interviews with Charles Palm, September 5, 2007, and David Abernethy, September 22, 2007.

105 To the mushrooming questions . . . Author interviews with Charles Palm, September 5, 2007, and David Abernethy, September 22, 2007; George Hackett with Gerald C. Lubenow, "Too Close for Comfort?" *Newsweek*, February 23, 1987, 30.

106 The Reagan library plan was coming . . . Author interview with David Abernethy, September 22, 2007.

106 He turned to his Hollywood Rolodex . . . Lucy Howard, "Living Legacy," *Newsweek*, April 27, 1987, 6.

106 The final blow . . . Susan Avallone, "Plans for Reagan Library Fought by Stanford Faculty," *Library Journal* 112, no. 7 (1987): 8.

106   "I was much in favor . . ." Warren Christopher, e-mail message to author, September 12, 2007.

106   Reagan himself made the decision . . . Author interview with Edwin Meese, September 19, 2007.

106   "Life is too short." . . . Author interview with Martin Anderson, September 21, 2007.

106   "not by a thoughtful . . ." Author interview with Donald Kennedy, September 11, 2007.

106   "The attorney general of the United States . . ." Ibid.

107   "One of the most dyspeptic . . ." Ibid.

107   more cars per household . . . Jack Smith, "Searching for a Pulse in Simi Valley," *Los Angeles Times*, April 3, 1989.

107   carbon-copied for the Simi Valley . . . Author interview with Charles Palm, September 5, 2007.

107   for the first time in history . . . Seth Mydans, "Elite Group to Dedicate Reagan Library," *New York Times*, November 1, 1991.

107   Simi Valley was an appropriate venue . . . Ibid.

107   Stanford would never have had the space . . . Author interview with Edwin Meese, September 19, 2007.

108   "They snubbed him . . ." Author interview with Marlin Fitzwater, September 25, 2007.

108   "It was better to have a library . . ." "Unburning Bush," *Economist*, November 8, 1997.

108   his team inked a deal with Texas A&M . . . "Aggies Celebrate Bush as One of Their Own," *Christian Science Monitor*, December 2, 1994; Paul Burka, "The Revision Thing," *Texas Monthly*, November 1997.

108   The College Station university . . . Author interview with Marlin Fitzwater, September 25, 2007.

108   At $83 million . . . Sam Howe Verhovek, "5 Years after Finishing 2d, the 41st President Is No. 1," *New York Times*, November 7, 1997.

109   longtime Saudi ambassador . . . Lisa Beyer and David Van Biema, "Inside the Kingdom," *Time*, September 15, 2003, 38.

109   followers of Sun Myung Moon . . . John Gorenfeld, "Bad Moon on the Rise," *Salon*, September 24, 2003, http://archive.salon.com/news/feature/2003/09/24/moon/index.html.

109   "George Bush War, Auto . . ." Roger Rosenblatt, "Underbooked," *New Republic*, December 1, 1997, 17.

109   "America has had a good man . . ." Sam Howe Verhovek, "Ex-Presidents Gather," *New York Times*, November 9, 1997.

110   "Whatever it costs . . ." Paula Span, "Monumental Ambition," *Washington Post*, February 17, 2002.

110   He would later teach . . . Doug Smith, "Skip Rutherford Quietly Gets Things Done," *Arkansas Times*, November 16, 2006.

111   almost $14 million in assets . . . "Clinton Library: $8 Million Added," *Los Angeles Times*, August 23, 2001.

111   Several of the midnight pardons . . . Van Natta Jr., "Going Is Tough for Clinton Library Campaign, Backers Say"; author interview with Warwick Sabin, April 18, 2007.

111   close friend of the Clintons . . . Author interview with unnamed source, July 24, 2007.

111   "there was no quid pro quo." William Jefferson Clinton, "My Reasons for the Pardons," *New York Times*, February 18, 2001.

111   "distinguished Republican attorneys" . . . Ibid.

112   "It was terrible politics . . ." Jesse J. Holland, "Clinton Has Regrets Over Rich's Pardon," *Houston Chronicle*, April 1, 2002.

112   "No big donors jumped ship . . ." Author interview with Skip Rutherford, June 26, 2007.

112   further pardon-related scandals . . . David Johnston and Don Van Natta Jr., "Clinton's Brother Pursued Clemency Bids for Friends," *New York Times*, February 23, 2001.

112   a chum of both Clinton and Denise Rich . . . "Former Democratic Official Won't Testify about Pardons," *St. Louis Post Dispatch*, February 27, 2001.

112   Burton's committee was primarily concerned . . . Richard Serrano and Stephen Braun, "Fund-Raiser to Stay Silent on Role in Rich's Pardon," *Los Angeles Times*, February 27, 2001.

112   ultimately found no illegalities . . . http://news.findlaw.com/hdocs/docs/clinton/pardonrpt.

112   emirs in Dubai . . . Author interview with unnamed source, April 18, 2007.

112   Clinton friend Casey Wasserman . . . Solomon and Birnbaum, "Clinton Library Got Funds from Abroad; Saudis Said to Have Given $10 Million."

113   Carlos Slim . . . Author interview with Warwick Sabin, April 18, 2007.

113   a billion investment dollars . . . Fred A. Bernstein, "Archive Architecture: Setting the Spin in Stone," *New York Times*, June 10, 2004.

113   more than three hundred thousand visitors . . . Author interview with Skip Rutherford, June 26, 2007.

113   "It is our arch." . . . Smith, "Skip Rutherford Quietly Gets Things Done."

113   "architecture as politics, played skillfully to please . . ." Clifford A. Pearson, "Polshek Partnership's Clinton Library Connects with Little Rock and the Body Politic," *Architectural Record* 193, no. 1 (2005):110.

113   "trailer on stilts." . . . Kane Webb, "A Big Deal in Little Rock," *Wall Street Journal*, November 17, 2004.

113   hope to spend a week to ten days . . . Bernstein, "Archive Architecture."

113   visited the library once or twice . . . Author interview with Skip Rutherford, June 26, 2007.

114   two former presidents . . . Jeff Zeleny, "Clinton Library Shines on Damp Day; Celebration of 'Bridge' Reaches Across Party Lines," *Chicago Tribune*, November 19, 2004; Scott Gold, "Clinton Library Opens with Bridge to the Past and Future," *Los Angeles Times*, November 19, 2004; Bill Nichols and Richard Benedetto, "Clinton Library Opening Draws Stars," *USA Today*, November 19, 2004.

114   "the exhibits tell the story of someone . . ." Nichols and Benedetto, "Clinton Library Opening Draws Stars."

114   "a place for people to talk . . ." Elisabeth Bumiller, "His Legacy and His Library Occupy Bush's Thoughts," *New York Times*, May 8, 2006.

114   "Part of [the] Institute's mission . . ." Marvin Bush and Donald Evans to John White, July 7, 2005. Letter in authors' possession.

115   Other universities submitted bids . . . David Glenn, "When History becomes Legacy," *Chronicle of Higher Education*, March 9, 2007.

115   "bathed [their] project in prayer" . . . Elliott Blackburn, Lubbock On-Line.com, November 15, 2005, http://www.lubbockonline.com/stories/111505/loc_111505026.shtml.

115   Bush paid a visit . . . Author interview with Charles Palm, September 5, 2007.

115   "Don't put your library at a university." . . . Author interview with Martin Anderson, September 21, 2007.

116   Bush gave the university . . . Todd J. Gillman, "Bush Library Donors Could Remain Anonymous," *Dallas Morning News*, January 25, 2007.

116   A fellow trustee . . . Dave Michaels, "Dallas Billionaire Ray Hunt Has Quietly Shaped His Hometown," *McClatchy-Tribune Business News*, December 9, 2007.

116   the Bush committee would seek . . . Author interview with James
      Hollifield, June 26, 2007.

116   SMU's bid for the library . . . Author interview with William K.
      McElvaney, December 10, 2007.

116   "Given the secrecy . . ." Bill McElvaney and Susanne Johnson, "The
      George W. Bush Library: Asset or Albatross?" *SMU Daily Campus*,
      November 10, 2006.

117   "recipe for long-term difficulties . . ." Author interview with Cal
      Jillson, June 24, 2007.

117   Bush had no desire . . . Author interview with James Hollifield, June
      26, 2007.

117   only after Hoover issued its press release . . . James Hohmann,
      "Stanford Think Tank Debate Could Be Headed to SMU: Debate
      Centers on How Much Oversight School Should Have,"
      McClatchy-Tribune Business News, November 14, 2007.

118   an untenured SMU historian . . . Author interview with Benjamin
      Johnson, May 10, 2007, http://bushlibraryblog.wordpress.com/.

118   "I don't think anyone would lie down . . ." Jost, "Presidential Librar-
      ies," 245.

118   "With overlapping donor pools . . ." Author interview with Benjamin
      Johnson, May 10, 2007.

118   Johnson and others called for . . . David Glenn, "When History
      Becomes Legacy."

118   "It will rise or fall on its own merits . . ." James Hopkins, e-mail
      message to author, December 26, 2007.

118   "If you have a strong university . . ." Author interview with James
      Hollifield, June 26, 2007.

118   "If Nixon's library had come to Duke . . ." James F. Hollifield, "The
      Biggest Man on Campus," *New York Times*, January 20, 2007; Glenn,
      "When History Becomes Legacy."

119   "ideological orientation" . . . "Regardless of one's perspective" . . .
      Matthew Wilson, "Policy Institute Is Part Most Likely to Enrich
      Students," *Dallas Morning News*, February 05, 2007.

119   "It will be one of the most studied presidencies . . ." Michaels,
      "Dallas Billionaire Ray Hunt Has Quietly Shaped His
      Hometown."

119   "I just think it a plus . . ." Glenn, "When History Becomes Legacy."

119   Ambivalence on the part of many . . . Author interview with Alexis
      McCrossen, November 11, 2007.

119   "lacking the self-confidence . . ." Author interview with Cal Jillson, June 24, 2007.

120   "if you can't stand a little politics . . ." Author interview with James Hollifield, June 26, 2007.

120   "As a graduate student . . ." James Hopkins, e-mail message to author, December 26, 2007.

120   "I really like our model . . ." Author interview with Betty Sue Flowers, August 30, 2007.

CHAPTER 3. WAR, CONFLICT, AND THE EX-PRESIDENCY

121   "When I was president . . ." Patricia O'Toole, *When Trumpets Call: Theodore Roosevelt After the White House* (New York: Simon & Schuster, 2005), 302.

121   "The lessons of World War I . . ." Richard Norton Smith, *An Uncommon Man: The Triumph of Herbert Hoover* (Worland, WY: High Plains Publishing, 1984), 258.

121   Many of his once . . . Jeffrey Goldberg, Letter from Washington, "Breaking Ranks: What Turned Brent Scowcroft Against the Bush Administration?" *New Yorker*, October 31, 2005, 54.

122   "Do they want to bring back . . . ?" Susan Page, "Father Defends Bush on Iraq War; Says Critics Forget Brutality of Saddam," *USA Today*, November 9, 2007.

122   "a big mistake . . . We never sent . . ." Rupert Cornwell, "Ex-President Leads the Critics," *Independent*, November 18, 2005.

122   "It's just not fair . . ." Greg Sargent, "Bill Speaks Out: Idea That Hillary Wanted War 'Just Not Fair,'" Talking Points Memo, March 23, 2007, http://tpmelectioncentral.talkingpointsmemo.com/2007/03/bill_speaks_out_idea_that_hill.php.

122   "opposed Iraq from the beginning." . . . Anne E. Kornblut, "Bill Clinton Says He Opposed War from the Outset," Washington Post. com blog, The Trail, November 27, 2007, http://voices.washingtonpost.com/the-trail/2007/11/27/post_214.html.

122   "a quagmire very similar . . ." Jimmy Carter, interview by Katie Couric, *Today*, NBC, September 30, 2004.

123   "since 2001, the U.S. government . . ." Jimmy Carter, *Beyond the White House: Waging Peace, Fighting Disease, Building Hope* (New York: Simon & Schuster, 2007), 272.

123 "I don't think I would have gone . . ." Suzanne Goldenberg, "Ford's Posthumous Rebuke to Bush over Iraq Policy: Late-President's View Was Kept Secret Until His Death," *Guardian*, December 29, 2006.

123 "pugnacious." . . . Bob Woodward, "Ford Disagreed with Bush About Invading Iraq," *Washington Post*, December 28, 2006.

123 "I just don't think we should go hellfire . . ." Goldenberg, "Ford's Posthumous Rebuke to Bush over Iraq Policy."

124 Reacting to France's hostility . . . James Thomas Flexner, *George Washington: Anguish and Farewell 1793–1799*, vol. 4 (New York: Little, Brown, 1972), 421–22.

124 "the Agents and Partizans of France . . ." Marshall Smelser, "George Washington and the Alien and Sedition Acts," *American Historical Review* 59, no. 2 (1954):331.

124 they were a black spot . . . Gordon Wood, "An Affair of Honor," *New York Review of Books*, April 13, 2000.

125 "by an intermixture with our people . . ." James MacGregor Burns and Susan Dunn, *George Washington* (New York: Times Books, 2004), 134.

125 "for the express purpose . . ." Ibid.

125 "seated in the shade. . . ." Marie Hecht, *Beyond the Presidency: The Residues of Power* (New York: Macmillan, 1976), 3.

125 "if a crisis should arrive . . ." Robert E. Jones, *George Washington: Ordinary Man, Extraordinary Leader* (New York: Fordham University Press, 2002), 187.

125 Directing the army . . . William J. Murphy Jr., "John Adams: The Politics of the Additional Army, 1798–1800," *New England Quarterly* 52, no. 2 (1979):242.

125 "predilection to French measures." . . . Burns and Dunn, *George Washington*, 135.

126 In a break. . . . Roger H. Brown, "Who Bungled the War of 1812?" *Reviews in American History* 19, no. 2 (1991):185.

126 Adams had made improving . . . David McCullough, *John Adams* (New York: Simon & Schuster, 2001), 566, 577.

126 "Oh! the wisdom! the foresight . . ." Page Smith, *John Adams, 1784–1826* vol. 2 (New York: Doubleday, 1962), 1,108.

126 Jefferson applauded Adams . . . McCullough, *John Adams*, 606.

127 Though weak and disorganized . . . Donald M. Jacobs, review of *Mr. Polk's War: American Opposition and Dissent, 1846–1848*, by John H. Schroeder, *New England Quarterly* 47, no. 4 (1974):619.

127 "a most unrighteous war" . . . Thomas Leonard, *James K. Polk, A Clear and Unquestionable Destiny* (Wilmington, DE: SR Books, 2000), 160.

127 "While he welcomed . . ." Edward Crapol, *John Tyler; The Accidental President* (Chapel Hill: University of North Carolina Press, 2006), 234.

128 "our god-like fathers created . . ." Ibid., 261.

128 Lincoln made clear to Tyler . . . Ibid., 262.

128 "In a choice of evils . . ." Hecht, *Beyond the Presidency*, 18.

129 "tottering ashen ruin . . ." Robert Gray Gunderson, *Old Gentlemen's Convention: The Washington Peace Conference of 1861* (Madison: University of Wisconsin Press, 1961), 10.

129 Tyler's own nineteen-year-old . . . Crapol, *John Tyler*, 262.

129 "Is there any human power . . ." Garry Boulard, *The Expatriation of Franklin Pierce: The Story of a President and the Civil War* (Bloomington, IN: iUniverse, 2006), 76.

129 "No man can with propriety . . ." Ibid., 77.

129 would have considered attending . . . John Niven, *Martin Van Buren: The Romantic Age of American Politics* (Norwalk, CT: Easton Press, 1986), 610.

129 Van Buren's vocal opposition . . . Ibid., 611.

130 While Pierce, unlike Tyler . . . Boulard, *The Expatriation of Franklin Pierce*, 111.

130 "their willing instrument . . ." Roy Franklin Nichols, *Franklin Pierce: Young Hickory of the Granite Hills* (Philadelphia: University of Pennsylvania Press, 1931), 521.

130 Some Republican newspapers alleged . . . Elbert Smith, *The Presidency of James Buchanan* (Lawrence: University Press of Kansas, 1975), 194.

130 Buchanan allowed committed Masons . . . Hecht, *Beyond the Presidency*, 22.

130 "the malign influence . . ." Jean H. Baker, *James Buchanan* (New York: Times Books, Henry Holt, 2004), 143.

130 "When we have conquered . . ." Robert J. Scarry, *Millard Fillmore* (Jefferson, NC: McFarland, 2001), 318.

131 "God's commission to deliver . . ." Charles W. Calhoun, *Benjamin Harrison* (New York: Times Books, Henry Holt, 2005), 163.

132 "it would be an outrage . . ." Alyn Brodsky, *Grover Cleveland: A Study in Character* (New York: Truman Talley Books, 2000), 416.

132 "the most inhuman . . ." Ibid., 417.

132 "I cannot rid myself . . ." Robert McElroy, *Grover Cleveland: The*

Man and the Statesman, vol. 2 (New York: Harper and Brothers, 1923), 272.

132 "general and ominous inquiry . . ." Henry Graff, "The Wealth of Presidents," *American Heritage,* June 1974, 133.

133 But Roosevelt claimed that Wilson's . . . Kathleen Dalton, *Theodore Roosevelt: A Strenuous Life* (New York: Alfred A Knopf, 2002), 445.

133 "President Wilson interfered. . . ." Theodore Roosevelt, "Our Responsibility in Mexico," *New York Times,* December 16, 1914.

133 Not surprisingly, Roosevelt . . . Kathleen Dalton, *Theodore Roosevelt: A Strenuous Life,* 445.

133 His thinking was shaped . . . Russell Buchanan, "Theodore Roosevelt and American Neutrality, 1914–1917," *American Historical Review* 43, no. 4 (1938):776, 778, 779.

134 "I am no anti-German" . . . Ibid.

134 Roosevelt skewered Wilson . . . Dalton, *Theodore Roosevelt,* 457–58.

134 His claim was doubtless . . . Louis Auchincloss, *Theodore Roosevelt* (New York: Times Books, Henry Holt, 2002), 129.

134 "the signatory powers . . ." "League to Enforce Peace Is Launched," *New York Times,* June 18, 1915.

135 During his Nobel Peace Prize . . . Nathan Miller, *Theodore Roosevelt: A Life* (New York: William Morrow, 1992), 507.

135 "heckling the Commander-in-chief . . ." Dalton, *Theodore Roosevelt,* 489.

135 "unpatriotic not to criticize." . . . Ibid.

135 "they misrepresent conditions . . ." Henry F. Pringle, *The Life and Times of William Howard Taft,* vol. 2 (New York: Farrar and Rinehart, 1939), 907.

135 After years of contempt . . . O'Toole, *When Trumpets Call,* 366.

136 Summing up their encounter . . . Ibid., 366–67.

136 "did not assume any of the powers . . ." "Judge Nation League Plan on Merits, Taft," *Los Angeles Times,* May, 30, 1919.

136 "you violate your duty . . ." Ibid.

136 "If George Washington were alive . . ." Ibid.

137 "that mulish enigma . . ." Pringle, *The Life and Times of William Howard Taft,* 949.

137 Taft rallied behind his fellow . . . John Milton Cooper, *Breaking the Heart of the World* (Cambridge, England: Cambridge University Press, 2001) 390.

137 met privately with Adolf Hitler . . . Smith, *An Uncommon Man,* 251–56.

138 "black breeches, varnished boots . . ." Ibid., 254.

138 "expressing his admiration . . ." John Lukacs, "Herbert Hoover Meets Adolf Hitler," *American Scholar* 62 (1993): 235.

138 Hitler offered the usual National Socialist . . . Ibid., 237.

138 "America was politically very different . . ." Ibid., 238.

138 "not West but East and South . . ." Ibid.

138 "it is in a certain sense . . ." Smith, *An Uncommon Man*, 255.

138 Such encomia may in part . . . "Hoover Blunt to Hitler on Nazism; Says Progress Demands Liberty," *New York Times*, March 9, 1938.

138 "sixteen trumpeters . . ." Smith, *An Uncommon Man*, 255–56.

139 he toured the country . . . David Burner, *Herbert Hoover: A Public Life* (Norwalk, CT: Easton Press, 1996), 332.

139 "we would be fostering . . ." Smith, *An Uncommon Man*, 258.

139 "far more likely" to be dragged . . . "Hoover Sees No Invasion," *Los Angeles Times*, November 1, 1940.

139 lobbied strenuously to weaken . . . Smith, *An Uncommon Man*, 294–95.

140 believed that if the United States had pursued . . . Justus D. Doenecke, "The Anti-Interventionism of Herbert Hoover," *Journal of Libertarian Studies* 8, no. 2 (1987): 9.

140 though others were skeptical . . . Burner, *Herbert Hoover*, 333.

140 "sane policies cannot be made . . ." Edward T. Folliard, "Hoover Attacks Democrats as Assassins of Freedom," *New York Times*, July 9, 1952.

141 He raised similar objections . . . Gary Dean Best, *Herbert Hoover: The Post-Presidential Years, 1933–1964*, vol. 2 (Stanford, CA: Hoover Institution Press, 1983), 309.

141 "under the most specious reasoning." . . . Smith, *An Uncommon Man*, 393.

141 "If he accomplished nothing . . ." "The Great Debate on Foreign Policy; It's a Fight Over Means, Not the End," *Los Angeles Times*, January 12, 1951.

141 As president, he backed . . . Stephen Ambrose, *Eisenhower: Soldier and President* (New York: Simon & Schuster, 1991), 321.

141 "The General doesn't know . . ." Steve Neal, *Harry and Ike: The Partnership That Remade the Postwar World* (New York: Touchstone, 2001), 290.

141 "Once you spend a dollar . . ." Norman A. Graebner, ed., *The National Security: Its Theory and Practice, 1945–1960* (New York: Oxford University Press, 1986), 55.

142 "We never knew the cunning . . ." Murray Kempton, "The Underestimation of Dwight D. Eisenhower," *Esquire*, September 1967, 156.

142   Kennedy not only had Eisenhower's . . . Richard Filipink, "An American Lion in Winter: The Post-Presidential Impact of Dwight D. Eisenhower on American Foreign Policy (John F. Kennedy, Lyndon B. Johnson)" (Ph.D. diss., University of Buffalo, 2004), 6.

142   "Kennedy thought there was something frightening . . ." Thomas C. Reeves, *A Question of Character: A Life of John F. Kennedy* (New York: Free Press, 1991), 33.

143   Eisenhower skewered the president . . . Stephen E. Ambrose, *Eisenhower: The President*, vol. 2 (New York: Simon & Schuster, 1984), 638.

143   "I'm going to have this page rewritten . . ." Ibid., 640.

143   Yet Eisenhower's reservations . . . Filipink, "An American Lion in Winter."

144   "a blockade, intense surveillance . . ." William B. Pickett, *Dwight David Eisenhower and American Power* (Wheeling, IL: Harlan Davidson, 1995), 178.

144   Eisenhower even went on record . . . "Eisenhower Bars Any Crisis Abroad as Election Issue," *New York Times*, October 22, 1962; Filipink, "An American Lion in Winter," 97–98.

144   Eisenhower did encourage his party . . . "Eisenhower Bars Any Crisis Abroad as Election Issue."

144   "The Russians have always backed up . . ." "Two Former Presidents Back Stand," *Chicago Daily Tribune*, October 23, 1962.

144   "There is only one course . . ." Ibid.

144   Ike thought the deal he struck . . . Pickett, *Dwight David Eisenhower and American Power*, 178.

145   "I didn't get you into Vietnam . . ." Randall B. Woods, *LBJ: Architect of American Ambition* (Cambridge: Harvard University Press, 2007), 548.

145   Johnson was keen to draw Ike out . . . Michael Gordon Jackson, "Beyond Brinkmanship: Eisenhower, Nuclear War Fighting, and Korea, 1953–1968," *Presidential Studies Quarterly* 35, no. 1 (2005):67.

146   "Johnson did the right thing . . ." "Johnson Did Right Thing, Truman Says," *Los Angeles Times*, August 6, 1964.

146   "Johnson knows what needs to be done . . ." "Truman Supports Johnson's Moves," *New York Times*, February 17, 1965.

146   "I need your wisdom . . ." Henry William Brands Jr., "Johnson and Eisenhower: The President, the Former President, and the War in Vietnam," *Presidential Studies Quarterly* 15, no. 3 (1985): 590.

146   "no moral courage whatsoever" . . . Ibid., 592.

146   "only part of the story . . ." William Pickett, "The Advice Not

Taken: Dwight D Eisenhower's Opposition to Lyndon B. Johnson's Strategy in Vietnam; 1965–1968" (paper presented at the September 12, 1987, conference of the Society of Historians of American Foreign Relations), 17.

146 "We should keep constant pressure . . ." Ibid., 17.

147 "we were not talking about military programs . . ." Fred I. Greenstein and Richard H. Immerman, "What Did Eisenhower Tell Kennedy about Indochina? The Politics of Misperception," *Journal of American History* 79, no. 2 (1992): 569.

147 "When you once appeal to force . . ." Brands Jr., "Johnson and Eisenhower," 596.

147 Eisenhower counseled LBJ to sideline . . . Ibid., 597.

147 "The current raucous confrontation . . ." Ambrose, *Eisenhower: The President*, 664.

148 When Johnson seemed to succumb . . . Ibid., 665.

148 "No person has been more help . . ." Filipink, "An American Lion in Winter," 187.

148 Two years after resigning . . . Jonathan Aitken, *Nixon: A Life* (Washington, DC: Regnery, 1994), 543.

148 Nixon then went on the offensive . . . Theodore Draper, "Nixon Redivivus," *New York Review of Books*, July 14, 1994.

149 "I am going to speak out . . ." Nick Thimmesch, "Richard Nixon Speaks His Mind," *Saturday Evening Post*, March 1979.

149 "rhetoric on human rights . . ." Ibid.

149 In reality, the Shah . . . Ronald Steel, "Perfectly Clear," *New York Review of Books* June 26, 1980.

149 "Did anybody suggest . . . ?" Thimmesch, "Richard Nixon Speaks His Mind."

149 "a fair and proper thing." . . . "Carter Defends Nixon Invitation," *Los Angeles Times*, January 17, 1979.

149 Reagan made it clear . . . Douglas Brinkley, *The Unfinished Presidency: Jimmy Carter's Journey Beyond the White House* (New York: Penguin, 1999), 58.

150 "a round-trip ticket to respectability" . . . Mary McGrory, "Richard Nixon Rides Again," *Chicago Tribune*, October 24, 1981.

150 "way back from Elba." . . . Haynes Johnson, "Nixon's Redemption," *Washington Post*, October 13, 1981.

150 In a meeting with select journalists . . . "Recognition of PLO Backed by Carter, Ford," *Los Angeles Times*, October 12, 1981.

151 "there is no way for Israel . . ." Haynes Johnson, "Ford, Carter Unite on Mideast," *Washington Post*, October 12, 1981.

151 "We thought it was wrong to label . . ." Douglas Brinkley, *Gerald R. Ford* (New York: Times Books, 2007), 153.

151 A little over a year later . . . Brinkley, *The Unfinished Presidency*, 103.

151 "I won't see Arafat . . ." "Carter, on a Middle East Trip, Rules Out an Arafat Meeting," *New York Times*, March 2, 1983.

152 "Quite often, my image and goals . . ." Wayne King, "Carter Redux," *New York Times*, December 10, 1989.

152 "the [U.S.] Ambassador had canceled . . ." Ibid.

152 the administration adopted . . . Elaine Sciolino, "U.S. Officials Urge Carter to Cancel a Damascus Trip," *New York Times*, March 3, 1987.

153 "I am not here to criticize . . ." Patrick E. Tyler, "Carter Assails President; Reagan Policies Hit in Cairo Speech," *Washington Post*, March 20, 1987.

153 "say what I please." . . . Ibid.

154 "When [the Russians] have 10,000 . . ." Robert Scheer, "Nixon Urges Sharing Data on 'Star Wars,'" *Los Angeles Times*, July 1, 1984.

154 "kept dying on me." . . . Bob Woodward, *Shadow* (New York: Simon & Schuster, 2004), 163.

154 "We want peace . . ." Rudy Abramson and James Gerstenzang, "We Have to Live Together, Reagan to Tell Gorbachev," *Los Angeles Times*, September 17, 1985.

154 "playing the China card . . ." Scheer, "Nixon Urges Sharing Data on 'Star Wars.'"

155 "Defend the President . . ." "'Not Another Watergate,' Nixon Says of Iran Crisis," *Los Angeles Times*, December 10, 1986.

155 "That was illegal, apparently . . ." Ibid.

155 "It is not going to be another Watergate . . ." "Defend the President for Trying to Seek His Goals, Nixon Urges," *Washington Post*, December 10, 1986.

155 "It was a covert action . . ." David Johnston, "Active or Passive Iran-Contra Role? Point-Blank Questioning for Reagan," *New York Times*, February 15, 1990.

155 "I, to this day, do not recall . . ." "Reagan Testifies," *Maclean's*, March 5, 1990.

156 "Goliath of totalitarianism . . ." Sheila Rule, "Reagan Gets a Red Carpet from British," *New York Times*, June 14, 1989.

156 "You cannot massacre an idea . . ." Ibid.

156 "I love those young people . . ." Steven R. Weisman, "Reagan Sees Virtue in Sale of Studio to Sony," *New York Times*, October 26, 1989.

156 "return to its isolation . . ." Daniel Southerland, "Nixon Urges U.S.-China Cooperation," *Washington Post*, October 31, 1989.

156 "The cultural, political . . ." Ibid.

157 "The hot-button issue . . ." Draper, "Nixon Redivivus."

157 "pathetically inadequate" . . . "penny ante" . . . Thomas Friedman, "Nixon's 'Save Russia' Memo: Bush Feels the Sting," *New York Times*, March 11, 1992.

157 even pushed Bush to offer a degree . . . David Postman, "He's Back Again," *New Republic*, April 6, 1992.

157 "those who overcommitted themselves . . ." Ibid.

157 "I would have hit the Russian-aid . . ." Monica Crowley, *Nixon in Winter: The Final Revelations* (London: I. B. Tauris, 1998), 103.

158 Nixon persuasively laid out . . . Richard Nixon, "Save the Peace Dividend," *New York Times*, November 19, 1992.

158 "Mr. Nixon is not only rehabilitating . . ." Thomas Friedman, "White House Memo; One Topic, Several Agendas as Clinton and Nixon Meet," *New York Times*, March 9, 1993.

158 Clinton, too, benefited . . . Ibid.

158 "should be supported . . ." Marvin Kalb, *The Nixon Memo: Political Respectability, Russia and the Press* (Chicago: University of Chicago Press, 1994), 181–82.

158 "the West runs the risk . . ." Ibid.

158 "The cold war is only half over . . ." "The Road to Respectability," *U.S. News & World Report*, May 2, 1994.

159 "It's a totally different attitude . . ." E. J. Dionne Jr., "Carter Begins to Shed Negative Public Image," *New York Times*, May 18, 1989.

159 "diplo-evangelist" . . . Art Harris, "Citizen Carter: Nicaragua and Beyond: The Peacemaker's Moral Mission," *Washington Post*, February 22, 1990.

159 Integral to the former president's . . . Brinkley, *Unfinished Presidency*, 270.

159 The Bush team's distancing . . . Ibid., 271.

160 but also helped answer a common complaint . . . Author interview with Stanford University political scientist Michael McFaul, April 23, 2008.

160 *"Son ustedes honestos, o ladrones? . . ."* Wayne King, "Carter Redux."

160 Carter's "guerilla diplomacy" . . . Hendrik Hertzberg, "Mr. Ex-President," *New Republic*, June 5, 1989.

160 George H. W. Bush formally authorized . . . Brinkley, *Unfinished Presidency*, 283.

161 He shared with Ortega . . . John Whiteclay Chambers, "Jimmy Carter's Public-Policy Ex-Presidency," *Political Science Quarterly* 113, no. 3 (1998): 413.

161 "put Nicaragua on the course . . ." Author interview with Robert Pastor, December 7, 2007.

161 "scrupulous neutrality" . . . Kai Bird, "The Very Model of an Ex-President," *Nation*, November 12, 1990.

161 "The United States government isn't in any position . . ." R. W. Apple Jr., "Carter the Peacemaker Now Turns to Ethiopia," *New York Times*, September 3, 1989.

162 "We don't want to duplicate . . ." Art Harris, "Citizen Carter."

162 "I urge you to call publicly . . ." Joshua Muravchik, "Our Worst Ex-President," *Commentary*, February 2007.

162 "It seemed to me that if there was ever a violation . . ." George Bush and Brent Scowcroft, *A World Transformed* (New York: Alfred A. Knopf, 1998), 414.

162 "negotiation is not capitulation." . . . Elizabeth Kurylo, "Carter Defends His Belief in Negotiations with Iraq," *Atlanta Journal Constitution*, February 1, 1991.

163 "not appropriate, perhaps." . . . Maureen Dowd, "Despite Role as Negotiator, Carter Feels Unappreciated," *New York Times*, September 21, 1994.

163 "Such is the pretentious effrontery . . ." Murray Kempton, "The Carter Mission," *New York Review of Books*, October 20, 1994.

163 "Carter did not simply write . . ." Jim Hoagland, "The Time Carter Went Too Far," *Washington Post*, September 29, 1994.

163 Former officials in Carter's administration . . . Terry Adamson and Jody Powell, "A Former President's Prerogative," *Washington Post*, November 14, 1994.

163 Clinton had also hired . . . Brinkley, *The Unfinished Presidency*, 366.

164 "a demagogue with unlimited . . ." Steven A. Holmes, "Carter Here, There, Everywhere," *New York Times*, September 19, 1993.

164 he limited his engagement . . . Neil Lewis, "Aidid Proposes U.N. Panel," *New York Times*, September 14, 1993.

165 "I think the sustained effort . . ." "Carter Acting as a Go-Between, Former President Responds to Fugitive Warlord's Request," *Houston Chronicle*, September 11, 1993.

165 It was later reported that U.S. forces . . . Walter Goodman, "Good Intentions Going Horribly Awry," *New York Times*, September 29, 1998.

165 "I don't know him . . ." Lewis, "Aidid Proposes U.N. Panel."

165 While Clinton discussed with world leaders . . . Bruce Cumings, "Korean War Games," *London Review of Books*, December 4, 2003.

165 "some of the important issues . . ." Associated Press, "Carter to Visit Koreas," *New York Times*, June 9, 1994.

166 Without Clinton's own diplomatic . . . David E. Sanger, "Carter Optimistic after North Korea Talks," *New York Times*, June 17, 1994.

166 "treasonous prick." . . . Suellentrop, "Jimmy Carter."

166 "Jimmy Carter, private citizen . . ." Kempton, "The Carter Mission."

166 "It is the beginning of a new . . ." "Finally, Talks with North Korea," editorial, *New York Times*, June 25, 1994.

166 "most important achievement" . . . Author interview with Morton Halperin, July 17, 2007.

167 Despite Aristide's occasional authoritarian . . . Raymond A. Joseph, "The Haiti Imbroglio," *Wall Street Journal*, April 6, 2004.

167 "classic negotiating stance . . . never [a matter of] two equal . . ." Author interview with Paul Farmer, November 21, 2007.

167 "slim and attractive" . . . Maureen Dowd, "Mission to Haiti: The Diplomat," *New York Times*, September 21, 1994.

167 "the most important and urgent visit . . ." Larry Rohter, "Carter, in Haiti, Pursues Peaceful Shift," *New York Times*, September 18, 1994.

167 He pledged not to take sides . . . Norman Kempster, "Carter Weighs Bosnia Trip at Request of Serb Warlord," *Los Angeles Times*, December 15, 1994.

168 Was the former president . . . "10 Questions for Jimmy Carter," *Time*, December 3, 2003.

168 Did the Bosnian Serb leaders . . . Douglas Jehl, "Carter Says He May Travel to Bosnia as Private Envoy," *New York Times*, December 15, 1994.

168 most were uneasy . . . Elaine Sciolino, "Carter's Bosnia Effort Provokes Skepticism," *New York Times*, December 16, 1994.

168 And while objecting to . . . Marjorie Miller, "Enemies Agree to Four-Month Bosnian Truce," *Los Angeles Times*, January 1, 1995.

168 Carter defends his methods . . . Brinkley, *The Unfinished Presidency*, xiii.

169 "We select a favorite side . . ." Douglas Brinkley, "Jimmy Carter's Modest Quest for Global Peace: The Missionary Man," *Foreign Affairs*, November/December 1995.

169 "at least a limited offensive biological . . ." David Gonzalez, "Carter and Powell Cast Doubt on Bioarms in Cuba," *New York Times*, May 14, 2002.

169 "there were absolutely no such . . ." Ibid.

170 Though Carter also used his Cuban . . . Christopher Marquis, "Bush Plans to Tighten Sanctions on Cuba, Not Ease Them," *New York Times*, May 15, 2002.

170 "a system of apartheid . . ." Jimmy Carter, *Palestine: Peace Not Apartheid* (New York: Simon & Schuster, 2006), 215.

171 "I chose that title . . ." Michael Powell, "Jimmy Carter's 'Peace' Mission to Brandeis," *Washington Post*, January 24, 2007.

171 "[Carter] seems to me no longer capable . . ." Scholars for Peace in the Middle East, December 26, 2006, http://www.spme.net/cgi-bin/articles.cgi?ID=1613.

171 "refuge to scoundrels" . . . Deborah Lipstadt, "Jimmy Carter's Jewish Problem," *Washington Post*, January 20, 2007.

171 "obvious that Mr. Carter . . ." Harvard Law School, December 4, 2006, http://www.law.harvard.edu/news/2006/12/04_dershowitz.php.

171 "a screw loose somewhere." . . . Author interview with Melvin Konner, November 7, 2007.

171 "from the storm generated . . ." William B. Quandt, *Journal of Palestine Studies* 36, no. 3 (2007): 89; author interview with William B. Quandt, September 3, 2007.

172 "For the first time since the State of Israel . . ." Philip Weiss, "Honest Broker," *American Conservative*, February 26, 2007, 9.

172 Carter apologized vehemently . . . Ibid., 11.

172 This did little to satisfy critics . . . Ibid., 9.

172 "wildly inappropriate" . . . Author interview with Joshua Muravchik, August 4, 2007.

172 "This is the first time . . ." Powell, "Jimmy Carter's 'Peace' Mission to Brandeis."

172 "I was taught by my father . . ." Dana Milbank, "Pass the Pinata, Please: A Former President Regards the Current One," *Washington Post*, April 5, 2007.

172 "bulletproof self-confidence" . . . Author interview with Richard Cohen, October 5, 2007.

172 While detractors like Deborah Lipstadt, feel . . . Author interview with Deborah Lipstadt, October 4, 2007.

172   contributions to the Carter Center . . . Jimmy Carter, interview by Evan Solomon, CBC News, December 2, 2007.

172   The book itself was a smash hit . . . Author interview with Norman Finkelstein, September 3, 2007.

173   "The problem is not that I met . . ." "Hamas Will Accept Israel's Right to Live in Peace," *Guardian*, April 21, 2008.

173   "I think as far as the adverse impact . . ." "Bush Is 'the Worst in History' in Foreign Relations, Carter Says," *Washington Post*, May 20, 2007.

173   "I think it'll be hard . . ." Lee Michael Katz, "A Conversation with Carter," *Guardian*, October 25, 2007.

Chapter 4. On the Road Again: Ex-Presidents on the Hustings

174   "They can use my name . . ." Robert Remini, *Andrew Jackson and the Course of American Democracy 1833–1845*, vol 3 (New York: Harper & Row, 1984), 501.

174   "I would greatly welcome . . ." Justus D. Doenecke, "The Anti-Interventionism of Herbert Hoover," *Journal of Libertarian Studies* 8, no. 2 (Summer 1987): 319.

174   "In 1984, I was very unpopular . . ." David S. Broder, "Carter Hails Party's Return to the Middle," *Washington Post*, July 15, 1992.

176   George Washington never abandoned . . . Douglas Southall Freeman, *Washington* (New York: Scribner, 1995), 738.

176   "too old and infirm . . ." Ibid., 731.

176   "earnest wish." . . . W. B. Allen, ed., *George Washington: A Collection* (Indianapolis: Liberty Fund, 1988), 662.

176   mounting recognition of parties . . . James Thomas Flexner, *Washington: The Indispensable Man* (Boston: Back Bay Books, 1994), 382.

177   "I shudder at the calamities . . ." James Grant, *John Adams: Party of One* (New York: Farrar, Straus and Giroux, 2005), 434.

177   in a private letter . . . Ibid., 449.

177   "prigarchy" . . . millercenter.org/academic/americanpresident/jefferson/essays/biography/3.

177   newspapers were suggesting . . . David McCullough, *John Adams* (New York: Simon & Schuster, 2001), 620.

177   "Yesterday was one of . . ." Ibid., 620–21.

178   Monroe even once briefly contemplated . . . Arthur Scherr, "James
      Monroe and John Adams: An Unlikely Friendship," *Historian* 67, no. 3
      (2005): 411.

178   "I cannot pass this opportunity . . ." Ibid., 427.

178   "The multitude of my thoughts . . ." Grant, *John Adams*, 449.

178   "ineffable feelings . . ." John Ferling, *John Adams: A Life* (New York:
      Henry Holt, 1992), 442.

179   "be ultimately reduced to . . ." Robert E. Shalhope, "Thomas
      Jefferson's Republicanism and Antebellum Southern Thought,"
      Journal of Southern History 42, no. 4 (1976): 551.

179   represented the true heir . . . Joseph H. Harrison Jr., "Sic et Non:
      Thomas Jefferson and Internal Improvement," *Journal of the Early
      Republic* 7, No. 4 (1987): 348.

179   "to keep aloof from . . ." Drew R. McCoy, *The Last of the Fathers:
      James Madison and the Republican Legacy* (New York: Cambridge
      University Press, 1991), 124.

180   former presidents should remain outside . . . Henry Ammon, *James
      Monroe: The Quest for National Identity* (New York: McGraw-Hill,
      1971), 558–60.

180   The huge turnout that year . . . Lynn Hudson Parsons, "In Which the
      Political Becomes Personal, and Vice Versa: The Last Ten Years of
      John Quincy Adams and Andrew Jackson," *Journal of the Early
      Republic* 23, no. 3 (2003): 422.

181   "My darling Harvard disgraced herself . . ." Ibid., 429.

181   "the golden calves of the people . . ." Paul C. Nagel, *John Quincy
      Adams: A Public Life, A Private Life* (New York: Alfred A. Knopf,
      1997), 360.

181   "immense assemblages of people . . ." Lynn Hudson Parsons, *John
      Quincy Adams* (Lanham, MD: Rowman & Littlefield, 1999),
      244–45.

182   "unwieldy mass[es] . . ." Ibid., 245.

182   "shallow mind, a political adventurer . . ." Ibid., 246.

182   abandon his dismal vice president . . . John Niven, *Martin Van Buren:
      The Romantic Age of American Politics* (Norwalk, CT: Easton Press,
      1986), 462.

183   "The election of Mr. Van Buren . . ." Remini, *Andrew Jackson and the
      Course of American Democracy*, 467–68.

183   "Young Hickory" . . . Michael Paul Rogin, *Fathers and Children:*

Andrew Jackson and the Subjugation of the American Indian (Piscataway, NJ: Transaction Publishers, 1991), 309.

183 According to one historian . . . Author interview with Michael Holt, September 6, 2007.

183 Polk was less concerned . . . Sean Wilentz, *The Rise of American Democracy: Jefferson to Lincoln* (New York: W. W. Norton, 2005), 571–72.

184 Pierce had modestly reentered . . . Garry Boulard, *The Expatriation of Franklin Pierce: The Story of a President and the Civil War* (Bloomington, IN: iUniverse, 2006), 70–71.

184 "a single lingering desire" . . . Donald B. Cole, "Franklin Pierce Charged with Disloyalty: 1861–1862," *New England Quarterly* 34, no. 3 (1961): 385.

184 "grog-drinking, electioneering Demagogue" . . . "Some Papers of Franklin Pierce, 1852–1862," *American Historical Review* 10, no. 2 (1905): 365.

185 "live or die, survive or perish." . . . Edward P. Crapol, *John Tyler: The Accidental President* (Chapel Hill: University of North Carolina Press, 2006), 256–67.

185 "The whole South would rally . . ." Ibid., 255.

185 "We have fallen on evil times . . ." Ibid., 257.

185 "Integrity of the Union . . ." Boulard, *The Expatriation of Franklin Pierce*, 72.

185 Probably casting his vote . . . Asa Martin, *After the White House* (State College, PA: Penns Valley Publishers, 1951), 228.

185 "distinct and unequivocal denial . . ." Roy Franklin Nichols, *Franklin Pierce: Young Hickory of the Granite Hills* (Philadelphia: University of Pennsylvania Press, 1931), 513.

185 remained faithful to the Democratic Party . . . Niven, *Martin Van Buren*, 610.

185 "not because I was a Democrat . . ." Robert Scarry, *Millard Fillmore* (Jefferson, NC: McFarland, 2001), 306.

186 "It is no time . . ." James Clark, *Faded Glory* (New York: Praeger, 1985), 60.

186 "national bankruptcy . . ." Martin, *After the White House*, 216–17.

186 "restored Union . . ." Ibid., 217.

186 "as a general rule . . ." Harold M. Dudley, "The Election of 1864," *Mississippi Valley Historical Review* 18, no. 4 (1932): 506.

186 "my interference should promise . . ." Martin, *After the White House*, 246.

187 "Have you ever reflected . . ." Philip Klein, *President James Buchanan: A Biography* (Norwalk, CT: Easton Press, 1987): 421.

187 "They have won the elephant . . ." Ibid.

187 "exterminate the South . . ." Martin, *After the White House*, 217.

187 "The little fellow . . ." Hans Trefousse, *Andrew Johnson: A Biography* (New York: W. W. Norton, 1997), 356.

188 threw his support behind . . . Ibid., 362.

188 "no reconstruction can be successful . . ." James M. McPherson, "Grant or Greeley? The Abolitionist Dilemma in the Election of 1872," *American Historical Review* 71, no. 1 (1965): 44.

189 Conkling often spoke . . . Thomas C. Reeves, "Chester A. Arthur and the Campaign of 1880," *Political Science Quarterly* 84, no. 4 (1969): 628–37.

189 "a very deep interest . . ." William S. McFeely, *Grant* (New York: W. W. Norton, 2002), 484.

189 "gladly attend any meeting . . ." "Grant to Come to New York," *New York Times*, September 3, 1880.

189 "monster demonstration" . . . "Last Hours of the Parade," *New York Times*, October 13, 1880.

189 "Probably a more brilliant . . ." Ibid.

189 "I have not taken any active part . . ." "General Grant Not Actively in Politics but a Supporter of Logan," *Chicago Daily Tribune*, March 22, 1884.

190 Hayes grew weary . . . Ari Hoogenboom, *Rutherford B. Hayes: Warrior and President* (Lawrence: University Press of Kansas, 1995), 482.

190 "a scheming demagogue . . ." Ibid., 483.

190 "I dread the turning back . . ." Ibid.

190 "For more than twenty years . . ." Ibid., 502.

191 But the former president's real interest . . . Ibid., 501–2.

191 "the man with the purest . . ." Ibid., 524.

192 Delighting in the Democrats' fissures . . ." "Harrison for the Party," *Boston Daily Globe*, August 28, 1896.

192 Harrison made forty speeches . . . Marie Hecht, *Beyond the Presidency: The Residues of Power* (New York: Macmillan, 1976), 126.

192 "in a constant state of wonderment . . ." Alyn Brodsky, *Grover Cleveland: A Study in Character* (New York: Truman Talley Books, 2000), 418.

192 Cleveland was unwelcome . . . *Chicago Daily Tribune*, July 4, 1900.

192 "My young man . . ." "Predicted Bryan Landslide," *Washington Post*, October 30, 1900.

192 "sanity will succeed insanity . . ." Brodsky, *Grover Cleveland*, 421.

192 "I think now we have . . ." Hecht, *Beyond the Presidency*, 127.

193 Some Democrats even urged Cleveland . . . Brodsky, *Grover Cleveland*, 425.

193 Democratic delegates began to fear . . . "Convention Wild over Cleveland," *New York Times*, July 7, 1904.

193 Cleveland gave what he could . . . Brodsky, *Grover Cleveland*, 430–32.

194 "out of politics" . . . "Taft Favors Root for the Presidency," *New York Times*, November 11, 1915.

194 "one of the greatest living Americans . . ." Ibid.; "Root as President Would Please Taft," *New York Times*, December 15, 1913.

194 "not a fit person" . . . "Taft and Root Come Out Against Brandeis," *Wall Street Journal*, March 15, 1916.

194 both felt America was in considerable need . . . "Taft Favors Root for the Presidency."

194 Root represented old-line . . . "Ask Roosevelt about Root," *New York Times*, May 4, 1916.

194 Taft himself skipped . . . "They'll Miss Taft at the Convention," *Los Angeles Times*, May 7, 1916.

195 "It was a bit stiff . . ." Henry F. Pringle, *The Life and Times of William Howard Taft*, vol. 2 (New York: Farrar and Rinehart, 1939), 860.

195 "make a particle of difference . . ." "Feud with TR Ended," *Washington Post*, June 29, 1916.

195 "anything in my power . . ." "Happenings on the Pacific Slope," *Los Angeles Times*, July 1, 1916.

195 "I will make no . . ." "Roosevelt to Give Cold Hand to Taft," *New York Times*, September 30, 1916.

195 "How do you do?" . . . "We shook hands . . ." "Col. Roosevelt and Taft Meet," *Boston Daily Globe*, October 4, 1916.

196 Taft never hid . . . Pringle, *The Life and Times of William Howard Taft*, 951.

196 "not of our intellectual . . ." Phyllis Lee Levin, *Edith and Woodrow: The Wilson White House* (New York: Scribner, 2001), 480.

196 the Democratic platforms of 1924 . . . Richard Norton Smith and Timothy Walch, eds., *Farewell to the Chief: Former Presidents in American Public Life* (Worland, WY: High Plains Publishing, 1990), 8.

196 "Ten years in Washington . . ." William Allen White, *A Puritan in Babylon: The Story of Calvin Coolidge* (New York: Macmillan, 2001), 361.

197 "When men in public office . . ." Robert Sobel, *Calvin Coolidge: An American Enigma* (Washington, DC: Regnery, 1998), 408–9.

197 a distinctly minor "Coolidge for President" . . . "New Movement Made to Name Coolidge," *New York Times*, June 16, 1932.

197 "economic recovery is beginning." . . . "The Week Reviewed," *Barron's*, October 17, 1932.

198 "the greatest struggle . . ." Gary Dean Best, *Herbert Hoover: The Post-Presidential Years, 1933–1964*, vol. 1, *1933–1945* (Stanford, CA: Hoover Institution Press, 1984), 41.

198 "fountain of fear" . . . "New Deal Policy Is Hit by Hoover," *Atlanta Constitution*, February 13, 1936.

198 After the wreckage . . . Albert U. Romasco, "Herbert Hoover: The Restoration of a Reputation," *Reviews in American History* 12, no. 1 (1984): 143.

198 "Fascist-Nazi state" . . . David Burner, *Herbert Hoover: A Public Life* (Norwalk, CT: Easten Press, 1996), 328.

198 the "five horsemen" . . . Best, *Herbert Hoover*, 59.

198 Ultimately he was distressed . . . Richard Norton Smith, *An Uncommon Man: The Triumph of Herbert Hoover* (Worland, WY: High Plains Publishing, 1984), 207.

198 a group Hoover loathed . . . Joan Hoff Wilson, *Herbert Hoover: Forgotten Progressive* (Boston: Little, Brown, 1975), 219.

198 "selfish and stupid" . . . Smith, *An Uncommon Man*, 219.

198 "The New Deal may be . . ." Best, *Herbert Hoover*, 61.

199 thirty-minute ovation . . . Burner, *Herbert Hoover*, 331.

199 "When you have a good story . . ." Samuel T. Williamson, "Herbert Hoover: A Friendly Portrait," *New York Times*, June 13, 1948.

199 casting off Hoover's ideological . . . Wilson, *Herbert Hoover*, 222–23.

200 One rumor even briefly . . . Richard Hofstadter, *The American Political Tradition: And the Men Who Made It* (New York: Vintage, 1948), 310.

200 "the three thousand miles of ocean . . ." Charles Peters, *Five Days in Philadelphia: The Amazing "We Want Willkie!" Convention of 1940 and How It Freed FDR to Save the Western World* (New York: Public Affairs, 2005), 82.

200 "the immense task . . ." Eugene Lyons, *Herbert Hoover: A Biography* (New York: Doubleday, 1964), 362.

200 Journalist Drew Pearson interpreted . . . Peters, *Five Days in Philadelphia*, 78.

200 the European democracies could hold . . . Best, *Herbert Hoover*, 155.

200 Hoover offered to make . . . Earl C. Behrens, "Hoover Will Talk for Him, Says Willkie," *Los Angeles Times*, August 13, 1940.

200 "actual dangers" . . . Smith, *Uncommon Man*, 301.

201 "it is evident that . . ." "Hoover Says Willkie Sentiment Growing in West," *Chicago Daily Tribune*, September 8, 1940.

201 "I shall do any proper . . ." Best, *Herbert Hoover*, 167.

201 preventing FDR from winning . . . Ibid., 231.

201 "a public revulsion . . ." Smith, *Uncommon Man*, 331.

201 Discreetly, he solicited . . . Best, *Herbert Hoover*, 256–58.

201 Yet the Dewey camp worried . . . Smith, *Uncommon Man*, 332–34.

201 "He's afraid that . . ." Ibid., 333.

201 "nation's leading political leper." . . . Michael Birkner, "Elder States-man: Herbert Hoover and His Successors," in *Uncommon Americans: The Lives and Legacies of Herbert and Lou Henry Hoover*, ed. Timothy Walch (Westport, CT: Praeger, 2003), 241.

202 "the hordes from . . ." Robert C. Albright, "Ex-President Sees Civilization Threatened by European Hordes," *Washington Post*, June 23, 1948.

202 "our difficulty lies . . ." "Herbert Hoover's Address at Philadelphia," *New York Times*, June 23, 1948.

202 no less than sixteen . . . Smith, *Uncommon Man*, 377.

202 "The governor held . . ." Ibid., 378.

202 former president occupied himself . . . Best, *Herbert Hoover*, 325.

203 "the once plump . . ." *Time*, June 23, 1952, http://www.time.com/time/magazine/article/0,9171,859804,00.html.

203 "they're not going to shut . . ." Ibid.

203 "provided the Republican party . . ." Hecht, *Beyond the Presidency*, 140.

203 "I have tonight come out . . ." Herbert Hoover, *The Constructive Character of the Republican Party*, October 18, 1952.

204 "Remember this and remember . . ." Steve Neal, *Harry and Ike: The Partnership That Remade the Postwar World* (New York: Touchstone, 2001), 298.

204 "time for moderation" . . . "If you're referring . . ." "Truman Has Say on 'Moderation,'" *Washington Post and Times Herald*, November 28, 1955.

204 "I did not promise . . ." Richard J. H. Johnston, "Truman Refuses to Give '56 Choice," *New York Times*, October 30, 1955.

204 "I like them both" . . . Bernard Kalb, "Kind Words Flow on Truman Walk, He Likes Both Stevenson and Harriman—Denies 'Plot' to Control Convention," *New York Times*, July 5, 1956; "Harry Truman as a Political Neutral," *Los Angeles Times*, July 8, 1956.

204 "more highly." . . . "Query on Harriman Parried by Truman," *New York Times*, May 11, 1956.

204 awash with rumors . . . "Truman Scoffs at Reports of Get-Adlai Plot," *Chicago Daily Tribune*, July 5, 1956.

204 "exploded an H-bomb" . . . Walter Trohan, "Truman Choice: Harriman," *Chicago Daily Tribune*, August 12, 1956.

205 was peeved by Truman's antics . . . Christine Sadler Coe, "FDR Widow Takes Issue with Truman," *Washington Post and Times Herald*, August 13, 1956.

205 In private she reminded . . . Hecht, *Beyond the Presidency*, 142.

205 "too defeatist" . . . "carry any more states . . ." Arthur Krock, "The Political Dagger," *New York Times*, August 15, 1956.

205 "conservatives and reactionaries" . . . Anthony Leviero, "Truman Pledges to Press Harriman Fight to Finish," *New York Times*, August 16, 1956.

205 "shocked that any liberal . . ." Ibid.

205 "is determined to use . . ." Arthur Krock, "Truman Chooses Role for Party Convention," *New York Times*, April 8, 1956.

206 "Harry Truman, the Goliath . . ." James Reston, "The Stakes at Chicago," *New York Times*, August 15, 1956.

206 he played a tamer role . . . Best, *Herbert Hoover*, 398.

206 Hoover's speech and his autumn broadcast . . . "Text of Speeches by Martin and Hoover at G.O.P Convention," *New York Times*, August 22, 1956; "Ike Fulfilling Needs of U.S., Says Hoover," *Chicago Daily Tribune*, October 30, 1956.

206 recruited Hoover to appear . . . Best, *Herbert Hoover*, 401–2.

206 "Republican radicalism can get nowhere . . ." Ibid., 410.

206 "to comprehend that . . ." Ibid.

206 "How do you think . . ." Burner, *Herbert Hoover*, 338.

207 "Unless some miracle . . ." "Herbert Hoover Calls for Spiritual Rebirth," *Chicago Daily Tribune*, July 26, 1960.

207 "frightening moral slump" . . . Ibid.

207 Truman's temper ran high . . . "The Monkey Wrench," *Chicago Daily Tribune*, July 3, 1960.

207 "Senator, are you certain . . ." George E. Sokolsky, "These Days . . .

The Morals of Harry Truman," *Washington Post and Times Herald,* July 8, 1960.

207 "poise and maturity." . . . "Harriman Lauds Poise in Kennedy's Answer; Truman's Favorite in 1956 Says Senator Showed Maturity in Reply to Attack," *Los Angeles Times,* July 5, 1960.

207 "It's not the pope . . ." Gary Donaldson, *The First Modern Campaign: Kennedy-Nixon and the Election of 1960* (Lanham, MD: Rowman & Littlefield, 2007), 72.

208 pincer strategy . . . Author interview with James Symington, August 3, 2007.

208 "If you vote for Nixon . . ." "Truman Calls Nixon a 'No Good,' Assails Eisenhower and Cuba," *New York Times,* October 22, 1960.

208 "The fact is that when . . ." "Sorry Spectacle," *Washington Post and Times Herald,* October 13, 1960.

208 "In human and historic . . ." James Giglio, "Harry S. Truman and the Multifarious Ex-Presidency," *Political Science Quarterly* 12, no. 2 (1982): 247.

208 "as big a crook . . ." Merle Miller, *Plain Speaking: An Oral Biography of Harry Truman* (New York: Berkeley, 1974), 187.

208 except for one detail . . . Donaldson, *The First Modern Campaign,* 149–50.

210 Eisenhower agonized . . . Felix Belair Jr., "Eisenhower Bids Arizonan Explain," *New York Times,* July 18, 1964.

210 Without Ike's endorsement . . . Rowland Evans and Robert Novak, "How Eisenhower Aided the Senator to Victory," *Los Angeles Times,* July 22, 1964.

210 "It is pretty hard to go back . . ." "Eisenhower Hits at Idea 'End Justifies Means,' " *Los Angeles Times,* July 20, 1964.

210 "Would Goldwater have sat frozen . . ." William F. Buckley Jr., "Goldwater's Views Really Differ Greatly from Those of Eisenhower," *Los Angeles Times,* July 27, 1964.

210 "I intend to come to grips . . ." *London Times,* October 7, 1964.

211 "He's a man of great . . ." James Yuenger, "Eisenhower Gives Nixon Endorsement," *Chicago Tribune,* July 19, 1968.

211 "a number of delegates . . ." Don Irwin, "Eisenhower Urges Nixon Nomination as 'Best for U.S.,' " *Los Angeles Times,* July 19, 1968.

211 a tactical move . . . "Eisenhower on Nixon," *New York Times,* July 20, 1968.

211 More than once, Ike had regretted . . . Roscoe Drummond, "Ike's

Endorsement to Clinch Presidential Bid by Nixon," *Washington Post and Times Herald*, July 10, 1968.

211 "If you give me a week . . ." Robert B. Semple Jr., "Eisenhower Backs Nixon, Praising His 'Experience,'" *New York Times*, July 19, 1968.

211 there were also family ties . . . Louise Hutchinson, "Campaign Only a Second Love for Eisenhower-Nixon of 1968," *Chicago Tribune*, July 5, 1968.

211 "the Communists reach ruthlessly . . ." "Eisenhower Urges Party to Be Tough with Reds," *Los Angeles Times*, August 6, 1968.

211 On his back, Eisenhower . . . "Last-Minute Appeal by Ike: Elect Nixon," *Chicago Tribune*, November 5, 1968.

212 "It doesn't make any difference . . ." "Truman Says Johnson Will Be Renominated," *Washington Post*, March 21, 1968.

212 With Johnson's egress . . . "Truman Backing for Humphrey," *London Times*, April 13, 1968.

212 "Let's be candid . . ." Russell Freeburg, "Truman Gives Humphrey and Muskie Advice," *Chicago Tribune*, September 22, 1968.

212 By 1972 there were two . . . "Truman Is Serenaded at 88," *New York Times*, May 9, 1972.

212 "the most important thing . . ." "Harriman Says Truman Calls for Nixon's Defeat," *New York Times*, April 23, 1972.

213 LBJ's public role narrowed . . . William S. White, "Who Came to Lunch," *Washington Post*, September 2, 1972.

213 it was not until . . . Jack Valenti, *A Very Human President* (New York: W. W. Norton, 1975), 381.

213 "President Johnson was a non-person . . ." Jack Valenti, ". . . But 'Dejohnsonization' Made LBJ a Non-Person," *Washington Post and Times Herald*, July 19, 1972.

213 trying to regain some legitimacy . . . Tom Wicker, "Something Funny's Going On," *New York Times*, August 22, 1972.

213 "one of the most treasured . . ." White, "Who Came to Lunch."

213 "with affection and respect." . . . Jack Anderson, "LBJ Getting His Affairs in Order," *Washington Post and Times Herald*, September 26, 1972.

213 He responded by offering . . . Valenti, *A Very Human President*, 385–86.

214 the insurgent candidate . . . Richard Bergholz, "Ford Vulnerable on Nixon Issue—Reagan," *Los Angeles Times*, July 17, 1976.

214 boxed into defending . . . "Ford Defends Nixon Pardon; He Would Do It Again, He Tells Newsmen," *Los Angeles Times*, July 19, 1976.

214   "We're trying to forget . . ." Jim Squires, "Watergate Label Dogs GOP Policy," *Chicago Tribune*, August 16, 1976.

214   "my predecessor" . . . Lou Cannon, "Ford Talks of Nixon, Draws a Favorable Contrast to Him," *Washington Post*, October 28, 1976.

214   "Joe, there's one very . . ." James M. Naughton, "Reporter's Notebook: Jet Lag and Talk of Ford's 'Mo,'" *New York Times*, November 1, 1976.

215   In February he moved into . . . Julie Baumgold, "Nixon in New York," *Washington Post*, July 6, 1980.

215   "You can never reject . . ." "Carter Errs, Nixon Says," *Washington Post*, April 4, 1980.

215   "unquestioned nuclear superiority . . ." Thomas Powers, "Nixon: A Hard-Boiled Look at 'Cold Realities,'" *Chicago Tribune*, June 1, 1980.

215   Nixon exerted an influence on his campaign . . . Jonathan Aitken, *Nixon: A Life* (Washington, DC: Regnery, 1994), 554.

215   After the independent candidate . . . "Nixon Hits Times on Reagan," *Chicago Tribune*, July 16, 1980.

215   "Nixon's name is never . . ." Haynes Johnson, "The Exorcism of the Phantom Delegate from San Clemente," *Washington Post*, July 16, 1980.

216   "If twelve percent was good enough . . ." "Ex-President Ford in Energetic Campaign for Mr. Reagan," *London Times*, November 3, 1980.

216   By 1984, Richard Nixon's lost years . . . John Herbers, "After Decade, Nixon Is Gaining Favor," *New York Times*, August 5, 1984.

216   "would be in the best interest" . . . Kenneth J. Cooper, "Ford Says Apology from Nixon Would Be in the Best Interest," *Boston Globe*, August 11, 1984.

216   hailing President Reagan for his "fairness" . . . David S. Broder, "Reagan Defended on Fairness Issue by Gerald Ford," *Washington Post*, August 22, 1984.

217   "America's future belongs . . ." Ibid.

217   "about as much respect as . . ." Jack W. Germond and Jules Witcover, "Oí Meany Carter," *Chicago Tribune*, July 10, 1982.

217   "I would hope I would not be . . ." John Balzar, "Upbeat Carter Eager to Speak at Convention," *Los Angeles Times*, July 16, 1984.

217   After first offering him . . . William Endicott, "Carter Receives TV Coverage at Lance's Urging," *Los Angeles Times*, July 17, 1984.

217   his signature mediational work . . . E. J. Dionne Jr., "Jackson Suggests Carter Might Heal Rift with Dukakis," *New York Times*, July 15, 1988.

218   "I still have a ways to go" . . . Morris S. Thompson, "Carter Tapped for Limited Convention Role," *Washington Post*, July 17, 1988.

218   "It is a sad situation when . . ." E. J. Dionne Jr., "Talks Yield Accord," *New York Times*, July 19, 1988.

218   "and not go back eight . . ." Thompson, "Carter Tapped for Limited Convention Role."

218   "kind of effeminate" . . . George F. Will, "Pin the Label on the Donkey," *Newsweek*, August 1, 1988, 62.

218   "northern-fried Jimmy Carter." . . . Sidney Blumenthal, "The Carter Constituency," *Washington Post*, July 21, 1988.

218   "My name is Jimmy Carter . . ." Dionne Jr., "Talks Yield Accord."

218   Ford put the long-term interest . . . Lou Cannon, "Carter, Ford Join Group to Help Next President Avoid Some Pitfalls," *Washington Post*, May 12, 1988.

218   "For the first time . . ." Martin Tolchin, "From Carter and Ford, an American Agenda," *New York Times*, May 24, 1988.

219   "independence" . . . "drive" . . . "trapped by the establishment" . . . David B. Ottaway, "Nixon Sees Narrow Bush Victory," *Washington Post*, April 11, 1988.

219   Still, not everyone had . . . "Editors Pick Dick," *U.S. News & World Report*, September 12, 1988,

220   But Reagan's gravitas . . . Steven A. Holmes, "Reagan Endorses Bush as 'Best Hope' for Nation," *New York Times*, February 9, 1992.

220   "He doesn't seem to stand . . ." Timothy J. McNulty, "Reagan Quote Throws Bush Team Off Guard," *Chicago Tribune*, February 26, 1992.

220   his final major public address . . . Robert Reinhold, "Reagan Now: Traveling, Working, Clearing Brush," *New York Times*, August 17, 1992.

220   "This fellow they've nominated . . ." Robin Toner, "Tribute by Reagan," *New York Times*, August 18, 1992.

220   "We need George Bush . . ." "Excerpts of Address by Reagan to G.O.P.," *New York Times*, August 18, 1992.

220   "Goodbye and God bless . . ." "a haunting aura . . ." Tom Shales, "Reagan, Back in from the Sunset," *Washington Post*, August 18, 1992.

220   "You cannot help the wage earner . . ." Herbert Mitgang, "Reagan Put Words in Lincoln's Mouth," *New York Times*, August 19, 1992.

221   "Whether we come from poverty . . ." Robert C. Rowland and John Jones, "Entelechial and Reformative Symbolic Trajectories in

Contemporary Conservatism: A Case Study of Reagan and Buchanan in Houston and Beyond," *Rhetoric and Public Affairs* 4, no. 1 (2001): 64–65.

221 "There is a religious war . . ." David Broder, "Coherent Message Elusive," *Washington Post*, August 19, 1992.

221 "the speech probably sounded . . ." Katharine Q. Seelye, "Molly Ivins, Columnist, Dies at 62," *New York Times*, February 1, 2007.

221 "are losing a chance to continue . . ." Cragg Hines, "Ford Has Advice for President: Promise New Team for Economy," *Houston Chronicle*, August 7, 1992.

221 "done" . . . "kaput" . . . Tony Freemantle, "Convention '92, Congress Needs Major Change, Ford Says, Ex-president Wants a GOP Majority," *Houston Chronicle*, August 21, 1992.

222 "the dullest of them all . . ." Monica Crowley, *Nixon Off the Record: His Candid Commentary on People and Politics* (New York: Random House, 1996), 107.

222 "He's so extreme . . ." Ibid.

222 "Today we hear the voice . . ." Peter Applebome, "The 1992 Campaign: Ronald Reagan; 'Vintage' Reagan Stumps in South," *New York Times*, November 1, 1992.

222 a dalliance with Paul Tsongas . . . Karen De Witt, "Carter Welcomes Tsongas to Plains," *New York Times*, February 23, 1992.

222 With integrity lapses . . . Gwen Ifill, "Carter, with Clinton at His Side, Praises the Candidate's Qualities," *New York Times*, May 21, 1992.

222 "This is a great city . . ." "Excerpts from Addresses by Keynote Speakers at Democratic Convention," *New York Times*, July 14, 1992.

223 "I have participated in the last . . ." Adam Nagourney, "As One President Nears, Another Stays Away," *New York Times*, August 27, 1996.

223 "Carter was a major pain . . ." Author interview with unnamed source, March 31, 2007.

223 "leadership means standing against . . ." "Excerpts from Remarks of Ford, Bush and Powell," *New York Times*, August 13, 1996.

223 "It breaks my heart . . ." Richard L. Berke, "Applause for Powell as He Delivers Call for Inclusiveness," *New York Times*, August 13, 1996.

223 bold letter to the NRA . . . Timothy Naftali, *George H. W. Bush* (New York: Times Books, Henry Holt, 2007), 160.

224 "That really irks me . . ." R. W. Apple Jr., "Dad Was President (but Please, No Dynasty Talk)," *New York Times*, January 31, 2000.

224 "knows every bit as much . . ." "Excerpts from Interview with
     Bushes," *New York Times*, July 8, 2000.

224 "I'm not here to attack . . ." Richard L. Berke, "Revisiting the Honor
     Issue, a Father Defends His Son," *New York Times*, September 23, 2000.

225 "show business" . . . Ibid.

225 "I tell you as a dad . . ." Associated Press, "For Jeb Bush, Vote of
     Support from Dad," *New York Times*, November 10, 2000.

225 "Do you really think . . ." George H. W. Bush, interview by Jim
     Lehrer, *NewsHour with Jim Lehrer*, PBS, September 2, 2004, http://
     www.pbs.org/newshour/bb/politics/july-dec04/hwbush_09-02.html.

226 "I never have believed that Saddam . . ." Jimmy Carter, interview by
     Katie Couric, *Today*, NBC, September 30, 2004.

226 "During the Vietnam War . . ." Jeff Zeleny, "Clinton Returns to
     Stage, Trumpets Call for Kerry," *Chicago Tribune*, July 27, 2004.

226 "showed up when assigned to duty . . ." John Aloysius Farrell,
     "Clinton Revs Up Dems," *Denver Post*, July 27, 2004.

226 "My name is Jimmy Carter . . ." Todd S. Purdum, "Crowned by
     Popular Acclaim, Clintons Return as Royalty to Spotlight," *New York
     Times*, July 27, 2004.

226 "I think that's the issue . . ." "Carter Urges Focus on Iraq," *New York
     Times*, September 23, 2004.

227 "Let's just shell down . . ." Dahleen Glanton, "Clinton Stumps for
     Kerry in Home State," *Knight Ridder Tribune Business News*,
     November 1, 2004.

227 "Jesse Jackson won South Carolina . . ." Jake Tapper, "Bubba: Obama
     Is Just Like Jesse Jackson," Political Punch, ABC News Blog, January
     26, 2008, http://blogs.abcnews.com/politicalpunch/2008/01/bubba
     -obama-is.html.

228 "may be the last day. . . ." Daily Intel, "Bill Clinton: "This May Be
     the Last Day I'm Ever Involved in a Campaign," *New York Magazine*,
     June 2, 2008.

228 "No one is better prepared . . ." Associated Press, "Former President
     Bush Endorses McCain," February 18, 2008.

228 "His burning issue now . . ." Mike Allen, "Talk Show Tip Sheet,"
     Politico.com, February 25, 2007, http://www.politico.com/news/
     stories/0207/2886.html.

228 had been "extraordinary and titillating . . ." Alexander Mooney,
     "Carter Praises Obama," Political Ticker, CNNPolitics.com, January
     30, 2008.

Chapter 5. A Return to Politics

229   "There is a lure in power . . ." Harry S. Truman and Robert H. Ferrell, *The Private Papers of Harry S. Truman* (Columbia: University of Missouri Press, 1997), 177.

229   "My hat's in the ring . . ." Allan A. Metcalf, *Presidential Voices: Speaking Styles from George Washington to George W. Bush* (New York: Houghton Mifflin, 2004), 46.

229   "Perhaps it is the comfort . . ." Henry F. Pringle, *The Life and Times of William Howard Taft: A Biography* (Hamden, CT: Archon Books, 1964), 148.

231   "a French President" . . . James Thomas Flexner, *Washington: The Indispensable Man* (New York: Little, Brown, 1969), 383.

231   "I am thoroughly convinced . . ." James MacGregor Burns and Susan Dunn, *George Washington* (New York: Times Books, 2004), 135.

231   "It would be criminal . . ." James Thomas Flexner, *George Washington: Anguish and Farewell (1793–99)* (New York: Little Brown, 1972), 429.

231   "set up a broomstick . . ." Ibid.

231   "I should be charged . . ." Ibid.

231   "I do not want it any more . . ." John William Perrin, "Presidential Tenure and Reeligibility," *Political Science Quarterly* 29, no. 3 (1914): 427.

231   "How I entreated him . . ." John Y. Simon, ed., *The Personal Memoirs of Julia Dent Grant* (Carbondale: Southern Illinois University, 1988), 321–22.

232   Should he be remembered for . . . Allan Peskin, "Who Were the Stalwarts? Who Were Their Rivals? Republican Factions in the Gilded Age," *Political Science Quarterly* 99, no. 4 (1984–85): 708.

232   more capable and attractive candidate . . . Jean Edward Smith, *Grant* (New York: Simon & Schuster, 2002), 617.

232   "nothing but an act of God . . ." Kenneth D. Ackerman, *Dark Horse: The Surprise Election and Political Murder of President James A. Garfield* (New York: Carroll & Graf Publishers, 2003), 48.

232   The months that followed . . . Josiah Bunting, *Ulysses S. Grant* (New York: Times Books, Henry Holt, 2004), 149.

233   Garfield reached the magic number . . . Ibid., 150.

233   Yet some held out hope . . . Henry F. Graff, *Grover Cleveland* (New York: Times Books, Henry Holt, 2002), 132.

233 "[Cleveland] is the only statesman . . ." C. S., letter to the editor, *New York Times*, June 17, 1900.

233 "never be in winning condition . . ." Alyn Brodsky, *Grover Cleveland: A Study in Character* (New York: Truman Talley Books, 2000), 419.

233 When Bryan once again . . . Ibid., 421.

234 "availability for re-nomination . . ." Joel Silbey, *Martin Van Buren and the Emergence of American Popular Politics* (Lanham, MD: Rowman & Littlefield, 2005), 162.

234 His hopes raised, the former . . . John Niven, *Martin Van Buren: The Romantic Age of American Politics*, ed. Katherine E. Speirs (Newtown, CT: American Political Biography Press, 2000), chap. 26, passim.

234 The Whigs found him intolerable . . . David Zarefsky, "Henry Clay and the Election of 1844: The Limits of a Rhetoric of Compromise," *Rhetoric and Public Affairs* 6, no. 1 (2003): 81.

235 "if the people showed they strongly . . ." Sean Wilentz, *The Rise of American Democracy: Jefferson to Lincoln* (New York: W. W. Norton, 2005), 568.

235 After serving during the catastrophic . . . Michael A. Morrison, "Martin Van Buren, the Democracy, and the Partisan Politics of Texas Annexation," *Journal of Southern History* 61, no. 4 (November 1995): 697.

235 "We hereby tender . . ." Denis T. Lynch, *Epoch and a Man: Martin Van Buren and His Times* (New York: Horace Liveright, 1929), 492–93.

236 "free soil to a . . ." Rich Haney, John Van Houten Dippel, *Race to the Frontier: "White Flight" and Western Expansion* (New York: Algora Publishing, 2005), 246.

236 "no more power . . ." Arthur Bestor, "The American Civil War as a Constitutional Cristis," *American Historical Review* 69, no. 2 (1964): 347.

236 its elevated rhetoric stopped short . . . Eric Foner, "Politics and Prejudice: The Free Soil Party and the Negro, 1849–1852," *Journal of Negro History* 50, no. 4 (1965): 239.

237 Free Soilers had vilified Cass . . . Eric Foner, *Free Soil, Free Labor, Free Men: The Ideology of the Republican Party before the Civil War* (New York: Oxford University Press, 1970), 153.

237 a reaction to the rapid influx . . . Tyler Anbinder, *Nativism and Slavery: The Northern Know-Nothings and the Politics of the 1850s* (New York: Oxford University Press, 1994), 3.

237 The party's high-water mark . . . Robert J. Scarry, *Millard Fillmore* (Jefferson, NC: McFarland, 2001), 278.

238 moderated its rhetoric . . . Foner, *Free Soil, Free Labor, Free Men*, 198.

238 he accepted without hesitation . . . Scarry, *Millard Fillmore*, 284.

238 "men who come fresh from . . ." Anbinder, *Nativism and Slavery*, 221; James C. Clark, *Faded Glory: Presidents Out of Power* (Westport, CT: Praeger, 1985), 5.

239 "I consider my political career . . ." Robert Rayback, *Millard Fillmore: Biography of a President* (Newtown, CT: American Political Biography Press, 1998), 415.

239 "I most emphatically desire . . ." Henry Pringle, *Theodore Roosevelt: A Biography* (New York: Harcourt Brace, 1984), 374.

240 In a decisive turn away . . . Nathan Miller, *Theodore Roosevelt: A Life* (New York: William Morrow, 1992), 515.

240 he'd made a poor judgment . . . Max Skidmore, *After the White House: Former Presidents as Private Citizens* (New York: Palgrave/MacMillan, 2004), 95.

240 brought his institutional power to bear . . . George E. Mowry, "Theodore Roosevelt and the Election of 1910," *Mississippi Valley Historical Review* 25, no.4 (1939): 529.

240 Roosevelt laughed last . . . Miller, *Theodore Roosevelt*, 516.

241 putting his faith in the new . . . Pringle, *Theodore Roosevelt*, 390.

241 the primary process was expected to . . . Kathleen Dalton, *Theodore Roosevelt: A Strenuous Life* (New York: Alfred A. Knopf, 2002), 383.

241 "as fit as a bull moose" . . . Ibid., 391–92.

242 "We stand at Armageddon . . ." Louis Auchincloss, *Theodore Roosevelt* (New York: Times Books, Henry Holt, 2002), 120.

242 able to deliver only half . . . Joseph L. Gardner, *Departing Glory: Theodore Roosevelt as Ex-President* (New York: Charles Scribner's Sons, 1973), 261–62.

242 Roosevelt's refusal to embrace . . . Dalton, *Theodore Roosevelt*, 395.

242 "I have been shot . . ." Marie Hecht, *Beyond the Presidency: The Residues of Power* (New York: Macmillan, 1976), 111.

242 "ruthlessly smothering his own party" . . . Richard Norton Smith and Timothy Walch, eds., *Farewell to the Chief: Former Presidents in American Public Life* (Worland, WY: High Plains Publishing, 1990), 5.

243 "That is the craziest deal . . ." Richard V. Allen, "How the Bush Dynasty Almost Wasn't," *Hoover Digest Research and Public Policy*, no. 4 (2000).

243 Ford began to back down . . . Ed Magnuson, "Inside the Jerry Ford Drama," *Time*, July 28, 1980.

243 "Kissinger carries a lot of baggage . . ." Ibid.

244 "I have to say the answer is no . . ." Allen, "How the Bush Dynasty Almost Wasn't."

245 "a nun taking the veil" . . . Lynn Hudson Parsons, *John Quincy Adams* (Lanham, MD: Rowman & Little Field, 1999), 201.

245 "into dejection, despondency, and idleness" . . . Paul C. Nagel, *John Quincy Adams: A Public Life, A Private Life* (New York: Alfred A. Knopf, 1997), 334.

245 "not the slightest desire . . ." Robert V. Remini, *John Quincy Adams* (New York: Times Books, Henry Holt, 2002), 131.

245 "deserted by all mankind" . . . Nagel, *John Quincy Adams,* 336.

245 "no election or appointment conferred . . ." Charles Frances Adams, ed., *Memoirs of John Quincy Adams: Comprising Portions of His Diary from 1795 to 1848* (J. B. Lippincott, 1876), 247.

246 "great and foul stain" . . . Eric L. McKitrick, "JQA: For the Defense," *New York Review of Books,* April 23, 1998.

246 "adopted cause transformed him . . ." Nagel, *John Quincy Adams,* 356.

246 "Well, that is the most extraordinary . . ." Hecht, *Beyond the Presidency,* 277.

247 Not having argued a case . . . Parsons, *John Quincy Adams,* 237.

247 "The moment you come to the Declaration . . ." Ibid., 239.

248 "made his exertions more than . . ." McKitrick, "JQA: For the Defense."

248 "His Accidency" . . . Edward Crapol, *John Tyler: The Accidental President* (Chapel Hill: University of North Carolina Press, 2006), 2.

248 "a political sectarian, of the slave-driving . . ." Parsons, *John Quincy Adams,* 247.

248 Tyler assumed the pose . . . Crapol, *John Tyler,* 231.

249 Tyler fantasized that he might . . . Ibid., 255.

249 Instead, his worst fears . . . Walter LaFeber, *The American Age: United States Foreign Policy at Home and Abroad since 1750* (New York: W. W Norton, 1989), 138–39.

249 "Virginia has severed her connection . . ." Hecht, *Beyond the Presidency,* 26.

249 With great fervor . . . Ibid., 27.

250 His funeral there was an occasion . . . Crapol, *John Tyler,* 268.

250 Tyler's passing raised nary . . . Ibid.

250 "He ended his life suddenly . . ." "Death of Ex-President Tyler," *New York Times,* January 22, 1862.

250 Failing to consider political equality . . . Foner, *Free Soil, Free Labor, Free Men,* 69.

251   "I had rather have . . ." Clark, *Faded Glory,* 71.

251   Johnson had skillfully balanced . . . Hans Trefousse, *Andrew Johnson: A Biography* (New York: W. W. Norton, 1997), 355–56.

251   "In the Senate [Johnson] will be of greater . . ." Homer F. Cunningham, *The Presidents' Last Years: George Washington to Lyndon B. Johnson* (Jefferson, NC: McFarland, 1989), 128.

252   Hoover let it be known . . . Gary Dean Best, *Herbert Hoover: The Post-Presidential Years, 1933–1964,* vol.1, *1933–1945* (Stanford, CA: Hoover Institution Press, 1983), 276.

252   "his disinterested counsels . . ." "Mr. Hoover for the Senate," *New York Times,* August 8, 1945.

252   "under an oxygen tent . . ." Drew Pearson, "The Washington Merry-Go-Round," *Washington Post,* August 2, 1945.

252   Hoover tried to disguise . . . Best, *Herbert Hoover,* 276.

252   Thomas E. Dewey offered Hoover . . . Eugene Lyons, *Herbert Hoover: A Biography* (New York: Doubleday, 1964), 421.

253   "There is no function more important . . ." Stanley I. Kutler, "Chief Justice Taft and the Delusion of Judicial Exactness: A Study in Jurisprudence," *Virginia Law Review* 48, no. 8 (1962): 1,407.

253   asserting that he would be abandoning . . . Judith Icke Anderson, *William Howard Taft: An Intimate History* (New York: W. W. Norton, 1981), 82.

253   "I have said to my wife . . ." Earl Warren, "Chief Justice William Howard Taft," *Yale Law Journal* 67, no. 3 (1958): 357.

253   "that this which I am now declining . . ." Ibid.

253   Taft's ambitious family . . . Miller, *Theodore Roosevelt,* 485.

253   "should be shelved . . ." Warren, "Chief Justice William Howard Taft," 356.

253   "preferred some other mode . . ." Ibid.

254   Afraid that the move . . . Pringle, *The Life and Times of William Howard Taft,* 882–84.

254   Harding consulted extensively . . . Cunningham, *The Presidents' Last Years,* 193.

254   "progressively conservative and conservatively . . ." Asa Martin, *After the White House* (State College, PA: Penns Valley Publishers, 1951), 401.

254   "It has been the ambition . . ." "Ambition of Life Fulfilled, Taft Says; Here July 7," *Washington Post,* July 1, 1921.

254 His reforms invested more power . . . Peter G. Fish, "William Howard Taft and Charles Evans Hughes: Conservative Politicians as Chief Judicial Reformers," *Supreme Court Review* (1975): 137.

255 "merely technical canon of propriety . . ." Walter F. Murphy, "In His Own Image: Mr. Chief Justice Taft and Supreme Court Appointments," *Supreme Court Review* (1961): 163.

255 Taft was eager to insert . . . Ibid., 191.

255 "an expert in attempting to save . . ." Michael E. Parrish, "Sacco and Vanzetti Revisited: Russell and Young & Kaiser," *American Bar Foundation Research Journal* 12, no. 2/3 (1987): 579.

255 "I don't remember that I . . ." "William Howard Taft," http://www .whitehouse.gov/history/presidents/wt27.html.

255 At the advanced age of eighty-four . . . Skidmore, *After the White House*, 21.

256 "advance of liberalism." . . . David McCullough, *John Adams* (New York: Simon & Schuster, 2001), 631.

256 James Madison and James Monroe participated . . . Susan Dunn, *Dominion of Memories: Jefferson, Madison, and the Decline of Virginia* (New York: Basic Books, 2007), 155–70.

CHAPTER 6. THE GREATER GOOD: PUBLIC SERVICE AND HUMANITARIANISM

257 "Being a politician is a poor . . ." Joslyn Pine, *Wit and Wisdom of the American Presidents: A Book of Quotations* (North Chemlsford, MA: Courier Dover Publications, 2000), 49.

257 "You can sit there and feel sorry . . ." David Remnick, "The Wanderer," *New Yorker*, September 18, 2006, 46.

257 "Unless you're Shirley MacLaine . . ." Ed O'Keefe, "The Odd Couple," *ABC News*, May 19, 2007, http://www.abcnews.go.com/ Politics/Story?id=3192296&page=1.

258 "something refreshingly American . . ." "After the White House," *San Francisco Chronicle*, February 23, 2005.

258 "When it comes to helping . . ." "Bush and Clinton, in Thailand, Start Tour of Tsunami Region," *New York Times*, February 20, 2005.

258 "maybe I'm the father . . ." Tony Freemantle, "'41' and '42'—No Baggage," *Houston Chronicle*, March 7, 2005.

258 "Bush and Clinton have created a new . . ." Michael Duffy, "Bill Clinton and George H. W. Bush," *Time,* April 30, 2006.

259 an estimated haul of more . . . http://bushclintonkatrinafund.org; Stephanie Strom, "Ex-Presidents Try to Decide Where to Send Storm Relief," *New York Times,* October 8, 2005.

259 discouraged the still popular Democrat . . . Remnick, "The Wanderer," 64.

259 "I always liked and I always admired . . ." Dave Davies, "Bush & Clinton Accept Medal, Hailing Our Unity, Differences," *Knight Ridder Tribune Business News,* October 6, 2006.

259 "came at some sacrifice to other objectives . . ." Author interview with Eric Schwartz, July 17, 2007.

260 "not going to tiptoe . . ." "George H. W. Bush Friendship with Bill Clinton Doesn't Translate to Support for Hillary," *Fox News,* November, 4, 2007, http://www.foxnews.com/story/0,2933,307257,00 .html.

260 "to send me and former President Bush . . ." "Bill Clinton: George H. W. Bush Will Help President Hillary," CNN Political Ticker, CNN Politics.com, December 18, 2007.

260 "never discussed an 'around-the-world-mission' . . ." "Bush Rejects Bill Clinton Idea," Politico.com, December 20, 2007, http://www .politico.com/news/stories/1207/7491.html.

261 "Let him . . . promote the welfare . . ." Ari Hoogenboom, *Rutherford B. Hayes: Warrior and President* (Lawrence: University Press of Kansas, 1995), 466.

261 "more individual contentment . . ." Ibid.

261 "the American people have a grave . . ." David Thelen, "Rutherford B. Hayes and the Reform Tradition in the Gilded Age," *American Quarterly* 22, no. 2, part 1 (1970): 153.

261 "the thrift, the education, the morality . . ." Ibid., 156.

262 Hayes's ethics derived principally . . . Ibid., passim.

262 "These millions who have been so cruelly . . ." Don Quinn Kelley, "Ideology and Education: Uplifting the Masses in Nineteenth Century Alabama," *Phylon* 40, no. 2 (1979): 150.

262 "a bit too aware . . ." Stanley Elkins, "A Presidential Diary," *New York Review of Books,* July 30, 1964.

262 "uplifting of the lately emancipated . . ." Henry L. Swint, "Rutherford B. Hayes, Educator," *Mississippi Valley Historical Review* 39, no. 1 (1952): 52.

262   In Hayes's view . . . Thelen, "Rutherford B. Hayes and the Reform Tradition in the Gilded Age," 157.

262   Hayes became president of the National Prison . . . Hoogenboom, *Rutherford B. Hayes*, 486, 496.

262   In an 1888 address . . . Ibid., 496.

263   "government of the people, by the people . . ." Ibid., 494.

263   Never seeing himself among the ranks . . . Thelen, "Rutherford B. Hayes and the Reform Tradition in the Gilded Age," 163–64.

263   "the capital mistake is to attempt . . ." Hoogenboom, *Rutherford B. Hayes*, 469.

264   Cleveland agreed to investigate . . . Alyn Brodsky, *Grover Cleveland: A Study in Character* (New York: Truman Talley Books, 2000), 434.

265   the idea of a conservative foe . . . Henry P. Pringle, *The Life and Times of William Howard Taft*, vol. 2 (New York: Farrar and Rinehart, 1939), 915.

265   Taft's experience with the NWLB . . . Judith Icke Anderson, *William Howard Taft: An Intimate History* (New York: W. W. Norton, 1981), 257.

265   Wilson's respect for Taft's leadership . . . Walter Licht, review of *The National War Labor Board: Stability, Social Justice, and the Voluntary State in World War I*, by Valerie Jean Conner, *Business History Review* 58, no. 1 (1984): 138–39.

265   The country's reliance on imported food . . . George H. Nash, *The Life of Herbert Hoover, Master of Emergencies, 1917–1918* (New York: W. W. Norton, 1996), 4.

265   "I did not realize it at the moment . . ." http://hoover.archives.gov/exhibits/Hooverstory/gallery02/gallery02.html.

265   Working in concert . . . Nash, *The Life of Herbert Hoover*, 4.

266   encouraged the patriotic conservation . . . "Another War Winter," *New York Times*, November 30, 1942.

266   Hoover parlayed his success . . . Sean Dennis Cashman, *America Ascendant: From Theodore Roosevelt to FDR in the Century of American Power, 1901–1945* (New York: New York University Press, 1998), 159.

266   As president, Hoover's attempt to support . . . Elliot A. Rosen, review of *As Rare as Rain: Federal Relief in the Great Southern Drought of 1930–31*, by Nan E. Woodruff, *Journal of Economic History* 46, no. 1 (1986): 294–95.

266   "his loyalty to the American folklore . . ." Richard Hofstadter, *The American Political Tradition: And the Men Who Made It* (New York: Vintage, 1948), 305.

267 Hoover's isolationist inclinations . . . Richard Norton Smith, *An Uncommon Man: The Triumph of Herbert Hoover* (Worland, WY: High Plains Publishing, 1984), 277.

267 The commission was instrumental . . . "An American Friendship: Herbert Hoover and Poland," exhibit at the Hoover Institution, June 2005.

267 "I do not believe . . ." "Food Lack Won't Beat Axis, Says Hoover in Plea for Plan," *Washington Post*, October 20, 1941.

268 "If your neighbors and their children . . ." http://www.trumanlibrary .org/hoover/intro.htm.

268 "We do not want the American flag . . ." http://hoover.archives.gov/ exhibits/Hooverstory/gallery09/gallery09.html.

268 "When the attack on Pearl Harbor . . ." Donald R. McCoy, "Truman and Hoover: Friends," *Whistle Stop* 18, no. 2 (1990), http://www .trumanlibrary.org/hoover/mccoyl.htm.

269 after the commission's findings were reported . . . William R. Divine, "The Second Hoover Commission Reports: An Analysis," *Public Administration Review* 15, no. 4 (1955): 268.

269 The former president was less inclined . . . Joan Hoff Wilson, *Herbert Hoover: Forgotten Progressive* (Boston: Little, Brown, 1975), 237.

269 "have disastrously advised on policies . . ." http://www.trumanlibrary .org/hoover/friends.htm.

269 Although Ike was skeptical . . . Robert H. Ferrell, ed., *The Eisenhower Diaries* (New York: W. W. Norton, 1981), 249.

269 "The only individuals [he] wanted . . ." Ibid., 247.

270 Even at eighty . . . "Will Limit Election Role, Hoover Says," *Los Angeles Times*, August 12, 1954.

270 Hoover II also pushed for an increase . . . William E. Pemberton, "Truman and the Hoover Commission," *Whistle Stop* 19, no 3 (1991), http://www.trumanlibrary.org/hoover/commission.htm.

270 "The name of Herbert Hoover has truly . . ." John F. Kennedy, remarks at a dinner honoring Herbert Hoover, Washington, D.C., February 4, 1957.

271 "Every former president is just as different . . ." Danna Harman, "Can Celebrities Really Get Results?" *Christian Science Monitor*, August 23, 2007.

272 countless speeches about her experiences . . . Sara Rimer, "Enjoying the Ex-Presidency? Never Been Better," *New York Times*, February 16, 2000.

273   "completely exhausted . . ." Jimmy and Rosalynn Carter, *Everything to Gain: Making the Most of the Rest of Your Life* (Fayetteville: University of Arkansas Press, 1995), 2.

273   "I know what we can do . . ." Wayne King, "Carter Redux," *New York Times*, December 10, 1989.

273   "not only the right to live in peace . . ." Ed Cain, director, Carter Center Global Development Initiative, "Global Development Initiative and Human Rights," speech, September 30, 2003, Cologne, Germany, at International Policy Dialogue.

274   By the next presidential contest . . . Jimmy Carter, "Still Seeking a Fair Florida Vote," *Washington Post*, September 27, 2004.

274   Whether Carter's concerns . . . "Carter to Head Elections Panel: Bipartisan Group Will Look for Ways to Improve Voting in U.S.," *Washington Post*, March 25, 2005.

274   Other core recommendations . . . Dan Balz, "Carter-Baker Panel to Call for Voting Fixes; Election Report Urges Photo IDs, Paper Trails and Impartial Oversight," *Washington Post*, September 19, 2005.

275   The Gates Foundation celebrated . . . http://www.gatesfoundation .org/GlobalHealth/Announcements/Announe-060515.

276   Even those unfamiliar with . . . http://www.habitat.org/how/carter .aspx.

277   "I had to reconvene my life . . ." Lawrence Donegan, "What Bill Did Next," *Guardian*, June 20, 2004.

277   newest former president soon made clear . . . Bill Clinton, *Giving: How Each of Us Can Change the World* (New York: Alfred A. Knopf, 2007), 5.

277   Clinton first noticed the scope . . . Remnick, "The Wanderer," 47.

277   "Some of the problems that have bedeviled . . ." John F. Harris, "Bill Clinton Takes Spot on Global Stage," *Washington Post*, June 1, 2005.

277   At the outset, Clinton was not actively sold . . . Jonathan Rauch, "This Is Not Charity," *Atlantic*, October 2007, 66.

278   "money and organizational problem." . . . Ibid.

278   "aggregate enough demand . . ." Ibid., 68.

278   Bruce Lindsey claims . . . Leslie Newell Peacock, "The Rainmaker," *Arkansas Times*, November 9, 2006.

279   Yet some experts have pointed out . . . Bethany McLean, "The Power of Philanthropy," *Fortune*, September 7, 2006, 86.

279   Some advocates have groused . . . Harman, "Can Celebrities Really Get Results?"

279 the Clinton Foundation did itself few favors . . . Author interview
     with unnamed source, December 11, 2007.
279 AIDS activists were on the front lines . . . Author interview with
     Jamie Love, May 29, 2008.
279 "It is a miscarriage of justice . . ." Author interview with unnamed
     source, December 11, 2007.
280 "while others made sincere progress . . ." Ira Magaziner, e-mail
     message to author, December 26, 2007.
280 "hit a wall" . . . Author interview with Ira Magaziner, December 24, 2007.
280 former president's stated regret . . . Lawrence K. Altman, "Clinton
     Urges Global Planning to Halt HIV," *New York Times,* July 12, 2002;
     Celia W. Dugger, "Clinton Makes Up for Lost Time in Battling
     AIDS," *New York Times,* August 29, 2006.
280 "to accomplish now what you didn't . . ." Dugger, "Clinton Makes Up
     for Lost Time in Battling AIDS."
280 "Everyone was worried . . ." Ibid.
280 "I think it's all a bunch . . ." Ibid.
280 As abject as Clinton's unwillingness . . . John F. Harris, "Bill Clinton
     Takes Spot on Global Stage," *Washington Post,* June 1, 2005.
281 "bystanders to genocide" . . . Samantha Power, "Bystanders to
     Genocide," *Atlantic,* September 2001, 84.
281 "we don't do AIDS . . ." Author interview with Paul Farmer,
     November 21, 2007.
281 "ideological" . . . "pragmatic" . . . Ibid.
282 "significant public good." . . . "The Clinton Factor: A Former Presi-
     dent's eBay of Giving," *Economist,* September 25, 2007.
282 amassed more than $10 billion . . . "How the New Philanthropy
     Works," *Time,* September 25, 2006; "President Clinton Concludes
     Third Annual Meeting of the Clinton Global Initiative by
     Announcing Historic Levels of Commitments and Expansion," CGI
     press release, September 28, 2007.
282 "grantors are incentivized . . ." Deborah Corey Barnes and Matthew
     Vadum, "What Is the Clinton Foundation Up To?" *Human Events,*
     February 4, 2008, 9.
282 plunge his next decade's profits . . . Andrew C. Revkin, "Global Gift
     of $3 Billion from Tycoon," *Chicago Tribune,* September 22, 2006.
283 "he'll probably make more money off this . . ." Andrew C. Revkin
     and Heather Timmons, "Branson Pledges to Finance Clean Fuels,"
     New York Times, September 22, 2006.

283 investors expect that participating nonprofits . . . Michael Edwards, "Philanthrocapitalism: After the Gold Rush," Open Democracy.net, March 20, 2008.

283 Philanthrocapitalism has its share of critics . . . Ibid.

283 Clinton fought a losing battle . . . http://www.pbs.org/wgbh/pages/frontline/hotpolitics/view/.

284 On a macro level . . . Rauch, "This Is Not Charity."

284 "is in my view . . ." Brad Knickerbocker, "Many Green Mayors Fall Short," *Christian Science Monitor,* November 8, 2007.

284 jump-started a climate change initiative . . . http://www.c40cities.org.

284 each committing $1 billion . . . "Clinton Foundation, Microsoft to Develop Online Tools Enabling the World's Largest 40 Cities to Monitor Carbon Emissions," Microsoft press release, May 17, 2007.

284 some environmental realists feel . . . Juliet Eilperin, "22 Cities Join Clinton Anti-Warming Effort," *Washington Post,* August 2, 2006.

285 "the idea of markets in emission permits . . ." Paul Krugman, "Party of Denial," *New York Times,* May 2, 2008.

285 "the long-term health ramifications . . ." Arthur Agatston, e-mail message to author, June 4, 2008.

286 "Everyone always asks me . . ." "Dunkin' Donuts 'Whips Up' Deal with Daytime TV Host Rachael Ray," Dunkin' Donuts press release, March 8, 2007.

286 major food conglomerates such as . . . www.clintonfoundation.org/cf -pgm-hs-hk-work4.htm.

287 "[I] notice that he is getting on . . ." Joan Gussow, e-mail message to author, May 7, 2008.

287 "really seem to have a whole picture . . ." Author interview with Toni Liquori, May 29, 2008.

INDEX